PSYCHOLOGY FOR LIFE TODAY is the out-
growth of an award winning manuscript
submitted in the American Technical
Society's 50th Anniversary Manuscript
Contest. This contest was designed to
stimulate research and to encourage the
preparation of functional instructional
material.

# PSYCHOLOGY
## FOR LIFE TODAY

# PSYCHOLOGY

## FOR LIFE TODAY

CHARLES R. FOSTER

*Professor of Education and Assistant Dean, College of Education, University of Florida*

*Former Trustee, National Vocational Guidance Association*

*International President, Phi Delta Kappa (Fraternity of men in education)*

ILLUSTRATED

AMERICAN TECHNICAL SOCIETY

Chicago USA

FIRST EDITION

The original edition was published under the
title PSYCHOLOGY FOR LIFE ADJUSTMENT

1st Printing 1951
2nd Printing 1952
3d Printing 1953
4th Printing 1955
5th Printing 1957
6th Printing 1957
7th Printing 1958
8th Printing 1959
9th Printing 1960
10th Printing 1960

SECOND EDITION

11th Printing 1961
12th Printing 1962
13th Printing 1963
14th Printing 1964

LIBRARY OF CONGRESS CARD CATALOG NO. 61-14464

PRINTED IN THE UNITED STATES OF AMERICA

# PREFACE

The growth of psychology as a field of study is the result of man's increasing desire to understand himself and his world. The development of guidance services in our schools and in our communities is proof of this, as is also the great increase in courses and books available to students in all phases of psychology, sociology, and human relations.

Also impressive is the growing attention to human relations in business and industry, and the development of personnel work. Psychologists have given special attention to these important problems affecting the worker and his job.

What do these include? Success in living will come as we become capable of learning, of earning a living, of establishing a home, of taking a place in society, and of making our own individual contribution, such as it may be, to the community of which we are a part. Psychologists have found out certain things about how people do these things.

Much that they have learned can be helpful to anyone, and the purpose of this book is to present that information in an understandable way.

To simplify the conclusions of psychologists and others working in the field of human relations is not easy. But it is necessary because much of the writing and reporting in the field has been complex and hard to follow. This book attempts to describe and explain, in the simplest terms possible, different kinds of human behavior that we frequently encounter and which we often do not understand. It is believed that if we have a clearer idea of why other people, as well as ourselves, act as we do, we will be more successful in solving our problems as well as their problems.

Actual statistics show that more people lose their jobs because they can't get along with other people, than because of inability to do the work. A man may be well trained in a field, even very competent in it, but he may fall by the wayside because of personality difficulties. Problems of attitude, feeling, emotion, and motivation are given much attention in this book because of their importance in our everyday affairs.

One of the things we all do is *learn*. How do we learn? How can we be better learners? These questions are taken up in some detail because they are so important to all of us.

Because of the great significance of occupations and vocational guidance, much attention is given to this; suggestions are made which we hope will help the reader in his own vocational problems.

Since we live in a democracy, we not only have to learn how to get along ourselves, but we also have a responsibility for understanding what is going on and for being ready to take intelligent action about the problems we all face. This is a responsibility we don't always like to accept, but we can't escape it if we are going to keep on having a share in determining our own destinies in the democratic way.

Consequently, we need to understand society as well as ourselves. Parts of this book are intended to help us toward that understanding. Chapters will be found dealing with the forces influencing people (advertising and propaganda, for example), the relations between employers and employees, leadership, and the various group pressures and forces affecting political and social life in America today.

Educators have found that *problem solving*—not just memorizing facts—is the best way to learn. At the end of each chapter are many questions and problems. If the reader will actually work on these, he is bound to increase greatly his understanding of the fields presented. Most of the questions deal with things in our everyday experience.

The first edition of this book has been used by hundreds of thousands of students and from reports received from the teachers and students together with accounts of current and recent developments in psychology, each chapter has been thoroughly revised to attract and hold the interest of the reader.

The author is grateful to students and faculty members of the P. K. Yonge Laboratory School of the University of Florida for opportunities to try out many materials from the book in classes, and for their helpful criticisms; to Henry Weitz of Duke University for his many suggestions; to the following members of the American School staff for their careful analysis of the manuscript and for their contributions: James McKinney, Chairman of the Board of Trustees; Dr. E. C. Estabrooke, Educational Director; Thomas E. Kennelly, Principal of the High School; and Instructors Bette Adler, Leona Prentice, and James L. Comas; and to Wayne F. Johnson of the American Technical Society for his work in the editorial preparation of the manuscript for publication.

CHARLES R. FOSTER

# CONTENTS

Hiking with groups of people is a fine way to learn how to get along with other people. This is part of a 360-person hiking party moving up the trail.

*Denver Post*

# CHAPTER ONE

# THE PROBLEMS WE MEET

In our everyday life we are continually meeting problems for which we do not always have a solution. We may, for example, have difficulty in adjusting to unfamiliar situations, such as a new job or a new school. We may be perplexed about which action is in accordance with our best interests and the best interests of others. We may be puzzled about our emotional life. We may learn that the way we see ourselves is not in accordance with the facts. We may discover our interests are not varied enough. We may find that our methods of learning are ineffective. Psychologists are concerned with these problems and in the following pages we shall attempt to describe how psychologists deal with them.

## QUESTIONS THIS CHAPTER WILL ANSWER

1. What is psychology, and what is there in it that might be helpful to me?
2. What are some of the big problems everyone faces?
3. Why are some of our most important problems connected with our homes?
4. Why is it so important to understand what the psychologists call *motivation?*
5. What are some of the main problems with which psychology is concerned?

Have you recently started on a new job, joined a new club, or moved to a new community? Or have you undertaken any type of activity unfamiliar to you?

If you have, you have discovered that you meet many problems. It seems that people are always running into problems or having to meet new and different kinds of situations. Life is full of them. They are what make life interesting. In fact, if there are no problems, we are usually bored until we find some. That accounts for the many games and sports we play. We like puzzles, mysteries, and stories.

Every new situation we meet is a test of what we can do. Do we measure up to what people expect of us? Do such experiences give

1

us a feeling of accomplishment? Certainly, while the problems create life's interest and challenge for us, it is important that we feel that we can face them with some promise of success.

This book brings to your attention some of the helpful, guiding principles that psychology and experience have to offer. Psychology means the study of the mind and its workings, or, as it is usually interpreted today, the study of *behavior*. Psychology analyzes *what* we do and *why* we do it.

Many of the problems that psychologists are interested in occur in our work, in our school, and in our home. They are all around us. Sometimes we fail to realize that maintaining a happy relationship with those around us is vitally important to our well-being.

## Meeting Life's Situations

When getting started on a new job, or in a new school, you find yourself in a new environment. The building is strange and may seem a little inhospitable. It may be located in a part of the city which is unfamiliar. You may have to make a long trip in the morning to get there, and a long trip to get home.

People are all around you, but they are strangers. They may pay little attention to you and your problems. Some of them may even seem hostile to you from time to time. Those to whom you have been accustomed to turn for help are not to be found.

You find yourself face to face with many new ways of doing things. People suddenly thrust responsibilities on you which you hadn't expected. You may be asked to do things which you had not anticipated in any way. You are expected to know things which you realize you don't know. It is evident, furthermore, that you aren't expected to lean on those around you for help.

Of course, the particular problems which you will face depend on the kind of situation you are in. In a new school, for example, a student may be assigned to subjects which are unfamiliar and for which his preparation was poor. In large schools he may be asked to choose from numerous subjects which are offered, and feel that he has no way of telling how to make the choice.

In business or industry, employers have a way of putting a new worker on his own to see what he can do. Often it looks as though no one is even slightly interested.

Millions of American men and women have found it necessary to adjust themselves to an entirely new way of life during their service in the Armed Forces.

*Official Department of Defense Photo*

Sometimes the people already employed in the shop or office have a way of showing that they are not too happy about another person coming along—possibly to compete with them. There are many side lights on human nature which appear in these common situations of life. Some of them are good while others are bad.

If you are a young man or woman just starting out in school or on a job, you will naturally be interested in the people around you. You are growing up, so you have a greater desire to impress them favorably than you did before. Almost without knowing it, you may try to "manage" things so you can associate with certain individuals, and it would not be surprising if some of those with whom you seek association are members of the opposite sex. Because of these motives, students have been known to choose one subject rather than another subject; and people have been known to turn down jobs and accept other ones for similar reasons.

The activities and opportunities of your new life gradually appear. You would like to be a part of these activities. You wonder

The newcomer may feel discomfort until he is "accepted."

what you should do to get into them and how you can discover the best ways to get ahead.

More and more you become aware of the importance of other people. You are likely to wonder why some people seem to like you more than others do, and what you should do or say to get people to like you.

You begin to have a new respect for those whose greater experience and background may make it possible for them to help you.

## Problems of Right and Wrong

In the middle years of growing up, every individual becomes very much concerned with the world and its problems. Ideals begin to develop and the young man or woman is impatient with failure and with wrongdoing. One of the big problems of life during these years and the years of early adulthood is how to reconcile the things that ought to be with things as they are. It is a task to learn how to face the disappointments of life, but it must be done.

In a world where so many kinds of things are done and people differ so widely in their activities, it is necessary to find out what is acceptable and what is not acceptable. We had thought, at first, that it was easy to decide between "right" and "wrong." But as we move about and become more widely acquainted, we find that this is no easy matter. What we had held to be "wrong" now seems, under certain conditions, to be "right." What we had thought of as being extremely improper, many people, who seem to be "all right" in other respects, accept as quite normal. This makes it necessary for us to give more consideration to what is "good" or "bad" and to revise, in some respects, our attitudes toward people whose ways of doing things are different from ours.

It bothers us when something happens that isn't "fair." We begin to see that in the world around us there is injustice as well as happiness and this is disturbing. We begin to wonder why some people have so much and others so little.

Assuming that "right" means a way of behaving and thinking that is in line with our best interests *and* the best interests of others and "wrong" means the opposite, it becomes increasingly important to find out what these "best" interests are. We try to find out where we are going and why. Instead of following paths set by others, we often learn that it is up to us to chart our own course.

## Problems of Home Life

Not the least of the problems about which we need more understanding and guidance are those connected with the home. Questions about how to get along with our parents develop in adolescent years. Problems about using the car appear. Controversies occur about when to go to bed, when to stay up, when to go to the movies, and when to have "dates."

Many Americans often get married early in life. Frequently they have problems relating to how to get along in *three* families—their own new family, the husband's family, and the wife's family. In addition to the personal adjustments of husband and wife, there may be adjustments to mothers-in-law, fathers-in-law, and brothers and sisters-in-law.

These young people are facing a bright and happy future. It will be, if they work diligently to establish the ideal home which, no doubt, is part of their dreams.

*The Bride's Magazine*

It is often hard to get the happy combination of give and take which is necessary in these relationships. Frequently parents have trouble in realizing that their children are growing up. Many parents try to control their children and keep track of them long after the children should be learning how to handle problems for themselves. Sometimes the children, instead of accepting responsibility for the things they do, want to put all of their problems off on someone else. They cling to their home ties when they ought to be learning how to stand on their own feet.

The relationships with brothers and sisters, and with other members of the family who may happen to be living in the home, have to be considered.

In a way, the home is a little world where, in miniature, all the problems of people everywhere are brought close to us. And yet, so important is this home, so vital is it to our security and well-being, that we are all doubly anxious to learn the secrets of happy adjustment here. And almost to the last man and woman, we are encouraged to think that eventually we may have homes of our own, for which the present may be a time of preparation.

## Understanding Ourselves and Others

Sometimes it seems that life would be so simple if: (1) other people wouldn't do the things they do, or (2) you could just manage everything for yourself without having to bother about what other people think or want.

But we soon realize that this is ridiculous. We are living in a world of people and it would be foolish to ignore it. In these pages an effort will be made to explain what happens when people are thrown together in situations in which they learn, live, and work together.

If we can understand *why* our neighbor acts the way he does, we will know better how to get along with him and deal with him successfully. Discovering what people want in order to be happy and successful will help to explain why they, and ourselves, do many of the things we do.

We are always trying to understand ourselves. As often as we ask, about the other fellow, "Why did he do that?," we probably ask ourselves, "Why did *I* do that?"

Certainly it is true that each human being faces the question of understanding himself, even though he may not put the question into so many words. Part of the answer to "Why did I do that?" is found in the way the individual looks upon himself, or, as some writers put it, the way he sees himself. Psychologists refer to this as the individual's *self-concept*. Morgan calls it one's self-perception.

The kind of experiences that the child has are important in determining what his self-perception will be like. The child finds that his behavior and appearance elicit kindness or hostility, respect or rebuke, attention or indifference from parents and fellows. He hears himself described by parents and playmates in terms of various personality traits, and when these traits are consistently applied, he often accepts them as descriptions of himself. Praise and love from parents, respect and attention from playmates, will contribute to the development of a picture of himself as a desirable person. On the other hand, rejection and excessive criticism at home and indifference from others can lead to a derogatory self-picture, with resulting inferiority feelings . . . . .[1]

Morgan points out that individuals often get ideas about themselves, or form "self-perceptions" which are quite different from the way the outside world perceives, or sees them.

Most of us have known people who constantly underrate their own performance. By the same token we have also known people with a grossly exaggerated view of their accomplishments and capabilities. Children surrounded by an admiring family who excessively praise even poor performance are frequently found to have excessive self-evaluations. . . . . If the person's self-picture is too different from the true or objective personality, serious adjustment problems may arise.[2]

We are all familiar with the individual who sees himself as a great authority on politics, or religion, or raising children. All too often his self-concept is really out of line with what he actually does know or can do, but we come to understand this, and so we tolerate him to a certain extent. Sometimes when a person does something obviously out of line with his personality or character as we know it, we may say, "Come on now, *be yourself.*" It is one of our characteristics that we try to explain what another does, even though the explanation we give may not be adequate.

It is obvious that we will tend to act with more self-control, and be happier, if we can gradually gain a better understanding of how we ourselves think and act, and what kind of individuals we really are. For example, a young woman may "see herself" as a poor conversationalist and a kind of "wet blanket" when she goes out with her friends. Actually, she is warm and friendly and well liked by all who know her. Here is a case where an individual has formed a "self-concept" which is definitely not in line with the facts. If she could come to realize the true situation, it would in all probability help her overcome this timidity and fear of meeting or being with other people. The importance of an individual's "self-concept" in influencing his behavior is plainly evident.

The question often asked when someone does something that is not understood is: How do you explain his action? We want to know the reasons for human behavior. If we did not seek to know why individuals act as they do, life would be very confusing.

The explanation of an act, is also important because if we know it we have reason to approve or disapprove of the act. In law this is all-important. When a man kills another, the judge or the jury must decide whether the man was sane or insane, whether it was in self-defense or not, and whether it was done in anger or in cold blood.

To understand people we must understand why they do the things they do. By a proper understanding we can be more successful in working with people. The salesman is a psychologist in this way. He wants to know how to get the customer to buy his product. The newspaperman is interested in writing a newspaper story that people will read. The teacher is interested in discovering how to tell his class about something in such a way as to make the class not only listen to his explanation, but also develop a desire to learn more about the subject. Even the little boy is interested in the problem of getting his mother to give him permission to go to the movies on Saturday afternoon. All of these everyday activities require that we know something about the way in which the other fellow thinks and feels, and what interests him. Psychology is concerned with such problems.

Another question we are interested in is: What desires do we have because of human nature itself, because of the way we are made? Are there some things we do *instinctively?*

What about that little boy in the back yard who is always getting into a fight with the small girl from next door? Practically every time we look out of the window, they are either playing peacefully or fighting and yelling for "mamma."

Is there an instinct that makes people want to fight? The psychologists have some interesting things to say about instincts and we shall examine them.

Then there are questions about why some things are more interesting than others. This is useful information. Why is it that we don't all have the same interests? Perhaps a parent would like to have his son be a doctor, but for some reason or other the idea doesn't appeal to the son. Why?

If you are interested in something, is it because you have ability in that thing, or don't the two go together—*interest* and *ability?* This question has a great deal to do with choosing an occupation.

How can we keep up an interest in something when our attention insists on drifting elsewhere? How can we maintain an even keel under conditions which make us "out of sorts" one day but happy on another? What can a person do about a friend who grows cold or indifferent "for no reason at all"? These and other questions concerning interest will be discussed in the forthcoming chapters.

## Learning

The main reason for going to school, we are told, is to learn. In every job we take, there is learning to be done. There are some things about learning which we ought to know. How can we learn best? What *is* learning? What are some of the things which make learning difficult? Can we improve our ability to learn?

At this point we should notice that the problems of learning are not always simple. There are different kinds of learning and learning takes place under different conditions. Some people learn more easily than others; some people learn some things more readily than they learn other things. Certainly we should all be interested in whatever suggestions can be made for better learning.

It is interesting to note here that many college professors complain that their students never learned *how to learn.* Suggestions for better learning methods can help any student, and these will be discussed.

### Monetary Value of Learning

Studies have shown conclusively that the completion of a high school education increases very substantially the average annual income of both men and women. The National Education Association[3] reports that men who graduate from high school received, in 1958, a median salary $1334 higher than their fellows with only eight years of elementary schooling.

Figuring the additional advantage to men of a high school education, for a *lifetime*, the report indicated that the individual with a high school education would earn $75,862 more than the

---

[3]*NEA Research Bulletin,* Volume 39, Number 2, May, 1961, pp. 58 ff.

Is the willingness to fight instinctive
or learned behavior?

individual with an elementary school education only.

In similar fashion, the study also showed a marked advantage to those who go on to earn a college degree.

In 1958 an expected lifetime income of a college graduate was $435,242 as compared with $257,557 for a high school graduate. On the basis of these data, then, one may conclude that, on the average, four years of college education would yield a return equivalent to $177,685 in lifetime income.

These figures are consistent with other findings developed through studies of educational values as measured in terms of income, and strengthen the ever mounting evidence that " education pays" in a very real economic sense.

## Emotions Can Help or Hurt You

Another topic of interest to all of us is the topic of *emotions*. We all know what emotions are—at least we see the evidences of them around us. The movies tell us that we are going to be "thrilled" or that we will grip our seats as we watch the most sensational struggle of the century, when "mighty armies clash" and "civilization hangs in the balance." We all know the exictement of

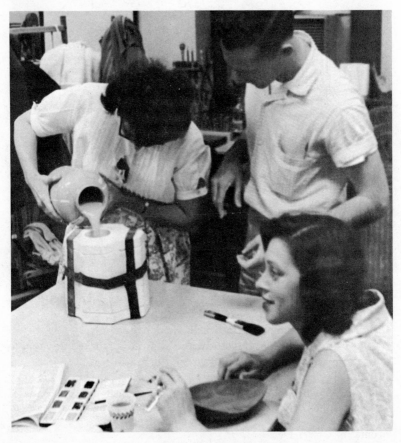

Even in casting material for a mold learning is involved. It requires interest on the part of the learner and careful attention to what the teacher is demonstrating.

*Florida Union, University of Florida*

It's just a game. So why does Harvard baseball coach "Stuffy"McInnis get so excited? Emotions are what give life its vigor and vitality.

*Photo by Marlow A. Sigel, Harvard Crimson*

a football game. We all know the sadness of leaving a friend or a dear one. We are familiar with the lovely scenes of Christmas.

The part which emotions play in our lives is so great that it is well for us to know some of the conditions which bring them about and some of the ways in which we need to deal with them.

Emotions add zest and color to life, but they also may either help or hurt us. When it comes to the possible harmful effect of emotions it becomes important to understand the ways and means of healthful control.

## Other Problems

Psychology has taught us much about individuals and how they behave, but it has also helped us to understand groups and the society in which we live. It has provided us with the means of guiding ourselves in achieving such understanding.

Without attempting to detail these here, we should simply note that there is much for us to learn about the many groups of people with whom we come in contact. In our world of politics and wars, actual or possible, it becomes more and more important to understand not only the people who live immediately around us, but the peoples of our country and its various sections as well, and indeed of the various parts of the world where our interests and values are involved.

We need to learn all we can about the *values* that people hold in our society and in other societies. Much has been heard about "social values"—the characteristics or ways of behaving of people that we consider important and toward which we tend to have rather strong emotional feelings. One of our values, for example, is respect for the dignity of the individual. When any strong or unusual punishment is meted out to some offender, we are shocked or hurt if it seems to interfere with our *value* concerning the rights and dignity of individual men and women.

There are some important problems about choosing and progressing in one's occupation, and about successful adjustment on the job, which must be considered, and finally, we must surely give some thought to problems which arise in the community in which we live.

### YOUR USE OF TIME

An exercise which is usually revealing is to make a chart or record of how you spend your time for a week. This is best done by taking seven sheets of paper, one for each day, and ruling them off in half-hour intervals, starting with the hour at which you usually get up in the morning and running through until the end of your day.

Having prepared the chart so that you have a place to write down items occurring in each half-hour, keep a record carefully for each day. So that you won't forget, it is suggested that you fill in the blanks for a day just before retiring, or early on the following morning before you have forgotten your activities.

For periods of time where you have been inactive, indicate by such expressions as "loafing around the house" or "sitting talking about nothing in particular with Jim," etc. However, where the conversation was a specific one on a specific subject, show that. The more specific your records are, the more it will show the nature of your use of time.

Be honest about it and wait until the week is over before you start examining it critically.

## A BUDGET FOR YOUR TIME

No one can write out a budget showing the best way for some other person to spend his time. To do so would be foolish under ordinary circumstances because people differ so much in their tastes and interests and in the effective use of their time.

However, each person can check his own use of time and prepare a budget for himself which is helpful. The following seven questions may suggest points to be considered in such a budget.

1. Does my time budget or plan of activities include sufficient time for sleep?

2. Do I include sufficient time to get my work done? (A student must include not only the hours spent in class but also the time needed for homework.)

3. Do I include sufficient time for transportation? (Some people are chronic late-comers because they never allow themselves time to get where they are going.)

4. Do I include sufficient time for personal care and cleanliness (dressing, bathing, care of the person, etc.)?

5. Do I include time for recreation, especially (a) physical activity, both outdoors and in, and (b) social activity involving *being with other people*?

6. Do I include time for personal improvement (reading, attending classes or lectures, attending church or related services, listening to and watching non-entertainment radio and TV programs, etc.)?

7. Do I include provision for doing my share of the work at home, including helping with the duties and responsibilities of the home?

The check list given is not exhaustive, but it provides the major points to be considered. The problem for the individual is to secure some balance in his activities according to his own needs.

It is safe to assume that some provision for each of the items on the check list must be made by the average individual for satisfactory adjustment to his life and surroundings.

## SOMETHING TO DO

It is revealing to make a list of the problems which occur under various main headings concerning our life activities.

One advantage of making such a list is that it gives the student some understanding of the great variety of adjustments we are called upon to make, and of the need for understanding them.

Suggest as many problems as you can think of under four main topics from the following:

| | |
|---|---|
| Problems of Home | Problems of Social Life |
| Problems of Study | Problems of Health |
| Problems in Your Town or Community | Problems of Religion |
| Problems of My Job | |

One suggestion might be to put each of the four headings you select at the top of a separate page and list the problems under it. The result would be a "problem book" of four pages. This could be useful in further study.

## QUESTIONS AND PROBLEMS FOR STUDY AND DISCUSSION

1. From the material which has been presented, write a page showing the *kinds* of problems with which psychology deals.

2. Make a list of the important activities in which practically all people engage.

3. Make a list of some of the ways you feel or ways in which you have behaved which have sometimes puzzled you, or take one such instance from your experience and describe it.

4. Give an example of something which was done which you considered unfair, and the reasons why you thought it unfair. Then give a possible reason why the unfair event took place and why the people involved did what they did.

5. Take a daily newspaper and make a list of about ten newspaper stories illustrating problems of human behavior. For each one of the events listed, write a question inquiring into the reason for the event. (A newspaper is a good source of illustrations since it is to a large extent a report of man's day to day problems and what he does about them.)

6. Make a short list of the people in your family and in your circle of immediate friends or school or business associates and indicate the nature of your relationship.

7. Taking the people referred to in Question 6 one at a time, indicate one trait of each which you have to take into account and about which you have to be careful in order to keep your relationship on a friendly basis.

8. Think of some situation in your school or in your work in which people are taking two different sides as to what is right and what is wrong. Try to describe the sides they are taking and give reasons or arguments which are used for defending each side.

9. Give an example, from people you know, of a person who shows that he is acting according to a high ideal. State what the ideal is and show how his behavior is being influenced by it.

# PART ONE

# WHY WE DO THE THINGS WE DO — MOTIVATION

How is our development affected by our heredity and our environment? To answer this question we need to know what characteristics are transmitted from parents to their children and how this takes place. We also need to know how certain surroundings cause some individuals to react similarly and others to react differently. We further need to know how individuals differ with regard to their intelligence.

When we ask the question "Why did he do that?" or "Why did I do that?" we frequently want to know what the motive was for performing the action. We want to know what moved the individual to act in the way he did. In this sense, *motivation* concerns all those conditions which are associated with the individual's needs and which arouse and direct his behavior toward the satisfaction of those needs. To understand other people's behavior as well as our own we must consider our various drives, appetites, and learned motives. In this chapter we will discuss our pyschological needs as well as our physical needs and their importance in regard to the individual and society.

## QUESTIONS THIS CHAPTER WILL ANSWER

1. What are the effects of the parents' experiences on their children?
2. What is a good environment?
3. How do people differ in their ability to learn?
4. How important is the physical side of our nature in determining what we do?
5. How can we maintain a good balance in our physical activity?
6. What can be said about the idea that human beings are seeking pleasure and trying to avoid pain?
7. How do people develop complicated *motives* or *ambitions?*
8. Why do people often do things that are actually dangerous?
9. Does everyone have a desire to be important and successful?
10. How much are we influenced by what other people think of us?
11. How important is "success" in everyday life for the average person?

## Heredity and Environment

Heredity consists of the physical and mental traits we get from our parents. Environment consists of everything around us which could possibly have any effect upon us.

What part of a person's make-up is due to what he obtains from his heredity and what part is due to his environment? Psychologists are continually thinking of experiences and the impression they leave on the individual. It is the environment which provides us with experiences. Your environment is different from mine, and your environment provides you with different experiences than are provided by my environment. The environment consists of the family, the social group, the community—in general, one's surroundings: places, people, and things.

It is clear, then, that you and I will differ from each other for two main reasons: (1) because our heredity (what we receive from our parents) is not the same, and (2) because we live in different environments, and therefore have had different things happen to us.

**The Mechanism of Heredity.** When the two *germ cells* unite in the body of the mother *at that moment the hereditary make-up* of the human being is determined. This hereditary make-up will

You inherit your physical structure.

include whatever traits, qualities, or possibilities for physical growth that were present in the germ cells of the parents at the time they united to form the new embryo or individual.

The technical method by which nature provides for this transfer of human qualities is a study of biology. We need not go into the details here, but it is known that the germ cells are constructed in such a way as to include particles of material called *chromosomes*. These contain still more minute particles called *genes*.

It is these units which carry the elements that provide the new individual with the qualities and characteristics which are to develop through growth.

Some of the person's qualities and traits come from his father and some from his mother. Since they, in turn, received similar traits and qualities from their parents, it can be seen that heredity goes on from one generation to another.

**The Effect of Parents' Experiences on Their Children.** Apparently, during the lifetime of each human being, these germ cells, which are the bearers of heredity, are simply housed and maintained in the body of the parent. The various things which happen to the parent in his lifetime, such as habits of eating and drinking, etc., have no effect on the make-up of these cells. This important fact was first observed and pointed out by a biologist named Weismann.

What the newborn individual receives as *heredity* through the germ cells of his parents has not been affected in any way by the kind of life his parents have led. Instead, what he gets from them, as heredity, depends solely on whatever traits or qualities were provided for by the make-up of the genes and chromosomes.

Therefore, it is nonsense to say that a baby has hair on its body because the mother was frightened by a horse or that, if a mother shows a great interest in music in the months before the birth of her baby, he or she will also show an interest in music. Nature has provided that the newborn child will have whatever traits the germ cells make possible and nothing more.

Of course, the health of the mother before the baby is born may have something to do with the *health* of the baby, but it will not have anything to do with the *heredity* of that baby.

**The Resemblance of Parents and Children.** It is generally agreed by those who have studied this problem that the traits and qualities of children are very likely to resemble those of their parents. Since the parents, in their turn, received traits and qualities from their parents, it is clear that what each person inherits comes from a long line of people starting with his parents and going back many generations. Generally speaking, about one-half of a human being's traits are received from his parents directly, and about one-half of the traits come from previous generations.

**Variations.** The student can see that we can never predict accurately what a child will be like just because we know what his parents are like. He will probably resemble them in many ways, but there will be other ways in which he will *not* resemble them. Sometimes an individual is born who varies a great deal from his parents. For example, a very bright father and mother may give birth to a child who is very dull or even feeble-minded. This means that somewhere in the germ cells of the parents there were what are known as *recessive* traits. When these appear, they may show themselves in such a characteristic as feeble-mindedness. That is, some feeble-mindedness is believed to be caused by specific recessive traits. A recessive trait which leads to the condition of feeble-mindedness must, according to the present theory, be combined with a parallel trait in the germ cell of the mate in order to produce this effect. Fortunately, it is not a common occurrence, but it can happen. This applies to other traits besides feeble-mindedness, of course, and probably to as many good traits as undesirable ones. But when we know that this can happen in connection with the working of heredity, it helps us to understand the fact that sometimes there can be sharp differences between children and the families from which they have come.

Occasionally a child is injured in the process of being born. Such *birth injuries* sometimes cause learning difficulties and damage to the nervous system. When this happens, the child would not owe his condition to heredity but to an accident in connection with his birth.

**The Main Ways in Which Heredity Affects the Child.** Let us examine what it is that a child does derive from heredity. These traits and qualities may be described under four main headings:

**1. Intelligence.** The child derives a certain amount of intelligence, or *mental ability,* from his parents and ancestors. Some persons are born with much and some with little of this quality which we refer to as mental ability.

**2. Emotionality.** The child derives a certain pattern of possible emotional behavior. This is due to the fact that heredity determines to a great extent the actual physical make-up of the individual. This physical make-up has much to do with the way he feels or his emotions.

**3. Physical Appearance.** The child's physical appearance is affected by his heredity. This is very important. We are likely to have the facial and bodily characteristics of our parents. The color of our eyes, the color of our hair, the general shape of the nose or chin, the forehead, the ears, our height, and our weight—these are all some of the ways in which our bodies are affected by heredity.

**4. Physical Stamina.** Also affected by heredity is the physical stamina, that is, the degree of physical energy and resistance that we are likely to possess or enjoy. Some people tend to be strong and vigorous; others tend to be weak and puny. Most are in between. Some recover quickly from disease; others are slow to be restored to health and vigor. Undoubtedly this vital quality is affected by the conditions we derive from our parents and those who have gone before. Longevity—or length of life—is also considered to be affected by the individual's heredity.

We should note that in each of these four ways, heredity merely *sets the limits* within which we may develop.

Whether we live up to the possibilities provided depends much on the conditions under which we grow and under which we live. It is probably true that most people never live up to the possibilities which heredity gives them. They may be able to learn much more than they ever do learn. They may be able to run faster than they ever do run. They may be able to make themselves look much more attractive than they actually do look.

It is the privilege of each individual to make as wise a use as possible of the gifts which nature has given to him.

## A Closer Look at Intelligence

Because of the major importance of intelligence in our lives, some further aspects of it should be considered.

Perhaps *mental ability* would be a better term to use. The question is: How do people differ in their ability to learn and to think, in their readiness to meet new situations in life, in their grasp of things, and in their ability to "get along"?

Before psychologists began looking into the matter, intelligence was simply taken for granted. People who had it were said to be "bright," and those who lacked it were called "dull." Now we know that hardly a human being is born who does not have intelligence. The question is: How much intelligence does he have and of what kind? It seems that intelligence differs from person to person in that some people are skillful with words and ideas, others with their hands, and still others in ability to meet with and get along with people.

Those who are quick with the use of words and ideas, who absorb things quickly from books and who can express themselves well in speech and writing, might be said to have *academic* or *abstract* intelligence. This does not mean that they don't have other kinds of intelligence too, but it means that they are particularly strong in the academic direction.

Others are skillful with their hands. They see how things are put together; they often like machines and motors. They are sometimes said to be strong in *mechanical* intelligence.

The group included under the heading of *social intelligence* would include the people who seem to get along especially well with other people. They know what to do when they are with people. They are quick to "size up" other folks; they know how to meet and talk with them; they often are good at leading them. They are usually well liked and play a very important part in our social life.

These three classes—the abstract, the mechanical, and the social—have been widely used by psychologists to indicate that people differ *in the direction* of their abilities. It is clear, though, that the differences between these three classes of ability are not well marked. And you will be able to think of people that seem to combine all three types of intelligence—the all-round people who are"good"in almost anything.

One thing that has become increasingly evident to psychologists is the fact that every human being has to have more than just intelligence in the narrow sense of the word. He has to have purpose, drive, and initiative. It is because some individuals lack this that they do not become successful, even though they may have a good deal of intelligence as we have defined it in the first paragraphs of this chapter. One of the problems we have is to enable people who have a considerable amount of ability to *use* it for their own good and the good of society.

Psychologists who have been most successful in trying to measure intelligence have followed the idea that the best way is to take a great many samples of what a person can do. If a man or a boy can perform well on a number of different tasks, jobs, or problems, we can assume that he has a considerable amount of this thing we call intelligence. In this sense, it is not abstract, or mechanical, or social intelligence of which we are speaking, but we are referring to this all-round general quality known as mental ability.

Psychologists have had some difficulty in giving a good definition of intelligence. One writer has written as follows about it:

There is little agreement as to just what kind of adjustment should be most emphasized by the word "intelligence." A person with a "large intellect" knows many facts. He is quick and clever in using what he knows. He spends long hours in reflection, is seasoned in judgment, and views problems with a broad perspective. He can readily apply himself to all types of practical situations. But some people are clever with their hands. We call them intelligent. Others can concentrate on problems, and they show strong purposes and motives. Some men stimulate us by the richness of their personalities. Are these factors also included in the word intelligence?[1]

There is the idea of "knowing" something, a great deal, in fact. There is the thought of being "quick and clever" with what one knows. There is the idea of being able to meet practical problems, to work with the hands, and to work with people.

There have been many times in the past when people failed to recognize intelligence when they came across it. Walter Percival brings this out as follows:

Today we can answer the question "how bright?" or "how dull?" The intelligence possessed by many people has been misjudged in former days. Oliver Goldsmith's teacher thought him one of the dullest children in the class. At twelve years of age, Sir Isaac Newton was placed at the foot of his class. Patrick Henry was "too idle to gain any solid advantage from the opportunities that were thrown in his way." Napoleon Bonaparte came forty-second in his class when he graduated. Such a failure to recognize ability would be inexcusable now.[2]

**Meaning of Intelligence Quotient or I.Q.** The *intelligence quotient* is simply a device for showing the relative intelligence or mental ability of the individual. It is found by dividing the mental age by the chronological age (number of years the individual has lived).

The following examples will illustrate:

Suppose John Smith's mental age, determined by the score he makes on an intelligence test, is 10. Suppose his chronological age is also 10. Then his intelligence quotient, or I.Q., will be 100:

$$\frac{\text{Mental age 10}}{\text{Chronological age 10}} = 1.00 \times 100 = \text{I.Q. 100}$$

[1]Coleman R. Griffith, *Psychology Applied to Teaching and Learning* (New York: Rinehart & Company, Inc., 1939), p. 50.

[2]Walter Pilling Percival, *Why Educate?* (Toronto: J. M. Dent & Sons, Ltd., 1941).

If the mental age which John Smith secured on the basis of the test turned out to be 12, and his chronological age is 10, the result is as follows:

$$\frac{\text{Mental age } 12}{\text{Chronological age } 10} = 1.20 \times 100 = \text{I.Q. } 120$$

But if John Smith's mental age was only 8, on the basis of the test, the result would be this:

$$\frac{\text{Mental age } 8}{\text{Chronological age } 10} = 0.80 \times 100 = \text{I.Q. } 80$$

Generally speaking, the average intelligence quotient, which we would obtain if we gave every human being an intelligence test so that his mental age could be tabulated, would be 100. Any person with an I.Q. above 100, therefore, is said to be above average; every person with an I.Q. below 100 is said to be below average.

But every citizen should realize that *there are just as many people* with I.Q.'s below 100 as there are people with I.Q.'s above 100.

If everybody would realize this, it would save a considerable amount of misunderstanding as to just what the I.Q. really means in life. It is simply a measure for showing how a person stands with reference to the matter of *general intelligence*, in comparison with his fellows.

We are justified, as we have seen, in assuming that any person with a very low I.Q. will have difficulty in learning; just as we are justified in saying that a person with a high I.Q. should be able to learn rapidly and do quite well in most problem situations.

It is important to emphasize here that there are no hard and fast lines between individuals who are placed in various I.Q. classifications. It would be impossible to discover differences of any importance between an individual whose I.Q. is 51 and one whose I.Q. is 49. For purposes of classification the line has to be drawn somewhere, and it is drawn at these points.

**Three Commonly Recognized Classes of Low Intelligence.** Those in the feeble-minded groups are often thought of as falling within three classes, described as follows:

1. Those whose intelligence is at the lowest level. Their I.Q. is below 25. These are known as *idiots*. They are so helpless that they must be cared for throughout life, and they are practically unable to learn.

2. Those whose intelligence ranges from an I.Q. of 26 to an I.Q. of 50. These are known as *imbeciles*. They are not able to learn

much, but, if taught patiently, they can be taught a few skills, such as picking up waste paper, carrying things, etc. They cannot take responsibility, and they must be constantly taken care of.

3. Those whose intelligence ranges from I.Q. 51 to I.Q. 70. These are known as *morons*. They are capable of considerable training, but it requires time and patience to teach them. They are able to learn to read. They can perform simple tasks and can be given many kinds of routine jobs. One, for example, held a job as a telegraph delivery boy until his death at the age of 55. He was faithful and well-liked by everyone who knew him.

It is important to remember that classifications and terms such as have just been presented are for convenience and for the purpose of clarifying our understanding of intelligence. Any given individual might not be easily placed—there are border line cases and the classifications tend to shade into one another. Above all the tendency to "brand" an individual by using these terms must be avoided.

## Distribution of I.Q.'s

The following shows the percentage of population in each of I.Q. ranges.[3]

| I.Q. Range | Percentage of Population in This Group |
|---|---|
| Below 68 | 2% (feeble-minded) |
| 68 to 83 | 14% (below average) |
| 84 to 116 | 68% (average) |
| 117 to 132 | 14% (above average) |
| Above 132 | 2% (superior) |

**How Are These Measures of Intelligence Obtained?** The measures of intelligence just cited were obtained on the basis of a very well-developed intelligence test known as the Stanford-Binet test. It is a test which includes a wide variety of little tasks or problems to be worked out at the direction of a trained person who administers the test.

As a result of giving the test to many thousands of persons, psy-

---

[3]M. J. Nelson, *Handbook of Educational Psychology and Measurement* (New York: The Dryden Press, 1941), p. 32.

chologists have been able to find out what score the average six-year-old child will make, what score the average five-year-old child will make, etc. When an individual takes the test, they can determine whether he has the *mental age* of a five-year-old, a six-year-old, or whatever age level it may be.

**Physical Appearance and Intelligence.** A question is often asked: Can we tell the difference between the feeble-minded and the normal by the way they look? The answer to this is quite clear: We cannot tell the difference between people on the basis of the "way they look."

One of the most attractive and cherub-like boys in a certain state institution has an I.Q. which places him in the low moron class. And it is possible to find, among the geniuses of the world, people who "look like" morons.

In other words, the "dumb" look which the world associates with morons is a general picture of morons which has no basis in fact and which has grown up somewhat like tradition. In the movies and cartoons, a "dumb" person is usually portrayed as a thick-skulled, dull-eyed, mussy-haired individual, and a general "picture" has developed in the public mind that this is the way morons appear.

There are, it is true, some deformities and physical features which are associated with certain types of low-grade feeble-minded whose lack of intelligence is the result of some birth injury or physical cause. The term *stigmata* is sometimes applied to these. It may be said, though, that, on the whole, the appearance of the feeble-minded is not different from that of their more intelligent fellows.

**Intelligence in Relation to Race.** Efforts have been made to study this question, but they have not been very successful. It is hard to compare two races because it is hard to find two groups whose members may be fairly compared.

Obviously, it not fair to compare a group of children who have grown up in favorable environments with a group of children who have grown up in a poor environment.

There is a great deal of evidence that many people of another race will have intelligence which is superior to that of a great many white persons, and there will be a great many white people whose intelligence is superior to that of other races. That is the important thing because it shows that if similar educational opportunity is provided to other races, many will come forth to benefit greatly by it.

The problems of relationship among persons of different races are great, but they are not problems of difference in native intelligence. They are problems involving social attitudes, customs, historical issues, and economic opportunity. They should be approached in that light.

There is no evidence from the investigations of psychology that any race is superior to any other race. The idea of "Nordic supremacy," which was the rallying cry of the German nation under Nazi leadership, was pure quackery.

Another fallacy which studies in psychology have upset is the belief that a person who is superior in intelligence is usually a weakling physically. Here again, we note the tendency of people to build up a stereotype or prevailing idea as to what some classes are like. The "bright" person has come to be thought of as a slight, short, hollow-chested person who wears tortoise shell glasses and keeps his head buried in a book.

Professor Terman has shown by careful study of a large number of superior children that they are not only the equals of other children in physical size, height, strength, and athletic ability, but that they *tend to be superior to the others in these traits too!*[4]

## Importance of Finding Out about Our Abilities

One of the things which a modern school hopes to do is to enable the individual to find out something about his intelligence and his abilities. Naturally, if we have some information on this subject, we can make a better educational plan for ourselves, and we can be more successful in choosing a vocation or profession toward which to point our energies.

It is wasteful for those with very high intelligence to spend their time and energies on activities which do not make the best use of their abilities.

It is also unwise for those with very limited general intelligence to work vainly toward an objective which their ability will never permit them to reach.

All individuals are endowed with some abilities which they can use to great advantage.

[4] L. M. Terman, *Genetic Studies in Genius*, Volume I, Mental and Physical Traits of a Thousand Gifted Children, Stanford University, 1925-26.

# PART TWO

# CHAPTER TWO

# WHY WE DO THE THINGS WE DO— MOTIVATION

We have considered heredity in relation to emotionality, physical appearance, physical stamina, and intelligence. We have also considered various kinds of intelligence, the meaning of the intelligence quotient, and the relation of general intelligence to physical appearance and race. We now turn to another important factor used to explain our behavior, that is, our environment, and explore it more thoroughly. We shall examine the effects of different environments on people. We shall discuss our physical needs as well as our learned needs, and show how they enable us to better understand our behavior. We shall mention the importance of maintaining a good balance between activity and rest. Reference will also be made to the pleasure-pain theory, considered by some people to explain all human behavior.

## The Importance of Environment

The student should realize that when a psychologist speaks of environment he means more than just the obvious things. Before the child is born, his mother provides his entire environment. After he is born, he is thrown into a new environment. This environment consists of the crib in which he sleeps, the bedclothes and small articles of clothing which surround him, the light or darkness of the room, the sounds made by people and objects, and, most important, the people themselves.

In fact, everything which is around him and which can possibly have any effect upon him is part of his environment.

**Why Environment Is Never the Same for Any Two People.** It has been said that the people who live in his home are part of the child's environment. When we look into it, we see that environment is different for every human being. Sometimes people think that it is the same for two individuals if they live in the same family.

Thus, when a high-school boy gets into trouble, we may hear it said, "I don't see why Henry doesn't get along well in school. His brother James never had any trouble. How can this be when both boys come from the same environment?"

Of course, both boys *don't* have the same environment. Henry is part of James's environment and James is part of Henry's environment. Each boy will have different friends and playmates. The parents probably do not treat the boys exactly alike. Perhaps they sleep in different rooms. One has a pet, and the other doesn't have one. All of these are differences in environment. All of them play a part in the matter of how the two boys grow and develop.

During the period of growth, every human being is much influenced by what happens to him. This is so to such an extent that it is not long after an individual is born that it becomes quite hard to tell which of his qualities are due to heredity and which are due to environment.

It is true that a good environment has a lot to do with producing a good person, and a bad environment has the opposite effect. But it must be remembered that many people who started out in life with rather poor environments rose from these surroundings to lead rich and useful lives. Others who were born in the midst of opportunity have failed.

It is a *combination* of qualities and opportunities which make for success. While it is the job of each person to *make the best of his opportunities* and of the traits which heredity has given him—for his own good and the good of society—still, we should certainly prefer to have a world where people could grow up in an environment which would give each and every one of them a chance to meet his own most important needs. Too often the opposite is true.

The most desirable condition is one in which the individual has what is usually called a good *biological inheritance* and a home and community to grow in which is stimulating and worthy. Of the two forces, heredity and environment, something can be done about the environment but there is little that can be done about one's heredity.

Both elements are vitally necessary. A good seed can't grow very well in poor soil; and certainly a defective seed can't produce a fine plant in good soil.

Every person has the right to an opportunity to grow into a useful member of society. Until that opportunity has been given to him, we have no right to say that he cannot become such a person.

## Two Main Types of Behavior

One of the most interesting questions in psychology is certainly the question: Why do people do the things they do? What are the reasons for the many types of behavior? It is a fascinating subject to study because there is so much variety to human activities.

It will be helpful to the student to note that we may divide our behavior into two principal types:

Where do they come from? What do they do? It is interesting to speculate on the ambitions and plans of people we meet—like these winter visitors to Atlantic City Boardwalk.

*Fred Hess and Son, Atlantic City Convention Bureau*

*The things we do because of the way our bodies have developed.*
We are physical organisms and organic needs often influence our
behavior.

*The things we do because of the changes that have taken place
in us through learning.* All learning is determined by the kinds of
experiences we have had. These experiences shape our personalities
and result in our having certain wishes, attitudes, and ideas.
Through them we develop rather definite notions of what is good
and bad for us, and, as mentioned before, certain "self-concepts."
How we see ourselves and how we think of ourselves is bound to
influence our behavior.

## Our Organic Needs

A great many of our responses are accounted for when we
study the biological nature of the human being. In the first place,
there are the conditions of an organic sort which must be met in
order to keep alive. These include the need for food to satisfy
hunger, the need for water to satisfy thirst, and the need for
conditions of life which will enable us to avoid pain or other
annoying discomforts.

One writer has summarized some of the more important physical
drives under the heading of "biological drives."[5]

The hunger drive
The thirst drive
Air hunger
Fatigue
The sleep drive
Warmth and cold drives
Pain as a drive
Bowel and bladder tensions

Under "appetites and aversions" Ruch considers the "sexual
appetite" and such things as appetites for certain foods and flavors,
for certain colors, for certain kinds of musical sounds and other
items. He notes that "the appetites have very much the same

---

[5] Floyd L. Ruch, *Psychology and Life* (Chicago: Scott, Foresman & Company, 1958), pp. 106ff.

function in directing human behavior as do the basic biological drives. The organism will persistently seek to maintain the pleasurable gratification of an appetite and will actively seek it when it is not present."[6]

Ruch describes an "aversion" as a "negative appetite"—something we dislike and strive to avoid. An example of this might be a disagreeable odor.

Appetites and aversions are not as closely related to the basic physical structure as are the biological drives; and they appear to be influenced by learning and experience to a considerable extent. Thus some odors which are disagreeable to certain individuals do not appear to be so in the case of others. Some odors do not appear to be offensive to very young children although they are offensive to adults.

It would also seem that aversions, although they influence what we do to a considerable extent, do not have the motivating force that is characteristic of the biological drives. The biological drives are fundamental and more demanding — aversions operate to influence what we do, but at a less powerful level. Aversions will yield to the demands of the basic biological drives.

Each of these drives and aversions could be analyzed in more detail. Thus when we are hungry, we experience a "gnawing" sensation which is the result of contractions of muscles in the stomach walls, resulting from the absence of food on which these muscles could be working.

It is interesting to note that when the stomach has been without food for a long time, the muscles tire, become relatively quiet, and then we no longer feel so hungry. This is the reason why one is sometimes able to fast for a lengthy period.

The condition of being hungry usually sets off a series of activities on our part, and a great many of the things we do can certainly be explained on that basis.

The young baby tries to satisfy this need simply by crying for its mother, who, it has already learned, will be able to care for its wants in this respect. Later on, after the baby has grown for two or three years, he will be making raids on cracker boxes and will gradually learn that there are times when this hunger can be satisfied and times when it can't be satisfied.

---

[6]*Ibid.*, p. 15.

The need to be more comfortable when cold, or hot, leads to an amazing list of human activities, including making and wearing of clothes, obtaining fuel to make fires, building houses, making heating systems, and manufacturing air-conditioning units. It takes but little imagination to see that changes in the weather lie behind a vast process of building and manufacturing which is one of the major sources of income for millions of workers.

Another interesting example of the motivating force of organic conditions might be the effects that disagreeable odors resulting from perspiration have on our behavior and on our economy. This would be an instance of what happens because of an aversion. Not only do we try to avoid conditions in which body odors are present, even to the extent of avoiding people whom we suspect might be disagreeable in this regard, but we spend millions of dollars annually to try to avoid being offensive because of this condition.

Rest and activity—we need a good balance
between the two.

Likewise our aversion to disagreeable odors makes it necessary that certain types of manufacturing plants be built at locations where they will not be disturbing to residential areas, and the same is true of noise-producing industries. We spend, and are willing to spend, large sums of money to protect ourselves from such sources of unpleasantness.

**Maintaining a Good Balance.** One of the things which is most important is that we maintain a good balance between activity and rest. Overexertion and lack of sleep make severe inroads on the physical health of many people. It is especially true in a society like ours when many people do not keep "in condition."

Students of human growth and development suggest that the question of the amount of sleep needed by individuals is a highly personal one—some people obviously are able to live alert, satisfactory lives with fewer hours of sleep than others. The amount of sleep needed by adolescent boys and girls is probably somewhat more than six or seven hours because they live rather highly "scheduled" lives.

A good rule to follow would be that a junior or senior high school boy or girl have a "bed time" hour that would allow "adequate" sleep for him—and this can usually be determined by the test of whether or not his day to day activities show that he is getting enough rest. There is little basis, apparently, for a uniform requirement applicable to all.

There are some practical suggestions that occur to us from our realization of the importance of a physical balance in connection with *motivation*.

We should try to see to it that our physical activities and opportunities for rest and recreation are in good balance. Time to play and time to rest are important. *Active recreations* are important, as well as *passive* ones. Passive recreations are those in which you are just a spectator or an observer. Include in your life program some recreations in which you do something of a physical nature, or, it may be, something involving both physical and mental activity. Don't be a victim of *spectatoritis* (so many Americans just go to see shows and games, and never take part themselves in health-giving activities).

It is necessary to culitivate some interests of the active sort. Some games require a whole team, others may be engaged in by one person or by just a few persons. Tennis, handball, golf, hiking, and swimming are good active sports to become interested in, since you can continue these activities at times and in places where there aren't other people around to form teams.

The importance of physical exercise is so great that it ought to be emphasized in any discussion of psychology. An illustration of its importance is found in the reports of biologists who have studied the life and health of people in tropical or subtropical climates. In these warm areas, it has been found that the people who take part in active physical exercise, or work, are healthier both physically and mentally than those who are indolent and inactive.

Young men and women, in their high-school years, engage in a great variety of activities because of the driving force of sex. This includes dating, going steady, "necking," reading material and looking at pictures having sexual connotations, sharing "stories" with a sexual theme, and in addition a host of manners and customs identified with the desire of the boy to impress the girl and the desire of the girl to attract the boy.

Less directly observed behavior which is *motivated* by the sexual drive might include a boy's working at a job in order to get money to spend on girls or a girl's preoccupation with matters of dress, hair styling, and grooming in order to be attractive to boys.

The problem for the individual is to keep these activities within bounds and within the limits of what is considered to be good for society and for the individual.

If we can keep in mind the fact that the body is continually striving to maintain a balance between its various needs and requirements, we get a very good picture of the basic importance of the physical side of life.

Of course, it is very seldom that any human being actually achieves a true state of balance. We always seem to have either too much or too little of the things we need. Either we are too hungry, or we have just eaten a big meal and feel overstuffed; we are very sleepy, or we have just had a long nap and feel very disagreeable. The room is either too hot or it is too cold. There are too many covers on the bed or not enough. The office has too little fresh air or the breeze is blowing everything onto the floor.

In other words, the human body is usually experiencing a shortage in something, or an excess of what is needed. Therefore, in the principle of keeping a balance, or equilibrium, we have a

very satisfactory explanation for many of the things we find ourselves doing in life.

**The Pleasure-Pain Theory.** Some people have tried to explain
human behavior in terms of avoidance of pain and seeking after
pleasure. It is true, of course, that we have a tendency to want to
do the things which make us comfortable and to avoid the things
which lead to discomfort and suffering.

But this is not always true. Sometimes people do things which
lead to suffering instead of pleasure. This is true of overeating, too
much drinking of intoxicating beverages, or overexertion. When
these things occur, we have to look to other reasons besides the
mere seeking of pleasure, or avoidance of pain, to explain things.

But, it is true, we are usually to be found doing quite a few
things simply because they bring us pleasure. We just like to do
them. We are very likely to avoid everything which is disagreeable
or which may bring discomfort. Making allowance for many
exceptions, it is safe to say that we seek most of the time the
conditions that promote our well-being and sense of happiness and
provide us with a measure of enjoyment.

## Some Motives Which Result from Learning

A little reflection shows that a great many things people do
seem tó have little relation to physical needs. Why does a student
spend hours in the library working on a term paper for history?
Why will a violinist give up many ordinary pleasures in order to
spend days practicing preliminary to appearing in a concert? Why
will a missionary risk the dangers of life in tropical jungles and
willingly separate himself from his friends and home for periods as
long as three years? Why do men risk their lives every day in such
activities as stunt flying, automobile racing, climbing rugged mountains, or driving through dangerous and crowded city traffic?
There are reasons for all of these things and they certainly do not
all find an explanation in the satisfying of physical urges. Many
things men do are clearly dangerous and may even lead to the
destruction of the individual himself.

The general answer to why men do these things is that man is
so made that he *learns* to want some things rather than others. The

things he does because he *learns* to want to do them are often of tremendous importance.

If we take the example of the boy who likes history, we will probably find that as he has gone to school and found that the reading of history brought him pleasure in one way or another. Perhaps his father has always been interested in history and has often pointed out historical places or talked about historical events.

Perhaps his parents or a teacher have congratulated him when he has said things in class showing that he knew something about

**Why does a student spend hours in study?**

history. Such experiences have made him feel that reading history is worth while. He may even go on to study history further and eventually decide that he would like to be a writer of history or a teacher of the subject.

These learned motives become so powerful as motivating forces that they may direct the entire future of our lives. Psychologists are not sure that they know just why one individual will develop an interest in one field, whereas another may become interested in something entirely different. But they are quite sure that the *learning experiences we go through,* year after year, have a great deal to do with it.

It would help our understanding of this problem of motivation to examine other examples.

**Desire for Social Status.** Why does a man become an engineer? Here again it is likely that his early experiences have much to do with it. Perhaps he liked to build things as a child. Perhaps he showed exceptional ability in mathematics and physics at school. Perhaps it occurred to him that if he could succeed in this line of endeavor, people would look up to him and he would earn a certain amount of prominence. Psychologists refer to this as *social status.* It is regarded by those who seek it as worthy of achievement.

What makes tennis interesting? Several kinds of motivations are at work in a competition like this one at Forest Hills. Can you identify some of them?

*NBC Photo*

To the thoughtful reader it will be apparent that such values are extremely important in the explanation of behavior.

**Joy of Taking Risks.** Men and women seem to enjoy taking risks. Climbing mountains and gambling illustrate this. There is a risk in climbing mountains because you may fall and injure yourself. There is a risk in gambling because you may lose something which is valuable to you. If there were no risks involved in these activities many people would not engage in them.

This university music professor clings to a rock corner halfway up Flatiron, with the city of Boulder in the background. He finds mountain climbing challenging, yet relaxing. It is obviously slightly risky!

*Denver Post*

**Desire to Escape from Monotony.** One of the motives which causes people to act in various ways is the desire to get away from conditions which are monotonous. It has often been observed that people who have little or nothing to do, and for whom practically all wants are satisfied, will become restless and turn to possible avenues of excitement or change.

Evidently whether a given type of activity is monotonous or not depends on all of the other conditions present, and on the attitude of the individual. Nevertheless it is a safe generalization that individuals will seek to *vary* their activities and that they are usually much more satisfied if there is some variety in what they do.

**Desire To Feel Important or Successful.** One other very important cause of behavior is the desire which people seem to have to feel important and successful. Psychologists often refer to the personality needs of the individual. It is recognized that a human being wants more than merely to eat and sleep. He wants to be recognized as a person, and he wants to *feel* that he is successful.

The "wanting to be recognized as a person" is a *social need*. The "wanting to feel that one is successful" is a *personality need*.

Here we have two immensely important drives in human nature and they are of great interest to the psychologist. They tie in with what we have said about some motives being organic, and some motives being learned, because in order to satisfy our biological or physical needs we have to be successful and we have to get along with other people.

These important drives tie in with what we have said about motives being learned, because it is through our experiences, especially our experiences with people, that we *learn* the value of social and personal success.

Certainly every individual feels better and works more efficiently if he is able to succeed in something and if he is able to feel that his own place in the world is important. Most students of social behavior feel that every human being has some untapped potential—that everyone has something he can do well, or better, if we can just discover what it is. The challenge is to look for these talents in ourselves and in others.

## SOMETHING TO DO

Since it is so important to all of us to find out what things we can do well, and what things we might reasonably expect to be able to accomplish satisfactorily, we should study our own make-up in this respect.

It is often true that we may be very much interested in some things for which we do not have the ability or aptitude which is necessary for success. Then there are other activities which we might be very good at, if we had a chance to explore them or try them out.

It seems probable that most people could do many things well which they have never tried, or have never even considered as possible.

On the chart which follows, make a little study of yourself along these lines.

To aid you in thinking of different possibilities, use the following check list of broad fields of activity:

A. Educational activities (school subjects, courses).
B. Activities around the home.
C. Activities and things which are going on in the community.
D. Occupations or jobs—full time or part time.
E. Games and sports.
F. Religious activities.
G. Activities in the field of art, music, crafts—hobbies.

*Some Comparisons of Interests and Ability*

| Activities Which Interest Me | My Probable Ability in the Activity: Very Good, Fair, Poor, Don't Know | I Might Have Some Ability if Given a Chance — Yes or No |
|---|---|---|
| 1. | | |
| 2. | | |
| 3. | | |
| 4. | | |
| 5. | | |
| 6. | | |
| 7. | | |
| 8. | | |
| 9. | | |
| 10. | | |
| 11. | | |
| 12. | | |
| 13. | | |
| 14. | | |
| 15. | | |

*Comment:*

## QUESTIONS AND PROBLEMS FOR STUDY AND DISCUSSION

1. Can you report on any example of the inheritance of a physical trait which you have observed or come across in your experience?

2. Since we inherit our traits from so many different human individuals, is it likely that a descendant of the Pilgrim Fathers will possess many of the particular traits of those individuals?

3. Do we inherit disease?

4. Do certain diseases run in certain families? Explain.

5. Do people inherit mental disease or insanity?

6. Do people inherit special ability, like musical ability?

7. Do you think it would be possible to produce better people by strict laws controlling who should marry? Do you think this would be desirable?

8. What are some of the characteristics of a good environment: (a) at home, and (b) in the school?

9. From your reading in history or literature, show: (a) how some man or woman was able to rise above his environment to honor and success, and (b) how some individual was restricted and handicapped by the environment in which he lived.

10. Write a little sketch indicating what you would expect to find in a city which provided a good environment in which to live and grow.

11. Make a list of some of the things you have done during the past week because of organic or physical needs.

12. How far will a person go in undertaking something which involves pain or discomfort?

13. Every winter several million people plan to travel to Florida to spend from a few days to several months. What is the motivation involved in this?

14. Mention some activity or interest you have which seems to have been *learned*. Can you indicate the experiences on which this was based? Sometimes we develop an interest or motive without realizing what brought it about. Do you have such an interest or motive which you could describe?

15. A boy was finally caught for taking small amounts of change from other students' desks and pocketbooks. Can you think of any motives which might have caused him to do this?

16. A bank cashier was arrested for embezzling large sums of money from a bank. What would be some possible motives which might have caused him to do this?

17. Sometime ago a New York City bus driver drove one of the city's large buses to Miami. His action was not discovered until he appeared in Miami with the bus. What possible motive could have been behind this rather unusual action?

18. Take some subject in school which you have liked or disliked. Analyze the reasons why you have liked or disliked the subject.

19. Take some hobby and show the kind of motivation which is involved in it.

20. In Minneapolis, a wealthy man, some years ago, constructed a tall skyscraper shaped somewhat like the Washington monument. In large letters atop the building his name appeared. What motivation does this suggest?

21. Interview a newsstand dealer on which magazines sell the most copies. Make a list of the five best-selling ones. See if you can analyze the features which probably caused this.

22. Note a motion picture which really attracts big crowds. Analyze the probable reasons for this.

23. Describe several kinds of motivation which you can see in a group of people attending a big football game. Which of the motives mentioned in this chapter can be identified in the actions of this group of spectators?

24. Note the conversational interests of some people. The topics they talk about evidently motivate them a great deal. What are some of these topics?

25. Select one of the topics discussed in the preceding chapter which held some interest for you. What motive caused you to have this interest in your opinion?

26. In your own words, describe what is meant by: (a) academic intelligence, (b) social intelligence, and (c) mechanical intelligence.

27. Describe a person who illustrates each of these three types of intelligence.

28. Make a list, in three columns, of some of your own abilities in each of the three areas: academic or abstract, social, and mechanical.

29. Why do we say that intelligence has something to do with choosing occupations or vocations? What are some of the things we should be careful about in this connection?

30. What is said about the relation between the way people look (appearance) and intelligence?

# CHAPTER THREE

# PERSONAL MOTIVES, INSTINCTS, AND COMPETITION

Some of our friends may show a lack of confidence in their relations with others while others may exhibit over-confidence in their behavior. We also may be shy or aggressive at times. The importance of understanding our behavior as well as others requires that we examine the conditions which are associated with each of these types of behavior.

Often we act on a particular occasion to gain the approval of others. On other occasions we may act without thinking of whether or not the social group to which we belong approves. Such actions are frequently intermingled but usually we are able to discern the difference. The way in which such purposes motivate us will be examined.

Some of our actions are said by some to be instinctive in nature. We are said to fight because we have an instinct to fight or to be curious because we have an instinct to be curious. The value of such explanations will be analyzed.

Perhaps one of the most discussed topics is competition. We hear a great deal about it in connection with business and industry, as well as in relation to games and sports. This chapter considers the nature and importance of competition from the standpoint of psychology and suggests how it may be used wisely for the betterment of ourselves and others.

## QUESTIONS THIS CHAPTER WILL ANSWER

1. What effect does failure have on our behavior? What are some of the peculiarities of conduct which may be traced to this cause?

2. What is the importance of a feeling of personal satisfaction? What do we mean by self-respect and self-approval? Why do psychologists consider them important?

3. Are there really instincts which drive us to behave in certain ways?

4. Are people inevitably driven to fight? Is there a fighting instinct?

5. What do psychologists say about competition? Is it good or bad? Is it necessary?

## Motives That Affect Our Personality

**Failure To Achieve Success.** If a person allows a feeling of failure to dominate him, he may attempt certain ways of "making up" for the things he is unable to do. This is true of all of us to a certain extent. People usually try to make up for shortcomings which they feel and are anxious to avoid. Thus a boy might want to keep away from other boys for fear his own faults might be talked about, or for fear he might not be able to say or do what would be expected of him. Sometimes this feeling is the result of previous experiences in which he has met with failure and has, as a result, felt discomfort and chagrin. But the causes of shyness are not simple and the same factors which produce shyness in some individuals, produce aggressive and hostile behavior in others.

Another way in which this idea might work out is that the individual might adopt a policy of being very blunt and forward, or *aggressive,* apparently hoping by this means to make people realize that he is not timid or weak in any respect.

Here we have, in rather simple terms, the explanation of *two* main types of human behavior. First, we have the shy or withdrawing behavior, which is defensive behavior intended to keep us out of situations in which we might be criticized for some shortcoming we have, either real or imaginary. Second, we have the bold, aggressive kind of behavior, which is intended to conceal some shortcoming, real or imaginary, by "putting up a front" in the presence of other people.

Of course, either extreme is undesirable. Each individual's constant effort should be to find ways of living and meeting with other people which will make him useful, helpful, and liked in society. He should avoid any extremes of behavior which, instead of being useful to him, might possibly interfere with his getting along in the world.

**The Need for a Feeling of Personal Satisfaction.** The need of the individual for a feeling of satisfaction in his own accomplishment is at least partly learned, because his idea of what will make for happiness depends very much on what other people do and how they treat him. We learn as we go along through life which things will enable us to receive credit, and which will be frowned upon.

It would be possible to make a long list of the things which a person can do for which he is rewarded and a similar list of things which bring criticism or scolding.

There is a large share of our behavior which is determined by the extent to which other people will approve or disapprove. This is what psychologists call the *social approval* motive. If people

This young man receives recognition for his work in providing employment opportunities for handicapped persons.

*Gainesville Daily Sun*

approve, we have the feeling of satisfaction which we have been discussing. If they disapprove, we have the opposite of a feeling of satisfaction—we have a feeling of disappointment or we feel hurt.

However, underneath all of this there is something else—a very personal condition which is sometimes called *self-respect*. This is a kind of *self-approval*. The self-respect which a man has may be the most important motive of all. Men will do things in order to satisfy this desire for self-respect or self-approval, even at the risk of bringing upon their heads the criticism of other people.

This is another way in which the need for a feeling of satisfaction shows itself. People have sometimes done things which brought them credit from others, but if the act performed was not sincere, and they didn't have this feeling of self-approval along with it, they had an inner feeling of shame and disappointment. This is just the way we often feel when we have "gotten away with something."

Some of the noblest deeds in history have been performed by men and women seeking to maintain their feeling of self-respect or self-approval. This element of self-respect is probably what some writers have in mind when they use the term *conscience*. A person may build for himself a high standard of behavior and be largely controlled by this standard.

A higher motive is at work in an act of saving a life.

**The Power of Higher Motives or Ideals.** We ought to note that it is this higher form of motive which probably accounts for those events in human affairs in which we see men actually doing things which, instead of promoting their lives, lead to their own destruction. Thus the soldier goes where duty calls, regardless of the consequences. The hero jumps into the rushing river to save another human life, and thereby takes his own life in his hands. The mother rushes out onto the street to save her child, risking death at the wheels of a speeding automobile.

In each of these cases it is the higher motive of self-respect or self-approval which is at work. If we failed to act, we would not be true to ourselves. This simply means that we have, through experience and learning, built up a standard of what is right which means more to us than anything else.

# What Psychologists Believe about Instincts

Psychologists have often debated the question whether or not instincts exist. Formerly, some of them believed that we do the things we do because of a whole series of inborn impulses, leading us to want to be with other people, to want to build things, to want a mate, etc.

Because so many of these so-called instincts did not seem to be in harmony with one another, and because so many people failed to show any evidence that they were gifted with certain instincts, there has grown up a considerable doubt in the minds of psychologists as to whether these instincts exist.

It seems likely that our many patterns of behavior are the result either of the efforts which we make to supply our physical needs, or of the things we have learned to want to do.

If we have found that it is pleasant to be with people, we will want to be with people; if we have found it unpleasant, we will avoid them. If we have found that it's fun to collect stamps, we will collect them; if it has seemed boring to us, we will not want to be stamp collectors. If it seems worth while to be kind to people and if it gives us satisfaction, we will develop kindly dispositions; if we find that we profit more by being mean and hard, we may turn out to be bullies.

Psychologists are inclined to accept the term *instinct* if it is used to describe—very specifically—some kind of behavior that is obviously not learned, but which results from organic conditions. For example, Morgan[1] points out that there are some kinds of behavior that can be shown to result from the presence in the organism of certain hormones or like materials. He notes that prolactin, which is secreted by the pituitary gland, has been shown to cause quite definite maternal behavior when it is present in rats. This behavior, he would say, is instinctive behavior.

But in the rather popular loose sense that the term *instinct* has often been employed, there are many reasons to believe that learning, or the influence of environmental factors, has entered in.

**Instinct of Curiosity.** Let us take one so-called instinct to make this discussion clear. It used to be taught that we have the instinct of curiosity. It takes but a little reflection to realize that we are not all curious about everything. Whether we are curious about things or not seems to depend on the kinds of experiences we have had.

Some men are curious about how machines work, others are curious about what is in books, and some are curious about how other people live.

If it was instinctive to be curious, we might assume that any new thing would arouse the curiosity of a child but that is not the case. He is likely to be curious about some things and not curious about others. Therefore, it would seem to be sensible to say that we are curious about the things we learn to be curious about.

The child does have a tendency to explore his immediate environment and to investigate the things surrounding him. But this seldom develops into a curiosity about everything. Many things in his environment he will take for granted, and never investigate at all.

There is an underlying tendency to be active which, given the right conditions and the right stimulation, may lead to curiosity in certain directions. But this is evidently a matter of learning, and a matter of the kind of stimulation the child receives.

If we had an instinct to be curious, most of us would be much more active and interested in the world around us than is actually the case. One is reminded of the Boston woman who was asked if she had ever ridden on a Pullman car.

---

[1]Clifford T. Morgan, *Introduction to Psychology* (New York: McGraw-Hill Book Co., Inc., 1956), p. 245.

"No, why should I?" she replied. "I'm already here."

Her experiences in life had evidently led her to feel quite contented just to stay where she was, and her curiosity about the rest of the world was apparently very small, if it existed at all.

**Is There a Fighting Instinct?** Certainly the subject of instincts should not be left behind without inquiring into the much-talked-of fighting instinct. When we find one who is a fighter in the sense that he seems to have a tendency to be getting into fights all the time and actually seems to want that sort of thing, we usually are able to explain his behavior without reference to an inborn fighting impulse.

We find that he fights because he has *learned* to fight. He fights because he has discovered that he gets social approval, or self-satisfaction, as a result of it. It is noteworthy that the individuals who are not successful in fighting are not usually the ones who get into fights, if they can help it. It is the individual who has learned that he can usually "lick" the other fellow who is apt to be a bully.

Psychologists now feel that when a man is placed in a situation in which his health, his safety, or his ideals are in danger, he will fight; but otherwise, he will avoid fighting as long as possible, because he has learned that his goals in life are more likely to be promoted by working with people, instead of against them.

Although fighting has been pretty well shown *not* to be the result of an "instinct to fight" in the older way in which the expression was used, it is important to note that fighting is one of the forms of *aggressive* behavior that may be employed when people are *frustrated*. Frustration is experienced when the individual is prevented from achieving a goal of some kind or of satisfying his wants. An individual may become frustrated if he hears the loud noise of a radio when trying to sleep or if he is unable to find the kind of work he desires or if someone disapproves of his friends. And if the situation is strong enough or persistent enough, he may well show *aggressive behavior.*

Aggressive behavior, or aggression, or, as it is sometimes called, *hostility* (to use a more general term), may possibly produce fighting, and often it does. But this is not necessarily so. There are times when a feeling of hostility, or aggression, produces activities which are harmless. Thus we have all heard of persons who, moved to anger, went out and "worked off steam" by spading up the garden or chopping some fire-wood.

## How Competition Motivates Us

In our country we hear a great deal about competition. Many people feel that competition is good—that it brings out the best that is in people and leads them to be original.

Others say that competition is harmful. They say that it gives people unworthy motives based on self-interest, that it makes them forget the rights of others, and that it makes them grasping and hard.

What do psychologists find to be the case? First, let us define the word more carefully. *Competition* is a word which refers to any situation in which individuals or groups are thrown into possible conflict, because they are trying to secure something which is desired, and which is available only to one or more of the individuals or groups, and not to all.

When it comes to getting oil out of the earth, we find that the supply is limited and that oil is found only in certain places. Therefore strong competition develops among people and companies which are seeking oil.

If we use marks in school to show which pupils are most successful in their work, then we immediately have competition because everybody can't be equally successful if some are to be called the "best."

**How Competition Results from the Fact That People Differ.** There will usually be competition wherever people of unequal ability are asked to perform tasks, or where they are, on their own initiative, striving to secure something which is limited in amount. We could also say that whenever a situation exists in which competition is present, it will bring out the individual differences which are characteristic of people.

There are usually two kinds of competition: competition between individuals and competition between groups. Both kinds of competition are important and both have a strong effect in causing people to do things, that is, in motivating them.

*The finding of psychologists is that of the two types, competition between individuals is more likely to bring out the best work of which the individuals are capable. Next most effective in bringing out the abilities in people is competition between groups.*

**Individual and Group Competition Compared.** Individual competition occurs when one person is trying to perform more successfully than another person or a group of persons. One car salesman trying

The competitive nature of our personality is evident in the games we play.

*Official U.S. Coast Guard Photo*

to outdo another car salesman is an example of individual competition. Often an automobile sales company will have a chart on the wall showing the record, day by day or week by week, of the various salesmen in "moving" new or used cars.

It is not a good thing to have individual competition in all cases where we are trying to get individuals to do better work. Individual competition has some bad effects, and we must keep this in mind. The people with the least ability may find that they are losing most of the time and we have just seen that one of the things every human being needs is a feeling of being successful. Therefore, we are not being fair to the less able people—in school or anywhere else—if we set things up so that they are always having difficulty and never enjoying the feeling of success.

Group competition occurs when one group is trying to perform more successfully than another group. One division of a sales company pitted against another division in terms of monthly sales is an example of group competition. In Community Fund drives it is often a custom to put various teams in competition on fund raising. Team captains are appointed to stir up enthusiasm among the workers. When a team seeks to outdo another team the driving force at work is that of group competition.

In group competition we build up the feelings of group loyalty and the interest of working with people for the benefit of the group. Also we know that people will work in groups and for groups, and that working together for the good of all is really more important, in the end, than is success for a few individuals.

**Competition with One's Self.** Many people believe that one of the best forms of competition is that in which the individual is striving to improve his own record. Instead of trying to outdistance some other person, his goal is self-improvement. He is motivated by the idea of doing better—not better than someone else, necessarily, but better than he has done in previous attempts. This is evident in the case of the pianist who studies recordings of his works to see how they might be rendered more desirable or of the accountant who examines his methods to determine how they might be made more efficient.

It is a common-sense observation that this is a motive which many people have and that it is probably a good motive. We can see, however, that in most cases there is more emphasis on motivation concerning individuals and groups, since so many of our customs and practices in society have traditionally been geared to that sort of rivalry.

## SOMETHING TO DO

Clip out some front page newspaper stories, including the headlines, and decide what kinds of motivation are shown in them. Why are they of interest and why did the editor put them on the front page?

Try to explain the reason for your choice of stories. What made you select each of them?

## QUESTIONS AND PROBLEMS FOR STUDY AND DISCUSSION

1. What is the principal cause of shyness?

2. Almost every school playground has a bully. What kind of behavior does the bully show, and what is the probable cause of it?

3. A man is working alone in a forest, chopping down a tree. After he finishes his work, he is not satisfied with the appearance of the stump, or of the fallen tree, so he spends some time trimming them. What is the motive which probably causes him to do this?

4. Occasionally a store, or a government agency (such as a tax collector's office) gets a check or some cash from some person who says that he has owed this amount for many years and feels that he should pay it. What is the motive for an act of this kind?

5. Every year the Carnegie Hero Commission awards medals to persons for acts of heroism, and publishes accounts of these awards and the reasons for them. In most of these exciting events, there is evidently a strong motive behind the act of heroism. What type of motivation is this?

6. Note the reactions of people to various kinds of situations shown in a motion picture feature.

7. How do psychologists explain the often discussed "fighting instinct"?

8. Give an example of each of the two kinds of competition which psychologists conclude are very useful and important.

9. Describe some activity in your own community which shows the constructive value of competition.

10. Give an example, from your own experience or your reading, of harmful results which have come from too much competition.

11. Analyze your own reaction in a competitive situation (for example, in taking an examination or in participating in a sport).

12. Give reasons why *all* schoolwork should not be set up on a competitive basis.

13. Discuss the extent to which competition should be used in a business or industry in connection with the promotion of employees, taking into consideration some of the facts about competition brought out in the chapter.

14. Describe your reaction to self-competition.

# CHAPTER FOUR

# INTEREST AND ATTENTION

This chapter takes up questions about interest and attention and presents the reasons why they are important to us and how they affect us.

This has a lot to do with many of our everyday experiences. Why are some speakers interesting and others boring? Why do some radio and TV programs have high ratings and others seem to fail? Why do we attend to some things in our environment and ignore others?

The reasons for certain practices and customs in advertising are explained in this chapter and, in general, we are introduced to the facts we must know in order to arouse and interest other people.

Psychologists have spent a good deal of time on this subject because of its importance in teaching, in advertising, and in politics. Once we know the basic principles, it is not too hard to apply them in many situations where they may be useful.

Incidentally, two very widely used terms in psychology, *stimulus* and *response,* are explained and their use illustrated.

## QUESTIONS THIS CHAPTER WILL ANSWER

1. Why should people need to understand the nature of interest and attention?
2. What determines whether or not we will be interested in anything?
3. Does the size of an object have anything to do with whether or not we will pay attention to it?
4. What is the psychology back of "moving" electric signs?
5. What are some of the other qualities about objects or events which determine whether or not we will pay attention to them?
6. What is the effect of "set" or "expectancy" on our behavior?

## What Makes Things Interesting?

It is a short step from considering the question of motivation to the question "What makes things interesting? Does interest come from within us, or is it partly in the nature of things? What determines what we attend to?"

Let us answer these questions immediately. *Both* the qualities of the situations confronting us AND the factors operating within us determine what we will attend to—what will interest us.

The observable qualities of things or situations which make them interesting or which cause us to *attend* to them are rather well known and will be identified and explained in this chapter.

Yet certain influences or forces within ourselves, based no doubt on biological drives and on previous experience, result in our responding to some things while not paying attention to others. Technically, psychologists are a long way from understanding these internal forces which direct our attention but it is rather well established that *both* the nature of the happenings in our environment, and our internal or subjective impulses cause us to respond as we do.

There are numerous examples in everyday life which show the variable nature of our acts of attention. The layman tends to put it in terms of "what interests us." The psychologist tends to deal with such matters in terms of our acts of attention, or attending. He is concerned with our acts of behavior as they relate to the situations which confront us.

If you will note a construction job in a large city, you will usually see some people gathering around to watch the steam shovels or the bulldozers at work. Other people walk rapidly by, their thoughts apparently on something else entirely. Men will hurry past a department store window displaying some beautiful new fall hats. Women, however, will almost always slow down, or probably stop, to have a look. Why?

So interested were people in the excavation work connected with building one of New York's great skyscrapers — Radio City — that the builder had a special platform built for them to stand on while watching the work. He put a neatly painted sign on it and called it the "Sidewalk Superintendents' Club."

Obviously these people were interested in what was going on. Yet there were other New Yorkers who thought the whole thing more or less a nuisance, and who grumbled at having to get out onto the street because the building materials were blocking the sidewalks. While it is true that this particular builder had a keen insight into the curiosity of many pedestrians, he had to concede

Being sidewalk superintendent interests some
people—but not everybody.

the fact that there were exceptions to the general rule. Everything
doesn't interest everybody.

## Getting Attention and Arousing Interest

Teachers have the problem of arousing interest among their
pupils in the subject to be studied. Newspapers have to decide
what will appeal to "reader interest." Theater men have to work
up public interest in every new motion picture or stage production.
Politicians have to get people interested in voting. American
industry pays large sums of money annually to advertising agencies
which make it their business to know how to arouse interest and
attract attention. The problem of getting attention is a major
concern of advertising specialists.

Ministers have the problem of getting people interested in their
religious services, and in many a town there is a conflict between the
churches and the movies to secure attendance on Sunday evenings.

The problem goes even beyond this. Each one of us, as a person,
is interested in getting other people to notice us and what we can do.

If a young man working in a department store wants to get a raise, it becomes quite important for him to get the boss interested in his work.

How disconcerting it is when you are trying to talk to people and they won't listen! Nothing is quite so disturbing to a person making a speech as to find that members of the audience are whispering, or turning their heads toward the side of the room every time someone comes in. Getting attention and holding interest is a major problem for the public speaker.

## How the Psychologist Analyzes Interest and Attention

The psychologist studies interest and attention in terms of *stimulus* and *response*. Here are two words much used in psychology. The word *stimulus* means something which causes an individual to react, or do something. When a mosquito bites you, it is giving you a stimulus. When the newspaper editor puts a headline on the front page, he is presenting you with a stimulus.

More than one stimulus are called *stimuli*. We speak of a person as being surrounded by stimuli, and by that we simply mean that there are a number of things around him which can cause him to act or respond.

The thing that a person does because of the presence of a stimulus is called a *response*. To illustrate, here are a few examples of responses to stimuli:

| *Stimulus* | *Response* |
|---|---|
| Intense bright light | Squinting or blinking the eyes |
| Door slamming in crowded auditorium | Turning eyes to see where noise came from |
| Comedian in movie slipping on a banana peel | Laughter |
| Green traffic light at corner | Going ahead across the street |
| "Itching" place above the ear | Scratching head |
| Something irritating in nose | Sneezing |
| Dry feeling in throat | Swallowing |

The above list of responses are usually regarded by psychologists as instances of *involuntary attention*. Attention in such cases involves little or no effort. There are cases, however, where attention is maintained only with effort. A student attending to a geometry problem (or to the problem of how to say what he means) may experience a continual temptation to wander from it and in order to solve it must exert conscious effort. Such attention is called *voluntary attention*.

The individual person selects the stimuli to which he responds from the many stimuli presented to him at any given time. If he were to respond to *all* the stimuli, he would be hopelessly confused. It is only physically and psychologically possible for us to respond to some of the stimuli which surround us.

Presenting gold watches to loyal employees make for wholesome attitudes in modern American Industry.

*Studebaker-Packard Corporation*

The psychologist finds that we will pay attention to certain things at certain times and not at others. For example, at certain hours, all of us pay considerable attention to food. But an ocean traveler, suffering from seasickness, is not interested in food. Indeed if we may believe reports, he is not interested in anything at all, not even in keeping alive! It is clear that whether or not we are interested in anything at any given time depends in part, at least, on (1) the condition we are in at the time, and (2) the nature of the outside thing or situation (stimulus) itself. We might say that under normal conditions we are interested in anything which has to do with our personal well-being. But it is quite obvious that a person suffering from a toothache, for example, is not likely to be very much interested in anything—whether it be an interesting book, a beautiful picture, or an attractive meal.

## The Shifting of Attention

There are several other aspects of the problem of attention which should be considered. One of these has to do with the shifting of attention which is an obvious fact when the matter is analyzed further.

Before we can become interested in anything, our *attention* must be attracted to it. But frequently our attention shifts rapidly from one thing to another. Why? Because the stimuli in our environment are constantly changing, and we, as individuals, tend to a great extent to *select* the stimuli to which we wish to respond.

Usually, we see, think about, or react to a familiar stimulus in *one* way, our usual way. "We see what we expect to see." Our *brain,* not our eyes, decides *what* we will see. Sometimes there may be two or more ways of seeing the same thing. The accompanying figure illustrates this point. The figure, a staircase, can be seen in two ways, either from above or below.

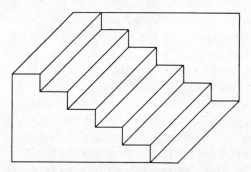

**Psychologists call this an ambiguous figure.
Can you see why?**

John Frederick Dashiell (noted professor of psychology at the University of North Carolina) points out that our previous experiences are what decide the impression this picture will make upon us.

What makes us see the staircase from *above* is the fact that we have had more experience in looking at stairs or steps from above than below. Yet we have also had some experience in looking at stairs from below. Therefore, when we study the picture for a while the picture as a stairway viewed from below will "catch" our attention. The fact is that if we continue to study the picture we will see it in a series of changing pictures. Psychologists have endeavored to explain this. One explanation is that there is a sort of fatigue or "satiation" which occurs and this results in the different perceptual responses.

## How "Set" Influences Our Attention

As has been noted, the factors which determine what will be central in our attention at any given instant are both external (what the situation *is*) and internal (our set or attitude of the moment).

Our set is determined by our biological needs, our interests, and social suggestion; and these, in turn affect our attention.

If you are hungry, stimuli related to food will be the ones that will attract your attention.

If you are a typist moving into a new office you will be interested in how well the new typewriter works. If you are the interior decorator you will be interested in the color of the type-writer—how this fits in with the general color scheme of the office.

If just before we view a film in a classroom, the instructor says that he wants us to notice how the people in the film walk, our attention will be directed to their legs and feet.

Properly used, the information which psychology provides about the causes of attending to stimuli of different types under various circumstances can help us in our understanding of behavior. The information may also be useful to us in our day to day work and responsibilities. Since all of us, from time to time, are responsible for attracting attention, or concerned with arousing interest, the information psychologists have gathered from their study of the nature of attention should prove useful.

**What Stimuli Do We Pay Attention to?** Let us now review the main facts about stimuli which help to determine whether we will pay attention to them or not. As we have said, our past experiences, and our condition at the time, will have much to do with it, but *other things being equal we will pay attention to stimuli which have the following qualities:*[1]

**1. We Pay Attention to Stimuli Which Are IN MOTION.** It is evident that motion attracts attention. The great interest in the movies and television helps to show this. People will watch a moving car more readily than they will one which is standing still. A man who is running attracts attention.

Advertisers have a tendency to favor moving signs—people like to watch the moving lights and figures. People like *action.* Races, athletic contests, speeding railway trains, speedboats, airplanes, fires and fire engines—these are sometimes so likely to attract our attention that we will temporarily stop whatever else we are doing to watch.

Realizing this, public speakers make use of gestures. They change their position on the platform or stage.

Motion, indeed, attracts attention.

**2. We Pay Attention to Stimuli Which Have INTENSITY.** Ordinarily, we will be interested in, and pay attention to, any stimulus which is *intense.* Examples would include loud noises, brilliant lights, and strong tastes.

Many examples of this come to mind. A group of people may be talking at a meeting. Suddenly, one voice is raised loud above the others. It challenges attention. The meeting comes to order.

We are apt to pay attention to the many cars and lights along a city street at night when we see the brilliant spotlight of a police car approaching, or the bright red flashing signal of an oncoming ambulance.

In fact, man spends a great deal of time and energy producing situations which will attract others or merely please himself because of the intensity of the stimulus produced. This might include anything from someone blowing up a paper bag in the kitchen just to explode it with his fist, to the chamber of commerce arranging for a gigantic Fourth of July fireworks display.

Intensity of the stimulus, then, is very likely to attract attention.

**3. We Pay Attention to Stimuli That Have SIZE:** The sheer size of anything usually causes us to attend to it. We notice the big man in the crowd. A large truck is more likely to attract attention than a small passenger car. The bus passengers will turn

---

[1]Adapted from J. F. Dashiell's *Fundamentals of Objective Psychology* (Boston: Houghton Mifflin Company, 1949).

to look at a big ship coming up the river. We read the big headline on the front page first.

Taking another example from the lighted city street at night, we are more likely to observe a large electric sign than the small ones. This is so well understood by advertisers that they try to outdo one another in an effort to put up the biggest sign. Sometimes

Elements of size and contrast help to direct your attention when you study this modern high voltage laboratory.

*The Anaconda Company*

advertisers erect huge billboards along highways. They understand that the bigger the sign, the more attention it will get.

The importance of this to people is shown by the tendency of Americans to build huge buildings. That it is not just an American idea is shown by the fact that the Russians, before World War II, started work on what was to be the highest building in the world (the Palace of the Soviets), even higher than the Empire State Building.

How many colleges have sought to attract attention by building the biggest stadium! How many students have tried to earn high marks by handing in a paper bigger and longer than any other in the class!

When the 1960 United States census figures began to come in, there was great interest in the factor of size. Which were the largest cities? Much attention was given by the newspapers to the fact that metropolitan Los Angeles had moved ahead of metropolitan Chicago into *second place*. In some towns chamber of commerce groups were protesting that the census figures "weren't right." They felt that their towns were "bigger" than the census figures showed them to be.

Size attracts attention. Size is interesting.

**4. We Pay Attention to Stimuli That Have CONTRAST.** When any object or sound is sharply different from those around it, it causes us to pay attention.

People will notice a big man and a little man walking together.

The audience will come to attention when the speaker either suddenly raises, or suddenly lowers, his voice.

Contrast is so important that it can be deliberately used to make programs interesting. Thus, a loud, humorous act will usually

Our attention is drawn to stimuli
that have contrast.

be followed by a quieter, more serious number involving different lighting, music, or dancing.

Contrast is almost certain to attract attention.

**5. We Pay Attention to Stimuli Which Are REPEATED.** Some alarm clocks are made so that the alarm will ring at repeated intervals. Signboards are erected, not just on one spot, but at intervals all over the city. The telephone rings repeatedly to attract attention.

Steamships in distress give quick, short blasts of their whistles. Radio programs often select some slogan or catchword and repeat it so often that everybody learns it and knows what it stands for.

If the teacher wants to emphasize some point, he will usually see that it is mentioned a number of times.

It is almost safe to say that any stimulus, if repeated often enough, will attract everybody's attention. There is one other fact, however, that should be remembered. If something is repeated *too* often, there is something about the human mechanism which causes it to cease noticing. A warning sounded too frequently is ignored. If the teachers say "Don't do that," too many times, we may possibly fail to hear it. This is also true of sounds—such as the noise of traffic which is repeated so often that it is almost continuous. It almost seems that we build up this resistance to too much repetition as a kind of self-protection against extremes.

But on the whole, repetition causes interest and produces attention.

**6. We Pay Attention to Stimuli Which Have DURATION.** This is quite like repetition, but introduces something else. It is the fact that if a sound or stimulus is long-continued, it will attract attention on that account, whether it is intense or not.

Sometimes at a meeting a man in the audience will get up and remain standing. He makes no sound, or disturbance, but just stands there. This is almost certain to attract attention.

A long, continuous blowing of a whistle arouses us, just as does the long-sounding automobile horn that is "stuck." One may ignore a telephone ringing for a short time, but if it continues long enough, it will usually get a response.

Some of our songs and games illustrate this. "Old McDonald Had a Farm" and "Frérè Jacques" are songs in which the interest is dependent on repetition and continuation or *duration*.

"See how long you can hold your breath" or "see how long you can hold that note" also involve this principle.

Jumping rope or walking on a fence or railroad rail depend on "how long you can keep it up" to hold interest. A few automobiles coming along the road will not attract attention, but a long "string" of cars is bound to make us look.

The duration of a stimulus attracts attention.

## SOMETHING TO DO

1. Get a copy of a newspaper and select an illustration showing how your attention or interest was successfully aroused by one of the factors connected with *the nature of the stimulus* (motion, size, intensity, etc.). In doing this, let your "being attracted to" the picture, advertisement, illustration, or whatever it might be, be the guiding factor. Then, after you have selected the example, see how you would classify it in terms of the points which have been made about the nature of stimuli.

2. Get a copy of a modern magazine and clip an example of the successful use of *color* to arouse your interest or attract attention. Keep these in a scrapbook.

## QUESTIONS AND PROBLEMS FOR STUDY AND DISCUSSION

1. Find a "human interest" story in a newspaper. What are the characteristics of the story which make it interesting?

2. Look through a newspaper or several newspapers for a number of "human interest" stories. Select several different kinds of stories and indicate the different types of interest they seem to appeal to.

3. The qualities of stimuli which arouse attention and interest were discussed in the chapter. They were shown to include (a) motion, (b) intensity, (c) size, (d) contrast, (e) repetition, and (f) duration.

Select one illustration from your reading or experience to show how each of these qualities operates to arouse attention.

4. Make a list of half a dozen things people ordinarily do. For each of them, show a possible stimulus. For example, a man on his way to work in the morning may break into a run. Possible stimulus: sight of approaching streetcar or bus.

5. Look through a mail-order catalog, and make a list of a dozen human interests to which the merchandise offered seems to have a strong appeal. How does the publisher attract your attention to various things in the catalog?

6. Take a profession or occupation which is familiar to you and show the interest-arousing things about it. Would these be the reasons the occupation would appeal to you?

7. You have been appointed chairman of a committee to "run" the

entertainment for a club gathering. What are some of the activities you might consider because they would probably prove to be interesting to the club members? (Any organization with which you are familiar could be used in working out this problem.)

8. Write a paragraph or two showing the relationship between *how you feel* and *what you are interested in* at any particular time.

9. Make a list of the principal departments or sections of a city newspaper. Show the interests which are the center of attention in each section. Check the departments which would interest you. For comparison, ask another person in your family to check the list independently.

10. People reveal their interests by tl.ings they do, their conversation, their choice of reading material, the things they look at, their clothing, adornments, purchases, etc. Watch the people in a store for a period of time, and see if you can make a list of their interests. Judging by their conversation, behavior, or other evidence, try to indicate one or more interest for each person observed.

11. Observe the magazines offered on a corner newsstand. What are the interests represented? Show some of the interests which seem to be common to many people; some which seem to be of probable interest only to a few.

12. Take a room with which you are familiar, in a home, club, hotel, or public building. Make an informal inventory of the objects in the room which attract your interest. Describe them briefly and indicate why they attracted your attention.

13. On a walk through the business district, keep in mind the various elements which arouse attention—as outlined in the chapter. When you get home, jot down some of the experiences, situations, places, or things which interested you and indicate why, in terms of these elements.

14. Explain the relationship between repetition and attention. Give an example of how repetition is effective; of how it may be overdone.

15. Consider one of your friends from the standpoint of interest and attention. What are some of the things you *know* would interest him, and which you could readily use in striking up an effective conversation with him?

## CHAPTER FIVE

# INTERESTS AND THEIR IMPORTANCE

Psychologists are particularly concerned with interests because of their importance in relation to education and choosing an occupation.

This chapter undertakes to show just what interests are and how they are formed. It is especially necessary to understand the tie-in between experiences and interests. Through our experiences, interests develop. This chapter shows how the process works out.

Tests have been developed to help us in exploring our interests. Some informal suggestions are also given to help us in this connection.

Much light has been thrown on interests and how they develop as a result of studies in growth. The more important findings in this connection are brought out in this chapter. They are particularly important in understanding and dealing with people of different ages.

## QUESTIONS THIS CHAPTER WILL ANSWER

1. How does an interest develop?
2. What are some of the different kinds of interests which people have?
3. Are interests permanent, or do they change frequently?
4. If we want to help someone to develop an interest, what do we do?
5. How are interests related to the choice of an occupation?
6. How can we decide what our own interests are? What are some tests which can be used for this purpose?

## What Are Interests?

Not only do we talk about a person being interested in something, or about the way in which a stimulus arouses interest, but we also say that an individual *has* certain *interests*.

This means that there are some activities in life to which his attention will return again and again. There are things, activities, or situations which repeatedly arouse him to action or thought. These may be objects, places, people, or ideas.

Sailing is an example of a pleasurable interest.

*University of Miami*

When you have developed a tendency to turn your attention again and again to any of these you have formed *an interest*.

**Importance of Interests in Our Lives.** Interests are important because they have a *very decisive influence* on our behavior. How we spend our energies, time, and money often depends on them. They also have a great deal to do with our choice of *occupations and careers*.

Interests have a further importance in that they furnish the purpose and often the objectives of life—keeping us occupied, busy, and happy. The lonely man, or the unhappy girl, is all too often one who has failed to develop interests.

Much could be said about the way in which interests add to the enjoyment of life. It is a fact that a person with wide interests receives more pleasure out of living. Life is full to him because so many things can awaken his interest and keep him alert and healthily alive.

This is not to imply, of course, that all persons should have the same interests. A farmer may have a wide variety of interests and have a rich and enjoyable life. Yet a city dweller's pattern of interests may be quite different.

**How an Interest Is the Result of Experience.** How does an interest develop? Undoubtedly it is created as the result of experiences—experiences which have proved interesting or valuable to the person forming the interest. In fact, there is no chance of an interest forming unless it is founded on experiences which are in some way or other satisfying or pleasurable, or which, at least, hold out the promise of being pleasurable.

Let us look at a few examples of interests.

Men have been known to "follow the races" from one part of the country to another. Men have developed such an interest in fishing that they will travel widely and put up with many hardships and much expense in order to reach places where fishing is good.

A man of the writer's acquaintance spends a great deal of money going around the country to places where dog shows are being held. A group of men make a practice of traveling once a week to a different golf course until they have now played on almost every course in a whole area. Another instance is that of a man who always makes it a point to see the public libraries in every town or city he visits.

Some young people try to see every movie which comes along; others to hear each new record that comes out.

It has already been said that interests result from experiences. This should be emphasized, because *many people who do not have a worth-while pattern of interests are in that position simply because they have not been willing to take the trouble to secure the necessary experiences.*

Camping and fishing can become a highly
developed interest.

There is no use saying that you are not interested in camping if you've never been camping. How many times a person will say he isn't interested in a certain game—when he *never even tried* to play it!

Of course, experiences work both ways. They may also destroy imagined interests, or at least change them. A city boy of fourteen may think he would like to study agriculture. But if he goes out on a farm and works there, he may change his mind. He may discover that it wasn't as interesting as he thought.

On the other hand, experiences often show an individual the occupations he would like, leading to interests which have permanent value. One boy moved to the city from a farm. He never had seen electric lights, motors, switches, or similar appliances before. He was so delighted with electric lights that he just liked to stand at the wall and turn the switch on and off. This led to curiosity about the way in which the switches worked and various other aspects of electricity. This boy continued his interest in electricity and became an electrician's helper; now he owns and operates an electrician's business and appliance service.

It is therefore recognized that experiences—preferably a variety of them under various conditions—furnish the most desirable background for developing some interests and rejecting others. This background may well serve as a means of selecting occupational careers.

Once the individual understands that interests are formed through experiences, he will, if he is wise, endeavor to secure a variety of experiences by selecting various courses in school, reading books of various kinds and in various fields, getting part-time jobs, looking for opportunities to travel and mix with people, and meeting and talking with individuals in all walks of life.

**Permanence of Interests.** Interests which are formed in childhood may and often do last a lifetime. Not all interests are permanent. Many of them are replaced by others as new experiences are gained. But it is true that the big, important interests which people develop are likely to endure. A man who, as a boy, develops an interest in writing, is likely to continue that interest; so also is a girl who is

These grownups have been out of school quite a while, but they are continuing their reading interests in an adult class for the study of the "Great Books".

*Pasadena City Schools, Library and Visual Service*

interested in caring for children likely to continue that interest late into life.

It is also true that interests can be developed (because they *are* the result of experiences) at any time in life. Many a person has picked up an entirely new interest late in life. One educator, in connection with his work, found it necessary to use statistics— that is, to work with mathematical methods and techniques. This led him to become so interested in statistics that he wrote one of the best textbooks in the entire field of statistics.

People are often misled into believing that a person's attitudes and interests are fixed early in life and never change. This is because they do not realize the basic psychological fact that interests and attitudes are the result of experiences. As long as we are capable of having new experiences, there is a possibility that our habits, interests, and attitudes may change.

A professor who had never used tools to build furniture or even simple objects was persuaded by his wife one day, after he was fifty years of age, to make a shelf for her. He found that it turned out satisfactorily, and she praised it and showed it to her friends.

He secretly began to wonder if he might not be able to do some other things along this line. Finally, out in the garage, he made a little chest.

**The professor — over fifty — developed a new interest out of a new experience.**

This also brought words of praise, and within a year's time he was engrossed in a new-found interest and activity. Over a period of several years he made several reproductions of antique furniture, and some of his work demonstrated great skill and beauty.

Another man who had previously made fun of people who had gardens, took up gardening in a small way after he established a new home in an area where there was space available for such purposes. He enjoyed the experience of seeing a few things grow which could be used on the table, and tried a few more the next year. It was not long until he had a varied garden of considerable size and—at the risk of the jibes of his friends who remembered his previous jokes about gardens at their expense—had developed a very strong and profitable interest.

It must be remembered that the main and the important interests of our lives will usually remain with us, especially if they are interests which are rewarding. If they contribute something to us, we will retain them.

**Interests Are Related to Our Growth and Development.** Another factor which influences interests is the factor of growth and development. We have already noted that boys and girls grow and mature

Training in the Industrial Arts develops interests that are often of great value in vocational guidance.

*Winnetka Public Schools*

rapidly in their early years. The interests a boy will have are definitely tied up with the stage he has reached in his growth. The same thing is true of girls. Interests are shown by the games and hobbies children like as they move on from one year to the next.

A boy who achieved distinction as a nationally known football player, Jimmy Robertson, of Carnegie Tech, did not play football in any competitive way throughout his high school years, but took it up after he went to college.

Jimmy Robertson was a boy of short and slight stature. It seemed that a certain amount of growth and development was necessary before he realized that he could take a successful part in such a difficult sport as intercollegiate football.

During adolescence, when boys and girls are growing into adulthood at a rapid rate, and when they are reaching physical and social maturity, there are certain types of interests which are especially prominent. These are identified by observations which have been made of their leisure-time activities.[1]

### Boys

A ranking of broad types of leisure activities for boys, according to the number reporting participation, places team sports first. Closely following are both formal and informal social activities, the latter including movies, radio, television and records. Also prevalent are outdoor activities, including camping, hiking, fishing, boating, hunting, and winter sports. Hobbies and individual sports are next. Whether or not they are widely available, swimming, hunting, and working on cars or motorcycles are specific leisure activities which are highly preferred.

### Girls

Among girls the broad classification of formal social activities is both first in preference and reportedly engaged in by the largest number. About as many take part in team sports and in informal social activities. This latter classification includes the mass media of entertainment, as mentioned in the previous paragraph, and also telephoning to friends.

In their recreational interests, boys and girls, before adolescence, may have preferred to play by themselves, or with one or two companions. They may have shown a tendency to want to be an "individual star." But in adolescence, as indicated by the above report, they become more willing to want to play on a team, to want to work with a group. It is true that the desire to be an individual star still persists in many men and women, but it is brought under somewhat greater control as they get older.

_____

[1]Edward C. Britton, and J. Merritt Winans, *Growing from Infancy to Adulthood* (New York: Appleton-Century-Crofts, Inc., 1958), p. 80.

## Why Are Interests Important to You?

As to gangs and clubs, there is little need to point out how important they are to the boy or girl in adolescent years.

Adventure and nature interests vary from person to person. Here again it depends on the experience the individual has had. It is true that as we get older, our chances of traveling around increase. The city dweller has more opportunity to get out into the country and the farm boy has more chance to get into the city. New experiences increase with each year. These new experiences create an interest in travel, adventure, and exploration.

One of the most striking developments of the mid-century period has been the great increase in outdoor camping and in boating. The national parks have reported increases in the use of their facilities to the point where they have become overcrowded at certain times in the year and must maintain a continuous program of expansion to keep up with the demand.

The annual expenditure on outboard motors, sailboats, and other types of marine equipment has reached new heights. Some people have seen a danger in the possibility that recreational activities may become too standardized for everyone. The older type of individual or small group experience, "off the beaten track," they think, has advantages, and ought to be encouraged. Thus we find, in one of the reports in connection with the 1960 White House Conference, the following:

". . . our society could well give attention to means for giving young people opportunities for vacations apart from their parents, so that both —parents and children—could find in recreation a fulfillment of their own interests. It could make sure that alternative forms of enjoyment are not neglected under the influence of forces which draw everything tightly toward the home circle—toward the family room, the patio, the barbeque pit, and the private swimming pool. I would suggest that organizations which encourage scouting, skiing groups, wilderness trips, and youthful tourism could be especially useful in the time ahead."[2]

Young people should seek opportunities to hike and camp not only because of the new experiences they make possible in the world of things and nature, but because they also make possible *many experiences with people.* And our interests will be very

[2]August Heckscher, "The Family and Social Change" in *The Nation's Children,* Edited by Eli Ginzberg, Vol. I for the White House Conference on Children and Youth (New York: Columbia University Press, 1960), p. 243.

one-sided indeed if they do not include interests in people, the result of fellowship and associations with one's fellow human beings.

**School Activities and Interests.** As to social organizations in school, a whole book could be written. Nothing can contribute more to the gaining of experiences than extracurricular activities. It is much to be desired that every boy or girl of high-school age take part in one or more of these.

Developing proper reading habits and an interest in the printed word are important steps in the growth of the personality.

*San Diego County Schools*

At the University of Minnesota it was discovered that fully one-third of all the students never took part in these extracurricular activities while in college. There were even hundreds of members of the upper classes who reported that they had never entered these groups.

Did not these young men and women miss something of importance? The values and rewards of taking part in school activities may be hard to measure, but it can hardly be denied that they do contribute very much to each person. Not only can they increase the likelihood of our developing these all-important interests of which we have been speaking, but they also aid us in developing the knack of getting along with people.

**Reading Interests.** What do you read? What magazines do you subscribe to? What parts of the newspaper interest you?

Here, in the world of books, newspapers, and magazines, is a great opportunity that is offered to everyone. We might not be able to travel to the ends of the earth for adventure and new experiences. But we can read.

Yet is is shown that a large number of Americans do not read. A study of people's reading habits brought out the fact that adult people, in the better residential sections of Chicago, read an average of ninety minutes a day. This was quite a lot of reading for busy people, yet most of it was in newspapers and magazines. Books were read by less than fifty per cent of the people studied. In fact, of the people covered in this study *who were college graduates*, only four per cent had read one book during the six months just before the study was made.

**Interests and Choosing a Vocation.** Psychologists have said that one way to find out whether or not a young person is going to like an occupation is to measure that young person's *interests* and then compare that pattern of interests with the pattern of interests usually found in people following a given occupation.[3]

For example, if a test shows that your interests are mainly scientific, then it might be said that (if you have the ability and other qualities you need) you should investigate occupations that are related to science.

But without the necessity of taking a test, any person can compare his own interests, in a general way, with those of persons engaged in an occupation. This will at least give him a start in the direction of considering whether or not he might find such an occupation agreeable.

But merely being interested in something is no guarantee that a person can do it well. Success depends on other things, too, such as intelligence, knowledge, perhaps skills, perhaps energy or "drive," and the ability to *complete* a given job.

Of course, it is true that the man who is interested in his work is likely to succeed better than the one who is listless about it. And we should be willing to work to learn or master the things we are interested in.

---

[3] A test known as the *Strong Vocational Interest Blank,* and the *Kuder Preference Record* are examples of devices used for this purpose.

**Interest Tests.** Several tests have been designed to aid the individual in finding out what his interests are and how they match the interests of individuals engaged in various occupations. An underlying assumption is that an individual would be wise to choose an occupation in which the activities are to his liking, and avoid an occupation which requires activities and interests which he does not like.

An example of such a test is the *Kuder Preference Record,* named after the man who designed it, G. Frederick Kuder.[4] In taking this test the individual makes choices from various kinds of activities which are suggested. His choices are compared to the kinds of interests and activities usually checked by persons engaged in various types of occupations. To the extent that your interests are like those usually checked by engineers, it would be reasonable to suppose that you would find their work congenial and that you would enjoy associating with them.

The author of the test points out that it can be used to avoid choosing occupations in which the activities are likely to be unsatisfactory to the individual. Of course, the individual must have the *ability* to do the things required in the occupation, and not merely be interested in activities associated with it. There is also a difference, as the author suggested, between taking an active part in some things and simply enjoying or appreciating them. This is especially noticeable in the case of music or art. If it should turn out on a test like the *Kuder Preference Record,* or on any other test of interests or preferences, that your interests were quite like those of musicians or artists, but your desire to *play* instruments or *paint* pictures was very slight, then such activities as *occupations* would hardly be suitable for you.

The *Kuder Preference Record* classifies the major interests which people seem to show when tested under nine headings, as follows:

| | |
|---|---|
| Mechanical | Literary |
| Computational | Musical |
| Scientific | Social Service |
| Persuasive | Clerical |
| Artistic | |

It is possible to classify, as Kuder does, many occupations under these headings or under combinations of these headings. It must be remembered that such suggestions as to possible occupational

---

[4]Published by Science Research Associates, 259 E. Erie, Chicago, Illinois.

choices are *suggestions only*. There is no sure way of choosing an occupation by simply taking a test or a group of tests and seeing "what comes out." The tests are very helpful in suggesting possibilities, however.

In connection with the *Kuder Preference Record,* it has been noted by psychologists that a student can *throw* a test of this sort by answering the questions in a manner that is deliberately untrue. In such cases, the findings of the test have no meaning, and the possibility of this sort of manipulation should be recognized. This is true of many types of paper and pencil "personality" inventories of tests.

**How Interests and Abilities Are Related.** It would be unwise to leave this discussion of the relation between interests and choosing vocations without pointing out very clearly that having an interest in something does *not* prove that a person is necessarily *able* to become successful in it.

Being interested in an activity does not mean that you can do it. All young people should check their abilities before coming to the final conclusion that "This is the occupation for me!" Many would-be actresses and actors found this out to their sorrow. Many boys and girls interested in engineering have discovered that their lack of adequate high-school training put the mathematics or science involved beyond their limited abilities.

We can have a strong interest in things all our lives and derive much pleasure from them, without necessarily making those things our life's work.

Another illustration that comes to mind is that of a young, underweight boy who was vitally interested in football. But he couldn't play football. He became water-boy to the team. A favorite of the players, he had a good time and enjoyed football, but *playing the game* was something else!

Society can find useful employment for a certain number of engineers, lawyers, and doctors. Standards in these professions are high and the education required is long and hard to get.

Hence it is wise for the individual to evaluate his own interests and abilities carefully, so that he can work most effectively toward a goal which is the right one for him.

Are your interests in a vocation real? Sometimes people have mistaken interests. They *think* they are interested in something, because they, perhaps, have been told that they *should* be interested in it. Or, they may have the idea that it is *the thing to do*.

Clearing up our own thinking as to just what our interests really are is an important thing for us all to do, especially when it

Diving may be either a fascinating avocation or a profitable vocation.

*University of Miami*

comes to selecting a course of study, a subject, an extracurricular activity, or a job. It is important to think carefully about this because the wrong choice of a vocational goal can lead to disappointment.

It is to the advantage of the individual to investigate what the probability of his obtaining employment in the vocation he desires to enter will be when he completes the requirements for the kind of work he desires to do. If it is low, it should be remembered that for the individual who has the ability and a strong interest to do the work he wishes to do, there is almost always a job of this kind available, even at the top.

## SOMETHING TO DO

On the accompanying chart, check the items given if they appeal to you. Check the things you like, or that you are interested in.

After checking, turn the page upside down and note the broad areas into which most of your checked items fall.

## INTEREST CLASSIFICATION CHART

| A | B | C | D | E |
|---|---|---|---|---|
| automobiles | doctors | science | design | hunting |
| airplanes | nurses | government | water colors | fishing |
| engines | teachers | politics | oil paintings | dancing |
| radio | children | law | decoration | hiking |
| electrical | boy scouts | ministers | music | baseball |
| equipment | girl scouts | psychology | symphony or- | football |
| bridges | workingmen | libraries | chestra | golf |
| railroads | labor unions | books | lights and shad- | tennis |
| highways | factory workers | technical | ows | swimming |
| mines | soldiers | journals | symmetry | rowing |
| medicines | airmen | ethics | pencil sketches | skiing |
| hospitals | sailors | logic | tone differences | tumbling |
| houses | crippled | formulas | color schemes | folk singing |
| painting | children | equations | flowers | community |
| (house) | old people | mathematics | flower arranging | singing |
| household | poor people | astronomy | gardens, flower | marching in |
| equipment | sick people | languages | architecture | band |
| rivers | people who are | translations | house styles | square dancing |
| harbors | out of work | novels | period furniture | weaving |
| game | young people | accounting | draperies | photography |
| fish | who are | newspapers | statues | amateur movies |
| trees | engaged | editorials | jewel settings | color photog- |
| ships | movie stars | essays | modeling | raphy |
| boats | actors | histories | fashions | gardening |
| subways | prisoners | biographies | streamlining | driving |
| elevated trains | family life | abstracts | sunsets | horseback |
| diesel engines | kindergartens | titles | rainy afternoon | riding |
| locomotives | little babies | courts and | winter scenes | bowling |
| machinery | boys and girls | judges | cloud effects | polo |
| pattern making | clothes and | treaties | sculptors | pool |
| tools | dresses | Unesco | murals | trapping |
| jig saw | Red Cross | banking | lamp shades | shooting mark |
| | insurance | cashier | oriental rugs | |
| | safety first | | | |
| Things | People | Ideas | Aesthetics | Physical Expression |
| A | B | C | D | E |

*Notes on Chart.*     Interests may be classified in the broad areas into which they fall. Such areas as are included in the exploratory check list are A—area of things B—area of people; C—area of ideas; D—area of aesthetics (art), and E—area of physical expression.

The area in which your checks are concentrated, after checking, may be considered to be your major area of interest.

In choosing or considering occupations, an individual might give careful attention to jobs or occupations closely related to the area in which his interests are mostly concentrated. The results furnish a clue as to whether you like best, for example, to work with people, or to work with machinery and equipment. A person who enjoys working with tools and equipment would probably not wish to become a language teacher or a librarian. The self-checking exercise is entirely informal and is suggestive only.

An individual's prevailing *mood* might affect his checking a list of this type. In order to discount unfavorable moods, it might be a good idea to put the list aside for a time after checking, and then check it again on another occasion.

*General range of interests.* From a mental hygiene point of view it is desirable to have a variety of interests. Unless the reader has interpreted the exercise very narrowly, a fair number of interests should have been checked. If a very few only have been checked, either (1) your prevailing mood has caused this result, or (2) you actually need to exert yourself in the direction of widening your interests and "getting around" more.

## QUESTIONS AND PROBLEMS FOR STUDY AND DISCUSSION

1. Take a boy friend and a girl friend, and write a description of their interests, as they seem to you. See if some of the differences can't be traced rather directly to their sex, or to different experiences.

2. Trace back the development of one of your interests. Show how it grew out of experiences.

3. Show how an interest can lead to a satisfying activity even though one's ability in that field may not be high enough to justify choosing it as a vocation.

4. Make a short list of the books you have read which you liked best. Could a person tell anything about *your* interests by looking at this list?

5. What is a good method for studying an occupation to decide whether or not it would be a possible occupation for you?

6. What kinds of reading do most people do, according to studies in this field?

7. Give some of the differences in interests of adolescent boys and girls as compared to younger children.

8. Using the main types of interests found in the *Kuder Preference Record,* write down, after each one, your own estimate of the extent to which your interests would probably fall in each type.

9. Bill W. says he is interested in engineering. A look at his high-school record shows that he has received grades of C and D in general mathematics, in algebra, and in general science. What should be taken into consideration in his case in deciding whether or not his interest in engineering should be encouraged?

10. Give some of the advantages of hiking and camping as means of developing interests.

11. What can you say about the permanence of interests? Are your interests of today likely to be the same when you are twenty years older? Explain.

12. From the field of travel advertising, select one advertisement which appeals to one class of interests, and another which appeals to a different class of interests. What conclusions can you reach as to the type of individual whose patronage each particular hotel or resort is seeking?

13. What can you say about the relationship of an individual's interests to his happiness?

14. Recall the most interesting course you ever had in school. What made it interesting? Did it touch on your own personal interests in any way?

15. Analyze a game, such as baseball, to determine what factors lead to the development of a strong interest in that game, such as we observe in an ardent fan.

# CHAPTER SIX

# THE PROBLEM OF HOW WE LEARN

Here is one of the main fields of psychology. To find out exactly how we learn has long been one of the main quests of teachers and scientists. The main reason for this is that if we know how learning takes place, it is likely we will know how better to teach (to say nothing of being better able to learn).

There are certain facts about the nature of learning that have been discovered, and there are certain generalizations regarding learning and teaching that have been shown to have great value. Of course, as the student of psychology will discover as he delves more deeply into the subject, there are many theories of learning and there are many unsolved problems having to do with what learning is and exactly how it takes place. Much experimental work will have to be done before our ideas of the nature of learning can be thoroughly verified.

In this chapter some of the generally recognized principles of learning are presented, especially those that have to do with "learning by association." The role of "conditioning" is explained as are the roles of trial and error, and guidance. Transfer of learning is discussed and we are reminded of the fact that "the way things belong"—the pattern into which they fit—has much to do with learning.

Some practical findings about remembering and forgetting are brought to our attention. And some of the most useful how-to-study ideas are outlined and discussed in detail. Note them carefully.

## QUESTIONS THIS CHAPTER WILL ANSWER

1. Do we learn different kinds of things? What are they?
2. What determines whether or not we shall learn something?
3. Is there any basic idea or principle which is found in all learning?
4. What are the main elements involved in learning?
5. What is meant by *conditioning*? Is it different from other kinds of learning?
6. What about *practice*—is it necessary?
7. Why do we forget?
8. What are some guiding principles that will make for better learning?

## Areas of Learning

Since learning is a thing we spend a considerable amount of time doing, it would be worth while to know something about it.

Higher learning in the United States centers in the many colleges and universities, one of the oldest of which is shown above.

Everyone is a learner and everyone is also a teacher. Even a young child showing another child how to play a game is teaching. Hardly a day passes, if we realize it, when we aren't either learning something ourselves, or teaching something to another person.

**We Learn Facts.** We pick up a vast quantity of facts about our friends, our neighbors, our city, our state, and our nation. We secure information about automobiles, about movie stars, about books, about games, and about animals. We learn people's telephone numbers.

We all learn other things, too, such as how to telephone, how to set the table—but that gets us to something else, for learning to set the table or make the bed is not learning facts, so much as it is *learning skills.*

**We Learn Skills.** How to dress, how to ride a bicycle, how to play baseball, how to telephone, how to add and subtract, how to skate, how to sew on buttons, how to drive an automobile — an enormous number of skills—these, too, we learn.

**We Learn Attitudes.** In connection with all of these things, we find ourselves learning to like or dislike making beds or meeting people. We find ourselves interested in games or bored by them. In short, we *learn* or form attitudes toward things, people, and activities. Learning attitudes makes up the third important kind of learning.

Here, then, are the big three of learning: facts, skills, and attitudes. They are what we learn.

## Learning and Values

What we learn often determines what we regard as important or worthy of achievement. Learning about the tragedies of World War II, for example, may lead us to regard a study of the United Nations as extremely significant. Learning to play new games may provide us with a new outlook toward people who played these games. Learning to change our attitude toward people who have different political beliefs than we have may result in our gaining new friends. In each case what we may not have regarded as valuable may, upon our learning more about it, become meaningful and significant.

It seems safe to say that almost everything we learn comes to have a value for us, and we are, as we travel along the route of learning, establishing our sense of values at the same time that we are learning skills, facts, and attitudes.

## The Learning Process

Some facts about learning may be stated in simple language as follows:

1. Most, if not all, learning takes place *when we want to learn something* (when there's *motivation*).

2. Most, if not all, learning is a matter of finding out what things go together—what things belong together.

Examples of this:

Finding out what the French word is for pencil.
Finding out how to put numbers together to add.
Finding out what city is the capital of Texas.
Finding out how a president of the United States is elected.

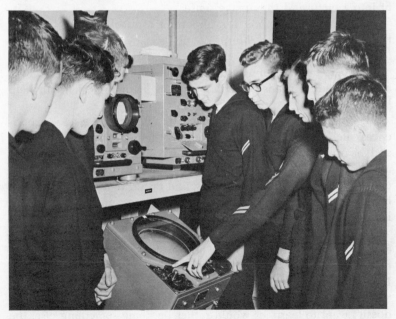

The U.S. Navy seeks to teach large numbers of technicians a maximum amount of information in a minimum amount of time.

*Official U.S. Navy Photograph*

Study these and you will find that they are all questions which can be answered when we find out what things go together.

3. An important thing in learning is *remembering,* and we remember things best which have (*a*) made a deep impression on us, or (*b*) which we have used or practiced a great deal.

4. The thing which makes most learning "stick" or stay with us is practice. Psychologists sometimes refer to this as the "law of exercise." It may be stated as follows: if we exercise or go over or use whatever it is we are learning often enough or long enough, we will remember it.

5. Learning is easier and more likely to take place if the thing we are learning fits into some whole picture or act. For example, it is easier to learn what to do in a game if we learn the whole game; easier to learn part of a song if we hear or learn the whole song and "know how it goes"; easier to remember things in history if we know the whole story of which the thing we are asked to learn is a part. In other words, things are learned better if they fit into a picture, if they make sense.

6. Words and symbols are important *tools* of learning because they *stand for ideas and things.* We tie facts, events, and experiences to *words.*

7. There are certain ways of going about learning that are good, and the student needs to form habits of learning which can help him.

8. Learning can only take place through *experiences* — experiences such as seeing things, handling them, working with them, and hearing about them. And to this should be added, *reading* about them. Reading is a short cut to learning because we can become acquainted with more things, and faster, by that method than by any other. Reading, therefore, is the most important way of learning.

**Wanting To Learn.** Learning is usually accomplished much more easily when we want to do it. The psychologist finds that this is a matter of the "set" or the attitude of the person who is learning. If a person is ready to learn something, and willing to learn it, teaching him becomes much easier. But if he is reluctant, and doesn't want to learn, or would rather be doing something else, the job of teaching him is harder.

Psychologists who have observed the way in which children grow and develop have noted that it is apparently a normal situation for a child to want to learn. He is almost always a source of questions, asking why, trying to find out about things. The drive of a child to learn is amazingly strong.

Some writers feel that the secret of good education is to adapt the activities of a school to the situations in which the child is already showing a desire to learn, that is, learning would be best if it could capture the enthusiasm which the child has to find out about the things which he sees as important *to him.*

It is obvious that this is a theoretically reasonable thing to do, but to apply this in teaching is difficult because of the enormous differences which will be found in class groups. Also, what a child sees as important to himself *today* may be something else *tomorrow* or the day after.

A vast amount of our learning, as we are growing up, is in connection with the things we want to do. Our games, playing with other people, our reading, or our exploration of our surroundings—these illustrate activities in which we have very often a good deal of interest. Because we are following our interests, and doing what we want to do, we learn easily.

In formal learning—in school, in class, and at home—we often find ourselves in a situation in which we are not very anxious to learn. When that is the case, we have to *try* harder. We have to make an effort. We have to make an attempt to see what it is that we are supposed to learn and why we are supposed to learn it. After we have become willing to do this, learning is not as difficult for us as it may have appeared at first.

Wanting to learn is the most important single factor in learning.

**Learning by Association.** Much learning takes place by this process. The facts about it are simple. We simply associate one experience with another experience that is already familiar to us. Hearing a word is an experience, and seeing an object which is familiar to us is another experience. Bring these two together and we have learning by association.

The baby sees a ball on the floor, and he hears his mother say, "Ball!" He already knows from experience what that round object is, which he now hears referred to as a ball. Because the *word* has now become associated with the *thing*, he learns to think of the *thing* when he hears the *word*.

By such incidents as these we gradually acquire the meanings of more and more words. We learn more and more expressions.

We find out what things are. We discover what animals do. We gain more and more ideas. One association is built on another association until we have formed a vast network of related facts and ideas. This process of learning by association is the groundwork of education.

**Learning by Conditioning.** Modern psychology refers to many kinds of learning as *conditioning*. We say that a child is *conditioned* to avoid touching a hot stove. He is *conditioned* to be afraid of a snake. He is *conditioned* to have a feeling of patriotism when he hears the national anthem, or when the flag goes by in a parade.

Conditioning is simply the process of linking up some new stimulus with any stimulus for which we already have a certain response.

**Pavlov's Work in Identifying the Nature of Conditioning.** Lindgren gives a good account of the basis of modern psychologists' understanding of the conditioning process:

For centuries before I. P. Pavlov evolved his theories of the conditional response, philosophers had been aware of the fact that learning is influenced by associations. However, Pavlov based his theories on physiological experiments. While studying the operation of the digestive system of the dog, Pavlov observed that digestive juices, which he had assumed were called forth by the presence of undigested food, actually began to flow when the dog heard the footsteps of the experimenter bringing the food. This led to his setting up an experiment in which he measured the flow of the dog's saliva in response to various stimuli. In a classic experiment, he placed meat powder in the dog's mouth, with the result that saliva flowed at an increased rate. Pavlov called this automatic response the "unconditioned reflex." The sounding of a bell in the presence of the dog caused no increase in the flow of saliva. However, when the bell was sounded a number of times just before the powdered meat was placed in the dog's mouth, the sound of the bell *alone* was sufficient to cause an increased saliva flow. Pavlov called this connection between the bell and the increased rate of salivation a "conditioned reflex" (termed a "conditioned response" by psychologists), and he called the sound of the bell a "conditioned stimulus."

The principle involved here is that when stimulus A produces response X and when stimulus B occurs with A, after a while stimulus B alone will be sufficient to produce response X.[1]

A further example of conditioning would be the way in which we become conditioned to jump back to the sidewalk if we carelessly step out onto the street and suddenly hear a loud automobile horn

[1] Henry Clay Lindgren, *Psychology of Personal and Social Adjustment* (New York: American Book Company, 1959), p. 379.

We are conditioned to jump out of the way
at the sound of a horn.

bearing down on us. We have become conditioned to respond this
way to the horn, because we have learned that a horn is associated
with an oncoming automobile.

Our jumping at the sound of the horn is a conditioned response.
We come running at the sound of the dinner bell because we have
formed a conditioned response to that stimulus. Our stopping at
the sight of a red traffic signal is another example.

Conditioning is sometimes capable of influencing people in important ways. Recently a story was told of a German government
official who occupied a high position in defeated Germany. He
was a socialist and very much opposed to militarism. In his capacity as a high ranking government official, he was explaining
some new policies to a group which included a former German
general.

During the conference this general suddenly "fired" a question
at him, whereupon he dropped his papers and snapped to military
attention.

Conditioning is an important factor in the training of combat troops.

*Official Department of Defense Photo*

This very embarrassing incident resulted because he had served, like nearly all other Germans, in the German army, and had been conditioned to instant and unquestioning obedience at any officer's command.

**Importance of Repetition.** While some of the things we learn are fixed in our minds by a single experience, most of them must be established by repetition. The repeated experience fixes a certain response to a certain stimulus. Otherwise we fail to make a well-established response or association, and our attention goes to something else.

Practice, or repetition, is therefore one of the most important things in learning. Anybody knows that unless the football player practices he can't be very good at the game.

In the same way, we must *use* words if they are really to be familiar to us, and if we are to know and understand them. We must *use* arithmetic and work at it repeatedly if we are to learn it.

Psychologists have found by experiments that repetition or drill is essential in learning, but they have also found out something else. They have found that the practice or the drill must have a purpose behind it. You have to be actually working at it, when you practice, to get results. Merely going over something again and again is not enough.

*Overlearning* makes learning more permanent. In memorizing, when that is necessary, it is a good idea to go over whatever it is you are learning several times. These extra repetitions produce what is called *overlearning*. The thing being learned is studied or gone over beyond the point necessary to learn or repeat it once. When this is done, provided *effort* is put into it, the material will be learned much better and remembered longer.

The trouble is that few people put in this extra effort, this additional practice. The wise student, keeping this in mind, will read over his notes more than once. He will find the time to read the material again—go over it another time. He will apply the principle that repetition or practice—drill as it is often called—is a "must" for efficient learning.

**Doing More and Learning More.** When we do much the same thing day after day we do not change much and we do not learn more. Learning depends a great deal on what we make of the situation.

If you take a trip to New York City and gaze with a passing interest at the scenery you will learn something about the city. But if you take greater advantage of this situation you will learn more. Perhaps you could plan your trip so as to visit the historical monuments in the parks, the Museum of Modern Art, Rockefeller Center, the United Nations, etc. Then your visit to New York will be a still greater learning experience. By doing more, making an effort, and being attentive to situations you encounter, you will be learning more and enjoying it more.

Many worth-while inventions have resulted because people have been observant of their surroundings. The manufacture and installation of change-making machines came about because some one noticed how many people were having trouble finding change to use in coin operated machines and dispensers. Self-service merchandising came about because some people noticed how time consuming and inefficient the old system of clerks-waiting-on-customers had become. All sorts of labor-saving machinery originated in a similar fashion, and in order to encourage such inventiveness, many industries have rewards for suggestions and invite their employees to be observant of ways to make improvements.

**Trial and Error in Relation to Learning.** Several concepts often discussed in connection with learning might be mentioned. Trial and error is a process which sometimes enters into learning. In learning to perform some act, we may "try" several approaches before we discover what will work. Actually, this is not so much a way of learning, as it is a way of pin-pointing or finding out what it is that we need to learn.

Trial and error is more frequently found in problem solving than in any other type of situation. When there is a problem to be solved, a difficulty to be overcome, we cast about, often through trial and error, to find the solution or the way to surmount a difficulty. Careful observation of the situation and planning will reduce the amount of trial and error involved or needed. There is also a mental sort of trial and error, as when we *do* things, or apply certain processes, in our minds, to see whether or not they might work. Mental trial and error, which is possible in man because of his ability to hypothesize and to imagine situations, is quite common. It lessens the amount of unprofitable effort likely to result from actual performance.

**Guidance in Learning.** Guidance, which may either take the form of showing someone how to do something, or making suggestions to lead him in profitable directions, has a place in learning. The coach shows the athlete a play, the artist shows the student how to achieve a certain effect, and the musician shows the student a way to achieve a certain kind of fingering.

In working with students about a problem in law or political science, the teacher may throw out suggestions to guide their thinking. Study outlines, with questions and problems, perform the same service. Questions also guide us by directing our thinking in worth-while ways.

Viewed in this way, guidance is an influence that can aid the learning process.

**Transfer of Training.** Especially among educators, it is important to know to what extent learning in one field helps us in another. Does the study of Latin make us better thinkers, better writers, or better debaters? Does the study of mathematics improve our minds, make us better able to solve problems?

Does learning how to be a good basketball player make a better airplane pilot?

Psychologists have devoted much time to the study of these questions. The answer in general is that there is a transfer of ability but only to the extent that the two activities are alike. If the two subjects are quite different, there will be little or no transfer.

Hence it is safe to say that the study of Latin will help only to a very limited extent any ability we might have to solve problems. It will help, to a greater extent, our understanding of the meaning of words when the words have been derived from Latin backgrounds, as is true of so many words in our language. The study of mathematics won't help us much to settle emotional quarrels. But it will help in the solution of problems in physics, chemistry, economics, etc.

There is another way in which transfer may be expected. Any program of concentrated, disciplined study may help us to develop habits of study which will be useful in other fields as well as in the field where they have been developed. In this sense, there is transfer —transfer of a way of dong things, of the willingness to work hard at a problem, of persistence. Yet these transfer values are not always to be found, because motivation, or the wanting to do something, varies from subject to subject, from activity to activity.

When the question arises whether there is transfer of training, we need to examine the area studied and the area to which transfer is expected. If the habits of work or the attitudes learned in one area are quite like those needed in the other, some transfer is possible. If the "things done" in one area are like the "things done" in the other area, some transfer is possible.

Ways in which there is transfer of training from one subject or field to another may be summarized as follows:

1. There is transfer of *facts* learned, or skills acquired, when the facts or skills are also useful in the second or in another area different from the one studied.
2. There is transfer of ways of doing things. Habits of working can be carried over to any other field where they apply.
3. There is transfer of attitudes. Points of view, liking or disliking something, or interests, may be carried over from the subject studied to some other area.

At the same time we need to remember that the large amount of transfer which some people claim is vastly overrated. No one subject has a tremendous advantage over any other subject insofar as transfer is concerned. Yet it is also true that even a small amount of transfer might be very important, because it could be in some life activity or some area of work which makes a great deal of use, for a long period of time, of that particular information, skill, way of doing things, or attitude.

**Words and Symbols in Learning.** Most of our learning which goes beyond merely forming habits or learning skills such as we use in making a bed, or riding a bicycle, makes it necessary for us to learn words, definitions, principles, numbers, formulas, or symbols.

It is very necessary that these words or symbols be understood clearly from the beginning. We have been pointing out that learning is largely a matter of associating things in our minds.

It is important to get the meanings clear. This process of association can be on a firm basis, or on a shaky one. If the student gets the *right* association at the beginning, and then repeats and practices it, he will learn well. Students should, therefore, make sure that they understand the meaning of words and symbols. And they should work with their friends and teachers until these meanings are perfectly clear.

Since words are so important in learning and in thinking, each student should build up a good vocabulary. It is wise to write down new words on cards, with their meanings, and go over them from time to time until they have become the property of the person learning them. This practice in understanding what words mean, in learning how to spell them, in becoming able to recognize them quickly, is so important in learning that each student should pay considerable attention to it. Many textbooks list the new words included in each lesson. This part of the lesson should get a good deal of attention, because the words are the framework of the subject. The words are the tools of the student.

Make a conscious effort to increase your vocabulary, for the man who really knows something, *also knows how to say it.*

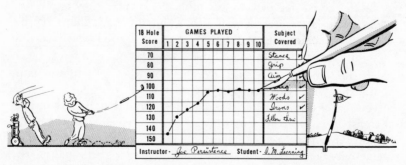

This golfer has evidently reached a plateau in learning.

**Plateaus in Learning.** A plateau is a high level area. The climber, when he arrives on a plateau, is unable to make any further progress upward as long as he remains on the plateau.

Psychologists say that there are plateaus in learning. That is, there are levels when we seem to make no progress, but seem to be standing still in our learning.

Nearly always, these levels are temporary. After a period of not making progress, learning is resumed.

This is a point worth noting in psychology, for it will help us to keep from getting discouraged. It is perfectly natural for the student, from time to time, to feel that he is not making much progress. The reasons for this may be that he is temporarily tired, or not interested, or perhaps something else is claiming his interest and attention. He may be consolidating or assimilating what he has already learned before taking on additional information.

The practical lesson we get from knowing about the fact that there are plateaus in learning and that they are rather common in our experience, is that we need not give up hope that there will ultimately be improvement in our skill. No doubt some people reach the point in learning any particular skill or body of information beyond which they will not likely go. But it is more common for people to *think* they have reached that point, when it is merely a plateau. Actually, continued effort will result in still more improvement a little later on.

**The Importance of How Things "Belong" in Learning.** Learning very seldom consists of isolated parts or bits. In studying the nature of how we learn, psychologists have become impressed by the fact that our experiences in life are usually organized into a sort of pattern. We don't just learn a lot of separate words in Spanish or French. We learn whole sentences, whole paragraphs, whole ideas.

The golfer doesn't just learn many separate things such as how to hold the club, where to put the ball, how to hold his head, etc. He learns *how to play golf*—which is all of those things and more.

When the person learning a new thing begins to see how the whole thing is put together, we say that he has finally acquired a "know how," or, as the psychologists sometimes put it, he has developed "insight" into the situation.

This is true of almost all kinds of learning. We reach a point where we "catch on" or "see through" the subject or problem.

It is important to see how ideas fit, how they belong and mean

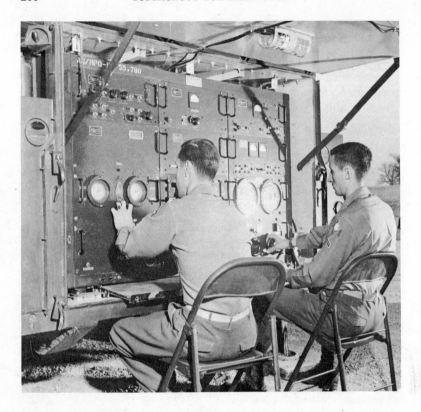

Constant practice enables these men to operate their radar sets with speed and efficiency.

*U.S. Army Photograph*

something. This means that as learners we should try to see the thing we are learning in its relation to the whole subject being studied. If we don't see any connection, we should read, ask questions, or discuss the matter until it makes sense. If we see a purpose in what we are learning, or a reason for learning it, this understanding will come more easily. Therefore the student needs to look over the whole subject and think about it, so that he sees a point or purpose to it. Then his studying will have more meaning to him and he will learn more easily. Without this over-all view of what he is doing, the student can literally get lost in his studies.

As a matter of fact, there appears to be a drive in the human being to organize things into patterns or into meaningful groups.

The desire to see meaning in things, to see how they "fit" or how they might go together, how they are related, is noticeable in man's effort to systemize his knowledge into the various sciences. This is demonstrated in psychology by various experiments in which the subjects have *completed* patterns in which only part of the information was given. *Gestalt* psychology demonstrates our tendency to conform to this drive, that is, to see wholeness in things.

One of the reasons for the difficulty which most people have in appreciating modern or abstract painting springs from the fact that they try desperately to see some meaning in the painting, to "organize" it into some meaningful whole. But being unable to do this they are frustrated with accompanying feelings of hostility toward the picture or the painter.

**Remembering and Forgetting.** It has already been noted that remembering is largely a matter of learning things well in the first place, and then in having enough opportunities to repeat them or use them or practice them so that they can be a *part of us* and be remembered.

If we have followed the rules, if we have learned something by getting it clearly in mind the first time, and then practiced it, why do we forget?

There are many reasons why things are forgotten, but perhaps the most important one is that we just don't get the practice. We don't have enough opportunities to use what we have learned. What we use frequently, we *don't* forget!

**Later Learning Tends To Crowd Out Earlier Learning.** Another reason for forgetting which psychologists have pretty well proved is that between the time when we first learn something and the time, later on, when we are called upon to use it, we have learned other things. These other things have a tendency to crowd out the earlier learning.

That is probably why seniors in college have been found, very often, to know less about some subjects than freshmen. In the years in between, they have studied so many subjects that they have forgotten much that was learned during the first year. Of course, if they had been practicing, or using, what they had learned during all of this time, then the material learned in between would scarcely crowd the earlier learning out. But the later learning does have the effect of standing in the way of what was first learned.

**Find Opportunities To Use What You Have Learned.** It is, of course, impossible to keep practicing and using everything we have learned, and so forgetting which is due to later learning can hardly be avoided. Yet the alert student, who is really interested in his history, his literature, his science, and his other subjects, will find himself thinking about them frequently, and will forget less than a student who has other things which interest him more.

The fact that what we learn in between one school term and another school term has a tendency to crowd out what was learned in the earlier term almost justifies us in saying that the more we learn the less we know!

That is an astonishing thing to say but there is some truth in it. The only answer to that is to keep our interests alive. We need to renew from time to time our interests in various subjects—in science, history, geography, reading, etc. That is the way to keep the information we have gained alive. This is good practical psychology for the student who wants to remember, rather than forget, a good share of what school has made it possible for him to learn.

It is good to be able to recognize things, even when we can't recall them. This is one other point in the psychology of remembering to be mentioned. Often we learn something so that we can recognize it and appreciate it, even though we might not be able to bring it up or recall it ourselves. Many of the things we have learned in geography, for example, help us to appreciate the newsreels and the things we read in the newspaper, even though we might find it hard ourselves to recall and bring up some item or point about the geography of the place referred to. Moreover, although we may not be immediately able to recall a fact that we have previously learned, we may be able as a result of our education to *find* it quickly, or at least to know where to look for the information. We learn to know what the great sources of information are and where to locate them.

## Suggestions for Better Learning

1. Get a clear idea of what it is that you are expected to learn. See how it fits into the subject, what it means.

2. Try to get a total view of the assignment. See what the whole assignment calls for. Then, very likely, the separate, specific items will fall into place in a way that is more understandable to you.

3. Get yourself into a frame of mind in which you really want to learn the assignment. That will usually come if you have done what has been suggested in Point One.

4. Try to fit in what you are learning with other experiences you have had—with things you already know about. This establishes associations, which, we have noted, are the basis of most learning.

5. Make a conscious effort to learn it. Close your mind to outside interruptions and pay attention to what you are reading or studying. A few minutes of concentrated effort will be worth more than an hour of dawdling.

New products, new ideas, different approaches to problems — these are but a few of the things that may be learned at International Fairs and Convention Exhibits.

*Fred Hess & Son*

6. Practice the thing you are expected to learn a number of times. If it is something to read, go over it more than once. Make sure you caught everything of importance in it. Ask yourself questions about it, and try to answer the questions. Often it is a good thing to talk it over with another student. You can ask each other questions. This will help immensely, for one of the best ways of making sure you know something is to try to explain it to someone else.

## Organize the Material You Are Studying

**Organize Your Materials.** Be sure, when studying at home, that you have a good place to study and that your tools (books, pencils, typewriter, etc.) are ready.

Efficiency in study is very much like efficiency on any other kind of job. If your materials are at hand where you can use them, it will help. Sometimes it takes a little time to get the materials ready, but this is important and useful. When you need an eraser, it is helpful to have it ready. When you need a dictionary, it is a good idea to have it where you can put your hands on it. Also, with paper and other materials, a little preparation can save you time and energy.

There is a more important side to it, though. Having your materials *ready* and *at hand* has a good psychological effect. It sets the stage, gives you a "mind set," puts you in a frame of mind to work. Why not use this psychological factor in order to make your studying easier and your homework more efficient?

Develop good habits of studying. Although this is discussed in connection with other aspects of psychology, it should be brought out here that there are a number of suggestions which might be helpful.

For example, some students find it helpful to outline their work. Making an outline of the important points in a chapter as you go along is a form of activity which helps to fix the important points in your mind. It also gives you something to go back to for reviewing.

This outlining may be of the formal, systematic type, where you try to get everything of importance in the chapter down in some logical order with headings and sub-headings, or it may be informal, in which you simply make brief *notes* on the important point, or points which seem new and important to you as you go along.

A variation of this would be to make rough notes, then write them up more formally afterward—possibly typing them on cards for easy reference. (See the following comments on taking notes in class.) The same technique might be used in taking notes on a book or other material you are reading.

Learning can take place any time, any place. Practical experience teaches us that learning is not all confined to that which is studied at home or in school in a place just set aside for that purpose.

Much productive work is done under anything but ideal conditions. Lincoln has often been reported as having written his famous Gettysburg speech in the form of rough notes while riding on the train toward Pennsylvania.

Many people have found that they can learn by the "few minutes a day" technique—utilizing odd times and places for a little study on some subject in which they are interested. In other words, if we have the motivation we can learn any time, any where, and under almost any conditions.

**Note-Taking in Class or at a Lecture.** One of the study problems every student has is connected with taking notes. He must organize what has been given in class for further study, for reference, and for review.

Do you know how to take notes when you attend a class or go to a lecture?

One of the best methods of taking notes is to write down very briefly what you hear in class—the things said by the instructor and also things brought up by other students—whenever they seem important or significant. *But don't try to write them down in final form as they are said in class.* Write rough notes, just enough so that you get the point.

Then, during your study period, or at home, *rewrite* them more fully, and in good order. This method of note-taking will be helpful for three reasons: (1) You will not spend so much time writing down notes in class that you miss some of the other important things that are said, (2) you will have time to think about what is going on, and (3) the very fact that you will go over the material again and think about it and write it up in good form will *in itself* help to impress the material upon you.

Your finished notes will be in good order, and they will make sense when you go back to read them over later. Many students who try to write everything down in a notebook as they go along come to the end of the term with a scrambled notebook (well illustrated with pictures and "do-dads"), so poorly written and so poorly organized that they can't tell what was important and what wasn't.

Of course when you take rough notes according to the plan just suggested, all you need in class or at the lecture is "copy paper" to take them on. The good paper or cards (some students use a file of cards for keeping their notes) are only used for the final transcribing after you get back to your study period, or to your home.

The only exception to this would occur when the teacher says that he wants you to take something down *verbatim*—that is, exactly as he says it, in which case he will dictate the material slowly so that you can do as directed.

## SOMETHING TO DO

1. Make a chart showing the things you are interested in learning in your present program of studies.

2. Make a list of things you are quite interested in learning, which are *not* in your present study program.

3. Take some of the main topics in any subject you are studying and under each one make a list of a few things which you would really like to know more about.

## QUESTIONS AND PROBLEMS FOR DISCUSSION AND STUDY

1. Make as complete a list as you can of the many different kinds of *facts* that you have learned.

2. Make two columns, one listing important things you have learned in school; the other, important things you have learned outside of school.

3. Compare your list of important things learned with some other student's list. Discuss your reasons for listing certain items as important.

4. Take some game with which you are familiar, and list carefully all of the different skills you can think of as necessary for playing the game.

5. Take a poem of about twenty lines length and deliberately set out to learn it by heart. See how many repetitions are necessary for the purpose.

6. Make a set of cards on which you will list, for two weeks, new words you come across in your reading, and their meanings.

7. What should one do when he is unable to remember something which is important?

8. Can a person improve his memory?

9. Give an example of someone you know who has worked very hard and studied a great deal in connection with some hobby in which he or she has been interested.

10. Give an example of something you have been required to learn which has been very hard for you. Analyze the reasons—as you see it—why this learning was hard.

11. Find a set of instructions for setting up some article or piece of machinery. Analyze them to find out in what respect they are clear and good; in what respect they are faulty.

12. To illustrate the importance of clear instructions, write out in careful detail directions for reaching some point several miles distant in your city or community. Have your friends criticize your instructions as to clearness and completeness.

13. Explain the meaning of *learning by association* and give an illustration.

14. Take a new game which you have recently learned and show very specifically what it has involved in the way of (a) skills, (b) facts, and (c) attitudes.

15. Explain what is meant by *conditioning*. Give an illustration from your own experience.

16. Give an example, from your own experience, of a *plateau* in learning. Explain the meaning of the plateau and, in connection with your example, give the probable reasons for it.

17. Explain what is meant by trial and error, and guidance in relation to learning.

18. Under what conditions does transfer of learning occur?

# CHAPTER SEVEN

# HABITS

Sometimes people think of habits as either good or bad, but they do not always think of them as being indispensable. This chapter brings out the importance of habits and shows that they are essential in our everyday lives.

This being the case, it is necessary to know the best ways of forming good habits; it is also necessary to know how to get rid of undesirable habits. The psychological principles involved are outlined in this chapter.

In order to show the great significance of habits and habit formation for everyday life, the latter part of the chapter takes up some of the more important habits most people have, or should have. These include work habits, study habits, health habits, and habits connected with exercise and recreation, as well as social habits.

Psychology offers some practical suggestions here which can help us. It is important to know the principles of habit formation not only for our own use, but also so that we may use the principles in working with others. They are necessary in the care of children, and in other situations where we are obliged to deal with other people.

## QUESTIONS THIS CHAPTER WILL ANSWER

1. To what extent are we "creatures of habit"?
2. How important are habits in our lives?
3. Can habits be changed? How is this brought about?
4. Assuming that there are some important habits to be formed, what is the best way to go about it?
5. What are some of the most important habits which all people should have, and how can they be developed?
6. What practical suggestions can be made to help us in establishing habits which are good for us in the more important areas of our lives?

## What a Habit Is

A habit is a fixed way of responding. It is a definite way of acting or thinking whenever the stimulus is given which usually "touches off" that particular way of responding.

For example, in scrubbing the teeth the individual usually starts out in the same part of the mouth every time. The stimulus for this is inserting the brush in the mouth. Movement of the brush in certain directions follows as a series of conditioned responses.

Once the TV cameraman knows his instrument, he operates it on the basis of habit and can devote his full attention to the assignment.

*NBC Photo*

In eating a meal like breakfast, the individual usually wishes to have some particular food to which he is accustomed first. If he is used to starting with fruit juice, then he wants fruit juice first. The strength of the habit is apparent when he is asked to take that item of food at a point later on in the meal, out of his customary order.

A thousand habits enter into our daily living. By habits our order of life is ruled; they affect the way we do our jobs and how we spend our leisure and recreational time as well. Some study of the nature of habits, how they are formed, and how they are changed, is therefore in order.

## Habits as a Result of Learning

We are not born with habits; they develop as we grow and learn. People recognize this indirectly when they say: "Teach the child before he is old enough to have formed a lot of bad habits."

We also hear older people spoken of as having their habits "pretty well set." The older the person, according to some, the more fixed his habits.

There is much truth in this, since the older we are and the longer we live, the more firmly established by practice and custom some of our habits become. Of course, as is shown elsewhere in this book, people are capable of learning *all of the time*—no matter how old they are—so many of their habits may change and be replaced by new habits.

The first time you drive a car with an automatic transmission you have a habit adjustment to make.

If a person used to driving an automobile with the conventional gearshift tries to drive a car with an automatic type of shift, he has a difficult habit adjustment to make. He reaches for the gearshift lever in vain. He fumbles with his left foot for the clutch pedal, but it isn't there. It is necessary to drive the new car many times before the force of the old habits is broken and the necessary new habits are acquired.

So strong are old habits, sometimes, that the individual can't make the change-over quickly enough, and he may get into real trouble in driving before the new ways of operating the car are learned. The story has often been told about the man who, when the automobile was first invented, bought his first car. Accustomed to driving a team of horses, which responded to shouts of "Gee" and "Haw" and "Whoa," this citizen found himself in trouble as his automobile moved swiftly down the street. He could not think quickly of what to do so he relapsed into shouting "Gee" and "Haw" and "Whoa," yelling louder and louder as the car jumped the curb and came to an inglorious rest in a shower of glass and a jumbled store window. The old habits failed in this emergency and the new ones were not established yet.

The essence of learning habits seems to be simply that a person responds or acts in a certain way which is practiced or repeated a sufficient number of times to become established as the customary response. The human being or the animal, it seems, is so made that repetition of this kind *fixes* the response. In fact, this is so important a form of learning that when we stop to think about it we realize that if this were not so we would be very helpless. Without habits of any kind, we would have to start out every day all over again, experimenting, fumbling, and stumbling around because we would not *know* what to do.

**Relation of Customs to Habit.** There is ample evidence that habits are learned. They are learned according to what we have been shown and taught in the particular environment in which we have lived and grown. The young boy is told to rise when a lady enters the room—it becomes a habit. The young girl is advised to remain seated when a young man enters the room and that becomes a habit. The young man is taught to walk between the lady and the street— it becomes a habit to such an extent that he feels most uncomfortable if, for some reason, he cannot assume that position.

Most of our customs are examples of habits. In many nursing schools the student nurses rise when the professor enters the room and remain standing until he is seated. In the army the private snaps to attention and salutes when a superior officer approaches. Also by force of habit, the superior officer salutes in return.

We stand for the playing of the "Star Spangled Banner," and for the "Alma Mater" of our own or another school. The men uncover their heads.

In many Protestant churches women may enter the church building without hats or head coverings; in others, and in churches of the Catholic faith, they wear hats or other head coverings to enter. Protestant men uncover their heads on entering churches, and would feel very uncomfortable otherwise. In Jewish congregations the men wear their hats in the synagogue.

These habits vary from individual to individual, reflecting the habits of the particular group in which the individual has lived, and so show that habits are the result of learning rather than of any other force. They come from day to day repetition.

## Circumstances Modify Habits

In the study of man and his behavior, one of the things which is noticeable and important is the fact that he is not always predictable. Now, if habits, which are so characteristic of people, as

Training to produce desired habits and attitudes is essential to the efficient performance of this U.S. Air Force crew.

*Official U.S. Air Force Photo*
*Department of Defense*

has just been seen, could be depended upon to show themselves uniformly and at all times without modification, it would be possible to say ahead of time just what John Smith and Alice Brown are going to do. This is not the case, as everyone knows.

For example, we may say that Mr. Jones has a "habit" of going home from the office at five o'clock every day. But when Mrs. Jones persuades her afternoon visitors to "Wait just a little while, I know Mr. Jones will be home," *that* just might be the time when Mr. Jones will leave at a different hour and go home by a different way.

Mr. Peterson "always" goes to church on Sunday morning, but on some particular Sunday morning, just when you are expecting to see him at the church, he goes somewhere else or stays at home.

Pennsylvania "always" votes Republican, but *this time* it doesn't. The people of the Solid South "always" support the Democratic ticket in a presidential election, but not in 1928, nor again in 1948.

The question we may ask, then, is how often does a thing have to be done the same way before we say it is a habit?

The difficulty which is presented here is that habits are not as binding nor are they as universally dependable as people have often supposed. They are the *usual* ways of reacting under *usual* conditions. They may be depended upon to serve as a guide to the behavior of the individual under those conditions. But when the conditions change, or whenever other conditions are presented, they may be shifted in favor of some other type of behavior.

If we realize that this is the case, we are in a better position to understand the role of habits and we are better able to understand people and their behavior.

## Importance of Habits in Behavior

As suggested above, habits are indispensable. They make it possible for the individual to meet the problems of everyday life with the greatest possible saving of his time and energy. The writer is able to typewrite this paragraph without a great waste of time and energy because he has developed *habits*. These habits include hitting the right key for the right letter, hitting the right lever to move the typewriter carriage, hitting the proper bar for spacing, and other steps necessary to typing.

Even such an apparently simple act as reading involves a great many habits. For example, it is necessary, in reading English, to read from the left-hand side of the page to the right, and to move the eyes back to the left of the page, and down one line, as the reading progresses. How important these habits are has been shown with children who have had difficulty in learning to read, and who have been found not to have developed these habits.

A man is able to shave and get dressed in the morning without taking too much time because he has learned certain habits. The housewife prepares the meal with a minimum of "fuss and bother" because she has formed certain habits. For example, if she wants a certain kind of knife, she knows in which drawer to look for it; she knows where to reach with her hand for a particular item in the closet where the groceries are kept and how long to keep something on the fire where cooking is involved; she knows these things in the sense that she has formed *habits* which enable her to work effectively.

A few considerations like this show us the importance of habits. We realize then that one might almost say that the successful man or woman is a person who has formed the *right* habits. In these particular activities, which we must perform every day, day in and day out, for years possibly, our habits keep us moving in the right direction. Thanks to having learned them, we have time and freedom to do other things and to think about other matters.

This immediately suggests to us the importance of habits and the need for deciding whether or not, in each of the major things we do in life, we have developed good ones. The efficiency expert in industry is often concerned with studying each operation to see whether or not the workers have developed the best habits.

The thought comes to mind that an individual's habits bear about the same relationship to his life as the underwater portion of the iceberg does to the iceberg. The one-eighth of the iceberg which is above the sea might illustrate that part of our lives which is the subject of our conscious effort and direction. The seven-eighths below represents that portion of our life which is controlled and provided for by habit. Incidentally, just as it would not be easy to swerve or change the course of the iceberg by pushing it at the top, neither is it, in reality, too simple a matter to change the direction or control of man. The force or control of the habits must be reckoned with.

What we are trying to bring out is that habits are important and necessary. The very power which they exert over us, and which sometimes makes us feel as though we, and others, are the creatures of habit, is what gives them their great value to us. It is because of the great service which they render to us, and of which they are capable, that we may use them to advantage. If they didn't have this power, in the sense of controlling us in the things we do from day to day, they would not be useful.

## Can Habits Be Changed?

Although it has already been suggested that habits can be changed, it is necessary to stress this point because there are so many conditions of life which are changing and for which preparation must be made. If habits could not be changed, man would be helpless indeed, because one of the most obvious things about our world is that it is changing.

We must change our habits to become accustomed to the changing conditions of life. Whether or not a person can change a particular habit or group of habits depends to some extent on how badly he *wants* to change. If he finds that the habits which he is now following are satisfactory, he will not want to change.

This leads us to a very important point in psychology. It is this: When an organism is set to respond in a certain way, for it to respond in that way is very satisfying, for it not to respond in that way is annoying. This suggests the reason for our often-noticed resistance to anything which interrupts our old habits. The same "ease-of-doing" which makes habits so useful and serviceable to us, means that if we cannot act according to them, we are unhappy and annoyed.

Hence we come to the point above mentioned, that whether or not we change our habits depends on how badly we want to do so.

If our usual way of doing things is interrupted and we see no particular advantage to it, we are annoyed and we will resist change. If, however, we can see a reason for it, we will make the change if it seems to us that it is a good reason or that the results will be good for us in the end.

The practical suggestion of this for us all is very clear: *If we are asked to change our habits for a new way of doing things, we*

*should try to find out the advantages of the new way; if we are
asking other people to change their way of doing things we must
try to show them how the new way will help them or be to their
advantage.*

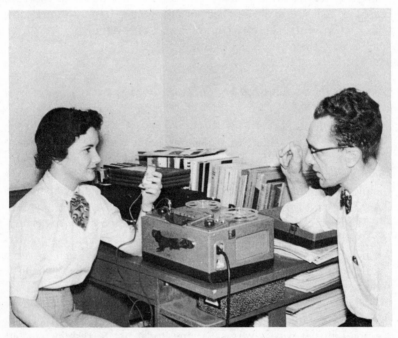

**Many occupations require the ability to speak clearly and correctly. With
study and practice, bad speech habits can be corrected.**

*Courtesy Myron Cunningham Photography*

There is another condition under which we will change our
habits without too much difficulty and without too much stress and
strain. That is when we are *forced* to change them and there is
no alternative. Thus, a person who has the habit of writing with
his right hand, will readily change his habit to that of writing with
the left hand if through some grave misfortune he loses the use of
his right hand. For a less frightening example, we might think of
the American who is used to driving on the right side of the road.
When he visits England he must change his habit to that of driving
on the left side of the road.

However, as long as there is an alternative, or as long as the individual feels that there is or should be an alternative, he may resist changing the habit if the established way of doing things has appealed to him strongly enough.

## Basic Principles of Habit Formation

Most psychologists agree on the nature of sound habit formation. Possibly the rules could be summed up as follows:

1. Know clearly what the habit is which is to be established.
2. Get the act or performance started correctly.
3. Practice it regularly.
4. Allow no exceptions.
5. Check for faulty performance and eliminate errors before they also become habitual.

These suggestions are written from the standpoint of the learner himself. As a teacher of others, the problem would be to see to it that these same rules are followed. If any suggestions were added, they would involve rewarding the learner when the right performance is accomplished, and encouraging him to "stay with it" until the habit has been formed.

**1. Know Clearly What the Habit Is Which Is To Be Established.** This means that in undertaking to learn anything new it is important to know what it is we are to learn. A man can't form a habit of getting to work at a certain time in the morning until he knows what time work is supposed to start. In learning a job, it is particularly important to know what the job requires. A person can't learn to swim successfully unless he knows what it takes to swim. Of course, we hear it said that one of the ways to teach a person to swim is just to throw him in the water. But there are just enough people drowned every year to make us suspicious of this as a recommended procedure.

Putting this principle to work in a few selected types of situations we might get suggestions such as these:

*a*) In learning the habits needed on a new job, find out what the job requires.

*b*) In learning the habits of study required for a new subject or a new course, study the subject to find out what it is about and what you are expected to learn.

*c*) In learning how to play a new game requiring a new set of habits, find out what the game calls for, what the principal rules are, and what the more important and most frequent plays will be.

*d*) In learning the habits needed to operate a machine, get the main functions of the machine in mind, determine what the essential steps are and set these steps up as the ones to practice.

In short, every one of these types of situations—indeed almost any learning situation we can think of—suggests the need for studying the situation to find out what is required. Many people fail because they really don't know what they are trying to do!

In connection with this principle it should be noted that habits are not usually learned in an isolated manner. Each habit is usually related to other habits. In typing, for example, there is a separate habit which results in the typist using a certain finger for a certain letter and another finger for another letter. There is also a habit which calls for hitting the spacing bar with the thumb of the right hand; another for hitting the bar which moves the carriage over at the end of the line.

In driving a car there is a habit for applying the brake with the foot; another habit for shifting into low gear, second, or high (if the car is a gearshift car) and yet other habits for turning to the right, the left, etc.

The learner soon learns to "run through" a series of habits with one being connected to the others in a smooth and orderly fashion. These series of habits are sometimes called by the psychologists *families of habits*, which simply means groups of habits used in carrying out a performance of any particular kind.

*The point is that the important habits which go into these groupings need to be learned in relation to one another* if the whole group of habits is to work smoothly. This can be illustrated in the case of driving a car. It would be foolish for the new driver to learn how to work the clutch pedal only, and not to know, at the very beginning of his learning, how to apply the brake. He must know the series of important habits needed to drive.

This again stresses the importance of finding out what is required in the new thing to be learned.

In an act like driving a car or playing a piano, the habits follow each other swiftly and it seems as though one habit leads to the next one. The piano player strikes a key or a chord and that leads to his striking the next key or chord and so on through the exercise he is playing.

The way in which these habits are all connected in a series is illustrated by what happens when the pianist is stopped in the middle of his exercise and his attention directed to something else. If it is an exercise he has "learned" (learned to play by *habit*) he may not be able to start again in the middle, but may have to start again at the beginning. He is "used" to playing it as a continuous melody, one part following automatically from the part preceding it.

It is because of this that many teachers advocate that the learner "go through the whole selection" first so as to see how the parts fit in together. This is called the *whole method of learning*. It is advisable in any performance which is not too long or complicated, because the learner then sees how the steps go together and how they belong.

This suggests one habit we all need to acquire, the habit of studying carefully any new thing we are to learn to make sure that we know what to do.

Sometimes when we notice a person who does this, we say "He is a methodical person," or "He is a careful worker."

**2. Get the Act or Performance Started Correctly.** Once we have decided what it is we are to do, we should start to do it, and then

This crew practices daily for months at a time in order to develop and perfect the habits which make for a winning combination.

*Harvard University*

we should make sure that we are doing it *right*. If we have a teacher, we may ask the teacher to tell us whether or not we have started the act properly.

If we are working "on our own" we must ask ourselves this question and check what we are doing to make sure that we are on the right track.

The reason for this is obvious. If we get started incorrectly, we will not be able to learn the right habit. Also, since we know that repetition or practice is what "fixes" a habit, or at least is what causes a habit to develop, we realize that the wrong habit can be started just as easily as the right habit and then we will have to undo what we have already learned and start all over again.

Many times we are in the position of trying to teach other people how to do things—to teach them habits of work or to train them. In this case it is very important to get them started properly in the performance of their duties.

Unsatisfactory habits can be formed so quickly that in starting a person on the job, an employer often finds that the new worker is doing his work in an unsatisfactory manner because he did not start out properly. Often this is the employer's fault because he did not take enough time to start the new worker in the right direction. Then he wonders why the new worker is so inefficient.

This is one of the main reasons why better industries and business concerns are setting up training programs, or schools for their new workers, in the hope that, among other things, the new workers will get off to a good start.

**3. Practice Regularly.** Any new habit, skill, or performance needs a chance to become developed. This requires practice. As we see elsewhere in this text, one of the principles of learning is that of practice or repetition.

Most habits simply won't "jell" unless they are practiced.

Few and far between are the good golf players who never practice. The once-a-month golfer is a poor match for the man who indulges in the sport two or three times a week.

Football teams spend weeks practicing plays, learning signals, and "toughening up."

Practice requires time and effort, and requires that we pay attention to what we are doing until we have *learned* the habit or set of habits we have in mind. If we want to learn to play the piano, hours of time and effort will be the price we must pay. The house-wife won't become a good cook by not practicing.

This seems like an elementary rule of habit formation but it is surprising how many individuals will resist it. The boy or girl who is taking music lessons is so often unwilling to practice. Of course, we have to want to do something to put much effort into it, but in every case we must realize that unless we "train"—which means practice—there are few good habits or worth-while skills which we will ever acquire.

How often have we listened to the good pianist, or watched the artist draw an interesting picture, and said "I *wish* I could do that!"

Here is possibly nine-tenths of the answer: We could do it if we practiced enough to learn.

**4. Allow No Exceptions.** In practicing an act which one is in-tending to learn, the act should be carried out the way it is supposed to be done *every time it is practiced.* Furthermore, there ought not to be interruptions in the practice.

If we are trying to form the habit of writing down our daily expenses every evening before going to bed, it must be done every evening until the habit is established. Otherwise, it is likely that the habit will not be established.

The person who is learning does not realize how difficult he is making his learning when he allows exceptions or says to himself "just this once" he will do it another way. After the habit has been thoroughly established an occasional exception may occur without damaging the habit.

**5. Check for Faulty Performance and Eliminate Errors.** This principle is easily understood, though possibly not so easy to put into practice because it takes effort to take time and energy to check and to criticize one's own performance. Whether the learner will correct his performance and get rid of the clumsy or unsatis-factory ways of working will depend on how anxious he is to do a good job.

It is clear that the wrong step or performance can be just as easily learned as the right one. An example of learning the wrong habit may be found in the case of table manners. It is possible for a person to form a habit of leaning on one arm on the table while eating—an unacceptable mannerism at the table. After this has been done a few times it becomes practically impossible for the person to sit down to a meal without lapsing into this bad habit.

Since this is one of the bad habits in the group of habits which enter into conduct at the table, it illustrates the importance of eliminating such bad habits before they can become fixed.

Teachers find many examples of bad habits getting started in connection with the writing of students—use of punctuation, spelling, pronunciation, etc. Some bad habits, if not corrected early in the learning period, may be troublesome to the student for the rest of his life. An example of this is the tendency to become confused in spelling some common word, like *their*, wondering whether the *e* or the *i* comes first. This results from not learning the *right* way of spelling at the very beginning and from allowing a bad habit to get started.

With the importance of habits in mind, and the possibility of changing them understood, the individual is in a position to consider the significance of habits for his own life and to make some effort to understand their meaning for him. A few examples and suggestions will be given in this connection.

**Work Habits.** Do you have good habits for your own particular job? Are you doing things the hard way or the easy way?

It has been found that the position in which tools are kept on a bench has a lot to do with the ease of a particular operation in a factory. The location of cooking equipment in a kitchen either helps or hinders the cook in developing good habits. The order in which things are done may change the outlook for success or failure in an operation.

There is no rule for all jobs, but it is possible for any worker to analyze his own job to see whether or not his habits are good or bad. Wasted motion may add up to a great deal of energy in the course of a day, a week, or a month.

By and large the key to applying good habits to a job lies in being systematic. By being systematic about it, almost any worker can improve not only the efficiency of his work, but also the ease with which it can be accomplished.

Orderliness in the keeping of materials may be illustrated in connection with work habits in an office or at a desk. The orderly filing of papers, letters, materials, and reports is a matter of habit.

Some office workers believe that keeping papers in a jumble on the desk suggests hard work. However, the psychologist would suspect that it merely means poor work habits. The habit of keeping papers in orderly fashion tends to make for more promptness and greater efficiency in handling the business at hand.

For this reason it is suggested that keeping the desk clear is in itself a habit which promotes other good habits.

**Study Habits.** Although this has been considered in another portion of this book, it ought to be noted in connection with our discussion of habits that this problem is much like that of work habits in general.

Matters of habit in connection with study include such points as:

1. Having a *time* to study and forming the habit of studying at that time.

2. Having a *place* to study and using that place for the purpose of studying.

3. Being surrounded by the *tools* of study—books, papers, cards, instruments, etc.—and *conversely*, keeping distracting items (like pocket novels, comic magazines, etc.) away from that place.

4. Forming the habit of fixing firmly in mind what the *study assignment* is for each study period. Forming the habit of going over, briefly but definitely, what is to be done before the studying begins.

5. Reading, studying, or working for the purpose in mind. To some extent one forms the habit of sticking to the subject at hand, the assignment to be read, the problem to be worked, and the exercises to be worked out.

6. Forming the habit of reviewing or checking what has been done to verify that the particular study assignment which was undertaken was correctly carried out, and was understood.

To the extent that the student will practice working under these conditions, the habits will gradually take over and his work will become more satisfactory and more efficient as a result.

**Health Habits.** General care of the body and health habits are so commonly known that they hardly need to be mentioned at this point. Suffice it to say that merely knowing what should be done is not enough; we need to have the habits established that will guarantee that they *are* done. Habits of keeping clean and brushing the teeth can be so routine that adhering to them becomes easy and departing from them becomes difficult. Usually this is a good thing for the well-being of the individual.

Some habits—like brushing the teeth—become permanently
fixed.

One or two examples of the application of habit principles to
healthful living might be added, however, to illustrate the point.

Sleeping is to a large extent a matter of habit. As is noted in
connection with the subject of conditioning, we become accustomed
to sleeping in a certain place and under certain conditions. The
habit factor also enters in, in the way we become accustomed
(habituated) to sleeping for certain lengths of time and at certain
hours. Regular sleep in sufficient amounts is important for health.
Accordingly, too many exceptions to our habitual hour of retiring
may prove troublesome and we may lose well-formed habits quite
necessary to our well-being. When we are away from home, or
whatever the circumstances should be, we ought to try—within
the bounds of reasonableness—to keep up the same health-giving
habits of sleep that we have already established.

The importance of regular hours for sleep is recognized in
camps, at schools, in all organized communities. These regulations
are not somebody's arbitrary whims, but just plain common sense
based on the importance of habit.

In addition to the habits of rest which have been mentioned,
food habits are also important. This includes forming good eating
habits from the standpoint of (1) the time of eating, (2) the kinds

of foods selected, and (3) the conditions under which eating takes place.

Bodily hygiene suggests that it is desirable to have relatively fixed hours for eating, and that we are happier and feel better if these are followed. When we are thrown "off schedule" (witness what happens to baby in this connection) our entire hygienic well-being may be disturbed.

Therefore, the student or the worker is only helping himself if he makes an effort to eat his meals on time. When traveling or away from home, a reasonable effort to keep "on schedule" is much to be desired. "Let's just drive a couple of hours more before we stop for lunch," may seem like an attractive proposition at the

Habits involving personal cleanliness and appearance are especially important to those people who daily meet the public.

*Chesapeake & Ohio Railroad Company*

moment, but it is not rewarding if health considerations are remembered. Keep to the good habits established, and the results will be worth-while.

With regard to the kinds of foods to be eaten, it need only be said that we already know what these are. When the selection of fruits and vegetables becomes habitual, as it will when we allow no exceptions, the individual will find that here again habit is working on his side.

There are many ways in which good habits concerning the conditions under which we eat may be suggested. Eating in unhurried and pleasant surroundings should obviously be something which becomes habitual.

The faulty habit of eating at drug store counters, in a hurry, might be just as easily formed. Pleasant conversation, in the family or with friends, if practiced regularly, will become the rule rather than the exception, and will help digestion.

Another important regulation for hygienic living has to do with elimination. Especially important is regularity of bowel movements. Habit enters here to a striking degree. Most people seem to develop good habits in this respect, but there are times when individuals are unfavorably affected. What we know about habits suggests that in this matter care should be taken to ensure that daily elimination is provided for, and that exceptions to this should not be allowed to occur even under unusual circumstances.

**Recreational Habits.** Habits of taking exercise and of securing the recreation which is needed for balanced living come under this heading. If a habit is good in relation to working, studying, and sleeping, it is good in relation to exercise.

Possibly few people realize the importance of this. Since the idea of *play* has traditionally been at war with the idea of *work* (probably due to our American Puritan background), many American workers feel that there is something *wrong* about taking time out for exercise and recreation.

However, if we have health and well-being in mind, we will take time out for exercise and recreation. We will find some time to exercise and we will form the habit of taking the exercise at that time.

If the habit is formed, the advantage will be obtained. If it is neglected we will probably find that other things have crowded the exercise out and our bodies and minds will be the sufferers.

Because of the physical necessity of an alternation of rest and exercise, exercise is something that cannot be left to chance. It must be provided for in the daily schedule, and if not daily, then at least weekly, so that the body can derive the important values that exercise gives.

Exercise, as has often been pointed out, does not have to be in organized games, though they have a big advantage in that they also include social advantages. Exercise may be in walking, swimming, riding (horses or bicycles), gardening, or other forms. The important thing is that it be provided for and that it become a matter of *habit*.

**Social Habits.** Elsewhere in this book there is discussion of the value of social contacts and friends for everyday living. Important in this connection is the matter of being with people and learning to like them and associate with them.

Do habits enter into this matter? Obviously they do, for the person who likes people and spends time with them might just as easily have formed habits of being alone and avoiding people.

Knowing, as we do, the importance of habit in controlling us, we will realize that spending a certain amount of time in the company of friends and associates will be more likely to take place if we make it a matter of habit. Especially would it be advisable for the conscientious type of individual—the student with a heavy leaning toward books and study—to try to establish the habit of visiting other people, spending time with them, and seeking out their company. The nature of habit being what it is, this procedure will reward the individual because it will tend to make sure that this side of his life will not be neglected, and it will make him (and this is more important) desire, need, and want the social experiences which for him are so essential and important.

As has also been noted elsewhere, there are various ways of achieving this goal. One way would be by belonging to groups or activities which are social in nature. This is much to be desired, and such activities should be sought after and promoted.

Another way would be through deliberately planning and setting aside time for the friendly hours of being with and talking with others. These friendly hours can be planned and carried out if the desire for them is present. It will be noted, too, that others will respond to these interests, and then the planning for social experiences will become easier itself.

## SOMETHING TO DO

Take a new habit in which you would be interested; some habit you think would be to your advantage. Write a clear statement of what the new habit is; make out a few short, specific things to do in getting the new habit established. Print or write plainly these instructions on a card. Keep the card in a visible place where you work or study, or at home, and make a positive effort to establish the new habit. See how many of the principles of habit formation will apply in this experiment, and how long it takes to establish the habit to the point where you feel that it has become fixed.

## QUESTIONS AND PROBLEMS FOR STUDY AND DISCUSSION

1. From your own experience show the importance of habits in conserving time and energy.

2. How can habits interfere with efficiency? Give an example.

3. What is meant by the statement that habits are learned? How are habits the result of learning?

4. What is meant by the suggestion that behavior is not always predictable? How does this involve habits?

5. Discuss the thought that a great majority of our activities are controlled by habits.

6. Explain why people don't like to be asked to do things which are contrary to their habits.

7. Explain why it is important for a person who is learning a new habit or set of habits to study the activity which he is supposed to learn.

8. What do psychologists mean by families of habits?

9. Take some activity or performance with which you are familiar, for example, playing a game of some kind, and show how the various habits involved are related to one another. How does this enter into the problem of learning to play the game successfully?

10. Give an example, from your reading or experience, of the force of habit as influencing an individual's behavior.

11. Discuss the importance of habit in the problem of traffic control in a large city.

12. Examine your own work habits closely. Make a list of proposed improvements which would involve changing some of your habits.

13. Give an illustration of how failure to practice regularly has interfered with the development of skill in some game or activity.

14. Using the problem of health habits as a subject, make a two column list of your own personal habits in this respect. On the left-hand column indicate your present habits which you would rate "good." On the right-hand column indicate those which you would consider "bad."

15. Take a bad habit and outline some steps which would be possible as a means of eliminating it or substituting a better habit for it.

16. Take a friend and make an analysis of his good and bad habits; ask him to do the same thing for you; get together in a friendly way and compare your lists.

# CHAPTER EIGHT

# THE ROLE OF ATTITUDES IN OUR LIVES

In this chapter, we come to one of the problems of psychology which has a great bearing on our relations with other people, and which has much to do with the stresses and strains of our democratic society.

The chapter endeavors to show just how important attitudes are. It explains what they are, as the psychologist sees them. It shows how attitudes are inevitable as resulting from our experiences and, consequently, that they are not entirely subject to our own control.

This leads to the problem of how some attitudes can be changed which is important when you consider problems of politics, of crime and delinquency, and of war and peace. If we are going to get along in a democracy we need to know how to cope with the attitudes which are found in different groups of people.

In the latter part of the chapter some suggestions are given as to how attitudes can be measured. The questions at the end of the chapter bring out how far-reaching attitudes are in influencing our behavior.

## QUESTIONS THIS CHAPTER WILL ANSWER

1. How do attitudes develop? Is there anything we can do about their formation?
2. What are some of the ways in which they influence our behavior?
3. If some undesirable attitudes have been formed, how can they be changed?
4. To what extent are attitudes involved in the present-day problems of society?
5. How can we tell what an individual's attitudes really are?
6. What suggestions have been made for studying attitudes and learning more about them in the lives of people?

## Attitudes and Their Importance in Controlling Behavior

An attitude, as pointed out by Morgan, is usually looked upon as "a tendency to respond either positively (favorably) or negatively (unfavorably) toward certain persons, objects, or situations."[1]

---

[1]Clifford T. Morgan, *Introduction to Psychology* (New York: McGraw-Hill, 1956), p. 351.

Attitudes are important because, just as it is true of habits, they have a great deal to do with our behavior. They control our behavior in many situations.

To illustrate this, we might look at the attitude of the *traditional* person toward school teachers. Through the years has come the idea that the teacher is a sort of prim, studious person who will be critical of what you do or say and toward whom you must behave differently than you would behave in dealing with other individuals.

This attitude actually affects or influences what people say or do when they are in the presence of school teachers. Just as true would be the effect of their attitude toward ministers or clergymen.

The attitude of a dignified club woman toward a patron of the local pool room or the downtown tap room would be very evident in her behavior toward that individual.

One way of studying attitudes and their importance is to consider one's own attitudes. What are some of your attitudes and how do they influence you? How did these attitudes develop? How important are they in your life?

Among the important attitudes which people have, a number may be readily thought of. The average person has attitudes toward the opposite sex; attitudes toward persons older than he and younger than he; attitudes toward members of other races; attitudes toward people engaged in various occupations.

Whether you have thought of it or not, you probably have an *attitude* toward plumbers, an attitude toward salesmen; an attitude toward taxi drivers.

Other attitudes which may be distinguished are attitudes toward persons of various nationalities and persons of various countries; also attitudes toward people in various sections of the same country. For example, the Northerner has an attitude toward Southerners; the Californian has an attitude toward New Yorkers. The American has an attitude toward Russians; toward Germans; toward Chinese.

There are attitudes which can be shown to exist between people living in different sections of the same city. This could be illustrated by the attitude of the resident of Manhattan toward the resident of Brooklyn. In most cities people who live in the older and more settled areas have a certain attitude toward those who live in the suburbs and probably they have different attitudes toward people from different suburbs.

There are attitudes toward people who may not happen to be in the same social or economic group; attitudes of the well-to-do toward the poor; attitudes of the laborer toward the capitalist.

From these examples it is easy to see that attitudes are very numerous and that in any one person there are many attitudes. It is also evident that it would take several pages just to make a list of attitudes which one person has developed toward various things, people, and situations.

## How Are Attitudes Developed and Changed?

We can see that attitudes are the result of learning and of the particular kind of experiences that the individual has had. It is also evident to the thoughtful person that we are very much influenced by all of these attitudes and that they more or less determine how we feel and what we will do or say in a great many of the situations of life. They are therefore like habits in that they guide our acts, influence our thoughts, and more or less rule over our behavior.

**Experience Is the Basis of Attitudes.** An attitude is developed by experience. The best way to explain how an attitude is formed is to take an example. We might take the attitude of a young boy toward the opposite sex to illustrate. His very earliest experiences are with his mother, then with aunts, nurses, friends, and others who are of the opposite sex. Then as he gets older and begins to walk and play, he encounters other young children who are of the opposite sex. Each one of these contacts with a woman or a girl adds a little more to his experience and with each of these contacts there is something of interest, something which he likes or dislikes, something which makes an impression upon him. Out of these repeated experiences he gradually forms an attitude toward the feminine sex. His attitude toward women is in the process of being built. He will grow older and mature, and with that the attitude will gradually be changed, because he will have new and different experiences.

In a sense the attitude that the growing child forms toward any person or group of persons or toward any situation or thing is beyond his control. It is the result of the kind of experience he *happens* to have.

If a young boy grows up in a rural area, he will have experiences with city people and with other country people which will cause him to develop an attitude toward city dwellers. If he grew up in a large city with many city people in a setting very much different from that of the country, his experiences with city people would be different and he would develop an attitude toward city people but it would be different from the attitude of his rural neighbor.

Each boy develops an attitude which grows out of the kind of experiences he has.

If people would only realize that attitudes are established out of experiences, they would understand the differences which arise and be much more sympathetic toward those whose attitudes happen to differ from their own.

Attitudes are inescapable. An attitude is whatever it is at any given moment because of the particular kind of experiences the individual has had. It may be a good attitude or a bad attitude. It may be the right attitude or the wrong attitude. This depends on what the standards set up by the group happen to be.

Another point which it is important to note is the fact that a person can develop an attitude on the basis of one experience or on the basis of fourteen or a thousand experiences.

A person may have met just one Chinese in his life, and yet have an attitude toward all Chinese. He may not have met any Chinese, and developed an attitude toward the Chinese as a result of what he has read or heard about them or been told about them. These indirect experiences are called *vicarious* experiences. They are important in their effect on our attitudes.

My attitude toward the Germans is the result of each and every one of all of the experiences I have had with the Germans, with the work of their hands, with their country and its products, with people who have talked about them, with books and articles I have read about them, with movies about them, and with every one of a countless number and variety of experiences in which something about the Germans may have been included. But if I had met only one German or just seen one movie about the Germans I would still have an attitude toward them.

We have gone into detail about this because it is important to realize the nature of attitudes and how they are formed. This is especially necessary if we are to understand how attitudes are *changed.* There is only one way in which attitudes are changed, and that is by having new or different experiences.

**How Changes in Attitudes Occur.** A person can change his attitudes very much as he grows older and goes out into life. For example, the attitude of a young man toward smoking or drinking may be one of hostility and disapproval. As he gets older and meets people who do these things in one way or another, he may find either that his attitude toward them is made stronger or that he becomes more tolerant and less hostile toward such practices.

Attitudes toward people of other races and creeds are subject to change as the result of experience.

*Official U. S. Coast Guard Photo*

It is interesting to notice how the attitudes of people change, especially attitudes toward other races, nations, or groups, as a result of travel opportunities and as a result of having contacts with them.

We should note in this connection, however, that whether an attitude will change or not depends on (1) the strength of the attitude already established, and (2) the importance which the individual places on it. An attitude may come to have such great importance to an individual that he will be conscious of preserving it and he will resist the natural tendency of experience to change it. Thus it is possible for an individual to nurture and preserve an attitude if he really wants to do it and if he thinks it is important for him to do it.

**Attitudes Don't Change on Demand.** One important fact to note about changing attitudes is that it is not possible to get a person to change his attitude by telling him that he ought to change it. It is not possible to change the attitudes of a group of people by just lecturing them, scolding them, or trying to talk to them about it.

The only way their attitudes can be changed is through helping them to get experiences that will have the effect of changing their attitudes.

The following story illustrates this fact. A man was driving south through the state of Oklahoma. A few miles outside of Tulsa, he picked up a hitchhiking high-school boy from Illinois who was dressed in a fine cowboy outfit. The youth obviously thought this was proper dress for those parts. When, however, the boy did not see a single outfit, other than his own, that even remotely suggested the elaborate costumes of the movie cowboys, his attitude about Oklahomans changed. Only through education, travel, and experience do we eliminate misconceptions and adjust our attitudes closer to reality.

The personnel man evaluates a young girl's attitudes when he considers her job application.

*Southern Bell Telephone and Telegraph Co.*

Our own *willingness* is also an important factor in changing an attitude. If a man has a special reason for keeping an attitude, he will not be inclined to change it. If, for example, an individual fears that his real estate will decrease in value because persons of a certain race or creed move into the neighborhood, he will resist efforts aimed at altering his attitude because he believes that it is to his advantage to maintain that attitude. Only when he considers it no longer so, will he be ready to change.

Attitudes have been shown to be our characteristic ways of thinking and feeling about things, about people, etc. It can be seen that they are very much like what we sometimes think of as *values* and *ideals*. These will be further dealt with in a later chapter, but it is worth noting that an attitude toward anything is like a value or ideal in that both of them grow out of our experiences and both are subject to change through new experiences.

Attitudes grow as a result of experience. They influence how we think and how we act. They are subject to change through experience. They can be nurtured or protected against change if we recognize a value in them and if we want, badly enough, to preserve them against change. We may do this deliberately or it may work out this way if the attitude or value is taking care of some important personality need which exists in our make-up.

## Relation of Attitudes to the People and Society around Us

In discussing the nature of attitudes it has already been suggested that they are very important in connection with our social lives; that is, in relation to our being with and dealing with other people.

Attitudes are involved in our *social relationships* particularly. For example, if a laboring man has an attitude unfavorable to banks and bankers, he will show this in his relationships with them and it will interfere with his getting along with them.

If the banker, on the other hand, has a hostile attitude toward the man who works with his hands, the banker will appear to be snobbish, bad-tempered, and ill-mannered when he deals with people of this group. The attitude which a man has developed toward a group comes into action quickly and at the slightest suggestion. Thus, if a businessman who is very much against socialism is introduced to a professor and discovers through just a word that is said or a hint that is dropped that the professor leans toward socialism, the businessman will almost immediately develop a feeling of resentment toward the professor and it will be hard for him not to show this feeling—this attitude—in dealing with the professor.

These examples are suggested to show the importance of attitudes in our social relationships.

A knowledge of what attitudes are, how they influence people, and how they develop is most important if we are to learn how to work with other people. If we understand how they developed their attitudes, we can discover how to work with them, or if we feel that we should take steps to influence them in another direction, we can find out how to go about it.

In the postwar period the United States was confronted by a great problem in the defeated countries of Germany and Japan. The problem was to determine a way of changing the attitudes of millions of people toward America and toward democracy. History will show whether the methods adopted have or have not been successful. But a knowledge of how attitudes develop should show us what some of the difficulties are. We can't just say to the Germans: We want you to have the right attitude toward democracy. Only by demonstrating to them the workings of democracy, only by arranging matters so that they can see the advantages and values in democracy can there be any hope of bringing about such a change.

Moreover, we will have to convince these people that the democratic way is *more to their advantage* than the methods they have been following.

**Attitudes and Law Enforcement.** Another example of the importance of attitudes in our society may be thought of in connection with law enforcement. A law can only be truly enforced if the people believe that the law is good and if they want it. It must conform to their accepted ideas of what the law should be.

People will enforce a law prohibiting stealing automobiles because they believe in it. They have learned through various ways that stealing is harmful to them, and their attitude toward such a law is favorable while their attitude toward such a practice as

Divided opinion about gambling makes control of it difficult.

stealing is unfavorable. Therefore a law against stealing is a good law and can be enforced.

A law prohibiting gambling may or may not be enforced. If any considerable number of people gamble and enjoy gambling, there will be difficulties in enforcing such a law because the attitude of the people toward gambling and toward such a law is not in harmony with the law. In some communities where gambling is more or less approved it would be impossible to enforce laws against gambling. In other communities where some of the people have an attitude favorable to gambling and some have an attitude against it, enforcement is very difficult and the community is always in a state of excitement over it.

## Ways of Measuring Attitudes

Attitudes tend to be *for* or *against* things. This means that they express an acceptance of the thing, or a liking for it on our part, or a tendency to disapprove of the thing, to not want it, to avoid it. The feeling side of attitudes is very strong. Of course, in some matters which do not seem to touch our lives closely, we may be more or less indifferent or neutral. But generally speaking our attitudes may be at any point between strongly favoring or strongly rejecting the thing in question.

Recognizing this fact psychologists have worked out attitude measuring devices. Attitude tests developed at the University of Chicago enable us to find out—within limits—about the attitudes of people toward such subjects as war, communism, religion, the constitution of the United States, the Negro, etc. The way in which these tests work out is as follows:

A series of statements are written, each of which expresses a feeling of liking or disliking, favoring or rejecting, a given practice or a given subject. These statements are arranged so that they include very strong statements *against* the idea, thing, or subject, and other statements that are strongly favorable, with a number of statements arranged in between in varying degrees of favoring or disfavoring the subject.

This group of statements, each of which is given a value or score, comprises an *attitude test*. The person who takes the test shows, by the statements he accepts or rejects, what his attitude toward the particular subject is.

Numerous variations of this have been employed in measuring attitudes. One that is sometimes used is to state a policy or a point of view and have the person taking the test indicate whether he agrees strongly, agrees in general, is neutral, disagrees, or disagrees strongly with the position. Attitude tests are relatively easy to develop if they are constructed in relation to a specific subject. They are useful in determining the attitudes of any group at any given time, and consequently are useful in indicating changes in attitude that may be reflected at different times.

The public opinion polls which have been conducted in recent years are in many cases measures of attitude.

In political life many issues are matters of *attitude*. They are determined according to what the attitudes of the people are, the decision often resting with the majority. The following are issues toward which many people develop very definite attitudes:

Federal financing of education
Government control of business
Maintaining a large standing army
Co-ordinating the army, navy, and air force into one military unit
Consolidation of rural schools
Free public junior colleges
Old-age pensions
Free medical care

Government provision of housing
Federal building of highways
Government operation of radio and television.

These are issues on which people develop attitudes which generally determine what the political parties are going to do on a national scale.


## How Attitudes Are Revealed in Behavior

Attitudes have much to do with the way we act in many everyday situations. If we are attending a party and the suggestion is made, "Let's play bridge," we may show by our manner or way of behaving what our attitude is toward playing bridge.

The more experienced person does not show his attitude so readily. But he has an attitude just the same, and his attitude (which is to a very great extent, as has been pointed out, how he "feels" about a given situation or thing) is almost certain to influence his behavior. If he is one who does not like to play bridge, possibly one who dislikes it very much, he may not say anything unfriendly when asked to play bridge if he is polite, but will in all probability become a little reserved and a little less cheerful in his manner and possibly show a trace or two of irritation. But if he is a well-trained and mature individual he will conform to the wishes of his host or the group in as cheerful a manner as possible.

However, the less well-trained person and the less mature person may show open hostility to the suggestion "Let's play bridge." He may show his attitude so openly that the suggestion is abandoned by the others, or, if not abandoning it, they may go on with the game but feel quite aware that he is opposed to it. We should say that from a social point of view the individual should practice controlling his display of certain feelings, that is, showing certain attitudes for his own good unless the matter is of serious importance.

The point is that our attitudes influence our day to day behavior and are therefore very important in our make-up.

We sometimes read in a newspaper account of a trial or a hearing that so-and-so showed a *belligerent* attitude, or that a witness displayed a *co-operative* attitude. These words are indications of the part which attitudes play in behavior. As Woodruff points out,[2] "Some form of attitude is being expressed by the person from the moment a situation occurs until it has completely ended," which means that our display of attitude is always present in us.

An individual's attitude toward his work is often revealed by his behavior and by the quality of the work he turns out.

*Chesapeake & Ohio Railroad Company*

At the risk of repeating something too often, we must again point out that our attitudes change with experience. The person who dislikes bridge may, a year or two later, as the result of associating with friends who play, come to have a more favorable attitude toward the game, so that he eventually welcomes the suggestion "Let's play bridge," instead of reacting with resentment.

## SOMETHING TO DO

Check to left if attitude is unfavorable, on a scale of 1 to 5. A check in space 5 indicates strongly unfavorable attitude toward item. Check to

[2] Asahel D. Woodruff, *The Psychology of Teaching* (New York: Longmans, Green & Company, Inc., 1946), p. 11.

right if attitude is favorable, on a scale of 1 to 5. A check in space 5 indicates strongly favorable attitude; in space 1, indicates mildly favorable toward item.

| 5 | 4 | 3 | 2 | 1 |  | 1 | 2 | 3 | 4 | 5 |
|---|---|---|---|---|---|---|---|---|---|---|
|  |  |  |  |  | Wall Street |  |  |  |  |  |
|  |  |  |  |  | Hiking |  |  |  |  |  |
|  |  |  |  |  | Sunday movies |  |  |  |  |  |
|  |  |  |  |  | Bridge |  |  |  |  |  |
|  |  |  |  |  | Sunday baseball |  |  |  |  |  |
|  |  |  |  |  | Dentists |  |  |  |  |  |
|  |  |  |  |  | Wednesday evening prayer meeting |  |  |  |  |  |
|  |  |  |  |  | Nurses |  |  |  |  |  |
|  |  |  |  |  | Mexicans |  |  |  |  |  |
|  |  |  |  |  | High schools |  |  |  |  |  |
|  |  |  |  |  | Baptists |  |  |  |  |  |
|  |  |  |  |  | College students |  |  |  |  |  |
|  |  |  |  |  | Daughters of American Revolution |  |  |  |  |  |
|  |  |  |  |  | Jews |  |  |  |  |  |
|  |  |  |  |  | Constitution of U.S. |  |  |  |  |  |
|  |  |  |  |  | Protestants |  |  |  |  |  |
|  |  |  |  |  | Catholics |  |  |  |  |  |
|  |  |  |  |  | Negroes |  |  |  |  |  |
|  |  |  |  |  | Democrats |  |  |  |  |  |
|  |  |  |  |  | Highway patrol |  |  |  |  |  |
|  |  |  |  |  | Republicans |  |  |  |  |  |
|  |  |  |  |  | Christmas |  |  |  |  |  |
|  |  |  |  |  | Socialists |  |  |  |  |  |
|  |  |  |  |  | Divorcees |  |  |  |  |  |
|  |  |  |  |  | Communism |  |  |  |  |  |
|  |  |  |  |  | Prize fighters |  |  |  |  |  |
|  |  |  |  |  | Russia |  |  |  |  |  |
|  |  |  |  |  | Apartment houses |  |  |  |  |  |
|  |  |  |  |  | Chinese |  |  |  |  |  |
|  |  |  |  |  | Labor unions |  |  |  |  |  |
|  |  |  |  |  | Bankers |  |  |  |  |  |
|  |  |  |  |  | Eskimos |  |  |  |  |  |
|  |  |  |  |  | Smoking |  |  |  |  |  |
|  |  |  |  |  | Poker |  |  |  |  |  |
|  |  |  |  |  | Public libraries |  |  |  |  |  |
|  |  |  |  |  | Whiskey |  |  |  |  |  |
|  |  |  |  |  | Mormons |  |  |  |  |  |
|  |  |  |  |  | Cigarettes |  |  |  |  |  |
|  |  |  |  |  | Short dresses |  |  |  |  |  |
|  |  |  |  |  | Chewing tobacco |  |  |  |  |  |
|  |  |  |  |  | Dogs |  |  |  |  |  |
|  |  |  |  |  | Dance halls |  |  |  |  |  |
|  |  |  |  |  | Cats |  |  |  |  |  |
|  |  |  |  |  | Pool rooms |  |  |  |  |  |
|  |  |  |  |  | Beer |  |  |  |  |  |

# QUESTIONS AND PROBLEMS FOR DISCUSSION AND STUDY

1. Give an example of how an attitude may influence an individual's behavior in a group.

2. Give an example of how an attitude may influence an individual's behavior toward a group or a nationality.

3. Explain the process of attitude formation in the matter of interracial relationships—how the attitudes involved came about.

4. Show how attitudes enter into political affairs.

5. Take a group such as a labor union, and show how a public attitude toward the union may result from experience.

6. Give an example of an attitude which has been based on very limited experience. Suggest how the attitude might be changed with further experience.

7. Suggest some attitudes which might change as people grow older.

8. What is meant by the idea that sometimes people can and will refuse to change an attitude? What conditions are likely to be affecting the individual in such a situation? Can you give an example?

9. Give an example of an attitude which you have observed between people in different levels of society.

10. Give an example of an attitude which you have observed which seems to be associated with the *places* in which the people live.

11. Show how favorable attitudes have helped in promoting some worth-while community enterprise.

12. See if you can identify any attitudes you have toward races or nationality groups which you think might be improved, and show how you might go about seeking this improvement.

13. Name some occupations which you would avoid if you could because of prevailing public attitudes toward them.

14. Give an example of where law enforcement has, to your knowledge, failed because of the public attitude toward the law.

15. Give an example of successful law enforcement, and analyze the reasons why it has been successful, in terms of attitudes.

# CHAPTER NINE

# THINKING — PROBLEM SOLVING

If you ask the average person what schools are for, he will often answer, "To teach people to think." To what extent this is possible is discussed in this chapter.

We need to know what thinking is. Psychologists have endeavored to throw light on this topic. They have succeeded in finding out what is involved in the thinking process itself. They have also discovered and examined some of the factors which influence our thinking.

This chapter discusses the role of concepts in thinking and explains why and how we think. Psychologists often say that thinking occurs only when we recognize or feel that we have a problem. It is also explained in this chapter that we can't think unless we have information with which to think. Another topic discussed is what is involved in "good" thinking, or logically correct thinking.

Since psychologists have thrown some light upon how faulty thinking occurs, the so-called "pitfalls of thinking" are discussed. Also included are suggestions for cultivating correct thinking.

## QUESTIONS THIS CHAPTER WILL ANSWER

1. How do concepts aid in thinking?
2. How are concepts formed?
3. Why do the concepts of a child differ from those of an adult?
4. What is abstraction?
5. What are some of the ways in which school training and other experiences influence how much and how well we will think?
6. What are the steps in problem solving?
7. What can psychologists tell us about improving our thinking?
8. What causes people to go "off the track" in their thinking?

## The Role of Concepts in Thinking

**Concepts.** Have you ever disagreed with someone as to whether an individual's action was *good* or *evil?* Have you ever argued with someone over whether something was *humorous?* If you have, you have used words which you thought referred to a quality or characteristic possessed by several things or actions. You have used *concepts*. And in this way you have communicated to another what you were thinking at the time.

The following are a number of concepts used in everyday speech:

| | | | | |
|---|---|---|---|---|
| toy | red | beautiful | good | house |
| dog | soft | ugly | evil | mother |
| humorous | hard | generous | triangle | democracy |
| traitor | patriot | selfish | fish | animal |

When we have formed a concept we recognize it as having a general application, and by referring to it we can direct others, in their thinking, into the same direction our thoughts are taking.

Because concepts have a wide application and because they convey meaning quickly, they are widely used in thinking and, indeed, are probably indispensable to thought. Concepts are useful to the extent that they *do* convey the meaning they are intended to convey.

Concepts give us a basis for comparing things, for choosing things, and for evaluating things. As is well known, an individual's thinking depends upon his developing concepts. Without a well organized system of concepts an individual's thinking is severely limited. He cannot solve problems except of the simplest kind. He can express only feelings and impressions of the most primitive type. He is unable to discuss problems with others and unable to understand how it was they solved certain problems. Consequently, his relations with other people dwindle as they continue to develop more adequate concepts to deal with the problems they meet. The individual who does not continue clarifying his concepts and developing new ones is constantly doing the wrong things and misjudging the worth of people and things.

Generally, when psychologists use the term *concept*, they are referring to an idea or set of associations *about* something which has grown up in an individual's mind through experience, and which conveys a similar meaning to others who have had similar experiences. When, for example, I say of a person that he is a patriot, the use of the term *patriot* suggests a concept to you and it is the concept of a person who is devoted to his country and zealously supports and defends it and its interests. In this way I quickly convey to you a partial description of the man even though you had never heard of him. This is possible because you have had experiences, either direct or indirect, with individuals who exhibited these qualities or characteristics. Of course, whether the statement is true depends on whether he actually exhibits these characteristics.

**Concept Formation.** It is helpful to note how concepts are formed and convey certain meanings. To take a simple example, *hard* represents a certain quality which we have come to recognize as appropriate to a wide variety of situations or things. Rocks are hard. Tree trunks are hard. Diamonds are hard. Shoveling gravel is hard. Pitching hay on a hot afternoon is hard.

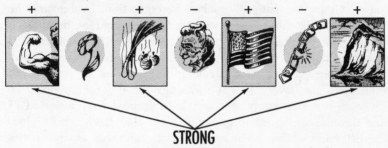

## STRONG

Concepts result from the experiences we have had.

The result of experiences with all of these matters has been to establish for each of us the concept *hard*. This is a concept we can use widely. If a student tells another student that such and such a course is "hard"—it has a certain meaning the other student grasps quickly. He has an idea of what the course is like, and so the concept has been useful. Of course, as a student considers the concept *hard* just used, it is obvious that he must distinguish between the "hardness" of objects and the "hardness" of an experience. The rock is not hard in the same sense that a course is hard. Yet there is common element which we have distilled from our many experiences, and which suggests *difficulty* of handling or "dealing with." This difficulty in handling is the basis of the concept and gives the concept an unmistakable meaning to all who hear or use it.

Each additional experience that a child has, as he grows up, may contribute to any particular concept that he is forming. Take the concept *house*, for example, and consider how it is formed in the young child's mind. When he is learning to speak he learns the names of things. A small boy looks out the window and points across the street. His mother says to him, "That's a house." Later that day the boy looks at some pictures, and his mother points out pictures of houses and sometimes of dogs and birds. But at first any building, an office building, a warehouse—anything that looks as though people could live in it—appears to be a house to the little boy.

Soon his mother will begin to correct his incorrect use of *house*. If he sees a school and says, "What a pretty house!" she will say, "That is not a house, that is a school." As he incorrectly identifies museums, government buildings, office buildings and factories as houses, his mother patiently makes the correction. In due time he has learned that *house* refers to a particular kind of building, a dwelling for people, as distinguished from all of these others. His concept of house has at last become firmly and correctly established.

**Some Concepts are Ambiguous.** It is important to realize that some concepts have different meanings for different people. To illustrate, our concept of tree has been formed over a period of time through seeing many growing things that have certain characteristics in common. The most obvious of these characteristics include bark, leaves, branches, and roots. Height is also a factor. One of the writer's northern friends thinks that palm trees aren't "really" trees. A child brought up in the tropics thinks they are trees, however. In a Miami school a child brought in a drawing of an apple tree to show his teacher. The tree had round objects which looked like apples hanging on to the branches, to be sure, but the leaves were shaped like palm fronds and the whole thing bore a resemblance to a cocoanut palm.

If a person who has always lived in the tropics has a different concept of tree from that of his northern neighbor, how much more difficult it might be, under some circumstances, for them to agree on the meaning of yet other concepts of a less tangible nature, such as *democracy* or *liberty*. These concepts have different meanings for different people. Much of the conflict in the world suggests that quite often different nations use the same term—like the term *democracy*, but with quite different meanings. It is necessary, more often than we realize, that we make sure of the meaning of each other's concepts.

**Abstract Concepts.** Especially important in adult thinking are abstract concepts such as *color, animal, mass, velocity, time*, etc. At first the child uses words which stand for concrete objects with which he is familiar, such as dog, cat, duck, etc. Later he develops abstract concepts which are *more general in nature*. For example, a young child may be able to name correctly various animals such as dog, cat, and duck but it is not until sometime later that he is able to group all of these objects under the single unifying concept of animal. And it's even later that he is able to group certain animals under the concept of warm-bloodedness and others under the concept of cold-bloodedness. This process of learning to group objects in terms of some isolated common property is called *abstraction*.

Abstraction is an extremely important factor in scientific thinking because the aim of scientific knowledge is the discovery of laws expressing the relation between such abstract concepts as *mass* and *gravitation, volume* and *pressure,* or *temperature* and *volume.*

## Why We Think

In psychology the term *thinking* is usually applied to that type of mental process which we identify as problem solving. There are, however, a number of kinds of mental activity which are sometimes referred to as thinking. There is a general "stream of consciousness" of which we are aware during all or most all of our waking movements. A succession of ideas, images, reveries, and associations streams through the mind, and we are aware, if we stop to contemplate it, of this activity of ours.

In most present-day psychology, however, when the subject of thinking is under consideration, the phase of it which has to do with reasoning, or problem solving is of chief concern. Hence, in this chapter we are confining our discussion to the psychology of *thinking as problem solving.* We are omitting any consideration of thinking as revery, or as daydreaming in the usual sense of the term —we are thinking mainly of what occurs, in our mental processes, as we deal with the everyday problems of life.

While discussing habits and attitudes, we emphasized the importance of *experience* in their formation. We also pointed out that new experiences are essential in changing our habits and attitudes. Let us now consider a little more closely how a new experience affects us.

When high-school students come up against the college entrance examination, as have these students at New Trier High School in Winnetka, Illinois,
they are compelled to do extensive thinking.

*The Educational Testing Board*
*Princeton University*

Earlier, in our discussion of attitudes, we mentioned, as an
example, the banker who might feel that any person who works
with his hands somehow cannot be very smart, must have poor
manners, and so on. His experiences with workers have tended to
confirm this attitude. But let us suppose that one day at a party the
banker meets a very nice young man with whom he discusses all
sorts of things, the weather, business, politics, etc. The banker finds
the young man to be intelligent, well-informed, and friendly, even
though he does not agree with all the young man's ideas. Finally,
the banker asks him what he does for a living, and it turns out
that the young man is a machine operator.

Of course, this is not what the banker has expected. At first he
is confused, and wonders why "such people" happened to be invited
to the party. But then he *stops and thinks*. The young man is a
*problem* to him because he does not seem like a "worker." Finally
the banker asks himself: "Can there be something wrong with the

way I feel towards workers, with the attitudes and ideas I have about them?"

This example can be used to illustrate some important aspects of thinking. In the first place, it is a fact that nobody "thinks" all the time, not even the "intellectuals." Most of our activities are directed by our habits; we don't think (in the sense of problem solving) because new problems are not involved. We think when we run into new situations or new experiences which we cannot handle by means of our previously acquired habits. New situations or new experiences are *problems* for us because we don't know what to do. Therefore we must start thinking to solve these problems. The *purpose* of such thinking is to solve our problems. To solve our problems correctly we must "see" them correctly.

How much a person thinks depends on the number of problems he runs into. In this respect people differ. Some can "see" many problems; others, in the same situations, can see no problems at all. Some people "never notice anything." Others see only problems that concern themselves. Still others are very alert and are aware of almost any problem. Awareness of a problem is the first step. Questions lead to the realization that problems exist.

**The Value of Asking Questions.** Developing the habit of asking questions is important. In the modern world, science, invention, and discovery are still going on only because people continue to ask questions.

Newton asked himself why it is that objects fall downward, when their support is removed. Columbus asked himself why he could not get to India if he started sailing westward from Spain and kept on going. Benjamin Franklin asked what lightning was, and wondered if it couldn't be brought under control and used for power. Galileo asked himself what he would see if he could just make a stronger telescope and look through it at the stars. Abraham Lincoln asked himself why it was that men, because they were black, should be bought and sold in slavery at a market place.

In modern times men and women are still asking, asking, asking. They are asking about electricity, about the airplane, about the weather, about atoms, about building materials, about insects, and about vitamins and medicine. Not a single important discovery was ever made except after someone asked a question. People are going forward to a better world because they are asking questions. They are asking why some people have to live in poverty while others

Columbus was seeking the answer to a question when he discovered America.

have abundance; why governments can't exist which are free from
corruption and graft; why clean, comfortable homes can't be the
right and privilege of every human being; why something can't
be done to check those who would prey on society—the gangster,
the criminal, and the racketeer; why an international society can't
be worked out that will keep the world from plunging periodically
into war; they are asking how diseases may be controlled so that
human suffering need not be so great, so disheartening and cruel;
they are asking the same kind of questions now about *man and
society* which they began to ask at an earlier date about *things and
machines.* Thus the age of science begins to penetrate the world of
men and human relations, and because of this we may expect another era of progress to open up in the years ahead.

**Reasoning and Thinking as the Result of Learning.** Thinking
and reasoning are said to be the highest powers of man. The thing

that makes men different from animals is their ability to reason. Some animals are capable of solving problems, but only the simpler kinds of problems.

Men can think through problems because they are capable of learning and of being affected by what they learn—of *remembering* and using *certain methods* to solve *certain problems.*

Thus learning, the result of experience, is the basis for our thinking and reasoning. The facts we acquire are the materials we think with. A dog can be *conditioned* to recognize many things and situations. Thus the dog will wag his tail and show interest and excitement when he sees the familiar can from which his food is taken. He is conditioned to *know* that the can means food. He wags his tail and shows signs of pleasure when his master reaches for the leash. The leash means going out for a walk.

Intelligent voting requires thinking which is based on learning and experience.

*National Education Association*

But the dog has no ability to think extensively. He runs and jumps into the car whenever he sees a member of the family is going out in it. The dog does not *reason* that he can't go along this time because the father is probably going on a trip and will be gone for a week.

Human beings are always finding problems. They reason about things, reach conclusions, and figure out explanations. They can do this because they have previously learned many things which they can consider in connection with any new problem. They make use of previous learning to solve the problem.

One of the most fascinating stories of how a man thinks about problems and solves them is the story of Robinson Crusoe, who worked out a very interesting and satisfying existence with the help of a few odds and ends from a wrecked ship. This is thinking.

The older a person is the more experiences he has had. Therefore we would expect the older person to have learned more. But this is not always true. What we have learned does not depend only on our age or the number of experiences we have had.

On the other hand a two-year-old child has no way of knowing what you mean when you say "I can't play with you now because I have to go to work." But when he becomes six or seven years old, this means more because he has gradually learned that adult people "go to work" and are therefore not at home playing with their children during daytime hours. Ten-year-old children begin to understand that this work is connected with the economic problems of earning a living. Fourteen-year-old children know something about the nature of the work and of its real significance in the home, and to the parent. Eighteen-year-old children know even more about it. They know something about the various job opportunities there are, and of the training required. They have done considerable *thinking* about vocations. They have had enough experience to be intelligent about the problems which arise in connection with their parent's work.

## How We Think

We have discussed *why* we think and learn. Now the question of *how* we think requires some attention. What is it we do when we attempt to solve a problem?

Most psychologists have accepted John Dewey's description of the stages in the process of thinking.[1] Most thinking can be broken down into these steps. We will consider them briefly:

**1. A Felt Difficulty.** Thinking usually does not occur until the individual runs across some problem. In driving a car, little thinking is required as we move smoothly along an unobstructed highway. But if we come to a barrier across the road, and see a sign, "Bridge Out," we are "up against something." We begin to *think*, we try to "figure out" what we can do in the situation we are in.

This would be a *felt difficulty*.

Situations which do not present difficulties, or which, at least, do not present enough difficulty to seem like problems to us, are usually met by our system of habits. A driver, coming up behind a car which is ahead of him but moving more slowly, usually does not "feel a difficulty." If the road is wide and nothing is in sight to disturb him, the driver just swings out to the left, blows his horn, and goes around the slower moving vehicle.

These responses are more or less automatic and the driver needs but to use the habits about passing cars which he has built up through experience. It would be interesting to analyze our activities for a single day to see how many of them are taken care of by the habits we have formed, and how many present problems which require thinking.

Coming upon a detour or a "Bridge Out" sign is out of our ordinary range of experience and we are obliged to replace *habit responses* with *thought responses*. We may or may not be able to determine what would be the best thing to do.

We will not do any thinking unless we are aware that a problem exists. Often we are confronted by problems but we are not aware of them. A philosopher lives in a world of problems because he is aware that problems exist. A lazy fisherman living along the river may not feel that the world is full of problems at all; he may just not recognize that the problems are there.

We might almost say that the first thing in thinking is to have something to think about.

**2. Location and Definition of the Problem.** Having a *felt difficulty* is not enough. We must see clearly what the difficulty is, and we

---

[1]John Dewey, *How We Think* (Boston: D. C. Heath & Co., 1933).

must *define* it. That is, the second step in thinking is to narrow the problem down.

The motorist, confronted by the "Bridge Out" sign, starts his thinking by considering just where he is, what route he is on, where the various "turn outs" are, what other routes he might take to get where he is going, etc. He takes out his road maps and studies them to ascertain these facts. But he must first of all know exactly where it is he is going, and where he has been. These activities illustrate *defining* the problem.

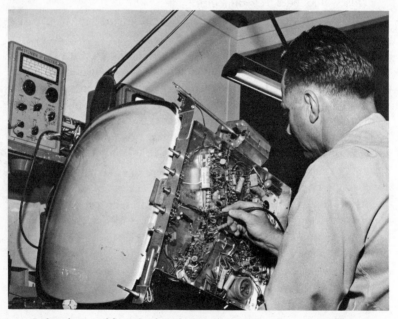

Before being able to fix the television set the repairman must locate the problem.

*Courtesy of Packard-Bell Corporation*

Suppose that a high-school senior is asked to explain the reasons for and purposes of the United States' immigration restriction policy.

Here is a problem which he must "narrow down" and define before he can answer it intelligently. He can reason about it best by breaking it down into such questions as:

*a)* What *was* the immigration restriction policy? Sub-question: what was immigration and how was it affecting our country?

*b)* Why did the United States adopt this policy? What were the needs the policy was supposed to take care of?

*c)* What good was the policy intended to accomplish?

Having decided just what the question was driving at, the student could proceed to write his answer to it. But he can never write a good answer to any question until he *knows what the question means.*

There is no doubt that many students "fumble" examination questions because they do not take the time to make sure what the question calls for or what it means. We must locate and define the problem if we are to do anything worth while about it.

**3. Suggestions of Possible Solutions.** The next step in thinking, after a problem has been *felt* or recognized, and after it has been *defined* or understood clearly, is thinking of possible answers or solutions.

Our motorist, at the "Bridge Out" sign, looks over his road maps and considers all the possible solutions of the problem, that is, the ways he might go. Perhaps he would be better off to take the left fork and go over a couple of miles to another road which goes in the same general direction, then cut back to the main highway further up.

Maybe he could go back to the last town and get directions there. Perhaps he ought to drive back to the last farmhouse and ask the farmer what the best route would be. Other things come to his mind as possible solutions.

The boy confronted by the question about immigration policy thinks about all the possible factors or reasons for the adoption of the policy by the American government. He tries to recall the various reasons why this policy was adopted and tries to remember any facts bearing on the problem.

This considering of possible solutions is a very important part of the thinking process, and it can readily be seen that the individual who is most adept at thinking of the various possible solutions will be most likely to arrive at the right answer.

**4. Reasoning the Possibilities of the Suggestion or Suggestions.** Perhaps we could call this *considering more fully the possibilities in the various suggestions which have come to mind.*

In this step of the thinking process, the individual goes a little further. He ponders on the full meaning of the suggestions and ideas.

He accepts in his own *thinking* some of the suggestions as good, and he rejects others as not very good.

This is clearly a job of "mulling over" the suggested solutions of the problem to find out what might work and what might not work, what might apply and what might not apply. Often as he does this, other ideas occur to him which may not have occurred before, or which are suggested by the ideas he is actively considering.

**5. Further Observation and Experiment Leading to Acceptance or Rejection of the Proposed Solution.** This is the final step in the thinking process, at which point the individual *decides* what to do, write or say. He makes up his mind on the basis of all that he has been able to think of concerning the problem, and puts his conclusions into action, speech or writing.

In the case of the motorist, he decides what he is going to do, and he does it. He may take that road to the left, and see if it works out satisfactorily. The student with the problem about immigration decides what the best arguments are, and he writes them down together with his conclusions.

If our driver at the "Bridge Out" sign decides on a course of action, he may or may not arrive at a good solution of his problem. If that road to the left turns out to be a dirt road, or longer than he had figured, he may say, "I didn't think that problem out very well."

The student may write down some reasons why the United States adopted its immigration policy, but he may not have remembered or thought about the best reasons, in which case he gets his paper back with a low grade.

But in all *problem solving situations* the general process or procedure is the same. Let us put it in our own words again, as follows:

*a*) We have to know that we have a problem. We have to face a difficulty and know that something has to be done about it.

*b*) We have to know just what the problem means and just what it is that we are called upon to do.

*c*) We have to think about it until we can figure out some ideas which may help us to solve the problem.

*d*) We have to take into consideration all the possible bearings or implications of these ideas.

*e*) We have to decide which idea or ideas are best and then go ahead and try them.

A few further thoughts are in order about these stages in the thinking process.

*a*) Some people see problems more readily than others. They get off to a head start because they quickly recognize a problem and sense that it has to be dealt with.

*b)* Some people are more adept at defining problems than others. They see "what the problem calls for" quickly. They see what the problem means.

*c)* Some people can think of more possible solutions than others. Here is the point at which information comes in handy. The person who has had the widest experience or who has more knowledge at his finger tips will be the person who is most likely to think of suggestions which will help in solving the problem. Someone has said that, other things being equal, the man with the most information is the man most likely to succeed.

*d)* Some people will be more skilled in evaluating the various suggestions which come to mind than others. Some people may not be able to tell, readily, which suggestion best fits the situation or problem at hand. Intelligence and experience will have a lot to do with this.

*e)* Some people will be better able than others to apply the suggestions or solutions that are proposed.

## Pitfalls in Thinking

Having discussed the role of concepts in thinking, why we think, and how we think, we shall now consider some of the common errors in thinking.

**1. Importance of Avoiding Snap Judgments.** One thing which ought to be mentioned especially in this discussion of reasoning and thinking is the matter of hasty judgments or conclusions. If we "jump to conclusions" the chances are that we are doing very little thinking.

Men have been arrested and put in jail because policemen jumped to conclusions about their possible connection with a crime. A man might just happen to be at the scene of the crime and because of that be suspected of having a part in it.

Many persons have been disappointed in buying a used car because they jumped to the conclusion it was a "good buy" since it had a good "paint job" and "looked okay." It is possible to get on a wrong train in a busy railroad station by jumping to the conclusion that the train which arrives at a certain time is the one expected. It could be a previously scheduled train which is late.

Occasionally we face problems where we have to make instantaneous or immediate decisions. In these situations we have to think and think fast and hope that we get the right solution. But in most situations in life we are under no such pressure.

If the man in our example a few pages back, coming upon the "Bridge Out" sign, had an injured person in the back of his car and was rushing him to a hospital, he would not have much time to sit in the car and study road maps or ponder about directions. He would have to think fast and then "get going" on what seemed to be the best route.

Snap judgments may prove disastrous.

However, few life situations are like that. If we learn to *take time to think* we will probably live more effectively and more happily. An educated man or woman will abhor the hasty decision of the crowd and he will react against the "hurry up" plea of the emotional orator. That much-to-be desired attitude of *thinking* instead of *acting* on hunches comes from experience and study.

**2. Importance of Making Sure the Basic Facts Are Right.** We can't do good thinking if the facts we are using are wrong. This requires accurate checking of information and testing.

In football, the players and coaches work out a play which "can't go wrong." It is based on certain anticipated movements by members of the opposing team.

However, in case after case the play does go wrong because the opposing players don't act the way they're supposed to. Chance occurrences may upset all of the offensive calculations. Furthermore, the defense may have some defensive plays which are entirely different from those the offensive team thinks it is going to meet.

An historic example of faulty thinking occurred in the Second World War when the Allied Powers (France and England) *as-*

Getting the facts right is indispensable to problem solving.

*Official U.S. Air Force Photo*

*sumed* (got the basic facts wrong) that the Germans could not get through the Maginot Line. The Germans practically sailed over the Maginot Line by (a) developing techniques for cracking it at key points, and (b) by-passing it entirely.

**3. Wishful Thinking.** Students will hear occasionally, and read, references to what is sometimes called *wishful thinking*. By wishful thinking we mean the kind of thinking which leads us to a certain conclusion, because that is the conclusion we would like.

The psychology of this is very definite. The person who has a very strong prejudice in favor of a certain point of view may hold this prejudice so intensely that no matter what all the facts may be, he thinks that they support his viewpoint.

A high-school student may be so anxious for his own high-school basketball team to have a successful season that he *thinks* the team is better than it actually is. His wishful thinking may lead him to make statements about the abilities of the team which are far out of line with the facts. What is more likely, he is apt to *think* that an opposing team is actually weaker than it is.

During a war, the people of one nation may *think* that the people of another nation, with whom they are in a life-and-death struggle, are discontented with their leaders and on the verge of revolution. Wishful thinking tends to distort our judgment. When we are *very sure* that a certain condition prevails, we would do well to ask this simple question: Do the facts justify our belief that this is the case, or are we engaging in wishful thinking?

Professor Clarke relates that after a Midwestern football game thousands of spectators denounced the "blindness" of the officials, declaring that in a decisive forward pass the ball had touched the ground. The unprejudiced and indubitable testimony of the motion picture showed, however, that the ball had not touched the ground. It likewise showed that the observation of the thousands was inaccurate.[2]

Although this is given as an illustration of the fact that these spectators were not in a position to see exactly what happened, it may be taken for granted that their *certainty* that they had been right and the officials wrong was due in large part to the fact that they *wanted* it to come out in a particular way.

The fact that wishful thinking occurs shows that the "mind set" of the individual, that is, the way in which he approaches a problem, a new experience, or a new fact, is instrumental in determining how he will understand and interpret the new experience.

---

[2]Edwin L. Clarke, *The Art of Straight Thinking* (New York: D. Appleton-Century Co., 1929), p. 109.

The way in which wishful thinking enters into our daily affairs and interferes with the successful carrying out of many projects will be clear to the student if he will think of experiences he has had in which this influenced his decisions.

In selling articles, salesmen frequently engage in wishful thinking as to the wants and desires of the public. So anxious is the salesman to think that Mrs. So-and-so ought to buy a new product he has to sell, that he actually makes himself believe that Mrs. So-and-so *needs* and *wants* the product, whether she does or not!

Manufacturers will place new products on the market and sometimes these products will fail — wishful thinking having led the manufacturer to think that the public wanted something it really had no interest in.

A teacher may be so interested in a particular subject that he thinks everyone ought to study that subject. And so wishful thinking—without actual reference to the needs and wants of the students—causes a subject or topic to be made a part of the school curriculum.

Newspaper editors and publishers indulge in wishful thinking about the importance of editorials. The editor is apt to wish that the public would read his editorials so much, that he continues to devote pages to them and to pour himself into writing them, despite the fact that actual studies have shown the editorial page to be one of the least read parts of the newspaper.

In this case, however, it would be erroneous to conclude that newspapers ought not to have editorial pages because even though a small percentage of the reading public reads the editorials, *that group may be an important group.* Furthermore, the editorial feature may have indirect values in strengthening the general quality of the newspaper, which would be lost if this feature were to be omitted.

The student will ask himself this question: How can I check this tendency to indulge in wishful thinking? There is only one way in which the answer may be given: by realizing that wishful thinking does occur frequently, and by *learning* to be on the lookout for it in one's own experience.

If we are aware of the fact that wishful thinking is indulged in, even by good thinkers, we may more readily "catch ourselves" when we are indulging in the weakness. There is no guarantee that we shall not engage in wishful thinking, because the strength of our

The editorial writer sometimes indulges in
wishful thinking.

wishes is so great, sometimes, that it clouds our own perspective
and discrimination. Yet an awareness of the nature of this tendency
can definitely help us to reduce the number of occasions on which
we are misled.

## Suggestions To Help You Think

One writer has compiled some suggestions for teachers to help
them in training their students to think.[3] We might rewrite these
suggestions as guides to students who want to learn how to think,
as follows:

1. Learn to define each problem clearly.
2. Learn to *keep your problem clearly in mind.*
3. Learn how to make many suggestions which might help in solving
the problem by:
*a*) Analyzing the problem into parts.
*b*) Thinking of other similar problems or instances, and the general rules
which apply.
*c*) Not being afraid to guess at possible solutions and stating these
guesses clearly.

[3]S. C. Parker, cited in Robert A. Davis, *Psychology of Learning* (New York:
McGraw-Hill Book Company, 1935), p. 201.

4. Learn to consider the value of each suggested solution very carefully by:

*a*) Waiting before you jump to a conclusion.

*b*) Looking ahead to possible difficulties or criticisms in your solution.

*c*) Learning to check up (verify) your suggested conclusions by looking up the facts, reading about other studies which have been made of the subject, or—in some instances—trying little experiments.

5. Learn how to organize your information and your facts by:

*a*) Making an outline for yourself.

*b*) Learning how to make and use diagrams or charts.

*c*) Checking up, from time to time, on what you have learned in various courses, and from books.

*d*) Writing down, or summarizing, the conclusions which you and your fellow students and teachers have reached in studying various problems.

## SOMETHING TO DO

Take some simple concept and ask of several friends what it means to them.

Compare the meanings which your friends have given to the concept.

See whether or not their answers can be related to what you know of their previous education or experience.

Examples: What does *democracy* mean? What do you mean by *patriotism*? What is *education*?

## QUESTIONS AND PROBLEMS FOR STUDY AND DISCUSSION

1. Explain why thinking does not occur until we recognize a problem. What type of behavior occurs in situations where we do not recognize a problem?

2. Give an example of the recognition of a problem leading to thinking —what results occurred?

3. What historic examples can be given of inventions or discoveries which grew out of *questioning*—the questioning attitude?

4. Explain why having many experiences is related to good thinking.

5. Give an example of a concept. Show what kinds of experience would probably go into forming the concept.

6. One of the ways in which people reveal their concepts is through drawing. Take some simple concept and ask a number of your friends to make a "rough sketch" of it. Note the various kinds of meanings which appear in their drawings. Note how these are related to their experiences.

7. Think of a problem you have solved and see if you can give the steps in thinking (outlined by Dewey) as they occurred in your solution.

8. Give an example of how you used past experience to solve a new problem.

9. Take a problem you have been assigned in a course and write down carefully the "breakdown" of the problem to show how it can be defined and the meaning made clear.

10. To see the difficulty of getting exact meanings in a problem, take some activity or project and write definite instructions for performing it. (Example: getting to a certain geographical location; assembling a piece of equipment; explaining some proposed game to a group.)

11. Give an example of fast and intelligent thinking which you have observed in your experience.

12. Give an example of how a person or group of persons "jumped to a conclusion" which turned out to be wrong.

13. Give an example of an error in problem solving which was made because someone did not get the facts straight to begin with.

14. Give an example of wishful thinking.

15. Write down a list of about ten problems that people are facing today which, in your opinion, will require careful thinking. In connection with each, show one or more facts which will have to be secured before a solution to the problem will be possible.

# CHAPTER TEN

# PROPAGANDA AND ADVERTISING

In a democracy, it is very important for us to know about propaganda and advertising because we do not restrict radio or television programs, nor do we censor magazines and newspapers. We allow freedom of the press, and we expect people to use good judgment about what they read and hear.

At the same time, there are so many ways in which a clever propaganda attack can affect us, that we all need to be able to recognize the tricks. We must know how to face the waves of propaganda which are sent our way by people who are using psychological principles to influence us—often for good, but not always. The agencies of communication—press, radio, television, and movies—are the leading channels employed to reach us.

There are some rather well-defined methods in propaganda. These are described in this chapter. They include name-calling, glittering generalities, transfer, the testimonial, plain-folk devices, card stacking, and the band wagon technique.

In addition to explaining some of the psychological methods used effectively in advertising, this chapter includes some important notes on how advertising affects our present American society.

## QUESTIONS THIS CHAPTER WILL ANSWER

1. What is propaganda?
2. What are the principal ways in which propaganda works?
3. What methods of propaganda should we be able to recognize and understand?
4. What psychological appeals are commonly used in advertising?
5. How can the average person protect himself against undesirable influences in advertising and propaganda?

## How Habits, Attitudes, and Ways of Thinking Affect Society

Habits "keep us running" from day to day and attitudes more or less determine our beliefs and ways of dealing with people and events. They both play a role in controlling society as a whole. By society we mean the groups of people and masses of people who make up the world of mankind. These people or masses of people in any given nation or in any geographical section seem to have habits and attitudes just as individuals do. We might say that there are sectional or national habits, attitudes, and ways of thinking. Of course, we realize that there are individual persons within any group who don't share these sectional or national ways of thinking. There are always dissenters and there are often minority groups within the larger section or nation. But the fact that some people think differently from the majority will not keep the entire group from thinking and behaving as a group. These group attitudes exist, and exert great pressure on every individual who comes into contact with them.

Examples of these group or national habits or attitudes may be seen in the Spanish liking for bullfights, the American fondness for baseball, and the English habit of taking tea.

Leaders count on the existence of well-established attitudes among groups. For example, political leaders take it for granted that people in certain sections of the country will respond to appeals of a certain kind and plan their campaigns accordingly.

In a workers' district where the attitude of the people as a whole is hostile toward employers and capitalists, the candidates will devote a good bit of time to denouncing the rich. In some southern rural sections politicians will paint alarming pictures, usually imaginary, of dangers said to result from "northern interference" with their affairs, and will rally voters by proclaiming the importance of "white supremacy."

Another example of appealing to established ways of thinking might be illustrated by the following campaign slogan in a city election: "Let's take this town away from the banks and give it back to the people!"

Here are some common appeals and the groups they are calculated to influence:

| | |
|---|---|
| Opposing Wall Street | Midwest and farming groups |
| Opposing public ownership of electric utilities | Businessmen and manufacturing interests |
| Favoring socialized medicine | Working classes and white-collar workers |

| Opposing socialized medicine | Doctors, lawyers, and other professional groups and business leaders |
| Favoring high income taxes and corporation taxes | Labor groups and low-salaried workers |
| Favoring large military defense program | Manufacturers and business groups |
| Opposing government planning and industrial control | Businessmen and financial interests |

All people are not swayed by these appeals but the probability is that large groups will be.

In the same way leaders who are able to appeal to the common interests of people will be effective; those who are intellectual or reserved may have difficulty. The usual preference for popular candidates who like to mix with common folks and who exemplify their ways illustrates the point. The election of political leaders who like to be friendly and democratic, whether they know anything about the important issues or not, makes us realize that many people can be depended on to be swayed by very simple methods if they are used widely and frequently.

A friendly voice over the radio, a genial smile, and a warm personality are said to be worth thousands of votes to any potential candidate for office.

Even more important is the fact that people, in groups, are usually for or against things which affect their traditions and customs. They are likely to behave according to their group beliefs and according to the things which they feel are important to them.

## What Is Propaganda?

*Propaganda* is a term often applied to methods used for the purpose of getting people to act in a certain way in accordance with their common beliefs. It is used to get people to accept both tangible goods and ideas.

The term *communication* is a more formal term used to describe the ways in which people influence their fellow men, through such media as the radio, movies, television, publications, and other forms of social contact.

Propaganda is made effective through printed circulars, moving

Propaganda may be employed for worthy causes as well as those which are undesirable. Modern propaganda may employ complex tools—like this master control console of the Voice of America which can select programs from 100 different sources and transmit 26 programs simultaneously.

*Voice of America*
*United States Information Agency*

pictures, radio and television programs, newspaper editorials, and books.

The principal method of communication among people is through the printed or spoken word or picture.

To show how powerful a word can become—how much meaning it may convey to those who see it or hear it—we have but to recall the early pioneer days in America. When the lonely settler in his cabin in the woods heard a sudden pounding on his door, and heard the rapidly riding horseman shout the single word, "Indians!" that was enough. He knew then the dangers which were at hand, and what steps to take to protect himself and his family.

The meaning of words is important to all of us. As we know, words have meaning to us just to the extent that we have had the experiences necessary to give them meaning. If we have had different experiences, the same word may mean different things to us. To the Englishman, the word *bonnet* may mean the hood of an automobile; to Americans it is a sort of hat worn by girls or women.

Propaganda and communication are important in psychology because they are influences which affect behavior. The devices of

Certain words are capable of provoking an immediate response.

radio, television, the movies, and the printed page are simply newer and more modern ways by which people communicate with other people and by which they frequently hope to influence what they do and what they think or believe. Propaganda can be an instrument for good as well as evil.

*Propaganda is what we say or do when we are deliberately setting out to get other people to think, act, or believe the way we want them to.* This includes the idea of planning, the idea of strategy. The aim is to influence the other fellow's opinion.

Probably we should note that in propaganda the main idea is to *influence* by appealing to the *emotions.* In education or debate we also seek to influence people's opinions or beliefs, but for good reasons which we hope will be understood and accepted because they are true. In propaganda the effort is to get the other fellow to believe something whether he understands it or not and whether it is right or not.

In education an effort is made to present all of the information bearing on any subject, so that the student can make up his own mind about the rightness or wrongness of any cause or issue.

Education is devoted to revealing the *truth*. Propaganda is often devised to *distort* it.

Propaganda intended to get large groups of people to vote *against* the Labor Party, in a recent British election, illustrated the point. Labor was pictured as a giant, a powerful machine trying to get a strangle hold on every detail of the life of the individual British man and woman. The propagandists did not care whether these ideas made sense or not, or whether they were true. The object was to get people to be *against* Labor.

A similar technique was employed *against* the Conservative Party in the same British election. Propaganda and politics frequently go hand in hand.

It is interesting to note that propaganda is more effective, and gets results more quickly, when the people have had but a limited education. Nevertheless, even the effect of education can be overcome by competent propagandists. Surely the people of Germany were an educated people, but their Ministry of Propaganda, during the Second World War, was able to mislead them very effectively.

Propaganda is a force for good or evil, and it is important that all citizens of democratic nations be familiar with it, and alert to the possibilities it represents.

## Agencies of Propaganda

It is important for people to realize not only what propaganda is, but to understand the principal *agencies* through which it works. The principal agencies of communication, as we know, are the newspapers, movies, radio, and TV. Also important are the magazines, books, billboard advertising, and public meetings and addresses. Word of mouth contact with other people is also used. Sometimes rumors are started by people talking to each other in ever-widening circles (whispering campaigns).

Newspapers may be instruments of propaganda through the kinds of news carried repeatedly and with regularity, the kinds of editorials printed, and the kinds of advertising favored. Headlines may "play up" or "play down" incidents.

The news stories themselves are usually accurate and as faithful to the truth as the newspaper reporter or editor can make them. At the same time, by the prominence or lack of prominence given to them, according to the policy of the newspaper, they may be a means of propaganda. Newspapers devoted to the highest ethics of journalism are constantly trying to be fair and impartial in handling the news. Nevertheless, all newspapers, since they are published by people who often have different interests and different points of view, do not handle news stories in exactly the same way. Furthermore, there is a limit to what can be printed in a newspaper (there is just so much room available in each edition), and the

America's belief in freedom of information led to the establishment of the Voice of America news broadcasting service. These VOA newsroom men are on the lookout for fresh and authentic news from all corners of the world.

*Voice of America*
*United States Information Agency*

editor must use his judgment in deciding what to use and what to omit. This means that in order to be sure that we are getting "all sides" to a story, we may have to read more than one newspaper.

Fortunately, in a democracy, freedom of the press is one of our fundamental rights, and so we can find newspapers reflecting different points of view and they are all available to us.

The newspapers also contain editorials and advertisements which carry propaganda freely. Advertisers pay for the space they use to carry a message, of course, and there is no question about the source of the message—it comes from whoever paid for the advertisement. The editorial pages—and to this we should add the cartoons and special columns—are also propaganda sources, but here again we know that the opinions are intended to be opinions and we know at least in part who is responsible for them. Often the editors represent the views of the people who own or who financially support the publication.

These are facts we must know if we are to be aware of the ways in which we are constantly being subjected to propaganda.

The same considerations apply to radio and to television. The broadcasting chains and the stations are like newspapers in that they select and edit the programs. The public assumes that this will be done in accordance with principles of fairness. At the same time, it is important for the public to be vigilant in demanding that these agencies adopt and maintain ethical practices.

In 1959 the nation was shocked by discoveries that certain television programs had been rigged. What appeared to the viewers as honest questioning and honest answering on certain quiz programs, had been "fixed" ahead of time so that programs were staged to appear honest when they were not.

Shortly afterwards, another scandal of this nature came to light. This was known as "payola." Some disc jockeys were playing records in order to "plug" them and make it appear that these records were in great demand by the public. The fact was that the disc jockeys were being paid on the side to play the records and the frequency of their playing had nothing to do with whether or not the public was requesting them.

As a result those involved lost their jobs and more strict policies were adopted by the networks.

Freedom of speech and freedom of the press give all people an opportunity to express their opinions. We, the readers and the listeners, must be responsible for our own opinions. We can listen and read intelligently, knowing what propaganda is and how it works, or we can be "suckers" and believe only what pleaders of special causes want us to believe and ignore the rest.

The intelligent person knows what propaganda is and learns how to distinguish what is true from what is false.

In a dictatorship there is no array of conflicting propaganda, but just one propaganda, as the Institute for Propaganda Analysis has shown. All of the propaganda is directed toward goals determined by one, central government. All contradictory propaganda is kept from the public or prohibited.

In such a situation people appear to *accept*, not to *think*. The tremendous influence of controlled propaganda has been seen in prewar Germany, in prewar Italy, in Communist Russia, in Communist East Germany, in Communist China, and in Cuba. The results are familiar to all Americans.

In our country we cannot, without changing the basic form of our government, prohibit various kinds of propaganda, and we would not want to. But we do need to know propaganda when we see it, and we need to know the psychological forces which are at work, all of the time, to influence us one way or another.

## Methods of Propaganda

The Institute for Propaganda Analysis developed seven classifications of propaganda which are useful and which may be briefly explained and illustrated:

**1. Name-Calling.** In this we call people names. The names carry a meaning to most people and so the person to whom we apply the name is immediately labeled, rightly or wrongly.

"He's a Red!" shouts the political speaker. So the person called a "Red" is immediately a bad individual who believes in communism and is an enemy of the United States.

Emotional appeal is very evident in this procedure, and it is obviously an attempt to appeal to emotions with complete disregard for the facts or any other consideration.

This is the commonest form of propaganda and the most widely used. Other examples of current name-calling include socialist, communist, Wall Streeter, labor agitator, egg-head, integrationist, scab, and others.

**2. Glittering Generalities.** This method uses broad general terms which have some suggestion of being very fine or good, or seem to stand for some ideal.

If we can tie in one of these words or several of them with whatever we are trying to promote or whatever we are trying to get people to believe, it influences them emotionally to be favorable toward our cause.

Truth, freedom, justice, liberty, democracy, progress, the American way, the American home, fair play, square deal, and others are examples.

"If you believe in justice, you will vote for Senator Wright. If you are for the American way, you will have to go along with Wright. The Wright way is the *right* way. It is the only way to preserve the America we love."

This kind of talk does not promise one single specific thing but suggests a lot of good things we all believe in.

**3. Transfer.** Transfer is a device by which the user of propaganda associates some goal or purpose with a symbol people already accept as good. A common example of this is the association of the cross with Christianity. The figure of Uncle Sam is another, and dur-

Propaganda can be a two-edged sword. This illustration could be used to demonstrate the futility of resistance to well-trained troops or it could be used to establish the ruthless cruelty of the enemy.

*Courtesy of Williams and Meyer Co.*

ing the Second World War the "V" sign came to stand for victory.

The basic principle is that the warm feeling of good will, the emotional approval, transfers to the idea the propagandist wants you to accept.

The symbol of clasped hands may be used to suggest brotherhood or unity of purpose. The figure of the blindfolded woman and the scales suggests justice. A picture of the rock of Gibraltar suggests permanent and unyielding strength and security.

It cannot be doubted that the Russians have used the symbol of the sickle and hammer, and the clenched fist, to win support of millions toward the belief in communism as the champion and defender of the interests of the working people. The idea has further been promoted by the slogan of many years standing, "Workers of the World, Unite!"

The American flag, to Americans, suggests the ways of life in which we believe and it is associated in our minds with much that we hold dear.

A recognition of transfer as a device of propaganda does not mean that we condemn it, but we do realize how frequently it may be employed in influencing what we and what others think and feel.

**4. The Testimonial.** Common in advertising and used extensively in propaganda of all sorts is the scheme of linking up a product or an idea or a point of view with a noted or prominent individual. Movie stars, athletes, and heroes are most favored in this connection.

Many magazines carry advertisements which feature the endorsements of certain products by well-known entertainers and athletes.

A noted television and Broadway actress endorses a beverage, illustrating a tendency which is especially common in advertising tobaccos, liquors, and beauty aids.

In propaganda, efforts are sometimes made to link up noted people of the past with present-day proposals. "How would Abraham Lincoln have felt about this?"—"Which side do you think Thomas Jefferson would have been on?" and similar suggestions illustrate the point.

Great names such as those of George Washington, Robert E. Lee, and Franklin D. Roosevelt, are often tied in with ideas which people are asked to support or work for.

**5. Plain-Folks Device.** The method of making us feel warmly disposed toward some policy by linking it up with the feelings and tastes or sentiments of the common people—the plain folks—is often employed, especially in political propaganda.

For example, a newspaper advertisement might suggest that "Bill Jones knows where he can get the best service for his car." Bill Jones is portrayed as a common sort of human being "just like the rest of us" and he naturally has unusual common sense and good judgment. If he gives his business to a certain firm, it would be a good example for us to follow, the argument runs.

In almost every election campaign of national interest some of the candidates make an effort to appear as "plain people." Any special advantages they may have had of education or wealth are "played down" and every interest they have shown, real or imaginary, in the lot of everyday people is "played up."

There can be no doubt but that we are, as a people, much impressed by a leader who is "democratic" and who laughs, cries, and makes mistakes just like the rest of us. This human, friendly touch may be very effectively used in propaganda.

**6. Card Stacking.** Card stacking is defined as using every argument and every possible supporting point, real or imaginary, to create an overwhelming opinion in favor of the position advocated. Thus by pointing out and underlining every possible point of weakness in American life and politics, the Russians have achieved considerable success in making our democracy seem like pretty much of a failure. Every incident of crime or delinquency is used to make it seem that law has broken down. Every business failure or labor crisis, such as a strike, is "played up" to show how poorly the capitalistic system works in America. Every lynching or riot is used to show our lack of consideration for justice and equality for all people. Every cheap or poor quality moving picture release is used to show the decadence of our screen industry.

These examples are sufficient to show the method of card stacking.

By a relentless presentation of all of the possible weaknesses of any plan which is proposed, the whole plan can be made to appear ridiculous to the unsuspecting reader or listener. This is a particularly malicious form of propaganda because it is contrary to our conviction in America that we should try to get both sides of any story.

**7. The Band Wagon.** In using the band wagon technique, propagandists make us feel that everyone is for a certain man, party, or idea, and we ought to "get on the band wagon" and go along, too.

This appeal is satisfying to the desire we have to share in the best things of life. We don't want to miss anything good. Therefore we will tend to "join up" with the others in any project, if we can be made to feel that the others are all joining up. Often we do not realize that the facts may not be just as stated. We may be led to feel that public opinion is practically unanimous on a certain point when, as a matter of fact, it is not.

Thus the American people might be led to believe, by certain propagandists, that "everyone" is against a certain medical program. The argument might be that all the doctors are against it, all the businessmen are against it, all the leading and thinking people are against it. Whether or not this is true should certainly be investigated, before a final conclusion is arrived at.

In the presidential elections of 1948 the newspapers from one end of the country to the other, the public opinion polls, and radio speakers generally were "sure" of a Dewey victory. The idea seemed to be that it was a Republican year and "everybody" was swinging along with the Governor of New York in his race for the presidency. Of course the "morning after" awakening, when it was shown that President Truman had been re-elected, brought home the weakness of the band-wagon argument in this case.

Another form of propaganda occurs when an entirely untrue story is made up and given such wide circulation that it is accepted as true. This is known as the Big Lie. The untrue story is repeated over and over again on the air and in the press, with increasing emphasis. This may occur for days and weeks on end until the people, hearing no other side of the story, accept it as true. Unfortunately this technique has apparently been used by some modern nations intent on sowing seeds of suspicion and mistrust concerning other nations. Such tactics are irresponsible and dangerous. It is very important for democratic nations to recognize it and be alert to its possible harmful influence.

In summarizing the effect of these devices on us, remember that all of them appeal to emotion and not to logical thinking.

Why are we fooled by these devices? Because they appeal to our emotions rather than to our reason. They make us believe and do something we might not believe or do if we thought about it calmly, dispassionately.

In examining these devices, note that they work most effectively at those times when we are too lazy to think for ourselves; also, they tie into emotions which sway us to be "for" or "against" nations, races, religions, ideals, economic and political policies and practices, and so on through automobiles, cigarettes, radios, toothpastes, presidents and wars. With our emotions stirred, it may be fun to be fooled by these propaganda devices, but it is more fun and infinitely more to our own interests to know how they work.

Lincoln must have had in mind citizens who could balance their emotions with intelligence when he made his remark ". . . you can't fool all of the people all of the time."[1]

## Psychology in Advertising

No people in the business world have been quicker to make use of the principles of psychology than advertisers. Businessmen who want to get people to buy things, or to act in certain ways, are certain to be interested in anything psychology can tell them about "what makes people do the things they do."

In addition to using all of the well-known techniques of propaganda, the advertiser makes specific use of the psychology of motivation. He is interested in the motivation based on physical drives and that based on learning.

As an example of an advertisement based on physical drives, we could cite a page in the *Saturday Evening Post* portraying a delicious looking baked ham, in beautiful colors. Exclamations such as "It makes my mouth water!" clearly show that this advertisement appeals to the physical drive of hunger.

Another advertisement appealing to physical drives is a travel advertisement by the state of Florida, which tells the reader to "Trade Icy March Winds for Sunny Spring Breezes." A beverage advertisement asks, "Haven't you been missing something?" And, a candy company says its product "fairly melts in your mouth." There is a suggestion that a certain perfume could lead to romance in the wording of this one: "Exciting as a flight through night winds, created to stir a mood of high adventure."

On the other hand, an appeal to learned interests is evident in a travel invitation from Williamsburg, Virginia, which urges us to

[1]Cited in *How to Detect and Analyze Propaganda* (New York: The Town Hall, Inc.).

"See Williamsburg as George Washington Knew It."

An appeal to motives which have been learned appears in an advertisement picturing a new model of an automobile, with a well-known movie star at the wheel. We might want to buy that car because it would appeal to our pride to have the same kind of car the movie star drives. We have learned that driving a car the "big people" drive adds to our prestige. Of course a little reflection shows that it might be quite foolish to be led into the purchase of an automobile, or any other advertised product, for such a reason. Yet we are led to act by such considerations quite frequently.

A search of advertising shows that many appeals are based on our appetites and desires, our love of luxury and comfort, our search for prestige, our interest in adventure and new experiences, our interest in sex, and a wide variety of personal needs for elements which could make for more satisfactory living. Often there is a mixture of physiological and learned motives but in most effective advertising there is a careful effort to approach us in an area in which the advertiser is sure we are vulnerable.

Frequently the eye-catching and attention-getting features of an advertisement have little or no connection with the qualities of the product advertised. Nevertheless, they are effective since they cause us to make note of the product and they have the effect of getting us to associate it with something in which we are interested or which appeals to us.

One of the most widely used devices of this sort is that of displaying an attractive woman with the product, whether it be an automobile, a new type of air-conditioner, or a winter cruise to Bermuda.

Increasingly, advertisers are appealing to us through the use of humor. Cartoons attract our attention and not only bring us enjoyment but tend to create a friendly attitude toward the product with which they are associated. Many of these humorous touches are developed and continued over a period of months or even years by business organizations.

**Some Important Influences of Advertising.** It has already been noted that advertising or propaganda can have either good or bad results. Advertising is good if it influences people to do the things that promote their own welfare and that of society. It is harmful if if it leads them into bad or unsocial behavior. It is also harmful if it makes them want things or develop ambitions they cannot attain, with the result that they become disheartened or discouraged. Many people have gone heavily into debt because they could not resist the appeals of advertising.

In connection with advertising, the problems of psychology, business, and industry are joined. This might be illustrated as follows:

1. Technicians and inventors learn how to make an electric refrigerator.
2. The electric refrigerator can be made at relatively low cost if there is sufficient demand for it to justify mass production methods.
3. Advertising is employed to promote the demand for the refrigerator.
4. As the demand grows, manufacturing by mass production is made possible and the cost of the article to the public can be reduced.
5. As the demand increases, it becomes more and more profitable to the men who are manufacturing the refrigerator, thereby increasing business activity and producing worth-while results for all concerned.

An objection to this is that the cost of the advertising has to be added to the cost of the refrigerator, or any other product which is manufactured and distributed. This may be true, yet because of the important role played by the advertising in making the whole manufacturing operation possible, this cost may be taken as legitimate.

However, the purpose here is not to enter into an economic argument concerning the justification of advertising, but to show that the use of psychological principles in this field is valuable and important.

Examples of the use of the same principles would take us into the matter of harmful advertising. The same principles that make a roasted ham attractive to us might also be used to make a bottle of whiskey attractive to us. Thus products which can be harmful in the extreme are advertised effectively and sometimes harmful or dangerous habits spread. A whiskey advertisement often makes use of the most skilled color photography, the most powerful attention-getting devices, and the cleverest psychological appeals.

A very comfortable and prosperous looking gentleman is seen sitting in his oak-paneled living room obviously enjoying his whiskey. It all looks very attractive indeed. Yet we have never seen a whiskey advertisement which portrays a "drunk" under the table, or staggering home, or slumped over the wheel of an automobile he has wrecked.

Therefore it is important for people to be "on guard" with reference to advertising and the effect it has on their impulses to act.

Some aspects of advertising are not always
to our best advantage.

Advertising frequently avoids mentioning unpleasant issues.

## Constructive Use of Propaganda and Advertising

We have already indicated that the advertiser uses devices
worked out in psychology for the promotion of commodities and
products, and often these are good; sometimes they are harmful.

The same powerful influences which make certain kinds of
propaganda harmful, may be used to work toward human better-

ment and the promotion of worth-while goals. For instance, a special play has been written, showing colorfully and dramatically just how public education operates in a democracy. It is justifiable to use all we know of psychology to interest people in worth-while things. It would be most unfortunate if we allowed the promoters of unworthy projects to use psychology, while ignoring its possibilities ourselves. The principles of motivation, of interest and attention are neither good or bad. They are simply principles governing human behavior. They themselves are only of value as they are used. One of the problems of leaders in society, in the school, in the church, or in other social institutions, is to learn about these principles and endeavor to use them for the promotion of worth-while ends.

The problem of each individual in society consists in learning, for his own protection, how the various principles and devices work. Then he must cultivate his own tastes and use his own judgment as to whether or not he is going to permit himself to be influenced by the various appeals which are made to him. No individual can protect himself entirely against propaganda, because the most effective propaganda is that which can be used without our being aware that it is being used.

At the same time, by familiarizing ourselves with these principles and devices, we can protect ourselves against the gross abuse of these methods. We can protect ourselves against the cruder forms. We can become less gullible.

The study of our own attitudes toward advertising and propaganda will aid us in building up some protection, and we can at least hope to appreciate the forces which surround us even though we may not always be aware of them or be sure that we are resistant to them.

If the methods which have been described are successful, they may be useful as well as harmful.

Propaganda which is employed to promote a worthy goal or object may be constructive; for example, in promoting a drive for the American Red Cross, for the war on infantile paralysis, or for some generally agreed upon useful movement.

In such instances all of the propaganda devices may be used and with good results. We do not need to feel that we are obliged to resist these appeals because the methods of propaganda are used. We may, on the contrary, feel that the methods used are very good, because we realize not only that the purposes of these movements are very much to be desired, but also that people—like ourselves—tend to be indifferent and often lukewarm toward worth-while projects, unless strong measures are taken to arouse their attention and interest.

This picture was used by the American Red Cross to promote giving to the worthy causes it represents. Who could resist being touched by Manfred's evident gratitude for his new pair of shoes?

*American Red Cross*
*Photo by Walter*

It is also to be noted that many useful products have been brought to the attention of people, and have found their way into their homes, because of effective advertising.

It should be clear that the methods employed are merely the methods of influencing people psychologically—methods which can be used for good purposes or bad. Our problem is to become alert to what is going on so that we can make sensible decisions as to what is good and what is bad.

## Suggestions to Help You Use the Means of Communication

1. Read freely, since it is well to be informed about many different points of view, including those of others as well as your own.

2. Ask yourself some questions about the source of the information.

Consider such questions as:

a) Is this news story reliable as indicated by the fact that it originated with one of the major responsible wire services such as the Associated Press or the United Press International?

b) Does the writer appear to have secured complete information covering all sides of the story?

c) Is there any indication that the story has been "cut," that is, does it appear that any paragraphs have been omitted?

d) Is the story objective or does it use language that shows a bias or prejudice on the part of the writer?

e) Does the news story convey the type of news or information suggested by the headline which appears with it? Frequently headlines are misleading as to the actual content of the story. (Don't limit your readings to headlines. Headlines have a purpose but they never were intended to be a substitute for the whole story.)

3. Does the newspaper you are reading appear to be truthful and fair in its coverage of news, or is it known to be partial to certain points of view?

4. What is the editorial policy of the newspaper you are reading?

5. What other newspapers or magazines might give a different treatment to the material you are reading?

6. Is it obvious that the story has been "played up" or "played down"?

7. Do you read one type of newspaper only or do you frequently read newspapers known to represent points of view somewhat different from those to which you are accustomed?

8. Do you read more than one magazine? Do the magazines you read represent different points of view?

9. Notice the cartoons published in the newspapers you read. Do these cartoons appear to favor one side or another in important political or social issues? (Cartoons are a good indication of the newspaper's editorial policy.)

10. Television:

a) Does the program appear to be partial or one-sided as judged by the following tests?

(1) The nature of the subject presented.

(2) The types of persons appearing on the program and their business or political connections.

(3) Occurrence of the common tricks or propaganda.

(4) The probable interests of the sponsors.

(5) Extent to which the program appears to be designed to arouse emotion and feeling or to appeal to reason or judgment.

b) Do you listen to one type of commentator only, or do you make it a point to hear a number representing different views and interests?

c) Do you listen to more than one station or network, or do you tend to listen to one station or network all of the time?

11. Movies:

a) Are you aware of the fact that a moving picture story can carry propaganda favorable to or opposed to a point of view in politics, economics, religion, or other areas of interest?

b) Do you realize that—like books and stories—moving pictures tend to play up certain interests of the characters represented and that they must be taken for what they are worth with this in mind?

c) Do you limit your movie-going to just certain types of films or do you select pictures, from time to time, which touch areas of life unfamiliar to you?

d) Do you "take with a grain of salt" the highly emotional treatment which sometimes is evident in a picture?

e) Do you thoroughly enjoy the films you see, but recognize that they are just stories and may overplay certain ideas or points of view for dramatic effect?

12. General suggestions:

a) Don't read just one newspaper all the time. Form the habit of purchasing other papers quite frequently so that you learn other points of view and can appreciate other ways of handling the news.

b) Become acquainted with a number of good magazines. Make it a point to read from a variety of publications rather than one or two.

c) Widen your radio and television listening and movie going so that you feel you are getting a real cross section of public opinion and dramatic interest.

d) Go out of your way to make sure that you are not the victim of a one-sided presentation of any important public issue.

Finally, don't forget that you can enjoy the things you read, the programs you hear, and the movies you see—and enjoy them very much—without necessarily allowing yourself to be influenced unwisely.

Life can be enriched by realizing that we can be stimulated by many books, articles, movies, or radio and television programs *even though we* don't agree with them. The man who would only listen to what he agrees with would find life extremely dull.

Read widely, see much, and listen often and you will enjoy the opportunities for free discussion which our democracy makes possible. You can do this and enjoy it to the fullest possible degree without fear if you have, at the same time, an understanding and appreciation of the techniques of propaganda which are a characteristic of our time.

## SOMETHING TO DO

1. In order to appreciate the way in which the various devices of propaganda are used, with special reference to the seven classifications discussed in the text (name-calling, etc.), write down an example of each kind, from your own experience.

2. Write a political speech deliberately using each of the seven techniques. After each type is used, indicate in parentheses the type you have illustrated.

## QUESTIONS AND PROBLEMS FOR STUDY AND DISCUSSION

1. In what way are propaganda and education similar? Explain an important way in which they differ.

2. Explain what is meant by group habits or attitudes.

3. What are some of the important groups in society? Give an example of a group which has one or more well-defined attitudes which are easily recognized.

4. Show what happens when a group attitude and an individual's attitude are different. Give an example.

5. From a political speech which you hear over the radio, or read in the newspapers, give an example of appealing to a group attitude.

6. Give an example of some group attitude which is "sectional"—that is, one which you feel is characteristic of some one section of the country.

7. Give an example of the "plain people" or "just folks" approach in propaganda.

8. Discuss the question of the possible good and bad uses of propaganda.

9. Show how propaganda works in a democracy and explain why it is not possible or desirable to prohibit propaganda by law.

10. What do we mean by saying that people can be educated to understand propaganda and protect themselves from undue influence in this respect?

11. Does a knowledge of propaganda methods prevent an individual from enjoying reading, radio listening, or the movies? Explain.

12. Describe some probable propaganda effects of a motion picture which you have seen. What groups or interests, in your opinion, were promoted by these propaganda effects?

13. Make a list of some organizations or groups which, in your opinion, may be expected to use propaganda considerably in promoting their objectives?

14. Write a paragraph supporting or endorsing a political candidate, using some of the tricks of propaganda described in this chapter.

15. Clip out several advertisements of movies, or of political candidates, which illustrate propaganda technique.

CHAPTER ELEVEN

# THE PSYCHOLOGY OF EMOTIONS

This chapter takes up the study of emotions and shows how they operate in our lives. The way in which emotions have a physical basis is explained, and the tie-in between emotions and our thoughts is shown.

Emotions are what give life its feeling and meaning. They enrich life. Without emotions, things would be quite routine and dull. The constructive side of emotions is sometimes overlooked, and this chapter brings out how important they are in this respect. In this connection, the importance of taking part in social activities, of adjusting to other people who have different ways of doing things, of practicing tolerance for others, and other similar problems are examined.

The chapter includes some explanations of humor—what it is and how it relaxes us and contributes to our well-being.

In the first part of this chapter, there is some discussion of how our emotions and feelings are conditioned through experience. It is evident that many of our emotions are learned. We learn when to be happy, when to be sad, when to be angry, etc.

## QUESTIONS THIS CHAPTER WILL ANSWER

1. What part do emotions, both constructive and destructive, play in our lives?

2. What is the machinery of our emotions?

3. How much of our emotional behavior is the result of what we have learned and the experiences we have had? How does this kind of learning take place?

4. How do psychologists study emotions and measure them?

5. What are some good ways to develop constructive and helpful emotional patterns?

6. What is the psychology of humor and relaxation, and what part does it play in our lives?

## Emotion Gives Life Its Color and Zest

The scene is a motion-picture studio. Actors and actresses are in position, brilliant lights are flooding the set with intense illumination, the motion-picture cameras are grinding and everyone is tense.

"Stop! Stop! Stop!" cries the director, jumping from his chair and waving his arms.

"For heaven's sake, put some *feeling* into it!" he cries. "Act as if you *meant* it. Don't you understand, we want people to grip their seats when they see this shot. Here, like this!" And the director steps forward to show the actors how to "put some feeling into it."

The director's face and gestures, themselves, are a portrayal of emotion—perhaps a mixture of anger, disgust, and impatience.

Motion-picture producers are well aware of the importance of emotion. Emotion "sparks" human affairs, makes the difference between monotony and routine, and adventure and excitement.

Emotion is the part of our living which makes life colorful, which often gives it what we call *meaning*. Feeling and emotion, we might say, keep us from being mere machines, make us real human beings.

Some of the emotions are very common. Anger, love, fear— these are the main strong emotions. There are mixtures of emotions, like those which the director felt when he didn't like the way the scene was going. These are mild emotions; not the strong ones, but those which we feel ordinarily. There are also joyful emotions, which give us a zest for living and a feeling of satisfaction. And there are the tender emotions of sorrow and sadness.

## How Ideas and Bodily Feelings Are Connected

In thinking of emotions we have to recall some facts about the nature of our physical make-up, because emotions are physical in nature — they are reactions of the body which go along with thoughts and ideas. The thoughts and ideas cannot be separated from the reactions of the body which create the feeling. They are joined together by special parts of the nervous system, centering in a lower section of the brain called the *thalamus*. Here the ideas and impulses from the various sense organs of the body unite or interact to produce the sensations which make up what we call *feeling*.

The actual bodily changes which cause emotional feeling are produced by the action of certain glands. Glands are special organs of the body which produce chemicals, and the chemicals, or

Millions of people have been emotionally stimulated by the Statue of Liberty.

*Acme Newspictures*

hormones, affect the other glands and the other organs of the body in such a way that the sensations produced within us are of the kind which we recognize as feelings.

But psychologists have also found that ideas have to go along with the chemical changes in the body if we are to have emotions. They have proved this by injecting glandular substances into the body, and have shown that unless there is some *idea* to accompany the chemical treatments, the person so treated does not *feel* any emotion.

Simple experiences, and what we have learned, can produce emotion. We now recognize, too, that some of our emotions are caused by very simple experiences and very simple stimulations, whereas others are the result of complex learning. We feel excited when a band and a parade marches by, and part of that is due to the fact that we have learned to become excited. We have learned to feel patriotic when we hear the "Star Spangled Banner." If we had not learned this, we would just hear the music without feeling any particular excitement. This is an example of conditioning, previously described.

Feeling and emotion may be caused, it has been said, by very simple experiences. One of the common causes of the feeling of fear is to suddenly lose our feeling of security. If someone kicks a chair out from under us, we will feel a sudden fear. If someone without warning strikes an iron bar behind us, the intense sound will make us afraid.

As the psychologists would put it, any sudden stimulation may make us afraid.

We are made angry by having something happen which makes us feel as though we are being restricted or held down. If the little child is held tightly so that he cannot squirm or move, he feels angry. He becomes red in the face; he is greatly disturbed.

The sensations which we describe as *love* are aroused when we are petted, or fondled, by those who are kind to us. In romantic love, stimulation of a sexual nature may be involved directly or indirectly. Part of this is just a physical feeling of pleasure, not unlike that which we observe in a little dog when we pet and caress him.

It is very important to realize the fact that there is a physical basis for emotions and feeling. People can no more *help* feeling angry or sad under certain conditions than they can *help* feeling tired or sleepy when they have been staying awake or working for many hours.

## How Emotions Are the Result of Conditioning

Gradually, as we grow older and have more experiences, a great many things become capable of arousing our emotions. The mere sight of someone we love can make us have a feeling of affection or love. So can the sight of his handwriting, or his clothes, or other belongings. Though the loved one may be a thousand miles away, the sight of a letter addressed by him to us and just delivered may arouse a very strong feeling of love. We have *learned* to associate the appearance of these things with the person. We have learned to feel emotion when these are brought to our attention. We have become *conditioned* to have these reactions. This emotional conditioning explains how our fears, our love, and our anger become attached to a wide variety of experiences in life — a wide variety of *stimuli*.

Many of the emotions which we learn through conditioning are acquired without our being aware of it. For example, our affection for home and the things in it, our feeling of pleasure on returning to "the old home town" or "the old school" after we have been away, could be explained in this way.

All of the things in the environment of the school, the home, or the home town were, without our being aware of it, *conditioned stimuli* and were associated with our feeling of affection for the place.

**Effect of Changes on Conditioning.** Sometimes when we have been away from one of these old familiar scenes for a long time, and return, we find that we are disappointed. "The old place has changed," we say, sadly. True, and as it has changed in the details, it has lost some of its power of arousing old feelings. The trees have grown larger; the buildings have been painted, changed, or torn down and replaced by others; the people we used to associate with certain places have been replaced by others; the people, and so in numerous ways the stimuli which were, taken all together, responsible for our emotional attitude, have been changed just enough to keep the scene from arousing the old familiar emotional response.

Many an "old grad" has been secretly disappointed when he

went back to his college class reunion a few years later, for just these reasons.

These emotions are very strong and play an important part in our lives. We could probably make a list of the places we know which arouse certain emotions in us and a list of the people we know who arouse emotions in us.

**Producing the Desired Effect.** When people are placed in an environment in which there are certain stimuli or situations which will arouse their emotions, it is certain that they will react in an emotional

The carnival atmosphere is designed to be emotionally stimulating.

way. This is a very important fact in psychology, because it means that if we want to produce certain emotions, all we have to do is to expose people to the stimuli or situations which we know will produce this kind of reaction. Thus, when we want to create a feeling of school spirit, we arrange things so that the stimuli which will arouse this feeling are present. We use flags, bands, people who are liked and who are leaders, songs, decorations, and other ways to produce the desired emotional effect.

Churches are familiar examples of design and decoration intended to produce atmosphere—a feeling of serenity, quiet, peace, and holiness. Europe's cathedrals have been known for centuries as marvelous architectural expressions of the religious feeling. The church, with its cloisters, its stained glass windows, its flickering candles or subdued lighting, suggests a mood of meditation and surrounds us with many stimuli likely to arouse the spirit of worship and prayer.

The midway of a typical carnival or circus offers another example of the part played by stimuli in arousing feeling. The gay pictures, the clowns, the dancing girls, and the colors are intended to arouse a carnival spirit in the people who visit the circus or the carnival.

Frequently, when a meeting or an assembly which was supposed to arouse community spirit has failed to do so, we will find that the people in charge of the meeting have made no attempt whatever to set the stage in such a way as to arouse the emotional responses desired.

Neglect of *planning* is evident in many gatherings. It often means that the persons responsible for the meeting have given no thought to the psychology of the emotions and how such information can be used to advantage. Successful meetings are planned in advance and attention is given to decorations, furniture arrangements, platform settings, etc.

Some of the most elaborate stage settings of all time were those created by Hitler at the Nuremberg rallies of the Nazi party. In a vast arena designed to accommodate as many as 200,000 people at one time, special stage and lighting effects were created to bring about a surge of patriotic feeling and a reaction of awe at the demonstration of might and splendor. Searchlights, Nazi banners, marching formations, music, and colors were used to produce the desired effect.

Square dancing would lose much of its appeal if the dances were held in more formal surroundings and if more formal attire were worn.

*San Diego County Schools*

These are examples of arranging things so as to present certain kinds of stimuli for the deliberate purpose of arousing particular emotional responses.

The other side of the matter is that when we want to *avoid* certain kinds of reactions, we *avoid* certain kinds of stimuli. So, when we want to avoid making people sad, or angry, we keep away from the stimuli which we know will lead to these responses. An occasion which is to be happy and cheerful calls for care in eliminating the conditions which usually produce the opposite results.

Gay parties, for example, are seldom held in auditoriums or rooms designed for more solemn occasions (such as chapels or churches). The *place* where an activity is to be held is important.

## Effects of the Adrenal Gland

Most notable of the glands, in emotion, is the *adrenal* gland. Here is an example of the way in which a physical part of the body is important in emotions. When this gland becomes active, it causes a flow of what is known as blood sugar. The blood sugar passes through the blood stream of the body, and has the effect for example, of dilating the pupils in the eyes, of causing the heart to speed up very much, and even of causing blood to congeal more quickly if we are hurt or injured.

The changes produced by the action of this gland, working through the blood stream, may be far-reaching. The intensity of the changes depends on the extent to which the individual is frightened or angered. But there is no question that these physical disturbances occur. They affect deeply the behavior of any woman or man who is wrought up.

The total effect of the changes caused by the adrenal gland, when it is active, is to prepare the body for intense activity. It is a part of the economy of nature that when a human being is confronted by a situation of danger, his body is prepared for it in this way. Perhaps this accounts for some of the superhuman feats which people have been known to perform when they have been in situations of danger. We have heard of people clinging for hours to precarious holds on cliffs, lifting heavy automobiles from injured persons, swimming for hours in cold water, climbing over high fences, and doing other things requiring strength and endurance. There can be little doubt that the extra energy is produced physically by action of the adrenal gland.

It is interesting to note that there should be an outlet for these extra energies when a person is thrown into a condition of strong emotion. Unless such an outlet is provided, these disturbances, if long continued, or repeated, may have an injurious effect on the body. Probably the best way to reduce any possible harm from such strong emotions is to engage in some active physical outlet, like taking a walk, or doing something requiring physical energy or muscular exertion. Then the energy-producing materials released into the body by the adrenal gland are used in a constructive or useful way, instead of harmfully.

## Anxiety

Perhaps anxiety is more like a complex of emotions. It is a general feeling of insecurity, of fear, of dread, usually associated with certain kinds of situations, either real or imaginary. Anxiety produces many of the sensations which are associated with other emotional reactions, especially the reaction of fear.

Because of its importance in connection with behavior, it is desirable to recognize anxiety and to understand its nature. Psychologists have pointed out that feelings of anxiety can range all the way from rather simple anxiety associated with some event which is about to happen which the individual fears because it will put him under a strain or put him in an insecure position (like taking an important examination) to abnormal anxiety which is all out of proportion to the situation a person is in, and which upsets the individual generally to such a degree that he can hardly perform the normal activities that are expected of him in everyday life. In the latter sense, anxiety is a form of neurotic behavior.

The kind of anxiety which is "normal" and rather common, is helpful in that it tends to make us prudent and careful.

Normal anxiety is . . . necessary to our functioning as emotionally mature individuals. Some people appear to lack normal anxiety altogether, for they are inconsiderate of the rights and feelings of others, show little incentive to learn, are unconcerned about the consequences of their own actions. . . . There are two important points to keep in mind. One is that anxiety is an inescapable part of everyday life. In its milder form, it helps us be concerned about the rights and feelings of others, it stimulates interest in the future and in learning, and it keeps us from behaving in ways that are essentially immature. The second point is that we must learn to tolerate anxiety and not permit ourselves to be overwhelmed by it. The more we are panicked by anxiety, the less mature and the more neurotic our behavior becomes. Learning to cope with anxiety is a necessary part of growing up, of becoming psychologically mature. Most people learn ways of coping with anxiety through the experiences of everyday living. Some learn their lessons better than others, but no one learns perfectly. Even the most mature and well-adjusted adult employs behavior mechanisms and has to cope with neurotic elements in his own behavior.[1]

Most people acquire control over anxiety as they grow up and go along through life enjoying a reasonable amount of success. Some, however, who find that anxiety is injuring their well-being more than is tolerable, may need to consult counselors, psychologists or psychiatrists in order to achieve a lessening of the damaging feelings with which they are coping. Generally speaking "anxiety reduction" is a desirable goal. The achievement of something we have worked for, or the successful carrying out of a responsibility that has been worrying us, is usually found to have a very definite anxiety- reduction value for us.

It often helps to discuss our anxiety with someone else. Sharing our feelings with friends or associates can often provide all the anxiety reduction that is necessary.

Psychotherapy is a process of helping individuals develop the psychological strength and skills to deal more adequately and effectively with themselves and with others. It may also be defined as a process of helping individuals to tolerate at least some of the anxiety that is a part of the stresses and strains of everyday living, to respond to the promptings of normal anxiety, and to resist becoming overwhelmed by neurotic anxiety. Through psychotherapy, individuals may learn to cope with the threats of everyday life—to turn "threats" into "challenges," in the terminology of Arthur W. Combs.

## How Physical Changes of Emotional Response Can Be Measured

Actual bodily changes produced by the emotions have been measured. One indication of emotional change in the body is a rise in blood pressure. Blood pressure can be measured fairly ade-

---

[1]Henry Clay Lindgren, *Psychology of Personal and Social Adjustment* (New York: American Book Company, 1959), p. 119.

quately as anyone who has had a medical examination knows. Instruments have been devised which measure such changes when a person is under emotional strain.

The lie detector which is used in police work records the changes in blood pressure, respiration, and the electrical properties of the skin. The prisoner who is suspected of having done something wrong is asked a series of questions. If, on the questions which have a close connection with the crime, he shows marked changes in blood pressure, respiration and so on, it is supposed that he knows something about the affair. However, there are many factors to be considered in the interpretation of the record. A habitual liar, for example, may show no circulatory changes, or some person may be able to convince himself that his falsehoods are true and thus not become emotionally disturbed.

## Tests of Emotions

Psychologists have been hard at work studying emotions and anxiety but there is much to be learned about this area of behavior. Tests have been worked out which can reveal areas of concern, or of emotional disturbance. Some of them involve answering questions such as: Do you laugh easily? Do you worry too long over humiliating experiences? Do you consider yourself a rather nervous person? Are your feelings easily hurt?

Projective tests are also used in which the individual is asked to tell what he thinks of, or sees, in pictures or designs which are presented to him. This provides an opportunity for the reporting of emotional experiences which are projected into the stimulating material. Analysis of his responses can show the psychologist something about the nature of the individual's typical reactions in the emotional field.

At the same time we should realize that much more experimental work must be done before we can completely understand the emotional make-up of an individual on the basis of such tests.

## Pleasurable Emotion

We have already noted that blocking a person, or holding him back—what the psychologists call *frustration*—will produce a feeling of strain, anger, or annoyance. But when we are successfully carrying out some idea or project, there is a feeling of joy in accomplishment. It has often been pointed out that real pleasure comes, not so much through obtaining something we want, as through making progress toward it.

There is a good bit of satisfaction in winning a football game, but the real thrill of it, for the players or for the spectators as well, is in the contest itself. The excitement of taking part in a race, a basketball game, a debate—this is the reward that is greatest.

When we look back upon our school days as pleasurable, we think of the "going to school" part of it, the daily lessons, and the daily associations; we do not usually think of graduation and the final winning of the diploma.

On the other hand, the feeling that we are "going somewhere," the feeling of success, is very important.

In mental hygiene psychologists often stress the importance of the feeling of success. One writer, Daniel Starch,[2] describes happiness as a "feeling of essential well-being." This means that everything is going along well. We have things to do which we consider worth while, and we feel that we are making progress.

The connection between the physical side of life and the feeling of pleasure and well-being is nicely told by Lin Yutang in this passage from *The Importance of Living*.[3]

To me . . . the truly happy moments are: when I get up in the morning after a night of perfect sleep and sniff the morning air and there is an expansiveness in the lungs, when I feel inclined to inhale deeply and there is a fine sensation of movement around the skin and muscles of the chest, and when, therefore, I am fit for work; or when I hold a pipe in my hand and rest my legs on a chair, and the tobacco burns slowly and evenly; or when I am traveling on a summer day, my throat parched with thirst, and I see a beautiful clear spring, whose very sound makes me happy, and I take off my socks and shoes and dip my feet in the delightful, cool water; or when after a perfect dinner I lounge in an armchair, when there is no one I hate to look at in the company, and conversation rambles off at a light pace to an unknown destination, and I am spiritually and physically at peace with the world; or when on a summer afternoon I see black clouds gathering on the horizon and know for certain a July shower is coming in a quarter of any hour, but being ashamed to be seen going out into the rain without

---

[2] Daniel Starch and others, *Controlling Human Behavior* (New York: The Macmillan Company, 1936), p. 354.

[3] Lin Yutang, *The Importance of Living* (New York: The John Day Company, 1937).

**Habits can cause us to be happy as well as unhappy.**

an umbrella, I hastily set out to meet the shower halfway across the fields and come home drenched through and through and tell my family I was simply caught by the rain.

Professor Starch emphasizes the fact that we often form *habits* which keep us from being happy, as in the case of a person who always seeks to blame everything which goes wrong on somebody else.

"The happy person," says Starch, "is usually too well adjusted to his world to bother about blaming anyone."

## Adjustment to Other People and Emotional Balance

It is most important to recognize that this is a big world, that it contains a lot of people, and that there is room for everybody. We must not expect everyone else to be exactly like ourselves. We must learn early in life that other people are quite likely to have a different way of doing things from the way we are used to. The trouble with many sour, disgruntled people is that they expect everyone to be, and think, the way they do. If we didn't expect everyone who comes along to think and act exactly the way we do, we would all be much happier people.

There have been many instances in which the telephone operator in a disaster area has demonstrated the importance of emotional stability.

*Southern Bell Telephone and Telegraph Co.*

**Learning To Be Tolerant.** This is one of the reasons why part of growing up is learning to be tolerant of "the other fellow." The young, serious student should not be unhappy because there are other young students who do not share his enthusiasm for learning. A young man who dislikes playing cards should not be unhappy because other people like it. It would help many people if, early

in life, they would find out that there are many individual differences in the world and that one way to be happy is to allow the
other fellow to be happy too.

It is an extremely serious matter if any young man or woman
gets the idea that he has the one and only notion of how to live
and what to do, and that everyone else should conform to that
pattern. The idea that is expressed in the old saying, "Live, and
Let Live," is the result of much human experience.

An instance was recently reported in which a young woman
was failing in her senior year in high school because she was in a
miserable frame of mind. She "couldn't stand" the other young
people in her class because "All they ever think about is dancing
and having a good time." So much concerned was she with her
own books and her own ideas, that she was unable to mix with the
group when they departed in the slightest way from agreeing with
her as to what was important and interesting in life.

**Importance of Social Participation.** As a matter of fact, the
serious, studious type of student should deliberately train himself
to take part in social life, "even if it hurts." He should put himself
out considerably to find opportunities to mingle socially with his
fellow students for the simple reason that his study interests—if he
isn't careful—will develop so strongly that they will crowd out these
other kinds of activities, and he will grow up with a very lopsided
personality.

Let the serious student reflect for a moment on the fact that the
best and greatest universities in Europe and America have *deliberately* insisted that their students be active *every day* in some kind
of sports or recreational activities. They don't want lopsided personalities, but real human beings, as graduates.

A friend of the writer once took a trip to Cuba. He thought it
was going to be a fine experience, but he was back in the United
States after one day.

"What in the world happened?" I demanded. "Didn't you like
it?"

"It was terrible," he explained. "I couldn't stand the people,
the food, or anything else. And I couldn't even get a good cup of
coffee."

He complained of the people, the hotel he stayed in, and on
top of it all said, "I couldn't understand the language, anyhow!"

Here was a man who had never learned that other people in the world might be different from himself. He *had* to have everything just the way he was used to it, or he was unhappy. What a pity to grow up with such attitudes! To such an individual the richer opportunities for experiences are entirely closed.

If psychology teaches anything, it teaches the *fact of individual differences*. It teaches the importance of learning to adjust ourselves to the other fellow whose ways and habits of doing things may be a little unlike our own.

**Size Up Your Abilities and Act Accordingly.** It has been suggested that mild, joyful emotions are present when we are functioning well. When we are getting along all right, and meeting successfully the problems of daily living, we feel pleased.

It is important that we maintain good health, secure adequate rest, and undertake only those tasks in which we have reason to believe we can succeed. This calls for considerable understanding of ourselves. Gradually, as we go along through life, we discover what our abilities are, and we gauge our work to meet our difficulties.

Many people are unhappy because they are always taking on jobs for which they are unprepared either in ability, physical strength, or previous experience. Young people need to study their own abilities. They should take advantage of the opportunities for help in this. These are provided in most schools by guidance departments or counselors.

**Learn To See a Job Through.** Once we have accepted a task or an assignment which seems appropriate, we should work on it with confidence and determination until it is completed. We should carry such tasks through, because it is only through successful experience in "finishing jobs" that we build up self-confidence. A feeling of self-confidence doesn't come just by pushing a button or rubbing a magic lamp. It only comes as the gradual result of carrying many different tasks through to a successful conclusion.

**Importance of a Sense of Humor.** It is interesting to note that numerous psychologists have recognized that when we laugh at something funny, there is a relaxation of the mind and body which is very refreshing.

Psychologists have shown that laughing at something *is* relaxation. It is common knowledge that people are much *relieved* if they can have a good laugh over something which has become a little too serious.

Laughter seems to be a natural form of relaxation. We "let ourselves go" for a few minutes or more. The usual result is that we come back to the point of attention quite refreshed.

Sometimes we go on a "laughing spree" as when we attend a humorous play or motion picture. In that case the release from tension is longer and more complete. When we use the expression *release from tension,* we simply mean that under the ordinary conditions of life and work we are all under a certain amount of mental and muscular control. This control requires effort. It produces a sense of strain. Part of it is mental, part of it is emotional, and part of it is physical. We hold ourselves in restrained positions when sitting in class or attending a meeting. The act of paying attention to anything requires a certain amount of this control and builds up tension. It takes bodily energy. That is one reason why there is a sense of let-down or a feeling of relief when something happens to release the control.

When something happens that strikes us as being illogical or peculiar, we are apt to let go of the control for a second or two, and we laugh. Thus it is always much funnier to see a very dignified man slip on a banana peeling, than it is to see a slovenly or careless person do so. Hence we are amused if a very carefully dressed person appears with a button unbuttoned, or with part of his shirttail sticking out—and the more careful he usually is about such details, the more amused we are.

This breakdown of tension often takes place when some highly rigid rule of conduct is unexpectedly broken.

But let us note that the *total situation* determines whether the "slip" is funny or not. We are amused if the circus clown gets pushed off a wagon and falls into the sawdust. We are horrified if he falls from a height and has a serious accident.

It is interesting to note that the relation which an incident has to you as an individual has a great deal to do with deciding whether a break in the tension is funny or not. If you are merely an onlooker at a school play or assembly program, and someone playing a part in the program comes out on the stage at the wrong time, or speaks out of turn, or forgets his lines and looks around uncomfortably for help, it may strike you as being funny and you will laugh with the audience.

But it isn't funny to the director of the play! He feels that he has too much at stake in the performance to see anything funny about it.

In the same way, we can laugh at the misfortunes of others, but find it difficult to be amused at our own misfortunes.

We are often amused when someone does something out of the ordinary.

We may conclude that we are amused when (1) something happens to suddenly disorganize a fixed arrangement of things, or events, or (2) some thing or event suddenly appears which was not expected.

Here are two stories which are funny because they have a "twist" in them which is unexpected:

A professor was working hard one afternoon pouring cement for a new section of the sidewalk in front of his house. A little neighbor boy who was watching him kept touching the new pavement with his foot and the professor didn't like the threat to his work which this situation was producing.

He became more and more annoyed and finally sharply ordered the boy to go home to his own yard.

"You don't like little boys, do you?" asked the small fellow.

"Yes, I like them *in the abstract*," answered the professor, "but not in *the concrete!*"

A superintendent of schools was traveling away from home and went into the hotel dining room for his breakfast. He found that he had forgotten his glasses, and asked the waiter to read the menu to him.

"I'm sorry, boss, I'm just as ignorant as you are," answered the waiter. "I can't read either!"

It is clear that laughter has a relaxing effect, and it aids us to reduce the amount of energy consuming tension which we build up in the ordinary course of our daily living.

Accordingly, we can say that there is a definite place for laughter in everyday life. It is entirely natural and desirable because of the beneficial influence which it has on our health and disposition.

We hardly need to be reminded, of course, that there are occasions when laughter is out of place and undesirable. In other words, we have to learn when it is proper to laugh and when it isn't. We need to avoid laughter when there are other important considerations or when things which have deep and serious meaning to other people are involved. At the same time, the situations in which a certain amount of humor is undesirable are few and far between. People are beginning to realize that it is healthy to laugh and that a smile is welcome.

One more caution: Extremes are to be avoided. No one likes a "wise guy" who is always turning everything into a joke. We might conclude this by noting what two psychologists have to say about humor:

Fortunate is the person who can readily smile. The smile need not be actually present, but if a person's state of mind is such that he may easily smile, he is in a splendid condition of relaxation. The attitude wins a warm social approval and prevents wearing of the nerves. By this susceptibility the mind is kept free from tension and goes on even keel. Humor is thus constantly at hand and the wheels of the mind are kept well oiled.[4]

And:

The world is thankful to the person who can create laughter. There is something about it which sweeps away annoyance, worry, jealousy, and even disgust. Laughter dispels timidity and takes the rough edge off the too aggressive act.[5]

## SOMETHING TO DO

1. Think of a meeting, sports occasion, celebration, or other event which was given emotional quality by planning. What methods were used

[4] William H. Mikesell, *Mental Hygiene* (New York: Prentice-Hall, 1939), p. 364.

[5] Floyd L. Ruch, *Psychology and Life* (Chicago: Scott, Foresman & Co., 1958), p. 214.

to present or suggest stimuli capable of producing the desired emotional results? Be specific and detailed and show the relationship between the details and the tone of the meeting or occasion.

2. Describe a meeting or other occasion which in your opinion was not particularly successful due, at least in part, to lack of attention to planning of this type.

## QUESTIONS AND PROBLEMS FOR STUDY AND DISCUSSION

1. Keep a lookout for some pictures which seem to you to portray various kinds of emotion. Tell why you think they do.

2. Can facial expressions and attitudes portray emotions even though the person himself does not really feel them? Explain.

3. Describe several different kinds of situations in which it is permissible to express some emotions, but not others.

4. Can you give any illustration of how the physical condition of the individual affects his emotional behavior?

5. Show how we can *learn* to make certain kinds of emotional responses to situations or stimuli which would not, in themselves, arouse any emotional response.

6. Prepare an illustration of how emotion *intensifies* behavior.

7. Analyze and make a list of the various kinds of emotions which you have felt in one day.

8. Make a list of various ways in which people react under emotional stress—such as an incident which produces anger. In how many different ways can a person show anger?

9. Can you give an example of the performance of some outstanding feat by someone under the influence of an emotion such as fear?

10. Try to write a description of exactly how you feel under some kind of emotional excitement.

11. From a story, novel, or play, select a passage which in your opinion is very successful in arousing a feeling of emotion on the part of a reader. See if you can pick out the words, expressions, or ideas in the passage which are most emotion-arousing. Can you tell why they have this effect?

12. Can you describe an example in which you think someone was made unhappy or uncomfortable because the behavior of other people was not as expected?

13. How far should people go in being tolerant of other people and their ideas?

14. What is the difference between "sticking to something" until you succeed or carry it through, and "being stubborn"?

15. Can you think of an example of how someone developed a spirit of self-confidence by having a series of successful experiences?

16. Describe an incident from your own experience, which to you was very funny. Then analyze it and indicate what caused it to impress you this way.

17. Can you think of an example of how someone developed a spirit of fear or lack of confidence, as the result of a series of failures? What might have been done to redirect these experiences so that this unfortunate outcome might not have come about?

18. See if you can find a story, joke, or humorous incident which is clearly based on the principle of something unexpected or unusual being done or said.

19. Prepare an illustration of how the use of humor relieved an otherwise unpleasant or tense situation.

# CHAPTER TWELVE

# THE CONTROL OF EMOTIONS

Everyone who realizes the importance of emotions, and who observes how definitely they are linked to mental and physical responses, also recognizes that we need to know as much as possible about how to control them.

While it is true that emotional reactions cannot be eliminated, there are some ways of controlling them. We can control their occurrence—particularly by controlling the situations which give rise to them—and we can do something about our own patterns of behavior. This chapter explains how we can approach this problem. Some suggestions for improving our emotional lives are included.

On the theory that prevention is better than cure, some suggestions are also given for eliminating the likely causes that prompt disturbing emotions to occur.

The chapter includes some further discussion of the importance of emotions in enriching our lives and character.

## QUESTIONS THIS CHAPTER WILL ANSWER

1. Is there any way in which we can control our emotions?
2. What role does habit play in the matter of emotions?
3. If we have built up or learned some unfavorable emotional patterns of behavior, how can they be replaced by better ones?
4. How can sharing emotions with other people help us to face difficult situations?
5. What are some practical rules for controlling undesirable emotions?

## What Psychology Says about Controlling the Emotions

Emotions may be either helpful or harmful. We know that they are both mental and physical in nature, and that their physical influence through the discharges of the glands is a very real thing.

We also know that overdoses of emotion, without appropriate outlet, can be harmful.

Of course, it is not only in a physical sense that emotion can be harmful. It can be harmful to our personalities and to our well-being in society, because uncontrolled emotion keeps us from getting

The injury and shock resulting from a serious accident usually leave the victim with little or no control of the emotions.

*Official U.S. Coast Guard Photo*

along well with people, from doing well in competitive games and sports, from succeeding in schoolwork, and from getting along well on the job.

## The Part Which Habit Plays in Emotions

One of the most important things to take into consideration in connection with controlling emotions is the fact that habits have a great deal to do with them. For example, we can form habits which lead us into emotional experiences, or we can form habits which keep us from emotion-arousing situations.

If some friend of ours, for example, is likely to become upset when a particular topic is referred to, we can avoid mentioning that topic. If particular people make us "mad," we do not have to associate with them, although in the case of business associates, co-workers, and the boss we sometimes do.

An English educator, Sir John Adams, once wrote that we can control our thoughts and feelings a great deal by taking care what subjects we choose to think about. We should not surround our-selves by emotion-arousing stimuli if we don't want to experience certain kinds of emotion or feeling.

We can hardly expect to avoid anger if at the same time we are constantly bringing up subjects which arouse it. A person who is frequently getting into arguments with other people is said to have a "chip on the shoulder attitude."

The important thing to note here is that we don't actually con-trol the emotions themselves (as we know they are the result of an interchange of ideas and physical responses) but *we can control the situations which produce the feelings.* We can control our emotions by keeping away from situations which give us reason to become emotional.

## How Emotions May Become Intense through Brooding

Often we pass from a feeling of slight emotion to one of great emotion because we allow ourselves to "cook up" the emotion. Someone offends us, and we ponder over it too long. We magnify it in our minds until it has ceased being something trivial and has become a thing of tremendous importance. This is usually quite unnecessary. We ought to realize the folly of allowing emotions to accumulate until they reach dangerous proportions.

Habit is involved in this, too. We can, if we want to and if we think about it, form a habit of passing over emotion-arousing situa-tions lightly, or we can form the habit of building them up.

Insofar as we are forming the habit of "shrugging our shoulders" to insults, real or imaginary, we are controlling our emotions. We are keeping them from accumulating to danger points.

## When Emotions Are Good

It would be a great mistake to assume that what has been said about controlling the emotions means that emotions are not of value. It would be a still greater mistake to think that there are not situations in life in which emotion is entirely justified.

There are some things in life about which we ought to get "mad." There is injustice, there is poverty, and there is selfishness. Some people exploit the weak and helpless. When we see these things we should be angry. The story is told of Lincoln, that, when, on his first journey down the Mississippi River to New Orleans, he saw a slave market, he felt so angry about it that he made up his mind that if he ever had an opportunity to break up that traffic, he would do so. In this sense emotion makes possible great deeds. It becomes one of the worthiest assets of human character.

This was recognized long ago when St. Paul wrote:

> And so abideth faith, hope, and love, these three,
> but the greatest of these is love.

The love of a man for his wife, and for his children, the affection of children for their parents; the attachment and loyalty of an individual to his home, his native state, or his own country— these are the things that make life worth while in the final analysis.

It would be difficult to think of life without emotion.

**Emotions Can Serve as a Drive.** How emotion colors the world about us and enriches life may be seen in the following verse which was written by a high-school girl who lived in Wilmington, Delaware. It was printed in a report by the Board of Education of that city. She was describing her school:

> It stands most like a living, breathing scene
> All dignified, this stone, this brick, this wood,
> This happy shell to hold so much of life
> This thoughtful wall preparing us for strife.
> This smiling site to teach us what is good,
> So full of heart, so vigorous, so keen
> It lives, for it is loved by living hearts.
> It smiles, for laughter echoes in the hall,
> Inspires, loves, pities, and imparts
> Its talents, its great knowledge offers all.
> Its beaming windows send out little darts

That shine their way into the soul—and fall.
This ceiling that has answered back
The shout of joyous laughter, bubbling out.
      —JOAN BRADLEY

While emotion can serve as a drive, it must not be stronger than our ability to handle ourselves. We must keep our ability to manage, to think, and to manipulate. The point is illustrated in driving an automobile. If a driver sees that he is approaching a road crossing, with other automobiles approaching at high speed, he must not become so afraid of the danger that he can't handle his car properly. Yet he must be aware of the danger enough to cause him to act quickly, and with accuracy, in handling his steering wheel, his brakes, and his engine.

The school teacher is an important factor in assisting the young person to learn emotional control.

*Courtesy of Myron Cunningham Photography*

Interesting examples of the role of emotions appear in connection with athletics. Should a football team be stirred up emotionally when entering an important game? After a great Yale-Harvard game, the *New York Times* wrote as follows:

## YALE UPSETS HARVARD
### By Robert F. Kelley

CAMBRIDGE, MASS., Nov. 25—Yale's football team today provided the complete answer as to why 52,000 persons would sit in frigid cold weather under sullen grey skies to watch two elevens which have no claims to anything in the way of mythical championships.

On the short end of ridiculous odds and suddenly without their captain and the mainstay of their line, the Elis refused utterly to fit in with the predestined scheme of the fifty-eighth game between Yale and Harvard and added one more wildly exciting upset to the history of this ancient classic of the gridiron.

Late in the afternoon, with one set of goal posts already down, the original ball the teams were playing with in the grip of hysterical celebrants, the game ended and the electric lights of Harvard's score board read: Yale, 20; Harvard, 7.

In those figures was all the drama of the unexpected, but in the actual play itself there was even more. Yale, granted only the slimmest of fighting chances, slammed from its own 42-yard line to a touchdown in the second period. Then, on the rising tide of emotion and fight, the Elis took full advantage of the two chances presented to them by Crimson miscues to add two more touchdowns and leave not the slightest doubt among those present as to which was the better team of the day.

Yale, probably, could not have done this in any other game. But the depth of tradition which lies behind these contests acted today to bring the Blue to the heights. Last week, against a really fine Princeton team, Yale almost accomplished the impossible. Today it did just that, and the excitement of the cold dark finale has not been equaled here in some years.

Harvard, scoring its only touchdown less than a minute from the end, kicked the extra point, and celebrants, already down on the field, grabbed the ball and fought over it. A new ball was provided, but the police had to fight off spectators from the goal posts before the game could go on into the last few plays. Then, before the end, one of the goal posts was tottering, and the instant the final whistle blew, Yale's stands poured their populace out on the field to dance in celebration and to subject their players to a worse mauling than they had received in the game.

For the Crimson there was only bitter disappointment. . . . In bare outline, that was the story of today's game. But it fails utterly to give the background which injected itself into its drama. Last night it was learned there was a chance Yale would have to play without its captain and center today. That news was reflected in the odds of 5 to 2 this morning when it was confirmed that the concussion suffered by Bill Stack in the Princeton game would keep him out. But the reaction was entirely different on the players of Yale. It meant simply there was more reason for them to play better than they knew how, and they went out and did it. . . . Yale made only four first downs to Harvard's eleven and gained fewer yards, but it also made fewer mistakes, and the Elis came through to an earned and clear-cut victory.

Here was a football game in which the underdog won by sheer fighting spirit, if we may believe what the reporters said. That is, they were "keyed up" emotionally to such an extent that they made every opportunity count, tried plays they would ordinarily have been reluctant to attempt, and by "fight" earned the gains and the touchdowns necessary to win.

We may be quite sure, however, that the Yale players knew the game of football. They already possessed certain knowledge and certain skills. When, to these, a high degree of emotional excitement was added (but not enough to interfere with their mastery of the skills), it made the difference between winning or losing the game.

Incidentally, it is rather well agreed that the teams are not easily kept at such a high pitch. Often a football team will "point" for a particular game, counting on the excitement of the day to bring victory. Then there will be a letdown—and often the same team will lose in a subsequent game to an inferior opponent. This is further evidence of the importance of emotions in behavior.

## Reconditioning Emotions

Two main methods recognized by psychologists for learning how to control emotions have been mentioned so far. The first one was to learn to avoid situations which produce undesirable emotion. The second was to work at building the habit of treating emotion-arousing situations lightly.

Another method of assisting in control of the emotions has been pointed out by psychologists. This is what is sometimes called the method of *reconditioning*. Without going into the technical problems involved, we can note that this simply means linking up stimuli which produce a feeling of ease, or confidence, with the situation or thing which is causing the emotion. If we take the emotion of fear as an example, we can see that one way to *recondi-*

*tion* people so that they won't be afraid is to have them experience some joy or pleasure in connection with or at the same time as they experience the thing which has been making them afraid.

One psychologist reconditioned a little boy who was afraid of a rabbit to like the rabbit by giving him some ice cream or candy to eat every time he saw the rabbit. In another case a boy who was afraid of the noise of fire engines was made to lose his fear by being taken to see the fire engines.

Unreasonable childish fears can be overcome by reconditioning.

Can we *recondition* ourselves? We can, to some extent. For example, if we are afraid to stay in a lonely house, we may make sure that we have some good book to read, or some interesting task to work on—something pleasant and agreeable to associate with the experience of staying in the lonely house. Whistling or humming when in a situation of danger has often kept a man from being overcome by fear. Possibly this is a form of conditioning in that a pleasure-arousing activity is associated with the thing which makes us afraid. There is also the fact that the actual physical expression of singing, humming, or whistling has the effect of producing a feeling of confidence, or well-being, which counteracts the impulse to be afraid or disturbed.

## Influence of Experience on the Control of Emotions

Although it may not seem so at the time, the actual meeting of emotion-arousing situations, if accompanied by success, tends to lessen the possibility of the emotion developing later. For example, many passengers are afraid of riding in airplanes. However, after they have tried it and have landed safely, they frequently feel very much less fearful. If they make a number of flights of this kind, their fear is lessened by each successful experience.

In the case of fear of any kind, it is possible to lessen the frequency of the occurrence of the fear, and the intensity of the feeling, by this method. William Burnham, in a book entitled *The Normal Mind,* gave us one of the prescriptions for overcoming fear, "Do the thing you are afraid of."

This is not always as easily done as said. However, if the individual can bring himself to a realization of the soundness of this principle, it may be used successfully on many fear-arousing occasions.

Needless to say, the admonition to "Do the thing you are afraid of," is not an invitation to foolhardiness in situations where danger is actually present to a serious degree. It is, rather, a suggestion which can be used effectively where the fear is largely the result of the individual's imagination.

A middle-aged woman was afraid to ride on the elevated railroad in Chicago, and for many years did not go downtown when this method of transportation was involved. It seems that in this instance her fear was quite unnecessary and that if she had tried it several times without alarming results, a source of considerable worry would have been removed from her life.

There are other kinds of fear which are sometimes caused by deep-seated conflicts or feelings of insecurity in the individual's life, which cannot be so readily overcome. But often these may be actually lessened or at least the number of situations producing them may be brought under greater control by "doing the thing you are afraid of."

## Effect of Group Activity on Emotions

Working in a group tends to lessen fear. Often a fear which the individual would find it impossible to overcome may be lessened by associating with other people.

In group therapy a group of individuals is formed for the purpose of studying each other's anxieties and problems together. This experience is helpful for many people because it gives them a chance to share their difficulties with others and it teaches them that other people, too, have similar problems. That this is successful

In present day labor-management conferences, men strive to replace emotions with intelligent reasoning. This group is comprised of labor union heads, directors of industrial relations of two large industries, and university personnel.

*Studebaker-Packard Corporation*

in dealing with activities which are partly emotional in nature is shown by the success of "Alcoholics Anonymous," widely known at the present time as an organization which seeks to bring together in friendly association individuals who have formed damaging habits of excessive drinking.

The *sharing* of experience with other people facing the same problem gives each individual a better chance of meeting his own personal problem.

We can certainly overcome many forms of fear by associating with other people. One of the most important things for us to realize is the fact that other people have emotional problems too. Other people are fearful. Other people get angry. Other people feel depressed.

This *sharing* of human experience is one of the keys to happier living. It is one of the reasons why social and religious groups have been successful in meeting the needs of people through the years.

## Sharing Emotional Experiences with Others

In connection with the emotion of anger it is possible to illustrate the value of sharing emotional feeling with others. Sometimes an individual who feels that he has been wronged or who feels as if he is being mistreated develops a very strong feeling of resentment or anger.

If he broods over this the resentment tends to grow and become more intensive. He gets "madder every minute."

Often it is helpful for the individual who finds himself in this situation to talk it over with a friend. The very act of "getting it off his chest" or "blowing off steam" as we may call it, helps to reduce the emotional feeling and restore the individual to a more normal balance. This is one of the ways of dealing with strong emotion which should be considered along with the others.

In individual therapy a counselor or a psychologist works individually with a single person in helping him to explore his problems and discover the causes of his difficulties. This is becoming increasingly available in communities, and in schools and colleges, as more people are trained for this type of work.

## Knowledge Lessens Some Emotions

Another suggestion which psychology has for us is that we may overcome many fears and worries by getting to understand better what it is that we are afraid of, and why we are afraid. Worry and anxiety are often caused because we do not understand, we do not know.

If we know the habits and behavior of rattlesnakes, we are less likely to be afraid upon meeting them. If we know the nature of certain diseases or ailments, and how they can be treated, we are less likely to be afraid. It is when we do *not* know the nature of the thing, the animal, the machine, or the situation, that we tend to be afraid.

Long ago it was written: "Knowledge casteth out fear."

We should add to our suggestions for controlling emotions, the idea that when we suspect a fear or worry is caused by lack of knowledge or information, we should get the information or knowledge which we need.

## Learn To Delay Action When Emotionally Aroused

Also important in emotions, particularly in connection with emotions of rage or anger, is the idea of doing something to delay giving in to the emotion. We are told to "think twice" before we act, or "count to ten." Here again, the old-fashioned advice is generally true and sound. The delay, the second thought, often causes us to be less emotional.

Some writers point out that every time we "give in" to a rash or emotional impulse to act, that type of action becomes easier, and restraint becomes harder. Evidently we become more and more capable of controlling our emotions if we will practice controlling them. We become less and less able to control our emotions when we continually yield to rash impulses.

A football player who later became quite well known had gotten into the habit of settling controversies with his fists. All his life this was the way he had settled his disputes with other boys.

But when he began to play on a college football team, he had to use greater restraint. It took him two years to learn to "hold back" when arguments arose. It was only after having the humiliating experience of being "benched" during a number of important games that he began to learn that he would have to curb his impulse to fight.

Penalizing emotional outbursts aids in teaching self-control.

The more intelligently we meet problems, the less emotional we become. Another suggestion of psychology is that the more capable we become in meeting different kinds of problems, the less likely we will be carried away by our emotions. Very often, it is because we don't know what to do that we yield to emotion. The more we study, the more we learn about meeting problems; the more we train ourselves, the less often will we find ourselves in "emotional jams."

This leads to the thought that one of the most important things of all is to learn how to get along with other people. Getting along with people is all-important. As one writer put it:[1]

[1] J. J. B. Morgan, *Child Psychology* (New York: Rinehart & Company, Inc., 1942), p. 187.

It happens that the most important part of our environment consists of people rather than things, so that effective emotional behavior must be the sort that will affect better adjustments to people.

If we can understand what causes other people to do the things they do, we have begun to learn how we should act toward them. This is the first step. If we can learn this, our inquiries into the nature of psychology will be worth while.

## Summary of Ways To Control Undesirable Emotion

The suggestions of psychology for learning how to control undesirable emotion could be summarized in these simple statements:

1. Learn to avoid situations which arouse undesirable emotion.
2. Cultivate the habit of passing over provoking situations. Learn to keep from allowing strong emotion to accumulate.
3. See if it isn't possible to connect pleasant or satisfying experiences with situations which you find are likely to arouse an undesirable emotion, such as fear.
4. Get more information or knowledge about things which make you afraid, or which make you worry.
5. Practice, as often as possible, the policy of holding back, or delaying, the act of giving in to an undesirable emotional impulse, such as anger.
6. Acquire understanding and skill in meeting life's situations and problems. Keep on with your education and training because it will help you to reduce the number of situations which make you unnecessarily emotional.
7. Study and practice the art of getting along with people.
8. Form friendships and associate with groups of people. Recognize that as a human being you need the fellowship of others.

### SOMETHING TO DO

Select some form of emotional response which you are making which is not good for you, and which you feel you should correct. Describe the emotion, the circumstances under which it is aroused, and the effect it has on you and on your behavior.

1. Outline a series of steps or things you might do which might be expected, over a period of time, to improve your behavior in connection with this particular emotion. Write these down briefly.

2. Refer to this list of suggestions from time to time and experiment for three or four weeks by trying to apply one or more of the suggestions.

3. At the end of the experimental period—say four weeks—write a brief account of what you did and what, in your opinion, the results were.

## QUESTIONS AND PROBLEMS FOR STUDY AND DISCUSSION

1. Describe some of the characteristics of a person who seems very capable in the matter of controlling his emotions.

2. Find a newspaper story illustrating an incident which resulted from apparent lack of emotional control.

3. Report on an example from your own or another person's experience of *reconditioning* emotion.

4. Give an illustration of how additional information or knowledge helped you to overcome an emotion or worry.

5. For your own use, make a list of some of the unnecessary situations which you sometimes allow yourself to get into, which arouse undesirable emotion.

6. Give an example of how an emotional feeling can be modified or reduced by engaging in some substitute activity.

7. Explain the influence of *belonging to a group* on emotional control.

8. Explain what is meant by *reconditioning* emotions.

9. Why are we sometimes told to "Do the thing you are afraid of"?

10. Explain how habit enters into the matter of emotion.

11. Give an example of how sharing an emotion with another made it possible for you to bring that emotion under control.

12. Suppose you came across this statement in your reading: "All emotions are physical. You have them because you are made the way you are. There isn't anything you can do about it." What would your comment be?

13. Can you give an example in which whistling or singing helped you to keep up your spirits in a situation likely to arouse fear?

14. Explain the statement that emotions are often good.

15. Explain why learning how to get along with people is considered important in connection with emotional control.

# CHAPTER THIRTEEN

# SOME ADJUSTMENTS WE MAKE

There are quite a few peculiarities of behavior which all of us show at times. Some of them can only be explained on the theory that we have problems to meet, and we don't always know how to meet them.

Some of these peculiarities of behavior are useful when you consider them as means of adjusting to difficulties—but they can also be harmful. We need to recognize these adjustment mechanisms for what they are. In this chapter we find the more common ones described and explained.

Understanding these adjustment mechanisms can help us in understanding other people, as well as in understanding ourselves.

Some adjustment mechanisms are quite common in the literature of psychology, but they are not always understood by the average reader. They include: rationalization, substitution, sublimation, projection, daydreaming, identification, repression, and regression. There are several forms of rationalization.

These adjustment mechanisms have some interesting influences on our social and political customs, and these are pointed out. In the latter part of the chapter, some useful suggestions are made for facing problems and coming up with satisfactory solutions.

## QUESTIONS THIS CHAPTER WILL ANSWER

1. What are some of the common, but important, adjustments we have to make?

2. What are the so-called *adjustment mechanisms* of which psychologists write?

3. How are these adjustment mechanisms explained? What kind of behavior do they lead to?

4. What are some of the *better* ways of adjusting to problems of this type?

5. Why is it said that goals or purposes will help us to make better adjustments?

6. How is this related to our philosophy of life?

## How Do You Behave When Facing Problems?

When people face problems, what do they do? If you answer that it depends on the problem, you are right—in part. It also depends on the person. It depends on his ability, his training, and his judgment. And it depends on a number of habits and attitudes which he has formed in past situations of a similar kind. It depends on those traits of his which we think of in connection with character and personality.

The problem of adjustment to an entirely different way of living is being facilitated for these eighteen-year-olds by an informal chat with Major General James C. Christiansen, C. G.

*Official U.S. Army Photo*

It also depends on how he perceives his problem, and how he perceives himself in relation to the problem. For example, what appears to be a problem to some people does not seem like a problem at all to others. From one point of view you don't have a problem unless you see that you have a problem. Moreover, whether a problem is a big problem or a little problem, to you, depends in part on how adequate you feel that you are in your ability to master the problem.

For example, many tests which are given in connection with schoolwork include questions having to do with arithmetic. If you are taking such a test, and you feel confident of your ability in arithmetic, you will regard these questions as relatively easy, and you will perceive yourself as quite able to do all right on them. On the other hand, if you think of yourself as very incompetent in arithmetic, you will feel unsure of yourself and you will consider this part of the test as "threatening" to you. So the same test will be differently regarded by different people, depending on how they perceive the test and how they perceive themselves in relation to it.

As a result of this, they will adopt different kinds of behavior toward the test.

But whatever else may be said, we may be sure of one thing. Everyone meets his problems *in one way or another*. It may be good or it may be bad. There are good adjustments and there are bad adjustments.

Certain rather definite ways of meeting problems are called *adjustment mechanisms* in psychology. These will be discussed presently, but first let's look at a list of some of the situations in life which we all face, and to which we must make adjustments. Sometimes we meet these situations successfully, sometimes we don't. Often they create conflicts and difficulties for us. They all present problems.

1. Meeting and getting along with members of the opposite sex.
2. Getting along with members of the family.
3. In school, getting along with the principal and the teachers.
4. Getting along with one's classmates, one's working companions, and with the neighbors.
5. Working out the problem of what to do with one's money.
6. Deciding what kind of job or vocation to take up—also getting ready for it, and getting it after we are ready for it.
7. Making progress in a job.
8. Making decisions about church or Sunday School. Deciding what to do about religious beliefs and faiths. Adjusting your own beliefs, or those of your parents, to those which other people hold.
9. Getting assignments done satisfactorily in school or on the job, especially when difficulties arise.
10. Facing examinations and learning how to adjust to passing or failing them.
11. Making decisions about joining clubs or organizations.
12. Deciding what to do and "facing the issue" when our friends want us to do one thing, and our parents, another.
13. Figuring out what to do about moral and ethical problems involving honesty, fair play, promises, and confidences.

14. Deciding what to do about clothes—what clothes to get, when to wear them, and *how* to wear them.

15. Making choices about how to spend leisure time.

16. Adjusting to serious happenings in life, such as the loss of friends or dear ones through death or accident or other causes.

17. Managing one's self and one's feelings when obliged to be separated from home and friends, as at the time of going away on a long trip or vacation, or moving to another town or place.

18. Meeting and getting along with people who are either older or younger than ourselves.

19. Making decisions about more education for self-improvement.

20. Making decisions about a change of job.

These are just a few of the problems in which we find it necessary to make decisions and to make adjustments. These are the places where we look for the stresses and strains. These are the problems which must be adjusted to.

Now here is a very important psychological fact. When we are not able to make these adjustments successfully, especially over a period of time, we often resort to or fall back on ways of behaving which may not be especially desirable. They may become habits and produce attitudes which are not good. These more or less unsatisfactory—though at times necessary—ways of behaving are the *adjustment mechanisms* which have been mentioned.

We shall consider some of the more common of them. We must remember that some of them are more serious than others. We must also remember that they are not always bad. They may actually help us over a rough spot in life—but when they are overdone, they may hinder more than they help. When they keep us from getting our work done, or from doing as well as we might, or from developing a full and rich personality, they can be distinctly harmful. It is well, then, to be aware of them and to recognize them for what they are.

In discussing them a few psychological terms or expressions will be used. The first of these is *rationalization*.

## Rationalization

Rationalization is a process in which the individual "thinks up" reasons for his failure to make an adjustment, or to accomplish something which should have been done. He gives reasons which are not the real reasons, but which sound possible. It is a way we have of excusing ourselves for our shortcomings and offenses.

The boy who is late in getting home from school, when questioned about it, may say, "I had to stop to see Bob about Friday's basketball game on the way home." The fact is ignored that this may have taken just ten minutes, and he was more than an hour late.

A businessman who takes off time to go golfing, may not simply say, "I like to go golfing", in explanation. He may say, and is more likely to say, "Getting out in the fresh air once a week is absolutely necessary for my health."

These are very simple examples. It is not hard to see that we may form a regular habit of excusing many things this way. Incidentally, most people seem to feel a need for explaining practically everything they do. This seems to show that we are constantly "on guard" lest we be criticized. How strong this is, is shown by the fact that the person who does not take the trouble to explain himself is thought, often, to be a little "peculiar." He is sometimes said to be "unconventional."

At the same time it is true that rationalization can be carried so far that we become less responsible and less dependable than we should be. One who makes too many excuses is not liked.

**The "Sour Grapes" Mechanism.** Several different kinds of rationalization can be noted. One type which some writers have called attention to is the *sour grapes* type. For example, a high-school student who fails to be selected for a part in the class play might comment to one and all "The play's no good, anyhow." He might say, "I wouldn't be in that show if they paid me for it!"

Or a student who could not be admitted to a college of his choice might remark, "That place is just an overgrown country club, anyhow." Students will probably not have much trouble in thinking of other examples of this type of mechanism.

**Giving Up Too Easily.** Another type of rationalization which occurs sometimes is the kind in which the individual takes a sort of Pollyanna attitude about his difficulties or failures. It is the "we're really very happy here" sort of thing.

Realizing that he can never obtain a desired promotion, the office worker may say, "The job I have now just suits me. I doubt if anyone could have a job more suited to himself than mine is."

The mother whose children have just gone through a siege of chicken pox may say, "We were lucky; they might have had the measles and whooping cough, too."

This "making the best of what you have" attitude is a satisfying way of adjusting to difficulties at times and is probably helpful.

But it can be a brake on progress if carried too far. The person, or the family, which "gives up" and does not strive for better things may acquire traits which are not desirable. Any city in which the people shut their eyes to crime, poverty, or disease—and say "Things might be a great deal worse here"—is certainly not likely to be a very good place to live.

During the depression which created much poverty and hunger and hardship in the United States in 1931 and 1932, a well-known man was quoted as saying that the depression was a blessing. He said it was "good discipline" for the people.

When we consider that undoubtedly this prominent man was very well fed and comfortable throughout all of the depression, the attitude is almost shocking. Instead of trying to do something about it, he rationalizes in Pollyanna style and says that after all a lot of good will come out of it. This must have been very consoling to the unfortunate and starving people!

Let's not rationalize like this if there is something we can do which would make things better.

**Evading Responsibility.** Yet another form of adjustment mechanism is the kind of rationalization in which we escape from blame by putting the responsibility somewhere else.

The child says, "I didn't soil my dress. Teddy (the dog) did it." A man is late for work in the morning because "the car wouldn't start." Sometimes the excuses are partly right. But often the individual should have been more careful.

Parents sometimes encourage their children to make excuses like this. The mother says, when the little boy runs into the door which is standing open, "That nasty door! To hurt little Johnny!" That doesn't teach Johnny very much about watching where he is going.

A student reports that he couldn't write an assignment because "The books were all out of the library." That does not really excuse the student if the real trouble was that he did not make an effort to get to the library before the last minute. Many a student blames the teacher—"She didn't explain it right." How hard did he try to understand it? Did he ask questions about the thing which was not clear to him?

The type of rationalizing in which we place the blame on someone else is our way of feeling comfortable about the mistakes for which we have actually been either entirely or partly responsible.

## Substitution and Sublimation

These mechanisms of adjustment occur when we are unable to carry out some activity which we would very much like to enjoy, or when some goal or wish is denied us by force of circumstances. What we desire is *blocked* or, to use a word often used by the psychologists, is *frustrated*.

Accordingly, we turn to something else as a substitute. In some cases the thing we do is not as good as the alternative behavior would have been. When the behavior we substitute is not as good as the other would have been, we call it *substitution*. But when we select another goal which is a good and satisfactory one, then we call the new behavior *sublimation*.

Skiing is a splendid activity. It often makes less satisfactory adjustments unnecessary. These young ski enthusiasts from the Denver area represent some 900 members of the Eskimo Club engaging in a week-end of fun.

*Denver Post*

**How Substitution Creates Bad Habits.** Substitution may be illustrated by the worker who, failing to get along well in his work, spends all of his spare time in a pool room or at some social club.

**Escape mechanisms do not solve problems.**

Perhaps he can be moderately successful at pool, or in playing cards, so he spends his time that way. He "forgets" the routine of the job. Many time-wasting things which people do are explained in exactly this way. When someone takes up gambling or drinking, it may be this mechanism which is at work.

These are also called *escape* mechanisms. In society men have often turned to drinking to escape from the feeling of failure or disappointment brought about by some inability on their part to get along, at work, or at home. A sign on a tavern bears this inscription: "Come in and drink your cares away."

This kind of drinking may become very dangerous. Drinking to escape from something is probably the worst form of drinking and is likely to lead to still more disappointment, failure, and misery.

**How Sublimation Produces Good Results.** On the other hand, when the alternate activity to which a person turns is a good one, we have an example of *sublimation*—and this may be a very useful form of adjustment mechanism. It probably explains many of the good things which are done in the world. We have many people in the world, who, failing to achieve success in something important to them, have turned to something else and having worked hard at it made an outstanding success.

A college professor had his heart set on a trip to Europe. Just at the last minute his wife became sick and he could not go. He turned to gardening in his back yard, and resolved that he would have the best garden in the whole community. He worked hard at it, overcame his feeling of disappointment, and actually did produce a garden which was the admiration of all the neighbors.

A young woman who was disappointed when her plans for

marriage failed, became a nurse. She was outstanding in her profession. There are many examples like this. People have *sublimated* some deep disappointment, and made good.

## Displacement and Projection

*Displacement* occurs when we transfer our feelings from one person or object to another person or object. One psychologist gives the following example.[1]

Having teased and irritated his wife to the point of explosion, Mr. Baker put on his hat and left for the office. Mrs. Baker was thoroughly wrought up. Her husband had dodged like a coward; he flung those taunts and accusations at her and lit out; she was chained to that house and the confining routine of it with no chance to get back at him. He could leave, yes, and he could forget it all in a few minutes, but she must wash dishes and sweep and make beds, and do all the things that give you too much time to think. The smallness of that last remark, the insinuating nastiness of it! After all she had tried to do to help him get somewhere in the world —no more appreciation than that! To trump up all those taunts and accusations!

Just then her five-year-old son came bursting into the house from his play outdoors. "Mother! Mother! Mother! Listen. Harold and I have got a swell stunt. We're going over to his house and get a wheelbarrow and make it into—"

That's as far as he got. He had tracked a little mud onto the porch. It was not much, but it was infuriating. Mrs. Baker fairly screamed. She jerked the child into the house; she shook him. She pointed at the mud and at his feet and harangued the child as if he had stepped in blood. He burst into tears, which only made her the angrier. She seized the hairbrush and whacked him vigorously. Howls of protest mingled with scoldings and recriminations.

Here the mother has transferred her feelings of hostility toward her husband to her son.

*Projection* occurs when an individual attributes the thoughts or feelings he has to another person. Thus an individual who has stolen merchandise from a store may find the thought of having done this so unbearable that upon the most innocent remark from Jones he convinces himself that Jones thinks he is guilty. To exclude the thought that he is guilty from his consciousness he accuses Jones of having stolen merchandise even though Jones did not do so. He

---

[1] Karl A. Menninger, *The Human Mind* (New York: Alfred A. Knopf, 1930), pp. 280, 281.

denies he stole any merchandise and ascribes to Jones his thought of guilt, thereby retaining a certain integrity or self-respect.

**How Projection Explains Many Things Which are Wrong and Cruel.** Undoubtedly this mechanism would explain the severe mistreatment which people sometimes mete out to others. It might explain the hard-boiled attitude of many a boss toward his employees. It might explain the harshness of a foreman toward the men working under him, or the severity of a farmer toward his hired man, or the cruelty of a poor southern white share-cropper toward a Negro.

The same mechanism is sometimes found to be showing itself in whole groups of people, perhaps even whole nations. When a large social group "picks on" a smaller group, or a minority group as it is called, and tries to blame that group for its misfortunes, we have an example of it.

Psychologists would say that the attitude of the Nazi Germans toward the Jews before and during World War II was an example of this mechanism of projection—this placing of the blame on some person, or group, or thing outside of or beyond ourselves. Sometimes it is called *scapegoating*. The person or minority group is the scapegoat for the crowd.

**The Danger of Projection in Our Own Group.** This sort of thing happens so often that it is well for us to understand it. In our own group there may be someone or even several persons on whom we— if we are not careful—might unthinkingly want to place the blame for things that go wrong. Or we might want to "take it out" on them. Thinking, intelligent people would abhor this, but it is well to know that it happens. In the United States such groups as the Jews, Negroes, Mexicans, and others are sometimes placed in this position.

Somehow or other this placing of the blame on someone else can be especially mean and cruel because it is done with such severity, as we have seen in the attitude of the Nazi Germans toward the Jews. It is a vicious tendency which accounts for many acts of injustice which occur in rioting and in war.

## Daydreaming

This is more easily recognized than some of the adjustment mechanisms we have been describing. We get a picture of an office clerk sitting dreamily at his desk, his head on his hands and his thoughts far away.

But daydreaming can occur almost any time and place when the duties and responsibilities of the situation are not forcing us to be active. We daydream on a bus or streetcar, while sitting in church, in assembly, or even in a social group if we do not find what is going on to be very stimulating.

Sometimes the important things are left undone because of daydreaming.

What happens is that in our imagination we dream of more pleasant and interesting things. We imagine ourselves to be enjoying experiences which in our present everyday life we are not obtaining. Perhaps we are making great speeches, or running football plays which will bring the crowd to its feet cheering. Or we may be a movie actress opening her fan mail. Or we may be going to a dance with someone we admire.

Yes, daydreaming is a make-believe world of pleasures not coming our way in the cold reality of everyday life.

It is not especially harmful—except when we are doing it so much and so often that it is keeping us from completing our work or when it is interfering with our necessary adjustments.

It is obvious that the student who spends too much time daydreaming may miss important information which he actually needs to get on with his subjects.

Aside from the pleasure of daydreaming, it may have some

positive values sometimes. If we dream of possibilities which we may sometime carry out—as Thomas Edison, Henry Ford, the Wright brothers, and Richard Halliburton did—then the daydreams may have a real value. Such dreams become motives leading to action.

But we need to beware of allowing the whole thing to end with daydreaming, while the important things we need to do go undone.

## Identification

Here is an adjustment mechanism which is interesting. Identification is the tendency to put ourselves in the role of others who are successful, or to connect up our own personalities with those of outstanding people we admire.

It explains the high-school girl who wants to wear the hair-do of a favorite movie star; it explains the high-school boy who dresses and imitates some star of stage or screen, or some noted athlete.

Here again, there can be little harm in such identification, unless it prevents the individual from developing his own good qualities. After all, perhaps some hero-worshipping is a good thing. The point is, though, that it ought not to interfere with "being yourself."

One other idea has been brought out in psychology. It is the thought that people have a tendency to link themselves up with organizations which are outstanding and successful or which have prestige. Thus boys and girls will want to be known as members of a school which is recognized and admired in the community. Or they will want to wear the badge of a club or fraternity which is well known. If athletes, they'll want to be "letter men."

This is such a prevailing tendency that it is a powerful force in our society. It makes us loyal to our school, branch of the service, club, town, state, and nation. It is important, because when we are loyal, we will usually work for the best things for our groups and our communities. This kind of identification is a good thing.

## Suppression and Repression

*Suppression* occurs when an individual will deliberately force himself not to think about a certain episode. When someone says to himself, "I will not think about my quarrel with my boss now when I am trying to study," he is suppressing this thought. It might also be thought of as deliberately not responding to some thought or wish which one considers undesirable. Thus an angry man may avoid showing his anger, a jealous man at a party may conceal his jealousy, or a saddened individual may hold back his manifestations of grief. You will note that suppression is voluntary.

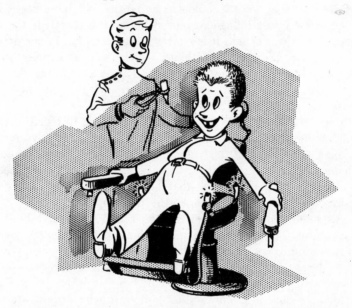

Suppressing an unpleasant experience with "No! It really didn't bother me at all."

*Repression* occurs when an individual's unconscious activity prevents some memory, feeling, or thought from entering the area of conscious attention. We force from conscious attention some wish or idea which is not acceptable to us.

If, for example, we promised to meet a friend, did not, and never apologized to him, we may "forget" this act toward him. This repressed experience may later result in an irrational dislike toward him even though we are unaware of its origin. We may imagine that our dislike arises from his acts, not from our own. The act of repression occurs without our being aware that it is happening. It is involuntary.

Some psychologists hold that it is impossible to repress entirely a wish or desire. This is usually referred to as the Freudian view. The reference is to the writings of the psychologist Sigmund Freud. He felt that all wishes and desires—if repressed—merely retire into a realm of the mind which he called the *subconscious*. From that point, the repressed wish or desire might exert an influence on us even though we would be unaware of it.

Many present-day psychologists agree that our basic needs and wishes exert a deep influence on us—whether it is exactly in the way Freud said it was or not. It is interesting to note that in our dreams we sometimes see or do the things which we can't express in our everyday lives. This suggests that there is some truth in the idea that just because wishes and desires are repressed, they are not gone entirely from our mental make-up.

Dreams are not to be ashamed of. It is absurd to regard dreams which involve some ideas and wishes which are seemingly immoral or "bad" as a sign that the individual having the dream should be ashamed. Quite the opposite is true. It is a sign that he is a person of character and self-control—that he *does* repress the wishes and desires which he considers unworthy or inappropriate.

Although some psychologists have raised questions about the advisability of repression or suppression as modes of adjustment, it is interesting to note that such forms of behavior are not only indispensable, at times, but they may be defended in certain cases on the ground that they allow the individual "time" in which to overcome some of the difficulties confronting him, or in which to mature sufficiently to permit other more satisfactory adjustments to develop.

Often talking over an unpleasant experience with a sympathetic friend, family member, or counselor can help us avoid unhealthful suppression as well as repression.

## Regression

This is the last of the group of adjustment mechanisms which we shall consider. It simply refers to the tendency to *regress* or go back to some childish form of response when we are confronted by difficulties or problems which it seems we can't face.

One of the commonest examples would be that of crying—or bursting into tears—when we are "in a jam."

Sometimes crying offers relief—when we are under great tension.

**Regression is generally ineffective in solving problems.**

There are times when our grief or disappointment is almost too great to bear. Crying makes us feel better. That is, it provides relief from the tension.

Usually regression isn't very constructive. We need to do something about the situations which present us with difficulties. Crying won't help very often.

In other words, regression to childish ways of responding is not ordinarily considered good. The world expects something of us. And growing up involves learning how to make better responses than we usually find in the adjustment of regression.

## Better Ways of Making Adjustments

These various adjustments which we have been describing contain many interesting explanations of why we do the things we do. Certainly knowing about them, and why they occur, can help us to improve our own adjustment.

From time to time we need to take a look at ourselves to see whether or not our ways of doing things are the way we would like them to be. It is very easy for us to fall into the habit of rationalizing, instead of correcting some slipshod way we have of working. It's a good idea to "stand off and take a good look at ourselves" occasionally just to check up on the extent to which we may be employing some of the more undesirable adjustment mechanisms—perhaps without even realizing that we are doing it.

But what are some of the ways in which we can make better adjustments? What does psychology have to say about these?

The first suggestion is that which many psychologists have pointed out. We need to learn how to face our problems honestly and fully, and make a direct attack on them.

**Analyze Your Problem and Plan to Meet It.** This means that we try to analyze the situation we are in. We face it squarely. We do not run away from the problem or pretend that the problem doesn't exist. We analyze the problem and our ability to meet it. Then we work out a plan which we think is the best plan. We might take two examples:

1. *The problem of not getting along well in one's school work.* The direct attack means that we will stop long enough to inquire into the causes of this situation. The student asks himself: What are the causes of my difficulty? Perhaps he asks his teachers to help him to analyze it. If the trouble lies in not having good study habits, he seeks to set up better work habits and better conditions under which to study and work.

If the trouble lies in the fact that he cannot read as well as he should, he practices reading and seeks advice on forming better reading habits.

If there are things he should know which he does not know, he tries to get the necessary training and background to make a better attack on his present problem.

These are direct ways of facing it.

2. *The problem of not getting along well with other people.* This problem may be faced squarely by studying what it is about us that keeps us from succeeding in our relations with others.

We subject ourselves to self-criticism. We raise the question: Why is it? What am I doing that is wrong? Do I have habits which are annoying others? What are they?

There is scarcely a person who cannot discover, by a little bit of self-analysis, ways of doing things or mannerisms which can be corrected or improved. But we have to know what these faults are before we can improve them.

We can seek the help of others, and the advice of counselors. Direct attack on the problem helps us to do this.

In studying our problems, we also need to be realistic. It has been previously suggested that we need to get a better picture of our own abilities and interests.

Counselors and teachers always like to talk things over with persons who have problems.

*NEA Counseling Picture*

**Choose Goals You Can Attain.** We need to choose goals which we have a reasonably good chance of achieving. One psychologist tells of a young man who did not have very much ability in school work, but who wanted to be a doctor. He undertook some tests of ability and aptitude which the counselor was able to provide for him. When he realized that he did not have the mental ability or scholastic ability to succeed in the long program of training necessary to complete the work of the medical school, he was ready to listen to other suggestions.

A *related* goal was suggested. The young man turned to the idea of being a mortician. After the necessary training and education —less extensive than would have been needed to be a doctor—he entered successfully into this line of work.

The famous American man of the theater—George M. Cohan—wanted to write a serious play. But he was not successful in this field. He decided, after one disappointing experience in trying to write a serious dramatic piece, that he ought to stick to writing and producing musical shows. This was something he could do well. This was where his abilities could be more wisely used.

**Work To Meet Your Basic Needs.** In connection with the problem of finding ourselves in life and working out well-adjusted personalities, it would be worth while to look again at the basic needs which people have and whose satisfaction, in the final analysis, is what makes them successful and happy.

Re-examining these fundamental needs, as outlined by Prescott,[2] we might state them like this:

1. A man should have the means of satisfying his basic physical needs, including such things as adequate food, rest, clothing, bodily comfort, exercise and recreation.
2. He should have a feeling of belonging to a social group or groups —the feeling of "belonging"—being a part of things, with people to love and appreciate, and with people who love and appreciate him.
3. He should be able to feel that he is worth while himself and that he is doing worth-while things—he should be able to respect and be proud of his own personality.

Each person, to fulfill these needs, must learn to sense and understand his own abilities and the nature of the world in which he lives. The world provides the opportunities for these things—we should learn to use the opportunities and to help others to have and to find these opportunities.

**How Time and Experience Can Help.** Working out a way of living means that each person must be ready and willing to reconcile his own ways of looking at things with the ideas and ways of looking at things which are held by other people. He must be flexible enough to make allowances for the breakdowns which occur. He must be tolerant, to a degree, of the other person's failures. The study of psychology enables us to understand the *why* of these things, but it takes time and experience to enable us to make the adjustments gracefully.

**Why Having a Goal or Purpose Is the Most Important Thing.** Usually an individual is more able to face the trials and problems

---

[2] D. A. Prescott, *Emotions and the Educative Process* (Washington, D.C.: American Council on Education, 1938), p. 113.

of life if he has deep affection for and belief in certain things that are fundamental.

He must think of life as a constant journey toward the achievement of those things which are right. A man who is undertaking a long automobile trip does not give up just because there is an occasional punctured tire or a blowout; or because of an engine breakdown. In the same way, a young person needs to have a conviction that he is on the way to a goal that is worth while. He must not lose sight of the final goal or purpose.

Biographies of great men all remind us that the leaders and the men to whom we look in admiration have plodded along this road to better things. The situations which block us — these frustrations—are not merely causes of the adjustment mechanisms we have been discussing. They are often stimulating and challenge us to greater effort and more activity.

Most men, when they are blocked or frustrated, try harder. Psychologists are sure that a determination to succeed, and the setting up of a worth-while goal, is the best way of assuring that the individual will make good adjustments.

Some call these ultimate values "a life plan," or "a purpose in life," or a "philosophy of life." The selection of the values we believe in and toward which we work is not done in an afternoon, or an evening. It is realized gradually as we study and work, and as we, through experience, see what the important things are, and what we as individual persons may be able to do about them.

One of the great men in the history of American education was Horace Mann. His ideals undoubtedly made themselves felt in his life. One thing that he said, can now be found on a monument to his memory on the campus of Antioch College.

"Be ashamed to die, until you have
won some victory for humanity."

Those who strive to understand the world and to realize their own abilities will probably come to have the best plan. Those who study other people and who try to realize the benefits arising from the situations of life through which they pass, will probably make the best adjustments as they go.

In our modern American schools and in business life today, we have the privilege of finding out what the men and women who have gone before us have learned about these things. This is the heritage which comes to us through books, through the contacts which we may enjoy in school, through the radio and TV, and through all the other means of communication.

The more we take advantage of these things, the wider our experiences will be. And the wider our experiences, if we have a determination to profit by them, the greater will be our chance of securing a satisfying and enriching *adjustment* in life.

## SOMETHING TO DO

One of the best ways to learn the meaning of the numerous adjustment mechanisms mentioned in the chapter is to think of an example of each one of them which you have come across in your own experience or in your reading.

After writing down briefly each example, go over the entire list and see whether or not you have classified each one correctly. Note that sometimes there may be overlapping, in that an example may illustrate more than one of the adjustment mechanisms. Some adjustment mechanisms are:

1. Rationalization.
2. Sour-grapes type of rationalization.
3. Pollyanna type of rationalization.
4. Substitution.
5. Sublimation.
6. Projection.
7. Daydreaming.
8. Identification.
9. Repression.
10. Regression.

## QUESTIONS AND PROBLEMS FOR STUDY AND DISCUSSION

1. Having a goal or a purpose is important to our well-being as all psychologists agree. Report on some of the purposes or goals which some favorite of yours in fiction or history held for himself. Show how his life was influenced by this fact.

2. What purposes or goals can an ordinary person work out for himself? Show how some of these can be of a kind which will enable him to lead a worth-while and happy life.

3. Some goals or purposes are short-term—others are longer in their nature. What are some of your short-term goals, and some longer goals which you may decide upon?

4. One noted psychologist said that the formula for working out a well-adjusted personality was to have "A Task, a Plan, and Freedom." Can you explain the meaning and importance of such a formula?

5. Explain what we mean by saying that everyone meets his problems in one way or another.

6. Check the list of typical problems presented early in the chapter.

Rate those which you find to be problems in your own case: (1) those which are serious for you, (2) those moderately serious, and (3) those which are mildly serious.

7. To illustrate the nature of the problems we must adjust to, consider a friend of yours and see if you can write down a list of problems which you know he has in his own life.

8. Taking two or three of the problems noticed in a friend (Question 7), indicate what method of attack on these problems he appears to be using. Comment on the value of his methods: Are they good or bad?

9. Make a list of four or five "good" and four or five "bad" adjustments which you recognize you yourself are making. Comment on the possibility of substituting better adjustments for the bad ones.

10. What mechanism of adjustment would be especially bad if found in the work of a policeman? Explain.

11. Name two adjustment mechanisms which *often* produce good results in the lives of people. Explain.

12. In your own words, describe the fundamental needs of all men, as outlined by Prescott.

13. What do you understand by the so-called "theory of repressed wishes"? Do you think that this theory is correct? Can you give an example of it?

14. Republicans frequently speak of their party as "The party of Lincoln." What adjustment mechanism is seen by this connection?

15. What is the commonest form of adjustment mechanism, in your opinion? Can you offer any suggestions as to why this is true?

# CHAPTER FOURTEEN

# PERSONALITY AND CHARACTER

This chapter takes up questions about personality which have created some difficulties for psychologists. The question, for example, of whether or not there are such things as types of people is discussed.

An effort is made to explain what we mean by character and personality. It is brought out that psychologists have found it worth while to think about this in terms of what people actually do—their behavior.

The so-called character traits are discussed, and it is pointed out that here, again, the most satisfactory information about them has been secured by studying what people do in real situations.

Much can be learned by studying the values people have. The chapter endeavors to show what is meant by values. Illustrations of the values some people hold, and how these values influence their behavior, are included.

In the latter part of the chapter, you will find some suggestions for analyzing your own values. This could be useful to you in formulating your own needs and plans.

The chapter includes some illustrations, from history and from our own American life, of how values have influenced the lives and actions of some of our great leaders.

## QUESTIONS THIS CHAPTER WILL ANSWER

1. What is meant by *character*, and what is meant by *personality*?
2. How does the psychologist explain these terms, and what does he consider important in connection with them?
3. What is meant by such traits as "self-confidence" and "honesty"?
4. Are there *types* of people?
5. What are *values* and *patterns of behavior*, and how do they fit in with our explanations of personality?
6. How can we analyze our own values and their influence on what we do in our everyday activities and what we want in life?

## The Nature of Personality

Each individual is a distinct personality. It is the nature of this personality that determines how he will act in any given situation.

Noting that there are many different ways of defining personality, two writers recently summed it up like this:

> . . . a generalized definition of personality would surely state that every person has a personality and that each personality is distinctive and individual. Personality is not only the impression one makes on others, but it is also one's knowledge of himself; it is a persistent disposition to follow certain patterns of life in making adjustments. Personality includes such things as traits, character, values, ethics, attitudes, abilities, drives, moral and philosophical beliefs, and emotional patterns—in fact the whole of what a person is in relation to the universe about him. Personality is more than the sum of its parts because it is an integration of all these. It is never static; it constantly develops and changes.[1]

Even though we recognize that what we call the personality of the individual is complex, and even though we know that what an individual does at any particular time is probably produced by numerous forces and influences *at work in him;* nevertheless we can very profitably study some of the more obvious of these influences and show what they are and how they affect behavior.

It does little good for us to say, in trying to explain why a person behaves the way he does, "It's because of his self-concept." We need to examine the way the individual feels about himself in more detail. We need to take a look at some of the common needs people have, and some of the common patterns of behavior that we find in them.

If we describe Bill Smith as a man who is youthful and good looking, who is prompt in getting to work and in meeting appointments, who is good at working out problems, who is always gentlemanly and who is fond of baseball and swimming, he seems like a real person. It is a combination of these things, and others, which make personality.

Usually we tend to *evaluate* personality. That is, we are inclined to say that it is good or bad, that it makes an impression, or that we like it or don't like it. We may use such an expression as "Joe has a lot of personality." If we use such an expression, we do not mean by "a lot" any particular amount or quantity, so much as we mean that Joe's personality is made up of traits, characteristics, and ways of doing things that we like.

This "ways of doing things" has much to do with it. If we in-

---

[1] Edward C. Glanz, and Ernest B. Walston, *An Introduction to Personal Adjustment* (Boston: Allyn and Bacon, Inc., 1958), p. 76.

clude in behavior what people do, what they say, how they carry themselves, how they *react*, together with all of the many little mannerisms, gestures, and facial expressions which they display, we have, certainly, a major portion of the traits or characteristics which are usually prominent in personality.

## The Meaning of Character

Character is the *value* of the person, his *worthwhileness* as a member of society. When you are looking for a job and are asked for references—you may be quite sure that the person who is considering employing you wants to know about such things as your loyalty, your honesty, your willingness to work, and your sense of responsibility.

The things that we like most about men and which are likely to impress us deeply are the things that have to do with character. Every American can appreciate this when we think of two outstanding characters of the Civil War. Abraham Lincoln and Robert E. Lee are remembered best as men of remarkable character.

A man of good character is a man who usually acts in accordance with what men think of as good. The person who doesn't keep his promises, who fails to meet appointments, who borrows money without paying it back, who is irresponsible, and who can't be trusted, is said to have a defective character.

In a way, character is the extent to which you and I measure up to the generally accepted ideals of our society. This, in turn, depends on how well we learn and how well adjusted we can become to the problems of life as we meet them.

Character and personality are hard to measure but they are easily recognized in people. They are sometimes thought of as *intangibles*—that is, as traits that are hard to put your finger on, sometimes hard to describe, but nevertheless traits which are all important in relation to whether we are going to succeed or fail.

## Patterns of Behavior

As the individual grows and learns, his behavior begins to follow patterns, which is another way of saying that he learns to do certain things in certain ways. A man's patterns of behavior are made of habits and attitudes. As has just been noted, the way in which these habits and attitudes are arranged, the way in which the individual behaves and does things, determine his personality to a very large extent.

The habit patterns of people differ widely. For example, Mr. Malone goes home after work, puts on his old clothes, and works in the garden until supper time. Mr. Porter heads for his favorite pool room every day when his work is finished, and plays pool "with the boys" until supper time. Sometimes he calls home and says he won't be in "till late."

Mr. Malone goes to church regularly on Sunday morning, Sunday dinner is always served at two o'clock, and the afternoon is regularly spent in reading the Sunday papers and in taking naps or watching television.

The Porters very seldom spend Sunday at home. Mr. Porter and his family usually go to the shore during the summer and visit relatives in near-by cities and towns during the winter. On Sunday they usually sleep late (until one or two o'clock), go out for dinner, and go to a movie, coming home about nine o'clock in the evening.

These are samples of habit patterns. The things that Mr. Malone and Mr. Porter do reflect their personalities; and their personalities are reflections of the things they do.

The individual differences among people which, after all, make them interesting, are in part a result of the great variety of *patterns of behavior* each one develops as he grows and lives in his own particular group.

Two traits of character or personality may be analyzed to throw light on this subject.

**Self-confidence.** This is a trait which is considered to be very important in our present society. It is harder to analyze self-confidence than one might suppose.

It is related to physical appearance and strength, but it is not always found in men who are large and strong. A large man may be a coward and lack self-confidence. An undersized, puny individual may show a great deal of self-confidence.

Whether or not an individual is self-confident depends on (1) the situation at hand, and (2) experiences he has had in similar situations. It can be frankly stated that no individual is self-confident in *every* situation. In some situations we will display self-confidence and in others we will not.

A football player who could handle himself with fearlessness

Through training these Navy recruits are acquiring an important personality trait, self-confidence.

*Official U.S. Navy Photo*

and skill on the field, before thousands of spectators, was nervous and fearful in the doctor's office when he had to have a slight injury dressed. Many hardened fighter pilots felt anything but confident in participating in their own weddings! In a motion picture (*Stand By for Action*), the brave officers of a United States destroyer were flustered and nervous when it befell them to take care of a lifeboat full of women and small babies rescued at sea.

When we talk about self-confidence we probably are thinking of it in particular situations. If a school principal, inquiring about a prospective teacher, asks, "Does she have self-confidence?" he probably has in mind how well she will handle herself in the classroom.

Self-confidence as a trait may be valued in some situations but not in others. If self-confidence means the kind of behavior which makes other people have confidence in us and feel warmly disposed toward us, then it is good. But if we carry self-confidence to such an extreme that it becomes pushing ourselves forward and making ourselves obnoxious or disagreeable, that is something else.

The trait of self-confidence is very close in its nature to a trait described as *ascendance* or *submission* by Gordon and F. H. Allport, who devised a scale to show whether or not an individual is ascendant or submissive.

What has been learned about this matter seems to show that individuals may tend toward one or the other of these directions in their behavior. Since the scale is based on a large number of specific situations, there is no doubt that an individual, by training or guidance, might learn a different way of acting in these situations, and accordingly become, instead of dominant or ascendant in these situations, submissive. The experiences we go through may "build us up" or "whip us down."

The following are the kind of questions such a scale includes:

If you saw an automobile accident, would you stop to see what you could do to help the people involved?

If you were standing in line to buy tickets, and someone got into the line in front of you, would you say something to him in protest?

Would you take the lead in organizing a game at a party if things were turning out to be a bit dull?

If you were riding in a train with a stranger, would you begin a conversation with him?

If you went to call on an acquaintance, and the doorbell was not answered the first time, would you keep on ringing it for a while?

**Honesty.** Studies of the nature of honesty as a trait show that whether or not people are honest depends to a large extent on the situation. Experience in everyday life seems to bear out the findings of the psychologists. We can all recall instances in which we have been honest and others in which we may have been lax.

Some persons will not hesitate to "get away with" riding on a bus or train without paying the fare—whereas they would be quite honest in making change in a store. Sometimes the truth is demanded and told; there are other times when it is "shaded."

It seems that people are able to build up characteristic ways of responding in most situations, but that there is no general trait of honesty which *always* determines an individual's behavior. *We do the thing which seems to be appropriate.*

Of course, we are able to build up a high regard for the ideal of honesty. This will undoubtedly influence us on many occasions. This is important and makes it worth while to work toward developing such an ideal. We want people to say of us: "You can trust him."

We must remember that it is necessary to understand each specific situation if we are to understand fully each act of behavior.

## Types of People

Jung's *introvert* and *extravert* types should be mentioned. These terms have become a part of everyday speech, and the ideas they represent have become more or less well-known.

It often seems that people can be divided into two general types—introverts and extraverts. The introvert prefers to work alone; the extravert prefers to work with or among other people. The introvert usually has few social contacts; the extravert enjoys being with people, either on or off his job. The introvert usually has but few friends and acquaintances, whereas the extravert is likely to have many. To Jung it seemed that these differences between introverts and extraverts implied a rather great and involved difference in their attitude towards life and the world. He sought to account for this difference by means of a rather involved and elaborate psychological theory. Most psychologists today do not accept Jung's ideas about why introverts are introverts and extraverts are extraverts, but they continue to use the two terms because they are "handy"—they express the fact that some like to work alone and some like to work with people, that some like a life of action and others do not.

Extraverts, then, are people such as salesmen, executives, trial lawyers, political leaders, public speakers, athletic coaches, taxi-drivers, and entertainers. Introverts are more likely to be bookkeepers, accountants, writers, file clerks, typists, scientists, and research lawyers.

Extraverts are usually much more flexible than introverts in dealing with people. This is natural, since they are more used to people. The introvert, on the other hand, may seem very ill at ease with people, especially strangers. Extreme introverts often offend others or seem to be unaware of their feelings; indeed, they may not understand other people too well.

But a *complete* introvert or a *complete* extravert is very rare. Psychologists feel that most of us possess both introvert and extravert traits. Therefore psychologists say that most people are *ambiverts*. What they mean is that most people are extraverts in some situations and introverts in another. For example, a young man might be the leader of his photography club, yet still be very shy in other social groups.

Then too, we can acquire certain traits that we lack. A person who is shy may make a special effort to learn to speak in public.

A businessman suffering from overwork and tension may force himself to read more or take up a hobby such as stamp collecting or music.

## Personality and Character as a Pattern of Values

Some further understanding of the nature of character and personality has resulted from recent studies of the nature of *values*. From one point of view it would be possible to say that a man or woman lives pretty much according to what his values are. The values he develops over the years are the conditions or situations he wants most, and accordingly they will influence his behavior and will have much to do with determining the kind of person he is.

**Values and How They Are Developed.** A value may be defined as a condition or situation which we find agreeable. Possibly it will be very agreeable, possibly slightly agreeable.

Unquestionably the desire for outstanding achievement has played some part in bringing these two men to their moment of triumph. They have just completed the ascension of never-before-climbed Diamond Cliff on the east face of Longs Peak.

*Denver Post*

High in our scheme of values are apt to be our loved ones, our home town, our school or college, and our favorite sport or hobby. People differ very much in their values, which is another way of calling attention to the importance of individual differences. The proud owner of a shiny new automobile is greatly concerned lest a scratch appear on the body or a fender; the high-school boy with his "jalopy" doesn't care one way or the other about such a detail. If he drives his father's car and has the same value about it that he has about his "jalopy" there is likely to be trouble.

Values are different for each individual, though a number of individuals may have the same value. Very few people, however, agree entirely in their values, a fact which can either make for friction or for enjoyment, depending on the seriousness of the matter under consideration.

**Influence of Values on Behavior.** Values may be very specific, having to do with particular things, or they may become general and become important in a wider sense because they set a *pattern* for our lives. Psychologists feel that people have a tendency to develop a set of values, thinking of them in this general way, which may influence everything, or nearly everything, they do. For example, if one of a person's values is a great fondness for people, that would influence his behavior in such ways as to cause him to want to be with people and to dislike anything which forces him to be alone; influence him to join clubs and organizations; cause him to have numerous friends visit in his home; and cause him to select games or sports in which many people are taking part.

If a person has as one of his values a great liking for machines he will be fascinated by mechanical equipment of all sorts; will want to read magazines like *Popular Mechanics;* will like to see and use trains, automobiles, and airplanes; and will possibly select a vocation which has to do with engineering or mechanics.

To show the difference in values as they are found in different people, the following two examples are given:[2] These are values which are general in nature. The two sets of values for the two girls are listed from the strongest to the weakest. That is, the values listed at the end of the list are not as strong in their appeal to the girls, as are those at the beginning.

[2] Asahel D. Woodruff, *The Psychology of Teaching* (New York: Longmans, Green & Co., Inc., 1946), pp. 29, 30.

PERSONALITY AND CHARACTER

| Helen | Alice |
|---|---|
| Personal improvement | Home life |
| Relaxation and recreation | Social service |
| Intellectual activity for its own sake | Physical comfort |
| Excitement | Intellectual activity for its own sake |
| Friendship within one's field of activity | Personal improvement |
| Home life | Security for the masses |
| Formal society | Relaxation and recreation |
| Wide friendships | Friendship |
| Physical comfort | Personal security |
| Wealth | Intellectual activity on the job |
| Social service | Society |
| Political power | Political power |
| Security | Excitement |
| | Wealth |

Alice presents an interesting contrast to Helen. She intends to become a home-economics teacher, and is enjoying her preparatory work. She is less interested in wealth, excitement, and leisurely living than Helen, and is more interested than Helen in social service, home life and intellectual work.

Helen, although preparing, like Alice, to be a teacher, seemed to be going in the wrong direction since the things she indicated as being her strongest values are not too likely to be associated with teaching. At least relaxation, recreation, and excitement, three of her first five values, would not be so considered.

**Practical Suggestions.** There are some practical suggestions which grow out of our consideration of values. They are important in connection with vocations. People will be likely to get along best in lines of work which offer them the chance to do things in line with their values.

Thus a truck driver may be satisfied and happy in his job if he enjoys driving and enjoys traveling. He might be very unhappy in an office job where he had to stay at a desk all day. A cattle grower, who prizes fine animals and considers the production of beef cattle to be very important, will be happiest when he is able to take part in activities of this sort and can be on the ranch with his favorite herds.

In selecting an occupation, a young person would be wise to consider what his values are, and to compare the opportunities of any particular occupation with these values as he finds them in his own make-up.

Another practical suggestion has to do with influencing the education and behavior of other people. Parents would be better able to deal with their children if they understood what values were important to them. A grownup who does not know much about the values of fourteen-year-old boys has a hard time working with boys of that age.

On the other hand, an adult who knows the values boys hold at such ages, and who understands them, can accomplish a great deal through applying this knowledge in handling them. It is clear that this is an important thing for teachers to understand and appreciate. An older person can find out what the values of boys and girls are by observing them closely and noticing what things appeal to them.

The boy who places a high value on a new automobile may quit high school and go to work so he can have a car. He probably won't admit it, but he has placed a higher value on owning a car than on a high-school education. Sometimes, as in this instance, a person will put a value on some short range objective that is not

Maturation has a pronounced effect on values.

nearly as important as some long range objective might be.

In handling young children, parents sometimes forget that the children are asked to do many things which are not in line with their values. For example, the trouble many parents have in getting their young children to wash hands, face, neck, and ears arises partly from the fact that the young children do not yet have personal cleanliness as a value. When the boy begins to value cleanliness and to consider it important, he will begin to keep clean without having to be prodded.

This does not mean that parents should not keep emphasizing the importance of being clean, but it shows why the child seems to resist the idea. He does not resist it to be stubborn, but simply because he does not see the purpose or value of it.

We are told that if we want to get people to do things for us, we should find a way to get them to see that taking the action will promote the values in which they believe.

**Great Men and Women Who Personify Values.** Reference has already been made to Lincoln, who was a great believer in honesty. "Honest Abe" was without doubt a great advocate of fairness and honesty in dealing with others. His devotion to this value led him to accomplish many remarkable things. It also caused him considerable trouble at times, since his desire to be fair resulted in his keeping men on his staff who were actually hostile to the things he himself believed in.

Harriet Beecher Stowe held individual freedom as a great value which caused her to devote herself to writing and working for the freeing of the slaves. *Uncle Tom's Cabin* became known as one of the greatest influences in promoting this idea.

Nathan Hale held the value of loyalty to his country above everything else. He became famous as the symbol of this spirit of patriotic devotion. Patrick Henry also became famed as a believer in loyalty to his country (". . . give me liberty or give me death!")

In the Second World War, Winston Churchill led the anti-Hitler nations with a stubborn and fearless belief that determination and effort would bring victory—a value which he not only followed personally but made the slogan of whole nations—V for Victory.

The pages of history are filled with accounts of people in religion, art, politics, government, and invention—people who were devoted to values which kept them active to the point where they made great contributions to the world.

Honored in the Hall of Fame at New York University are many great men whose personal values and goals have meant much to American civilization.

*New York University*

Benjamin Franklin is regarded as a man who was very intelligent and who did many great things for his country, but he is probably best known for his interest in the simple values of hard work, thrift, and honesty in everyday life.

Henry Ford was a great believer in industrial power and in the possibilities of modern machine methods in manufacturing—also in extending purchasing power to the masses of people so that they could buy the products of their own industry.

Thomas Edison was devoted to the value of "sticking to it" in the discovery of the electric light and a believer in better ways of doing things.

Madame Curie, who, together with her husband, discovered radium, was a believer in the value of women in the field of science.

We think of Cyrus Field and his patient work in laying the first transatlantic cable; of Roebling and his efforts to build wire suspension bridges; of Marconi and the radio; of George Westinghouse and the airbrake; of the Wright brothers and the development of the airplane. In all of these instances it was devotion to beliefs and values which carried these inventors through despite many obstacles.

**Importance of Values and Character in Our Society.** While it is possible to discuss the influence of values in the lives of great men and women, it is just as important to consider the need for values in the lives of people in all walks of life.

Regardless of the theories about personality, types of individuals, and character, the hope of all groups of people, of all society, must be in the development of worth-while values for all men and women in everyday life.

Scientists who do not have worth-while purposes are dangerous to all men. Political leaders who are dishonest are a constant threat to our well-being. Businessmen who are selfish and cruel, and who disregard the welfare of others, cause much unrest and work real hardship in their communities.

Our world needs men and women who learn what values can be of the greatest good and who work to realize them. All the way down the line from the leader to the average workman, this is necessary for the welfare of us all.

Each individual person who has low or faulty values is a cause of weakness in the city, the state, and the nation. This is one of the reasons why education must be in terms of values, purposes, and goals, as well as in terms of techniques and skills. All people need to recognize this and to understand the importance of values in society.

## SOMETHING TO DO

To get a pictorial representation of some aspects of your personality, think of the many separate activities in which you engage, and for each of them fill in or shade a block in the diagram on the following page as directed. It is not necessary to shade in every segment.

1. For each activity involving doing things with other people, (such as dancing, playing cards, playing volley ball, eating, etc.) shade in one of the segments in the outer ring.
2. For each activity mainly involving things (such as working in a photo lab, building a radio set, fixing something in the house, etc.) shade in a segment in the middle section of the frame.
3. For each activity that is strictly personal (such as writing poetry, writing letters, keeping a diary, reading books, etc.) shade in a segment in the inner section.

After you have shaded in the various segments, the concentration of shading should give you a visual picture of what your behavior patterns look like.

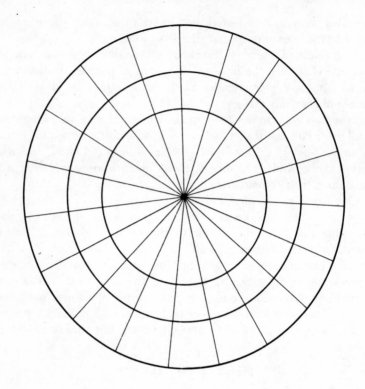

## QUESTIONS AND PROBLEMS FOR STUDY AND DISCUSSION

1. Write your own definition of character and of personality. Would you add any elements to those which have been presented?

2. Think of a man or woman who is considered to have good character in your community. What traits are especially noticeable in his make-up?

3. If you were employing a person to work in your office, what kind of references would you like to have concerning him?

4. Explain what we mean by suggesting that behavior patterns are closely related to personality.

5. Does a person have self-confidence in all situations? Explain.

6. Take someone who is considered to have a great deal of self-confidence. In what situations does this self-confidence seem to be most noticeable? Are there any situations in which, in your opinion, it is not so noticeable?

7. Explain in your own words the meaning of extravert and introvert. Can people have some qualities of both kinds in their make-up? Illustrate.

8. What is meant by the suggestion that individuals can, by training, become more or less ascendant, more or less submissive?

9. How do psychologists consider the trait of honesty?

10. What are values as defined in this text?

11. Describe some of the values you would probably find in a typical sixteen-year-old girl; in a typical twelve-year-old boy.

12. Compare the values held by two persons you know—for example, your father and your mother. In what respects are they different?

13. Make an analysis of your own values by listing some five to ten values under each of the important areas of life activities (such as education, home life, citizenship, occupational life, recreation, and leisure).

# CHAPTER FIFTEEN

# LEADERSHIP

Every time a group of workers organizes, or a club elects officers, or a town holds an election, there is the problem of finding leaders. Selecting leaders is one thing we all do, and we do it frequently.

In this chapter we consider what good leadership is. We look into the question of how the leader performs his work as a leader, and we examine the various behavior patterns that are found among leaders of different kinds.

Psychologists have found that men or women who are often leaders in some situations are not in others. Leadership usually involves bringing the right man and the right situation together at the right time. Another factor which is involved has to do with values. A person's leadership ability will often depend on what his values are, and how well they coincide with the values of the group he is leading.

Leadership is very important from the point of view of the psychologist, because the very essence of leadership is the ability to manage, direct, guide and inspire others.

Many industries are experimenting in an effort to find better ways of discovering and training leaders. This is also true in the military services and agencies of government. In this chapter we try to bring together certain important principles which are particularly significant for a democracy.

## QUESTIONS THIS CHAPTER WILL ANSWER

1. How do leaders become what they are? What abilities or ways of doing things must one have to become a leader?
2. What brings leaders and followers together in a working organization?
3. Can any one person be an all-round leader—a leader in everything?
4. As citizens, how can we go about finding leaders?
5. We are all followers in some situations. How can we be better followers?
6. Can leaders be "trained" for specific situations in life?

## Influencing the Behavior of Others

Leadership from the point of view of psychology is the ability to influence the behavior of other people. One writer defines it as "the ability and readiness to inspire, guide, direct, or manage others."[1]

This definition suggests that leadership is much more than just telling people what to do. It brings in the idea of inspiring and guiding them—as well as the suggestion of directing or managing them.

The minister of a church is a leader. He influences the behavior of others. He secures their co-operation in various activities and—

To achieve maximum efficiency and co-operation from employees, the supervisor should have the qualities of leadership.

*Ford Motor Co.*

at least in certain areas of life—inspires and guides the individuals in his group. He also has influence in the community in which he lives and even beyond.

There are political leaders and leaders in government in the local community, the city, the county, the state, and the nation.

The teacher is a leader in his class and to some extent in his

[1] Carter V. Good, Editor, *Dictionary of Education* (New York: McGraw-Hill Book Co., 1959).

community. The professor is a leader not only in his class and college but also in the whole field of s⁺udy he represents.

The automobile dealer is a leader in that field of business and may be influential in his community in financial, social, and civic activities.

Wherever there are groups of people there are leaders. There are many different kinds of leaders for different kinds of things, and very few "over-all" leaders, or leaders who are influential in everything.

It is also evident that people who are leaders in one situation may be followers in another. The President of the United States may be a leader in the government of his country, but when he goes to church on Sunday morning he is a follower; the minister is the leader.

The President may also be a follower when he meets with his cabinet and his advisers, any of whom may take the responsibility of being a leader in some problem which comes up. Probably what happens often is that at one time the President is a leader and at another time he is a follower, even in these close groups.

We are all sometimes leaders and sometimes followers.

This makes it important to understand the nature of leadership. Especially is this true in a democracy, because a democracy allows its members much freedom of action. We must know how to find leaders and how to follow them. And frequently we must know how to be leaders, when the situation calls for it.

Sometimes we are followers and sometimes we are leaders.

## Relation of Values to Leadership

A leader is one who shares the values of a group. He has purposes very much like those of the people in his group and has the initiative to do something about it. He wants to take action of some kind toward accomplishing the things his people are interested in. A real leader is a person of action.

He either does something, says something, or writes something that will influence the behavior of other people.

For example, the president of a social club plans dances, parties, and activities for the club. He makes arrangements about orchestras, places for dances, and refreshments he thinks the club members would like. He gets in touch with people who can do things for the club. He is a leader in that he shares the values of his followers and helps them to realize their aims and goals.

There is a difference between a leader and one who is merely the head of an organization. People often choose individuals to be heads of organizations when they are not leaders at all. The mere fact that a man is president of a group does not necessarily make him a leader. In one high school recently a boy was made president of the senior class because he was a football player and popular. He allowed the affairs of the class to drift so badly that he finally resigned, and a new president was chosen who could actually be a leader.

**Status Leaders.** A term used in discussions about leadership is the expression *status leader*. This is a person who is in a recognized *position* of leadership—a chairman, a foreman, the president of a company, or a school principal. Many political leaders, such as mayors, governors, members of Congress, are also *status leaders*.

A status leader—by virtue of the fact that his position usually assigns certain power to him—always exerts some leadership, but the extent of this may vary considerably. Sometimes status leaders are not very important as leaders because their followers, or the people in the group they purport to lead, do not *recognize* them as *real* leaders. In such cases we may ask, who are the real leaders in the group—who are the individuals whether they have high *positions* or not, who influence the policies and activities of the group?

These individuals, when we have identified them, are not status leaders but they are nevertheless leaders, because of the fact that they are held in high regard by the others in the group, and because they have what some writers refer to as *esteem*.

Sometimes, in fact quite often, the status leader is also the real leader. But sometimes the actual leadership of the group is to be found elsewhere.

Generally speaking the leader—whether he has *status* or not, is an individual who exerts influence in the direction of producing something of value to the group. He behaves in such a way that the members of the group feel that he is promoting their interests and that he is helping them to find the satisfactions for which they are looking as members of the group.

**Choosing Leaders.** When groups have leaders who are leaders *in name only*, they usually begin to break up or disappear as influential groups.

This makes it necessary in choosing officers for a group to select persons who have the interest and ability to be leaders—if the group is to amount to something. How many people think about this when they vote for the officers who are to lead them? We should choose a leader who has values and goals similar to ours and who will be likely to work for and promote them.

On election day it is important to vote, but it is more important to vote for the people who will represent our views and our values and who will do something to promote them.

Franklin D. Roosevelt was a leader who saw that the people wanted certain things and took steps to get these things for them. Among the *values* which he recognized and which he felt were the values of the people who voted for him were: security for their savings; security in their jobs; security in old age; right to have labor unions; repeal of prohibition; government help in building homes; national security and adequate defense.

We cannot deny that Hitler was a leader who became powerful because he gave leadership in the things the people of Germany wanted. He included in these: formation of a strong industrial organization; security in jobs; health and old-age insurance; vacations; development of a powerful army; encouragement for scientists and research workers; mass production of goods people wanted; development of highways and public buildings.

Hitler's downfall came not because of these but because of wrong national goals and errors in military judgment.

In our own country, we often find that local political leaders are successful because they get things for the people, or they support values or goals the people want.

Sometimes political leaders fail because they have goals which are different from those of the people or they support values which the people do not share. To have political success, it is important for leaders to show that they are working for values the people want. It is interesting to study history to discover how this has worked out over the years.

## Relation of Values to Followership

The point has already been made that we are sometimes followers as well as leaders. Just as it is important to *find* leaders we can follow because they will support the values we want, so it is important to *know what we want* and to give actual support to the leaders who share them.

We can see the importance of this if we will stop to consider our own attitude in a political campaign. How many people ever stop to ask themselves what it is they want their leaders to do? If we do not know what our own values are, and if we have not decided what values we want our leaders to represent, how can we vote intelligently for any candidates for political office?

On what basis can we organize support for, or opposition to, our elected representatives — unless we establish our own values first?

One of the causes of poor government is the fact that so many voters do not have very much of an idea of what kind of government they want. They vote for a candidate because he is good looking, or comes from "the right side of the tracks," or belongs to the same political party as they do.

Once we realize that the best leadership can occur when the leader and the followers share the same *values,* then we can make an effort to associate ourselves with the leaders and groups who share the values which we have.

It is hardly necessary to add that a good follower, once he has become a member of a group whose values are similar to his own, must give the group *support* as best he can. He isn't a knocker or a petty critic, because he recognizes that this only interferes with the chances of success for his group. He may give constructive criticism when it is needed, but on the whole he will support his group and his leaders, if he knows that through this process and only through this process can his values or goals be realized.

It is very important for us, when we are followers, to accept the responsibility that goes with it.

This takes a certain amount of willingness to subordinate our own interests and ambitions for the welfare of the group. Unless we can do this we are unlikely to be good followers.

Many different traits and ways of doing things go into leadership. Leaders may be very good leaders and at the same time have some glaring weaknesses. For example, sometimes good leaders are very conceited. Sometimes they are tactless. Sometimes they don't even seem to be very bright. But when these things are true, we have to look somewhere else for the quality that makes them leaders—that makes them "click."

One of the most fruitful ways to study leadership is to study actual leaders—what they do and how they do it. We can observe in others the practices which are successful and the practices which fail.

## Bringing the Leader and Followers Together

In addition to his ability to know what people want and to share their values, the leader usually has to know how to get along with people. He may not always know how to get along with *everyone*, but he must have the ability to get along with the people he works with and those able to support him.

It will be evident that leadership for one type of activity may be different from leadership in another type of activity. The one who wants to be an intellectual leader will be different from one who seeks to be a political or military leader.

If you want to be the head of the English department in a university, it will be necessary for you to become a student of English literature and you will have to learn to speak and write well. You will probably have to write some articles or a book, and you will probably have to obtain a doctor's degree. Your leadership will require the ability to get along well with students and with other professors, and it will be particularly necessary for you to be something of a scholar in the field of English.

If you want to be the district representative of an insurance agency, you will have to know as much as possible about insurance, but you will especially need the energy and "drive" to get a lot of work done, to secure other people who can and will work, and a great deal of ability in getting along with the people you will be working with.

If you are anxious to be a member of your state legislature or of Congress, you will need — among other things — a considerable amount of physical energy to campaign for office. Making speeches, working with committees and groups, and traveling require this. You will need a great deal of ability to meet and talk with all sorts of people about all sorts of subjects.

In other words, different kinds of leadership require different kinds of abilities, interests, and skills.

Sometimes popular impressions are wrong—the leader does not *have* to be tall or good looking. He does not *have* to have a commanding voice. He does not *have* to have unlimited physical energy. But he *does* have to include in his personality some traits which suggest to followers that they will be justified in placing their confidence in him.

Otherwise it will be impossible for leader and followers to be brought together to achieve their goals.

It cannot be too strongly emphasized that leadership is a combination of traits adapted to a particular situation. A man may have the qualities of leadership sufficient to enable him to be elected President of the United States at a given time, yet he may fail when he runs for the office under different circumstances.

## Qualities of a Good Leader

Some facts to be considered in connection with leadership are presented in the following comments from a book on this subject which appeared during the Second World War when there was a great need for work along these lines in the military forces.[2]

True leadership involves all that is finest in a man. To list all the desirable qualities would involve cataloguing all that is considered best in human nature. There are so many such qualities that enter into proficient leadership that it is impossible to reduce the attainment of true leadership to a formula. No one person, furthermore, can have all these desirable qualities.

Every leader must have certain of those qualities, however, that cause men to look up to him, to respect him, to have faith in him, and, consequently, to follow him. In any army, men will respect and follow an officer who knows his profession. This is true because the men always realize that their lives and the success of their cause depend upon his professional skill. In addition, an officer must be able to inspire his men. To do this he must be decisive. He must be forceful and aggressive. He must possess a thorough knowledge of human nature in general and his men in particular. He must be loyal to his men at all times and under all conditions. He resents a criticism of them as much as a sharp criticism directed at him. He stimulates a feeling of community of interest between himself and his men. He fosters the belief that they are all comrades-in-arms. He is fair at all times

[2] L. A. Pennington, Romeyn Hough, Jr., and H. W. Case, *The Psychology of Military Leadership* (New York: Prentice-Hall & Co., 1943), pp. 124, 125.

and he shows no favoritism. He can be relied upon to reward meritorious performance and to punish for misdeeds. While it is not essential for the leader to be popular in the ordinary sense of the term, the effective leader gives no cause for unpopularity, other than those actions required for the good of the service and the betterment of the organization. Necessarily these actions do not always please everyone. Tact in administration and in personal relationships, however, always yield beneficial results.

Soldiers respect energy, initiative, and enthusiasm in their officers. They will follow a leader who inspires the development of these qualities in themselves. While an officer must have dignity, this must not be carried to such a degree that his men consider him too remote to be interested in them and their problems. He must be human!

No coward is ever well liked. The successful leader must have both moral and physical courage. He must accept full responsibility for his acts and his orders.

Finally, the successful leader must be deeply and thoroughly imbued with the justice of the cause for which he is fighting. He must be able to impart this feeling to his men. He must be able by sheer ability, bearing, and enthusiasm to inspire them to follow him even into death itself.

Although these suggestions were written for military leaders, many of them are just as applicable in any type of leadership.

In the Second World War many men came to the front with qualities suggesting what is necessary for leadership. General Patton was recognized for courage and determination; General MacArthur for expert organizing ability and the capacity to act with strong authority; Prime Minister Churchill for his ability to inspire confidence and faith in ultimate victory; General Marshall for over-all understanding of the military and political situation; Admiral Nimitz for rugged naval heroism; General Eisenhower for ability to handle large-scale operations and men of many types of personality and temperament; General McAuliffe for fearless disregard of danger in the light of overwhelming odds in the siege of Bastogne.

Another quality often mentioned in connection with leadership is *intelligence*. Leaders tend to be above the average in ability and intelligence. However, it has been brought out that those who are rated "very superior" in intelligence do not tend to be selected as leaders. This is an interesting fact. Possibly the reason for this is that the "very superior" individual is likely to be a bit isolated from the group because his ideas and thoughts are too far beyond them. Appreciating and understanding the average person — especially his own followers—is absolutely indispensable for the leader.

Leadership is supposed to be more likely in the man of tall and

commanding appearance, yet we have Napoleons, Hitlers, Stein-
metzes, and LaGuardias—all men of short stature. Leadership is
said to require a good voice and speaking ability, yet George Washington is reported to have been very ordinary in this respect.

Leadership is said to require advanced education—college training and higher degrees—yet we have those who have lifted themselves by their own bootstraps. Many American presidents, including President Truman, were not college graduates.

The captain entrusted with this ocean liner must have, among other qualities,
the ability to command the respect and obedience of the crew.

*Moran Towing and Transportation Co., Inc.*

Often leadership develops when a particular man or woman has
some ability or quality which happens to be very much needed
by a group at a particular time. Again, however, it is a question
of values—the leader must represent and be able to make a contribution toward the values of the group.

While it is true that it would be difficult, if not impossible, to
make a list of traits or qualities which all leaders must possess, much
importance is usually given to the following:

| | |
|---|---|
| Ability to get along with people | Likeable personality |
| Imagination | Intelligence |
| Sense of responsibility | Initiative |

## How Leaders Work

A few comments may be given on ways in which leaders work. As we have seen, people may be encouraged to follow a given course of action by a leader who helps them to see that it is to their interest to do so. It is still better if he can cause these followers to feel that the line of action proposed is one they themselves have chosen.

It can be seen that such a leader might be just a demagogue— one who does whatever the crowd seems to prefer, regardless of truth or values. The good leader, however, will select those values toward which he wishes to see progress made, and direct the attention of his followers toward them.

The followers must secure satisfactions which will make them want to co-operate. The leader must be able to show his followers that they will derive some benefit from the course of action he is proposing.

The leader also endeavors to establish a point of contact between himself and his followers. He wants them to believe that he and they have points in common. The political leader is usually shrewd in this respect. He hopes to make the working man feel that he, too, was once a working man. A candidate for Congress, addressing a teachers' convention, may begin by pointing out that he taught school himself at one time. Addressing a veterans' meeting, he may refer to the time when he was in the service. He makes it a point to drop in at meeting places where people may be found, perhaps to share a meal with them or exchange some gossip on an informal basis.

The leader also tries to learn what interests people in any given situation. He studies the newspapers and listens to the radio and "keeps an ear to the ground." Although all too often the crowd will follow a leader just for emotional reasons, whether he is informed about issues or not, it must give the people confidence in him to discover that he knows something about the problems at hand. The fact that there are some leaders who are uninformed about important problems does not mean that a person who wants to be a leader can avoid examining important problems. In most fields it will be necessary for him to study, and work hard. A successful leader cannot be a lazy man, whatever else he may be.

The successful leader must recognize the ambitions of the people who work for him. He must be willing to give credit where credit is due. He must praise his followers for what they accomplish. He must be willing to delegate authority—that is, he must be ready to allow people in positions under his care to go ahead with their work with a feeling that they are responsible for it and that they are trusted with it. He must not endeavor to do everything himself—must avoid trying to "be the whole show." Many leaders fall short of real greatness because they can never learn to do this. They are afraid that nothing will succeed unless they personally take charge of it. No leader can move beyond very narrow limits unless he learns this lesson.

## Importance of Leadership

In this connection we ought to notice what some of the services of the leader are—keeping in mind the psychology of influencing people, and our definition of leadership as the influencing of behavior.

The leader provides stimulation. He encourages people to go ahead with their problems. He challenges them to do better. He gives them new confidence in what they can do. He reminds them of their abilities and he "talks up" whatever is going on.

The leader provides goals. He suggests things that may be accomplished. He often puts into words what the people are vaguely thinking about or considering. He points out the direction the group should go to achieve a given result.

The leader is a symbol of the values the group wants. He may be said to stand for its purposes. Washington stood for liberty in the time of the American Revolution and served as a symbol of the dreams and aspirations of the people. He really was the "Father" of his country and was almost worshiped by the American people at that time.

The leader is a means of tying together the various members of the group in terms of their common purposes. He is a bond between individuals who may not be able to work directly with each other. We go to the leader, and others go to the leader, and he is able to give us both direction. He also interprets to the various individuals and groups what the other individuals in the organization want and what they are striving for.

The leader provides direction. He ties together the various efforts of the individuals in the group and is able to see how the efforts of each can contribute to the welfare of all. He is in this sense a captain or pilot of the enterprise, whatever it may be. Any group, consisting of individuals or groups, needs this *co-ordination* of effort, and the leader is responsible for this task.

Finally, the leader *evaluates* or sizes up what is going on and tries to estimate the extent to which the group is succeeding or falling short. He is responsible for keeping track of the activities of his group and for advising the members of the group as to how well their efforts are succeeding.

## Finding and Developing Leadership

In any group—and we all belong to a number of groups—it is necessary for us to be constantly looking for, choosing, and supporting leaders.

This is true whether we are students in school, workers in a factory, members of a church, or members of a fraternity or lodge. The discussion of what goes into leadership, and how it works, is of value chiefly in helping us to realize the importance of leaders and in helping us to determine who will be good leaders.

The following check list may be helpful in this connection in situations where we are called upon to assist in finding or developing a leader:

1. Does he have a personality we can like and respect?
2. Would he enjoy working with us; would we enjoy working with him?
3. Does he have the same *values* as we do? That is, does he have the same goals and purposes which we have?
4. Does he have an interest in this activity or in this organization?
5. Would he probably enjoy working for this organization—would he "put something into it"?
6. Does he have or is he likely to have some *plans* or ideas for the benefit of the group?
7. Would he respect the members of the group and their ideas?
8. Would he share the responsibility with them, or would he want to "run things" himself?
9. Would he be the kind of person who could and would make a decision when necessary?
10. Would he be *responsible*, that is, could we depend on him to do the things the organization requires?

11. Would he help to promote the individuals working with him, or would he tend to hold them down?

12. Is he the type of individual we would like to have represent the group?

We read a good bit about training people to be leaders. It is obvious that to the extent that leadership depends on things that can be learned, we can do this.

For example, if it requires knowing about people and how to get along with them, there are many points we can learn from a study of people and from a study of psychology which could help us in this respect. That is a form of training.

Leaders often develop (i.e., are trained) through experience. In military activities, leaders of men often grow with experience—*learn* how to handle men.

If we say that part of leadership depends on knowing what people want and in helping them to realize their values, then it is possible to train leaders by helping them to know these values and what is involved in reaching them.

Of course leaders are trained, but it must be remembered that they are best trained in connection with the actual type of thing for which their leadership is being sought. We can't train leadership "generally," so that an individual will be a leader in everything. We *can* give him training in many of the specific kinds of duties and responsibilities which he will have as a leader. Yet for other types of leadership jobs, he will require more experience and more training.

We can train a person to be a better teacher in the classroom. But we will have to provide further training for that same person if he is to become a successful principal of a school, or a successful superintendent. We can train a man to be a good foreman in a shop —or at least we can train him to be a better foreman; but he will need more and different training to become a division superintendent.

Our training must be in specific things that are to be learned. We cannot increase a person's native intelligence greatly, nor can we give him a fine sense of humor, or the quality of imagination, patience, or understanding. In some of the broad, deep essentials, it will be necessary to select the right persons first, and then proceed with the necessary training in specific things.

## SOMETHING TO DO

To illustrate the possibility of studying leadership through observing actual leaders at work, take a leader and analyze his work as follows:

1. _____ is the leader of _____.

2. His physical appearance is as follows:

3. He has the following mannerisms which are noticeable in his work:

4. He is especially interested in:

5. When working with people he seems to have the following assets:

   Liabilities:

6. He has done the following things which show evidence of leader-ship:

Insofar as his particular leadership task is concerned, I would give him the following ratings on the following points: 10 points for exceptionally good; 7.5 points for good; 5 points for fair; 2.5 points for barely satisfactory; 0 points for complete or nearly complete omission.
   1. Pleasing appearance.
   2. Pleasing personality.
   3. Speaking ability.
   4. Grasp of the values and goals of the group.
   5. Interest in working for the values and goals of the group.
   6. Ability to get the members of the group to work.
   7. Ability to delegate authority and responsibility to others.
   8. Ability to handle problems as they come.
   9. Intelligence and originality of ideas.
   10. Ability to inspire the members of the group.

On a 100-point scale, the above rating should give a fairly good picture of the percentage of effectiveness, as to leadership, of the individual being rated.

# QUESTIONS AND PROBLEMS FOR STUDY AND DISCUSSION

1. Explain what is meant by the statement that leadership is the ability to influence the behavior of others.

2. Think of four or five men and women leaders in your community and indicate the type of leadership they provide.

3. Give an illustration of your own showing how someone is a leader in some situations and a follower in others.

4. Make a short list of ways in which you yourself are a leader and a similar list of ways in which you are a follower.

5. Explain the statement that a leader is one who shares the values of a group.

6. Explain the statement that a leader is essentially a person of action.

7. We often see or hear the expression "Vote as you please, but vote!" In view of what has been said about leadership and followership, what would you add to this admonition?

8. Give an illustration of a would-be leader (possibly a candidate for office) who failed because his goals or values were not in harmony with those of the people.

9. Select some position of leadership and show what abilities, interests, or qualities would be necessary to attain it.

10. Take a leader in some smaller group to which you belong and write down the qualities which in all probability have been important, or played a part, in making him a leader.

11. Give an example of a leader who was notably lacking in either appearance, intelligence, or tact. Why, in your opinion, was he able to succeed in spite of such shortcomings?

12. Comment on the idea that it is possible, to some extent, to train people to be leaders.

13. What are some of the things leaders do as leaders; in other words, what is their *role* in society?

14. Discuss the idea that a good leader must be able to delegate authority. Can you give an example of a good leader who does this?

15. Why do we say that one of the best ways to understand leadership is to study a leader and observe how he works and behaves?

# CHAPTER SIXTEEN

# FACTS AND VALUES IN OCCUPATIONS

Few indeed are the people who do not have to make a choice of an occupation, sooner or later. Choosing or entering an occupation is an important act that almost everyone has to do.

Therefore, it is important to know what to do and how to go about it. Psychologists and vocational-guidance workers have given a great deal of study to this matter ever since Frank Parsons, in Boston in the early 1900s, realized that too many boys were stumbling along blindly in this regard.

It is possible to make a very careful analysis of what goes on in choosing an occupation. You can study the occupations, and this chapter makes suggestions as to how to undertake such an inquiry. You can also study your own abilities, interests, and possibilities. This chapter shows what are the important things to consider, and how to go about considering them.

The chapter concludes with some very practical suggestions which any individual might use with good results in his own or another person's problem of vocational guidance.

## QUESTIONS THIS CHAPTER WILL ANSWER

1. What are the main things to consider in choosing an occupation?
2. In what ways does an occupation influence the nature of a person's life? How does it influence his opportunities in ways other than those strictly connected with the job?
3. How can we learn more about the characteristics and possibilities of any particular job or occupation?
4. What are the more important kinds of occupations which people should consider in planning a life's work?
5. How can you, as an individual, go about the problem of finding a suitable occupation?
6. Can you be sure that you will succeed in the occupation you choose to enter? How can you tell about this?
7. What can you do if the job opportunities seem to be very limited?
8. What are the most important things to consider in vocational guidance?

Important to everyone is his job—the job he has now and the job he will have in the future.

Your job is important because to a great extent your patterns of life depend on it. Where you spend your time, the kind of training you need and get, and the amount of income you will have, and, therefore, the possibilities of developing and enriching your life—all these are involved.

## Kinds of Jobs Available in the Years Ahead

One of the most helpful discussions of the actual nature of job opportunities ahead for young people in the 1960s was included in the volume entitled *Children and Youth in the 1960s, Survey Papers,* published for the 1960 White House Conference on Children and Youth.

In these reports the Department of Labor was quoted as estimating that for every 100 people in the following categories who were in the labor force in 1955, the nation in 1965 will demand:

137 professional and technical workers
127 clerical and sales workers
124 skilled craftsmen
122 managers, officials, and proprietors
122 semiskilled operatives
 96 unskilled laborers
 85 farmers.[1]

The survey made it clear that there has been a trend toward work demanding more education and more training.

It also emphasizes the fact that young people entering the world of work in the future will be affected more and more by *automation,* that is, the application of technical discoveries to jobs with resulting changes in what is demanded of the people who are working in them.

Citing various sources and references, the survey seems to point to these conclusions:

Automation is just a newer form of technological change.

Every new application of automation results in some workers being displaced, at least temporarily, and this means hardship for some.

---

[1]Marciak Freedman, "Work and the Adolescent," in *Children and Youth in the 1960s Survey Papers,* for the 1960 White House Conference on Children and Youth, p. 146.

However, in the long run, there is no great lessening of industry's need for workers.

The application of automation to industry is coming faster and faster, and we are just beginning to feel some of the resulting problems.

Quoting from the report:

Trade unions point out that there will be no automatic way to retrain workers, to meet the demand for higher levels of skill, or to obviate the dislocating effects on workers and on entire communities. Expansion in the electronics and machine tool industries that produce automation equipment will not take up the slack, because these industries are also being automated.

For young workers, it is clear that automation will tend to increase still further the necessary level of skill for entry jobs. One expert concludes that ". . . the age and grade level at which vocational training is offered will continue to rise. The added responsibility needed in many jobs—as well as other factors—will tend toward a higher entrance age into industry."[2]

What are the implications of this for the individual? Obviously, no one—whether he be mechanic, office worker, or professional man—can read the future well enough to know when and where, if at all, his own particular career will be affected by automation. But it is well to know what the trends are, and to take them into account in planning.

It is also evident that an increasing level of education will be needed for many kinds of work, and certainly for *moving ahead* in many fields of activity.

Manpower reports published by the Department of Labor indicate that the biggest increases (in employment) will occur in occupations requiring the most education and training. The table on the following page indicates this.

The same report gave the following characteristics of society as being the reasons for the changes in employment predicted for the years to follow 1960:

The continued shift from an agricultural economy to one that is predominantly industrial
The rapid expansion in research and development activities
The increasing size and complexity of business organization
The widespread growth of record keeping among all types of enterprises
The growing need for educational and medical services.

While it is not likely that every individual will be interested in, or able to, plan his vocational career precisely in line with these trends

[2] *Ibid.*,p. 147.

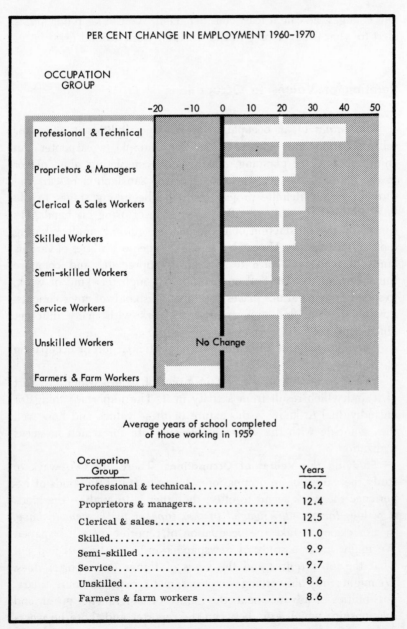

PER CENT CHANGE IN EMPLOYMENT 1960–1970

OCCUPATION
GROUP

|  | -20 | -10 | 0 | 10 | 20 | 30 | 40 | 50 |
|---|---|---|---|---|---|---|---|---|
| Professional & Technical | | | | | | | | |
| Proprietors & Managers | | | | | | | | |
| Clerical & Sales Workers | | | | | | | | |
| Skilled Workers | | | | | | | | |
| Semi-skilled Workers | | | | | | | | |
| Service Workers | | | | | | | | |
| Unskilled Workers | | | No Change | | | | | |
| Farmers & Farm Workers | | | | | | | | |

Average years of school completed
of those working in 1959

| Occupation Group | Years |
|---|---|
| Professional & technical.................... | 16.2 |
| Proprietors & managers.................... | 12.4 |
| Clerical & sales........................ | 12.5 |
| Skilled................................. | 11.0 |
| Semi-skilled ............................ | 9.9 |
| Service................................. | 9.7 |
| Unskilled............................... | 8.6 |
| Farmers & farm workers .................. | 8.6 |

From *Manpower, Challenge of the 1960s,* U.S. Department of Labor, 1960, p. 11.

and changes, he can at least consider them. We can keep our minds alert to what is developing in the world of work around us.

## Relation of Values to Occupations

The *values* of an occupation are the possibilities it offers for self-realization and self-expression. For example, a carpenter can enjoy the thrill of planning, making, and completing some object of usefulness or beauty. He can enjoy the satisfaction of carrying through a very definite project from the beginning stages to the final product. He can enjoy the satisfaction of using his hands. He can enjoy the satisfaction of manipulating, guiding, and operating tools and machinery. He can learn to enjoy the possibilities of various kinds of materials—learn to recognize, appreciate, and compare them. Perhaps he can find opportunity, through this kind of work, to spend time in various places and in various kinds of environments. Possibly he can find opportunities to work with many different kinds of people.

These are some of the *values* in the particular job or occupation of carpentry.

Every occupation has a certain group of values which are part of it and which result from activity in it. The important thing for an individual to know is the nature of these values and how well they coincide with the values in his own life for which he seeks realization.

**Studying the Values of Occupations.** There are two ways to study the values of an occupation: One is to study the kinds of experience the work seems to offer; the other is to analyze the kinds of values *the people engaged in that type of work seem to have.*

For example, take the occupation of reporter on a newspaper. We might make a study of newspapers and reporting to find out what the job requires and the kinds of things the reporter does. We might study his working conditions; matters such as hours, salary, possibilities of advancement, the nature of assignments given, and relationships which exist between the reporter and those he works with and for.

We might study the kinds of reporting jobs there are — straight news reporting, police reporting, political reporting, society reporting, and feature writing, to mention a few. We could watch these reporters at work and note the kinds of materials they handle, how they go about it, and the responsibilities they have to meet.

A large newspaper offers a wide variety of occupations in an interesting field.

*Chicago Sun-Times Photo*

We could study the profession of journalism by reading books on the subject. We could inquire into the kind of training or experience required in reporting.

In other words, we could make a careful *job analysis* of the occupation, and this would give us much information on the values it has to offer. This would show us the possibilities of the job in terms of realizing goals, purposes, or interests any individual considering it as a field of work might have.

The other approach would be to make a study of reporters as people. We could get acquainted with reporters and observe them.

We could find out what they are interested in and how they spend their time. We could inquire into their values and what they enjoy or do not enjoy. We could acquire a considerable amount of information about the values of newspaper work as a result of studying *the people* who are in it.

In a similar way, we could study any particular occupation, and the values it represents, in terms of human wants and activities. We could, then, compare these with our own interests and values.

## Opportunities in the Various Kinds of Occupations

Many individuals do not realize how many different kinds of jobs there are. Often they do not have very much information about the kind of work one would start with in entering an occupational field.

Information materials on both of these important points are available in counseling and placement offices, and in the offices of the various state employment agencies, in the *Dictionary of Occupational Titles*. This is so important to the counselor and to the young person who is considering the world of work that some description of it follows.

The *Dictionary of Occupational Titles* is a standard guide to jobs published by the United States Government, in several volumes. The first volume, entitled "Definition of Titles," gives the definitions and code numbers of occupations. It carries (the second edition) over 22,000 separate jobs. Volume II presents classifications of jobs at various levels.

Part IV of the *Dictionary of Occupational Titles* entitled "Entry Occupational Classification" is, according to Shartle,[3] probably the best source of information concerning the many "entry occupations" in the various fields of work. He defines an entry occupation as an occupation "in which a person without previous work experience may obtain employment."[4] As he points out, it is important for young people to know what the entry occupations are in areas of work in which they are interested, or which are available. "Counselors," says Shartle, "know that young persons must learn to work under supervi-

---

[3] Carroll L. Shartle, *Occupational Information: Its Development and Application* (Englewood Cliffs, N. J.: Third Edition, Prentice-Hall, 1959), p. 209.
   [4] *Ibid.*, p. 209.

sion and to adjust to the social environment of the job. This can be a valuable contribution of the entry job."[5]

The *Dictionary* uses an entry occupational classification which, according to Shartle, "classifies fields of work on the basis of similarity of tasks performed and worker requirements of entry occupations. Worker requirements include individual types of previous training required and apparent interests and abilities required."[6]

Here is an example of a job definition from the *Dictionary of Occupational Titles:*[7]

Interior Decorator (profess. & kin.) 0-43.40 consulting decorator.

Designs artistic interiors for homes, hotels, clubs, boats, and motion-picture arts: Makes a sketch of room showing arrangement of furniture, wall decorations, and the color scheme, and presents to client for approval. Estimates cost and the amount of material necessary. Makes necessary purchases, utilizing knowledge of period furniture to obtain correct size and authentic decorations, decorations in position.

Please note that by careful reading of the definition one can get a fairly good idea of the nature of the work. The fact that the *Dictionary* defines and describes so many different kinds of occupations makes it a valuable tool for studying the nature of jobs and the world of work.

## Occupational Families

Many occupations are similar in the sense that to engage in them the worker must have certain skills and perform certain kinds of work regardless of which occupation he is following. Such groups of occupations—all alike in that they require some common abilities—are called *occupational families*. It is useful to think of jobs in terms of families because in so doing we tend to realize a much greater variety of job opportunities than we would otherwise think of.

For example, the job of clock and watch repairman is related to such highly skilled occupations as instrument maker, camera machinist, speedometer repairman, typewriter serviceman, statistical-machine serviceman, lock assembler, aircraft mechanic, tractor mechanic, and cigar-making-machine mechanic.

---

[5] *Ibid.*, p. 210.
[6] *Ibid.*, p. 211.
[7] *Dictionary of Occupational Titles,* Vol. I, p. 708.

These occupations are all selected from the occupational family of clock and watch repairman. This simply means that there are activities and skills that are common to all of them.

The way in which occupations have skills and activities in common was brought out during the Second World War and was used as a means of finding men and women for quick training for new lines of work where shortages existed.

In planning careers, it is helpful for young people to consider the great variety of occupations related to those which appeal to them and to think of job or occupational families.

## Occupational Classifications

Closely related to the occupational families in usefulness are the broad classifications which have been developed. *The Dictionary of Occupational Titles* gives the following broad classifications of occupations. They are listed here because of their value in showing the different types of work which may be found.[8]

*Professional and Managerial Occupations*

Professional Occupations

Occupations that predominantly require a high degree of mental activity by the worker and are concerned with theoretical or practical aspects of complex fields of human endeavor. Such occupations require . . . either extensive and comprehensive academic study, or experience of such scope and character as to provide an equivalent background, or a combination of such . . . .

Typical professional occupations are those of doctor, lawyer, architect, mechanical engineer, chemist, physicist, astronomer, editor, actor, and musician.

Semiprofessional Occupations

Occupations concerned with the theoretical or practical aspects of fields of endeavor that require rather extensive education or practical experience . . . typically confined to relatively restricted fields. . . .

Chiropodists, tree surgeons, draftsmen, aviators, laboratory technicians, and fingerprint experts are typical semiprofessional occupations.

---

[8]Adapted from Carroll L. Shartle, *Occupational Information* (New York: Prentice-Hall, 1946), p. 115 ff.

## Managerial and Official Occupations

Occupations that are involved primarily with responsible policy-making, planning, supervising, co-ordinating, or guiding the work activity of others, usually through intermediate supervisors. Typical of these occupations are managers or presidents of business enterprises, superintendents of construction projects, and purchasing and advertising agents. Executive secretaries and treasurers, although not usually involved in extensive administrative or managerial duties, are nevertheless included because of their official capacities.

## *Clerical and Sales Occupations*

## Clerical and Kindred Occupations

Occupations concerned with the preparation, transcribing, transferring, systematizing, or preserving of written communications and records in offices, shops and other places of work where such functions are performed. Other occupations, such as collectors, telegraph messengers, and mail carriers, although not strictly of this character are included because of their close relationship to these activities.

## *Service Occupations*

## Domestic Service Occupations

Occupations concerned with the usual functions in the maintenance of households and their environs, the cooking of meals, the care of children, and similar services that are performed in private homes.

## Personal Service Occupations

The typical examples are barbers, waiters, bootblacks, and practical nurses.

## Protective Service Occupations

The services performed by such workers range from the routine duties of a watchman who guards the property of some organization, to the more complicated duties of a traffic policeman or detective, or to those of soldiers and sailors.

## Building Service Workers and Porters

Miscellaneous occupations that are concerned with cleaning the interior and equipment of buildings, offices, stores and similar places, and with moving or carrying equipment, baggage, and other articles.

*Agricultural, Fishery, Forestry, and Kindred Occupations*

Agricultural, Horticultural, and Kindred Occupations

Occupations directly associated with the processes of growing and harvesting vegetables, fruits, grains, and other farm crops; in the raising of poultry, livestock, and other animals and fowls for consumption, for their products, for pets, or exhibition; and in the various phases of horticultural activities. . . .

Fishery Occupations

Occupations of workers who earn their livelihood by actively engaging in catching or gathering all types of sea food and aquatic shells and plants by any one or more of numerous methods.

Forestry (except Logging) and Hunting and Trapping Occupations
Occupations concerned with the development and care of forests and the growing and gathering of forest products; also occupations of workers who guide hunting or trapping parties or who engage in the hunting and trapping of wild animals and game.

*Skilled Occupations*

This category includes craft and manual occupations in manufacturing and related activities, in nonmanufacturing activities, in miscellaneous skilled occupations, and foreman.

*Semiskilled Occupations*

Includes work "limited to a fairly well-defined work routine". . . may require the performance of part of a craft or skilled occupation, but usually to a relatively limited extent.

*Unskilled Occupations*

Manual occupations that involve the performance of simple duties that may be learned within a short period of time and that require the exercise of little or no independent judgment.

Classifications of occupations like these are in part based on the nature of the work, in part on the amount of skill or training needed for the work, and in part on the amount of responsibility involved.

It can be seen that there are hundreds of separate kinds of jobs within these broad classifications. The purposes of referring to them here is to direct attention to the great ranges of opportunity in the world of work.

EXPERIENCED CIVILIAN LABOR FORCE,[1] BY OCCUPATION GROUP AND SEX, 1957-59

| OCCUPATION GROUP | BOTH SEXES 1959 | BOTH SEXES 1958 | BOTH SEXES 1957 | MALE 1959 | MALE 1958 | MALE 1957 | FEMALE 1959 | FEMALE 1958 | FEMALE 1957 |
|---|---|---|---|---|---|---|---|---|---|
| ALL OCCUPATION GROUPS: NUMBER (THOUSANDS) | 68,952 | 68,213 | 67,596 | 46,315 | 45,951 | 45,689 | 22,637 | 22,261 | 21,907 |
| PERCENT | 100.0 | 100.0 | 100.0 | 100.0 | 100.0 | 100.0 | 100.0 | 100.0 | 100.0 |
| PROFESSIONAL, TECHNICAL, AND KINDRED WORKERS | 10.5 | 10.4 | 9.7 | 10.1 | 9.8 | 9.0 | 11.5 | 11.7 | 11.1 |
| MEDICAL AND OTHER HEALTH WORKERS | 1.8 | 1.8 | 1.7 | 1.1 | 1.2 | 1.1 | 3.2 | 3.3 | 3.1 |
| TEACHERS, EXCEPT COLLEGE | 2.5 | 2.3 | 2.0 | .9 | .9 | .7 | 4.9 | 5.1 | 4.7 |
| OTHER PROFESSIONAL, TECHNICAL, AND KINDRED WORKERS | 6.2 | 6.4 | 5.9 | 8.1 | 7.8 | 7.7 | 3.4 | 3.3 | 3.2 |
| FARMERS AND FARM MANAGERS | 4.4 | 4.5 | 4.9 | 6.3 | 6.5 | 7.3 | .5 | .6 | .6 |
| MANAGERS, OFFICIALS, AND PROPRIETORS, EXCEPT FARM | 10.2 | 10.1 | 10.0 | 12.8 | 12.7 | 12.6 | 4.7 | 4.7 | 4.7 |
| SALARIED WORKERS | 5.0 | 4.9 | 4.5 | 6.4 | 6.2 | 5.8 | 2.3 | 2.1 | 2.1 |
| SELF-EMPLOYED WORKERS IN RETAIL TRADE | 2.5 | 2.6 | 2.7 | 3.0 | 3.1 | 3.2 | 1.6 | 1.8 | 2.0 |
| SELF-EMPLOYED WORKERS, EXCEPT RETAIL TRADE | 2.6 | 2.6 | 2.7 | 3.5 | 3.5 | 3.6 | .9 | .9 | .9 |
| CLERICAL AND KINDRED WORKERS | 14.0 | 14.0 | 13.9 | 6.7 | 6.7 | 6.7 | 29.1 | 29.1 | 29.0 |
| STENOGRAPHERS, TYPISTS, AND SECRETARIES | 3.5 | 3.4 | 3.3 | .2 | .2 | .2 | 10.3 | 10.1 | 9.8 |
| OTHER CLERICAL AND KINDRED WORKERS | 10.5 | 10.6 | 10.6 | 6.5 | 6.5 | 6.5 | 18.8 | 19.1 | 19.2 |
| SALES WORKERS | 6.6 | 6.4 | 6.3 | 6.0 | 5.8 | 5.7 | 7.8 | 7.5 | 7.6 |
| RETAIL TRADE | 3.9 | 3.8 | 3.8 | 2.5 | 2.4 | 2.4 | 6.9 | 6.8 | 6.8 |
| OTHER SALES WORKERS | 2.7 | 2.6 | 2.5 | 3.5 | 3.4 | 3.3 | .9 | .7 | .8 |
| CRAFTSMEN, FOREMEN, AND KINDRED WORKERS | 13.1 | 13.3 | 13.3 | 19.0 | 19.2 | 19.2 | 1.0 | 1.1 | 1.1 |
| CARPENTERS | 1.4 | 1.4 | 1.4 | 2.0 | 2.1 | 2.1 | (²) | (²) | (²) |
| CONSTRUCTION CRAFTSMEN, EXCEPT CARPENTERS | 2.7 | 2.6 | 2.6 | 4.1 | 3.9 | 3.9 | .1 | .1 | .1 |
| MECHANICS AND REPAIRMEN | 3.1 | 3.2 | 3.1 | 4.6 | 4.7 | 4.5 | (²) | .1 | .1 |
| METAL CRAFTSMEN, EXCEPT MECHANICS | 1.6 | 1.7 | 1.8 | 2.4 | 2.5 | 2.6 | (²) | .1 | .1 |
| OTHER CRAFTSMEN AND KINDRED WORKERS | 2.6 | 2.6 | 2.5 | 3.7 | 3.6 | 3.4 | .4 | .5 | .5 |
| FOREMEN, NOT ELSEWHERE CLASSIFIED | 1.7 | 1.8 | 1.8 | 2.3 | 2.4 | 2.4 | .4 | .5 | .4 |
| OPERATIVES AND KINDRED WORKERS | 18.6 | 18.8 | 19.8 | 19.9 | 20.0 | 20.9 | 16.0 | 16.5 | 17.5 |
| DRIVERS AND DELIVERYMEN | 3.6 | 3.6 | 3.6 | 5.3 | 5.2 | 5.3 | .1 | .1 | .1 |
| OTHER OPERATIVES AND KINDRED WORKERS | 15.0 | 15.3 | 16.2 | 14.5 | 14.8 | 15.6 | 15.9 | 16.4 | 17.3 |
| DURABLE GOODS MANUFACTURING | 5.5 | 5.5 | 6.0 | 6.1 | 6.2 | 6.7 | 4.3 | 4.2 | 4.7 |
| NONDURABLE GOODS MANUFACTURING | 5.1 | 5.3 | 5.5 | 3.5 | 3.6 | 3.8 | 8.3 | 8.7 | 9.0 |
| OTHER INDUSTRIES | 4.4 | 4.5 | 4.7 | 4.9 | 5.0 | 5.2 | 3.3 | 3.5 | 3.6 |
| PRIVATE HOUSEHOLD WORKERS | 3.3 | 3.4 | 3.2 | .1 | .1 | .1 | 10.0 | 10.2 | 9.7 |
| SERVICE WORKERS, EXCEPT PRIVATE HOUSEHOLD | 9.1 | 8.9 | 8.6 | 6.4 | 6.4 | 6.3 | 14.5 | 13.9 | 13.4 |
| PROTECTIVE SERVICE WORKERS | 1.1 | 1.1 | 1.1 | 1.6 | 1.6 | 1.6 | .1 | .1 | .1 |
| WAITERS, COOKS, AND BARTENDERS | 2.6 | 2.5 | 2.5 | 1.1 | 1.1 | 1.1 | 5.6 | 5.4 | 5.4 |
| OTHER SERVICE WORKERS | 5.3 | 5.2 | 5.0 | 3.7 | 3.7 | 3.6 | 8.7 | 8.4 | 7.9 |
| FARM LABORERS AND FOREMEN | 3.9 | 3.9 | 4.2 | 3.8 | 3.8 | 3.9 | 4.2 | 4.2 | 4.8 |
| PAID WORKERS | 2.3 | 2.3 | 2.4 | 2.8 | 2.8 | 2.9 | 1.3 | 1.4 | 1.3 |
| UNPAID FAMILY WORKERS | 1.6 | 1.6 | 1.8 | 1.0 | 1.0 | 1.0 | 2.9 | 2.8 | 3.5 |
| LABORERS, EXCEPT FARM AND MINE | 6.2 | 6.2 | 6.0 | 9.0 | 9.0 | 8.7 | .5 | .5 | .5 |
| CONSTRUCTION | 1.5 | 1.6 | 1.5 | 2.2 | 2.2 | 2.5 | (²) | (²) | (²) |
| MANUFACTURING | 1.9 | 1.9 | 1.9 | 2.7 | 2.7 | 2.2 | .3 | .3 | (²) |
| OTHER INDUSTRIES | 2.8 | 2.8 | 2.8 | 4.0 | 4.1 | 4.1 | .2 | .2 | (²) |

[1] Includes the employed, classified according to their current job, and the unemployed, classified according to their latest civilian job, if any; excludes the unemployed person who never held a full-time civilian job.

² Less than 0.05 percent.

³ Not available.

From *Special Labor Force Reports No. 4*, U.S. Department of Labor, 1960, p. A-15.

Most modern business concerns are glad to provide help and information to prospective employees through their employment counselers.

*Southern Bell Telephone and Telegraph Company*

**Job Area Jobs.** Within any particular job area—for example, education—there are a great many different jobs. For example, the following list of job opportunities in education[9] is suggestive of the great variety of things you could do and still be a teacher or a worker in education. Yet most people think of education as offering just three or four different job opportunities.

I. Pre-school and Elementary Education

    A. Pre-school
        1. Director of research in child growth
        2. Teachers of pre-school children
        3. Nurses in pre-school
    B. Kindergarten
        1. Kindergarten teachers
        2. Kindergarten assistant
        3. Supervisor of kindergartens

[9]*Careers in Education*, mimeographed report by A. R. Mead.

C. Elementary schools
   1. Teachers for combined grades
   2. Teachers for separate grades
   3. Elementary school principal
   4. Elementary school supervisor
   5. Visiting teacher
   6. Teachers of integrated programs (shortage)
   7. Supervisors of
      a) Arithmetic
      b) Reading
      c) Music
      d) Art
      e) Health and physical education
   8. Child psychologist or counselor
   9. School nurse and director of health service

II. High-school Area
   A. High-school principal
   B. High-school teachers
      1. Mathematics
      2. Science
      3. Social studies
      4. French
      5. Spanish
      6. Latin
      7. English
      8. Industrial arts
      9. Agriculture
      10. Home economics
      11. Trade and industrial education
      12. Co-ordinator co-operative vocational education
      13. Commercial (business education)
      14. Health and physical education
      15. High-school art
      16. High-school music
      17. Department head in large high school—one for each field
      18. Visiting teacher
      19. Teachers of integrated programs (shortage)
      20. Recorder
      21. Counselors or directors of guidance

III. General Administrative Positions
   A. Superintendents of schools
      1. Full-time positions in counties and cities
      2. Part-time positions in small communities
   B. Assistant superintendents of schools usually allocated to certain parts of work

    C. Directors of school attendance
    D. Elementary and high-school principal (previously mentioned)
    E. Director of research and tests and measurements
    F. General and special supervisors of instruction
    G. Business manager
    H. School secretaries
    I. Assistant principals
    J. Director of curriculum
    K. School physician

IV. Special Schools
    A. Schools for deaf, blind, crippled, and delinquent
      1. Principals
      2. Teachers
      3. Attendance officer
      4. School psychologist
      5. School physician

V. Private Schools Usually Have Same Type of Positions as Public Schools with Some Exceptions

VI. Junior Colleges
    A. President and dean
    B. Teachers of different fields (English, mathematics, science, etc.)
    C. Registrar
    D. Business manager
    E. Health service personnel

VII. Teachers Colleges
    A. President
    B. Dean of women
    C. Dean of men
    D. Dean of instruction
    E. Business manager
    F. Registrar
    G. Secretarial workers
    H. Teachers of
      1. Subjects like English, science, etc.
      2. Subjects in education
      3. Teachers in training schools (need is great)
    I. Heads of training schools
    J. School psychologist and director of guidance
    K. Health service personnel

VIII. Liberal Arts Colleges—Positions Like Those of Junior Colleges except More Varieties and Larger Numbers of Them

IX. University Positions
    A. President
    B. Dean of instruction
    C. Dean of men
    D. Dean of women
    E. Registrar
    F. Director of guidance
    G. Deans of separate colleges

        1. Arts
        2. Education
        3. Engineering
        4. Agriculture
        5. Law
        6. Medicine
        7. Fine arts
        8. Pharmacy
        9. Social service
        10. Dentistry

    H. Assistants to deans
     I. Teachers of all subject fields included in a large university—about 300 separate fields
     J. Business manager
    K. Secretaries and accountants
    L. Research workers—part and full time in many fields
    M. Director of research
    N. Field workers for finance, or recruiting students
    O. Field workers for carrying services of university to the people
    P. Health service personnel

 X. Extension and Correspondence Teaching
    A. Head
    B. Teachers in field
    C. Secretarial workers

XI. Private Research Foundations
    A. President
    B. Financial officers
    C. Research workers

XII. Professional Organizations Like National Education Association; other National and State Educational Associations
    A. Head
    B. Executive secretary
    C. Research worker
    D. Field worker

XIII.  Positions in State Departments of Education
    A. State commissioner or superintendent
    B. Deputies
    C. Special field workers

XIV.  Educational Directors in Religious Education

XV.  Educational Directors for Noneducational Agencies Such as Chamber of Commerce, Labor Union, Religious Association, Manufacturing Firm, Wholesale Business, Retail Business, etc.

All of these jobs within the over-all field of education have elements of interest for different people, and all of them provide variations of activity which make them different from one another. When a person is asked to consider teaching as an occupation, he ought to review many of these to determine whether or not some of them are more challenging and interesting to him than others.

The vast network of American railroads offers many interesting, well-paid, and steady jobs.

*Chesapeake and Ohio Railroad Company*

All of the great areas of occupations have similar varieties of jobs within them. Much of this is due to the fact that we live in an age of *specialization*. This is especially evident in industry where there is a tendency for men and women to perform rather narrow operations when compared with the jack-of-all-trades activities of some years ago.

## Women in the World of Work

Among the changes which have been taking place in recent years none has been more noticeable than the marked increase in the number of women who work in almost all phases of the national life.

According to reports issued by various government agencies for the 1960 White House Conference on Children and Youth, there were about 24,000,000 women workers in 1960, and it was expected that the number would increase to 30,000,000 by 1970. It has been anticipated that one out of every three workers, in the United States, by 1970, will be a woman worker.

It has also been observed that there is a tendency for women to work at two or three different periods during their lives. The first is a period of employment prior to or in the first months or years of marriage. The second is a period of employment likely to begin after their children have become old enough to be adequately taken care of while the mother is away at work.

Looking at this from the point of view of the individual, it is possible to see that a young woman needs to be realistic about her working career. Marriage will probably interrupt her work for a period of several years while the children are very young; then, later, when they are older, she may wish to return to work. This means that her work plans should be thought of in terms of (1) beginning work, and (2) later work which might last for a longer period of time.

Of course, we don't always work out our plans this carefully, but it might be wise for young women to look ahead to these possibilities when they are thinking of possible careers.

Women, whose children are far enough along to permit their return to work, may in some cases need further training, or retraining, in order to re-enter the world of work at some level which appeals to them. For this purpose, it might be helpful if they would consult guidance counselors or advisers who are available in the various offices of the state employment services.

It is necessary to realize that with the passing of a few years, there are often changes in business practices or procedures that may make it necessary for them to "catch up" with what has been going on. Secondary schools and junior colleges, as well as other colleges, universities, and Y.M.C.A.'s, often have courses available that will serve as "refresher courses" to help with these problems.

## Kinds of Jobs Available to Women

With the increase in service occupations which seems to be a characteristic of mid-century America, there is a growing demand for clerical workers, a field long available to women. The public schools have particularly emphasized the preparation of women for clerical work.[10]

At the same time, there have been increases in available opportunities for women in teaching and in quite a few professions. Technical fields employ women, and a great number of industrial operations are available to women.

Women should, generally, give full attention to all their possibilities. They should not, it is certain, "write off" any occupation other than the most physically demanding or the most hazardous. Professional and technical employment is available to women on a scale never before dreamed of, and all women should know this and take it into account as they think ahead to the possibility of work and service.

Educators have been emphasizing the fact that it is a mistake for women to shorten their educational careers because they are going to get married. Every sign points to the fact that the nation will need all of the abilities it can get, on the part of both men and women, and that the opportunities for a rich, satisfying life are open to women just as fully as they are to men in our modern world.

---

[10]Figures cited in the 1960 White House Conference on Children and Youth showed that one-third of the girls in high school are enrolled in commercial courses.

## Job Opportunities in Your Community

Usually people are not too familiar with the jobs to be found in their own communities. This is especially true in smaller cities and towns where very often different kinds of business and industry may be carried on without much publicity and almost without the knowledge of the community as a whole.

Each community should have an occupational survey to determine what is going on in the job world, but these have not been made in most American communities.

However, each individual can make a survey of his own to determine what kinds of job opportunities exist in his particular area. Ways of doing this include: (1) looking through the classified section of the telephone book (you will be surprised to find out how many different kinds of businesses and industries there are in your own home town), (2) consulting such groups as the chamber of commerce for published information on business opportunities in your own community, and (3) consulting the officers of the state employment service in your area for a list of occupations which are available. There are interviewers and counselors in these agencies who will be glad to talk over job possibilities with you.

Just as an example, the following may be of interest as showing the range of job opportunities in a small American Community (Griffin, Georgia) in which an occupational survey was made:[11]

| | |
|---|---|
| Automobile and automobile accessory dealers | Automobile service stations |
| Department stores | Automobile garages |
| Dry goods and general clothing | Automobile painting shops |
| Five- and ten-cent stores | Blacksmith shops |
| Dairies and ice cream companies | Electrical companies |
| Grocery stores | Plumbers |
| Restaurants and cafes | Cabinetmaking shops |
| Furniture stores | Printing shops |
| Bicycle shops | Sheet Metal shops |
| Feed stores | Express companies |
| Florists | Government offices— city, county |
| | Georgia experiment station |

---

[11]Occupational Survey of Griffin, Ga. (National Youth Administration).

Coal, ice, and gas dealers
Jewelry stores
Drug stores
Barber shops
Beauty shops
Cleaners, launderers, and
   pressers
Photographers
Shoe shops
Advertising
Banks
Finance corporations
Life insurance
Real estate and fire insurance
Lawyers
Dentists
Hospitals
Opticians
Chiropractors and osteopaths
Physicians
Veterinarians

Public welfare department
Hotels
Moving and hauling companies
Newspapers
Railroad stations
Taxicab service
Telegraph company
Theaters
Cotton dealers
Grocery companies
Livestock dealers
Petroleum companies
Warehouses
Bottling companies
Box manufacturers
Cotton mills (major industry of
   the city)
Cotton oil manufacturing
Grist and flour mills
Hosiery and knitting mills
Mattress companies

## Importance of the Pattern of the Job

The pattern of a job is very important to the individual. Probably a great many people enter an occupation without giving this enough thought.

For example, a dentist usually finds a rather definite pattern of activity within which most of his work falls. If he is a practitioner, he finds himself cleaning teeth, locating and filling cavities, extracting teeth when necessary, straightening teeth, making false teeth (plates, bridges, etc.), and taking care of the general maintenance of hygienic conditions for his patients. Of course, along with this he must perform many activities—a great variety of them—learning how to use X-rays, various kinds of equipment, materials, etc. He must study the anatomy of the mouth and relationships between the teeth and the other important parts of the body, including the nervous system and the whole realm of hygiene. He has to know a good bit about medicine in general.

But the point is that the *job* sets a pattern of activity which will determine to a great extent the way in which the dentist will spend his energy and his time.

Similarly the work of an automobile mechanic, a refrigerator repairman, a draftsman, a printer—any of hundreds of jobs—might be explained or described. The variations in the work are often unpredictable and sometimes are indirectly related. For example, a telephone lineman who is employed by a big organization may perform much the same kind of work from day to day. However, he may find himself working in many different parts of the country and under conditions which vary from repairing equipment in southern Florida following a summer hurricane to patching up communications in the windswept prairies of North Central States after a winter snowstorm. He may be working at one time in some downtown office building area and at another time in a lonely forest section in the mountains.

Jobs should be analyzed for their possibilities, if they are being considered for a life's work.

## The Job as a Means of Setting a Life Pattern

It should be clear that the choice of an occupation does determine, to a greater extent than is commonly realized, the life pattern of the individual and, for that matter, of his family.

For example, traveling men are away from home for a month or longer at a stretch. Their lives are spent on the road, talking with customers, and in hotels. When they are home, they must crowd into a short time many relationships with their families and neighbors which they have not been able to attend to while away.

A college professor spends many hours in activities connected with his teaching duties or with the college. He attends committee meetings; meets with student groups; is expected to put in an appearance at assemblies, at lectures and musical events; and more or less moves in a circle which has the college or university as its center. His friends tend to be other faculty members and, to some extent, students. He has few contacts with businessmen and professional men in the community; his whole life is related to his job. There are quite a few activities in the community which take up a good bit of his time because, as a professor, he is expected to take part in them. We are much ruled by what people expect of us. We are very reluctant to do things which are not expected or approved by the groups whose good wishes and esteem are important to us. For example, the college professor is unlikely to take much part in some amusements which other members of the community expect him to avoid—even though they enjoy these same activities themselves. In other words, the pattern of the professor's life is set to some extent by his job.

Similarly, we could describe the way in which the farmer, the auto mechanic, the nurse, the clerk in a department store, or the painter finds that his life falls into a pattern pretty much determined by the occupation he has chosen.

This gives an importance to wise choosing of occupations that goes far beyond the things that are actually done on the job itself. The nature of our work may determine the kind of place in which we live, the geographical area in which we live, the friends we have, and the way in which we spend our leisure time. It may determine the amount of time we can have to spend with our families; it may determine the kinds of activities and friends that the members of the family can have. It might even determine the kind of political beliefs we have and the nature of our activities in politics. (For example, we might have some kinds of government jobs which would keep us from voting or from taking any part in the activities of political parties. Federal laws prohibit United States Government employees from taking an active part in some kinds of federal political activities, and some states have similar laws or regulations which limit the political activities of state employees.)

Perhaps these suggestions are enough to show what we mean when we emphasize the point that the job is a means of setting a pattern of life.

## Types of Occupations for Consideration

It should be noted briefly that there are not only many varieties of jobs in the world, and within each of the broad job families, but that there are types of jobs according to the nature of the things done.

Some jobs require working with things, some require working with people, some involve working with ideas, and some require combinations of these.

The constant challenge of solving problems in this telephone trunk relay system is what makes the job interesting for these two men.

*Southern Bell Telephone and Telegraph Company*

Since many positions require combinations of these (working with things *and* working with people, for example), the individual who is considering future occupational possibilities should keep these in mind and study the characteristics of any proposed occupation accordingly.

In this connection, the value of thinking of job families is apparent. For example, a young man with some rather evident personality shortcomings but with considerable academic ability was recently advised to try for a research job which would enable him to work with ideas and with materials, making use of his knowledge but at the same time requiring little contact with people. This was a change from a previous objective of being a teacher, but it was a much better and more satisfactory job outlook for this particular young man in his vocational planning.

## Self-Realization Through the Job

One of the most important things in a person's life is his job. The job gives the man or woman a chance to keep well occupied, to earn a living for himself and his family, to make a contribution to his fellow men, and above all to earn the satisfaction of self-realization.

Work experience teaches the individual not only to make good use of his abilities but also how to get along with people—the most important single consideration of all. It provides him with interests to occupy his time and activities to use his energies. It enables him to learn the habits and skills which are necessary for successful living.

Psychologists would naturally place the greatest emphasis on the values to one's own personality which result from a worth-while occupation.

## Practical Suggestions for Vocational Guidance

Choosing a life's work involves quite a few things. Let's note that: (1) It isn't easy. You can't put a quarter in a machine, turn the crank, and have an answer come out. (2) It takes time. Some people have required several years of study and tryouts before they have come to the *right* vocational decision. (3) There are certain things that have to be done. Some of them are outlined in the pages that follow. (4) It is entirely possible for anyone to find the occupation which would be right for *him* if certain important principles are kept in mind.

You might approach this problem by first asking, "What kind of jobs are there?" Or, you might begin with the questions, "What can *I* do best? What do my interests and abilities fit me for?"

One approach starts with the world around us — the world of jobs. The other approach starts with *us*—what we are, and what we can do, and then looks out at the world of jobs to see what is available.

It seems best to look at the world of work first. This is not so limiting a way of going about it. Furthermore, we realize that there are many occupations which require, at least in part, the same abilities. Let's find out what the world of work has to offer, first, and then see how we might fit into it. *Keep in mind that choosing a job is choosing a pattern of life. The values in the job, compared to your own values, are what count.*

**Study the Various Possible Occupations.** Reference has been made to the *Dictionary of Occupational Titles.*[12] In one section of that series, Part IV, called "Entry Occupational Classification," six main fields of work are given. These are occupational families in a *very broad* sense. They are as follows:

## SUMMARY OF MAJOR OCCUPATIONAL GROUPS

(Numbers Refer to Number Classification in Dictionary)

0-X Professional, Technical, and Managerial Work

| | |
|---|---|
| 0-X1 | Artistic work |
| 0-X2 | Musical work |
| 0-X3 | Literary work |
| 0-X4 | Entertainment work |
| 0-X6 | Public service work |

---

[12]The list might be a good starting point for any person who is exploring occupational possibilities.

It is suggested that the following types of information would be helpful in deciding which of the classifications an individual might place himself in: (1) personal traits; (2) leisure time activities (your hobbies, etc.); (3) work experience (jobs you have held, even short ones, might show likes and dislikes); (4) any training you have had.

|       | 0-X7 | Technical work |
|-------|------|----------------|
|       | 0-X8 | Managerial work |
| 1-X   | Clerical and Sales Work | |
|       | 1-X1 | Computing work |
|       | 1-X2 | Recording work |
|       | 1-X4 | General clerical work |
|       | 1-X5 | Public contact work |
| 2-X   | Service Work | |
|       | 2-X1 | Cooking |
|       | 2-X3 | Child care |
|       | 2-X5 | Personal service work |
| 3-X   | Agricultural, Marine, and Forestry Work | |
|       | 3-X1 | Farming |
|       | 3-X8 | Marine work |
|       | 3-X9 | Forestry work |
| 4-X   | Mechanical Work | |
|       | 4-X2 | Machine trades |
|       | 4-X6 | Crafts |
| 6-X   | Manual Work | |
|       | 6-X2 | Observational work |
|       | 6-X4 | Manipulative work |
|       | 6-X6 | Elemental work |

Note that these are kinds of work given in the main occupational groups. Within each kind of work there are many *jobs*. For example, there are many occupations connected with "entertainment work" or with "general clerical work."

If there is something about the kind of work that appeals to you—entertainment work, working with machines, or whatever it may be—then *the next step* will be to see what kinds of *jobs* or *occupations* are found in that general area.

To do this you may want to make use of the "Entry Occupational Classification" which the government has prepared. You might want to get a copy either at the library or at the office of the state employment service in your community. Look at the jobs which are listed under your chosen classification. If you visit a state employment office (state employment offices are affiliated with the United States Employment Service), talk with one of the vocational advisers about it. If you have access to a school counselor, discuss it with him.[13]

---

[13]Another way to get job suggestions is to consult the books which deal with occupations. Some of these are mentioned in a later paragraph in this chapter. An example of the variety of occupations found in a typical American community is given in the excerpt from the Griffin occupational survey, also cited in this chapter. The important thing is to select some occupational possibilities for further study.

**How To Find Out about Occupations.** Here are some suggestions to help you find out about different occupations.

1. Read pamphlets and books which have been written to describe them.

2. Find people engaged in the occupations. Observe them. Note the kinds of lives they lead and the things they are interested in. Talk with them if possible.

3. Get a part-time or full-time job in the occupation and try it out.

*First,* you could get, from the library or from a counseling office, if one is available to you, books and monographs describing occupations. There are a great many of these. Some information may be obtained from such sources as SRA's *Job Family Series and Occupational Briefs.*

The SRA's *Job Family Series* is described by the publisher[14] as "a series of booklets which classify specific occupations into job families, based on common tasks and required interests and abilities. The *Job Family Series* is designed to acquaint students with several jobs in the occupational fields in which they might be interested and successful."

Here are the job families or groups included in the above, as of 1960:

Jobs in Science
Jobs in Mechanical Work
Jobs in Outdoor Work
Jobs in Technical Work
Jobs in Selling
Jobs in Clerical Work
Jobs in Engineering
Jobs in Mathematics
Jobs in Building Construction Trades
Jobs in Health
Jobs in Agriculture
Jobs in Art
Jobs in Publishing
Jobs in Performing Arts

This publisher also makes available some 280 or more *Occupational Briefs,* describing in four-page, illustrated form, some 286 occupations. Occupational information of this type may be secured either from the publishers, or through the services of guidance counselors and libraries.

---

[14]Science Research Associates, Inc. 259 East Erie St., Chicago, Illinois.

Helpful information regarding careers and occupations may also be found in the bi-monthly publication *Your Future Occupation*, edited by Max F. Baer and published at Washington, D.C. (P.O. Box 7408).

Other sources are:

The H. W. Wilson Company's, *Occupational Literature* (New York: H. W. Wilson Co., 1958).

Walter James Greenleaf, *Occupations and Careers* (New York: McGraw-Hill Book Company, Inc., 1955).

John M. Brewer and Edward Landy, *Occupations Today* (Boston: Ginn & Co., 1943).

Mildred A. Davey, N. Smith, and Theodore R. Myers, *Everyday Occupations* (Boston: D. C. Heath & Co., 1945).

Mary Ford Detjen and Erwin W. Detjen, *Your Plans for the Future* (New York: McGraw-Hill Book Co., 1947).

There are many separate pamphlets describing occupations, including those published under the heading of *Vocational Guidance Monographs* (Commonwealth Book Co., Chicago); *Career Research Monographs* (Institute for Research, Chicago); *Vocational and Professional Monographs* (Bellman Publishing Co., Inc., Boston); and the *American Job Series of Occupational Monographs* (Science Research Associates, Inc., Chicago).

## WHAT THESE MONOGRAPHS WILL TELL YOU[15]

1. Something about the history of the occupation.
2. Importance of the occupation, and its relation to society.
3. Something about the size of the occupation (number of workers, etc.).
4. Number of workers needed in it. Something about the trends in the occupation (is it expanding?).
5. Duties, things done, and what is expected of the worker.
6. Qualifications to enter the occupation.
7. Preparation and education needed for it.
8. How to go about entering it.
9. Length of time before skill is attained (including information about union membership and apprenticeship where that is involved).
10. Advancement possibilities.
11. Related occupations to which job may lead.

[15]Adapted from National Vocational Guidance Association, *Content of a Good Occupational Monograph* (available from the National Vocational Guidance Association, 1424 Sixteenth St., N.W., Washington, D.C.).

12. Earnings, rates of pay, etc.
13. Hours, vacation time, etc.
14. Regularity of employment—conditions which might affect it.
15. Health and accident hazards of the occupation.
16. Organizations—of employers in the occupation, unions, etc.
17. Typical places where you would work.
18. Other information and places where you can secure it.

*Note:* All occupational monographs may not contain all of the above items, but many of them will include a majority of the items.[16]

Information about many occupations is published in booklet form by agencies of the United States Government. For example, descriptions of a great many jobs may be obtained by writing to the Superintendent of Documents, U.S. Government Printing Office, Washington, D.C., or to the U.S. Office of Education, Department of Health, Education, and Welfare.

A valuable source of information for young people interested in exploring the world of occupations is the *Occupational Outlook Handbook.*[17] The 1959 edition contains 785 pages and is considered by vocational guidance counselors to be one of the most important sources of job information available in the United States.

One reviewer of this important document points out that it is designed to provide occupational information young people need to help them in career decisions, and that the 1959 revision includes information on the following:

. . . nature of the work; where employed; training, other qualifications, and advancement; employment outlook; earnings and working conditions; and sources of further information. It also expands the *Handbook's* coverage of the world of work to a new total of more than 600 occupations and 30 industries. Among the important kinds of work new to the *Handbook* are electronic computer programmers, occupations in missiles and spacecraft, technicians, instrument repairmen, school counselors, clergymen, motor vehicle drivers, protective service occupations, and occupations in the baking and the paper and pulp industries. Among the major trends influencing outlook changes in these and other occupations since 1957, we are informed, are the continuing growth and changing composition of the population and labor force, advances in science and technology, and the rising levels of education being required and attained for both job entry and job advancement.[18]

---

[16]For a full discussion of many of these, see Chapter XX.

[17]*Occupational Outlook Handbook* (U.S. Department of Labor Bulletin No. 1255. [Washington, D.C.: Superintendent of Documents, U.S. GPO, 1959]).

[18]David H. Pritchard, *The Personnel and Guidance Journal* (American Personnel and Guidance Association, February, 1961), p. 514.

*Second,* Talk with someone engaged in the occupation. You can establish contact with a person in the occupation by: (1) calling at one of the industries in your area employing workers in this field and making your request known, or (2) by arranging for such an appointment through the state employment service office in your community or one of the school counseling offices (if available). Usually the chamber of commerce in your community will be glad to help establish a contact of this sort in case the other agencies are not available. Most people are glad to be of what help they can to young people who are interested in finding out about occupations. However, since there are "all kinds of people" engaged in many of these occupations, it might be *better* to arrange for an interview through the vocational advisers at the state employment service or through a school counseling office, since either of these two agencies would be more likely to be helpful in establishing the best kind of contacts.

*Third,* visit, if possible, the industry or occupation you have in mind. The same method of arranging for this is advisable that is suggested for arranging for an interview with one of the workers. On the other hand, many of the larger industries, especially, have regularly conducted tours through their establishments and are glad to show visitors around during business hours.

*Fourth,* arrange to get a part-time or tryout job with the industry or in the occupation you are considering. You would hardly take this step or want to do this until you had made some investigation of the occupation and come to the conclusion that you might really be interested. However, there is nothing like an actual experience on the job to give one an understanding and appreciation of its possibilities and its good and bad points.

**These Suggestions May Help You.** There are moving pictures available which describe different occupations and industries. These usually can be seen through arrangement with counseling offices in schools or through other organizations having access to the films. Sometimes church groups, Y.M.C.A.'s, and similar organizations can arrange to get and show films of this nature to interested persons.

Newspapers and magazines are sources of information, from time to time, about industries and occupations.

One way to find out about many occupations is to write to one of the business firms engaged in the occupation for printed and illustrative material. Many organizations publish descriptive material about their work. They are glad to send it to interested persons.

In fact, a person could—without too much trouble—build up a fair-sized library of his own about almost any occupation or industry in which he felt that he had sufficient interest to justify looking for, and writing for, books and materials.

It can be seen from these suggestions that finding out about occupations and jobs is not a hard thing to do, provided you are interested enough to make some effort in that direction. One book lists and gives notes on about 3,000 different pamphlets, leaflets, books, and other materials describing occupations.[19] This suggests that there has been a large volume of material produced on the subject covering a wide variety of occupations.

## Kinds of Skills and Abilities a Job Requires

Many occupations require the ability to work with machines. Shartle estimates that about 20 percent of all jobs do.[20] Likewise 45 percent of all occupations require the ability to learn to use tools.

It is obvious that the amount of training necessary to use tools or machines will vary greatly from job to job. In some cases, the training will be long and extensive because of the complex nature of the machinery—in others the training can be given on the job in a few hours.

Yet it is one of the things that the person who is examining an occupation needs to consider.

Shartle also notes[21] that about 10 to 15 percent of all jobs require the ability to supervise other people; about 10 percent of all jobs require working under hazardous conditions; 30 percent of all jobs require "ability to adjust to repetitive operations" and 40 percent require "average aptitude" in eye-hand coordination.

In addition, there are other questions that the prospective job-seeker might consider about occupations he has in mind.

---

[19]Gertrude Forrester, *Occupational Literature* (New York: H. W. Wilson Co., 1954).

[20]Carroll L. Shartle, *Occupational Information* (Englewood Cliffs, N.J.: Prentice-Hall, Inc., 1959), p. 254.

[21]*Ibid.*, p. 254.

Does the job require any special knowledge or ability? (knowledge of mathematics, of a foreign language, or ability to write, for example.)

Does the job require any special physical strength or endurance?

Just how much education is necessary to be considered for the job?

These are just examples of the kinds of questions about job requirements that might be asked.

**The Values To Consider.** These are in many ways the most basic considerations of all. But in connection with choosing jobs, it is necessary to realize that one must *start somewhere*. The important thing is to know where the path leads or might lead. Often a beginning job will have to be accepted or rejected along the lines of the facts mentioned in the preceding paragraph; but we must have the long range view in mind if we are to make a truly satisfactory occupational choice.

*Keep These Questions in Mind.* They have to be thought of in relation to you as an individual.

1. Does the job involve working with people? Do I enjoy working with people?

2. Does the job involve working with *things?* Do I enjoy working with things?

3. Does it involve using machinery or tools? Would that be interesting to me?

4. What kind of people would I be working with and what kind of people would I be working for?

5. Would the place in which I would be working be in harmony with my tastes, interests, and desires? (For example, outdoor *vs.* indoor work, etc.)

6. Would the kind of life I would have to lead in connection with this kind of job be suitable? How would it affect me in connection with such things as: having the kind of home and home life I would like, having the kind of friends I would like, taking part in leisure time activities I would enjoy, etc.?

7. Would the occupation have any important bearing on my present or future home life?

8. Is the kind of work done in harmony with my social and ethical ideals? Is it useful and important work? Would I feel that I was making a contribution to society that would be, or could be, worth while?

9. Would this kind of work give me a chance to develop as a person and to make the best of my own talents and abilities?

## Finding Out about Yourself

The material thus far presented has to do with discovering the occupational world and what it has to offer. The other side of the twofold problem has to do with your own aptitudes, capacities, and interests.

Every clue to these interests and aptitudes is worth considering. Much of the information you can obtain about yourself will be picked up informally as you go along. You find that you like this or dislike that, that you have the "knack" for doing one thing, and that you have an apparent inability to handle something else.

"I guess that isn't in my line," you will comment about some of the activities you try. About others: "There's something I could really go for!"

In connection with determining our interests, aptitudes, and capacities for important occupations, however, we must be more careful. We must not rely on the informal, casual experiences too much. Instead we must put together *all* of our experiences and contrast what we have to offer with the actual requirements of the field.

Choosing a life's work is too important to leave to snap judgments.

**Finding Out about Yourself through Tests.** Tests can tell you something about your general ability and something about your probable aptitude for certain areas of work.

However, most of the tests must be administered through counseling offices by persons who are qualified to do this. If you can have access to a reputable counseling office, in a school or privately operated organization, you might find it to your advantage to undergo a battery of tests.

Tests of intelligence (verbal, social, and mechanical), tests of aptitude, and tests of personality and character are available, as well as tests which can give you a picture of your interests. Unless the tests are administered by a qualified person, they can be very misleading indeed.

No one should use the services of a private counseling agency unless it is on the approved list of the National Vocational Guidance Association, or it is without question responsible to a well organized school program. In the better staffed offices of the state employment services, affiliated with the United States Employment Service, reliable counselors and vocational advisers may be found who can help.

*Pointers about Tests.* Here are a few pointers that may help you.

1. Intelligence tests measure general intelligence in a fairly satisfactory manner. Highly complex occupations and professions require a considerable amount of general intelligence, particularly intelligence of the "abstract" or "academic" kind. If, on the basis of general intelligence tests, it appears that your intelligence (abstract or academic) falls somewhat below the intelligence level of people usually found in any particular profession or occupation, you would do well to "think twice" before choosing it as a career, realizing that the obstacles for success would be considerable.

2. There is considerable overlapping in the *range* of intelligence required for various occupations. In almost any occupation you could think of, there will be some people of very high general intelligence and some with very low general intelligence. Consequently, intelligence test scores are not to be thought of as the *only* factor of importance in connection with choosing a career.

3. Tests of aptitude (such as tests supposedly measuring clerical aptitude, mechanical aptitude, and other forms) have *limited* value. Although much experimental work has been done and is being done, we must not expect to be able to take a single test or even a series of tests and come out with an accurate picture of what we should do. *The information we get from aptitude tests helps, and is useful, but it is not conclusive.*

4. The battery of aptitude tests provided by the United States Employment Service,[22] the so-called *General Aptitude Test Battery,* is useful in suggesting broad fields of work for which our abilities may fit us.

5. Personality tests are also useful, but they are not to be considered as able to determine with finality what we should do in the world of occupations.

6. An entire group of tests, including all of the above types, can provide us with a very useful body of information. If we can take the tests and go over this information with a person who is trained in interpreting them, and who will not draw too many conclusions from the information they supply, they can be very useful in vocational guidance.

7. *Interest inventories* are available which can help us to determine the fields of work in which we might have *interests.* They are very useful for this purpose. They do not tell us what kinds of jobs we would succeed in but only suggest kinds of work we might be interested in. One of their greatest advantages is that they may suggest fields of work to us which we might not otherwise think about.

**Finding Out about Yourself through Counseling.** Talking with other people about your occupational interests and ambitions is

---

[22]Consult your local state employment office about these.

useful. Counselors are available, as has been suggested, in the various state employment offices. Many schools and colleges have counseling services, and there are some private counseling services. As has been noted, select them with extreme care. Do not employ counseling services, no matter how "dignified" or "high sounding" the persons conducting them may appear to be, unless they are recognized and accredited. You would not go to a quack doctor. Do not go to a quack counselor.

Counselors who are trained for their work can be very helpful in discussing your plans and problems with you. You will also find some advantage in talking over your vocational interests, generally, with people engaged in educational or social work. Some of them may not be able to tell you just what you should do, but they might help you to see occupational possibilities which had not occurred to you, and they could help you to define your own problems and your own goals and purposes. They might help you to decide what some of your own *values* are.

Training in the industrial arts develops interests that are often important in vocational guidance.

*Courtesy of Myron Cunningham Photography*

When you know what the important things are in connection with wise occupational choices, you can evaluate for yourself many of the things which these people will tell you or which they will offer as opinions.

**Finding Out about Yourself through Tryout Experiences.** This is one of the most important ways of all to find out about yourself. By trying farming, we can soon discover whether we are interested in it and whether or not we have "what it takes" to be a good farmer.

Tryout experiences are available in some schools through such courses as general shop where some of the things which are done in various trades are "tried out." You can discover something about your aptitudes as well as your interests through them.

Extracurricular activities in school are excellent forms of tryout experiences. Working for the school paper can show you whether you would like, or be good at, reporting or not. The business side of activities is excellent tryout experience for business, clerical, and financial types of work. Selling advertisements for the school paper is a good tryout for selling.

Out-of-school activities provide many similar experiences. Part-time selling jobs can try out your selling ability for you. Part-time or evening selling has shown many a man whether or not he should consider the insurance business seriously.

All sorts of hobbies of your own could give you a tryout along many lines. Here are a few suggestions:

1. Try making something out of wood, metal, or plastics.
2. Try your hand at drawing, water coloring, or painting.
3. Try your hand at musical activities.
4. Try your hand at writing something—a poem or a story.
5. Take a job as an officer in a church or young peoples' organization and get some leadership, financial, or secretarial experience.
6. Try gardening.
7. Make a plan to collect some things—shells, timetables, insects, old coins, stamps. Be systematic about it and see whether or not there are any things about this type of activity you would like or could be "good" at.
8. Get an opportunity to go on a camping trip and see how you like some of the many things that have to be done outdoors: the water, the woods, and the recreational side of camping.
9. Look through the magazines or newspaper for some selling opportunities and try one or two of them out.
10. Look through some popular magazines in the area of mechanics, or arts and crafts (such as *Popular Mechanics*), and try your hand at making or producing one of the articles suggested and described.

In connection with any of these, you should "get into it" far enough to see whether or not you really would like it—really could do it. A halfhearted try is no try at all, nor would it be a good test. Some of the activities require "staying with them" long enough to get over the beginning difficulties and get to the point where some of the satisfactions of the activity begin to appear.

Finally, when and if you have given a good bit of study to a possible job, and you feel that it would justify the time and effort involved, there is no substitute for an actual period of time spent in the work, that is, a "real" tryout on the job itself. Usually there is not much lost, and there is much gained from such experiences. A football coach recently said that, after two years of coaching and teaching athletics, he was persuaded to try his hand at selling insurance. He thought he might be able to make a much better income.

The monetary compensation for a job is not the only one to be considered.

"I tried it," he said, "and I really was making money. But I couldn't keep my mind on it. Every afternoon found me wandering in the direction of the athletic field to see how the boys were getting along. Money or no money, I found out where my heart really was, and now I'm glad to be back in the teaching field again."

If a tryout experience shows that the occupation is the one we like and for which we are really suited, the investment made in time and perhaps money is completely worth while. Perhaps it is just as worth while if the experience shows us the type of occupation we are not suited for. There is not the slightest doubt but that there is a degree of satisfaction as to whether a job is the "right" one or not, which the tryout gives, that can come in no other way.

**Testing What You Have Learned about the Job and Yourself.** Although the tryout experience has these values, it is not possible to arrive at sound conclusions without a careful comparison of one experience with another.

It is necessary to be systematic about it—to write down the advatages and disadvantages, the rewards and the "not-so-good" elements of the job.

If you are trying to compare possible occupational choices, we might suggest writing down, on parallel sheets of paper, the advantages and disadvantages of each of the occupations under consideration. You can then decide where the strong points and weak points lie. You can decide whether, with more training, you could qualify for the work and whether or not it would be worth the effort.

You should also check on the availabilty or possibility of training. On pages to come, a check list or guide sheet is provided which might be suggested for the purpose of charting your course or coming to a decision.


## A Word of Caution

In a free industrial democracy such as ours, it is not always possible to enter an occupation you have chosen just when you would like to enter it or under the conditions that you would consider ideal.

Occasionally, there are periods when our industrial economy has variations in its speed and certainty of operation, and some times occupational openings are not available. You may find that if this happens, the doorway to entering the occupation of your choice is closed.

In such cases, it may be necessary to take any job that comes along—any job, that is, within limits. Try to find one that will be related to your choice, at least. Try to find one that will give you worth-while experiences or at least a tryout in some of the activities you would like to explore.

And in the event that fails, take the job you can get, but *remember this:* no job is a total waste of time so far as you are concerned. Every job has in it the problems of getting along with people, of adjusting to difficult situations, of finding out about your own abilities and limitations. Every job has something worth while to offer. Take the job you have to take in order to "buy the groceries"; then, when the situation in our industrial life improves, you will be just that much more used to the world of work and that much more likely to "know how" to make successful progress in the occupation of your choice.

Sometimes, in the period of time during which you must be satisfied with a job other than one in your chosen field, you can be studying or training yourself for the opportunity that will, in due time, be yours. Many a man who had to be in the armed forces for a long period of time, during the Second World War, took advantage of his spare time to take correspondence courses and other kinds of training, in preparation for his real life's work upon separation from the Service.

## SOMETHING TO DO

In occupational surveys made by the National Youth Administration before the Second World War, the following occupational fields were used to classify job opportunities and to show changes in occupational patterns in different communities: manufacturing and mechanical; transportation and communication; trade; public service; domestic and personal service; professional service; clerical service; and agriculture.

Under each of these headings, write down the names or descriptions of several jobs which you consider to be interesting or important. Then check those in which you know someone personally. Can you see any ways in which the work he does influences the character of his life, way of living, or ways of doing things?

## QUESTIONS AND PROBLEMS FOR STUDY AND DISCUSSION

1. Explain what is meant by the statement that a person's job sets a "pattern of life" for him.

2. Give an example of an occupation, and name several other occupations which might be related to it in an occupational family.

3. What would the psychologist consider to be the most important value a job has for the individual?

4. Mention three main types of work which are important from the standpoint of interests.

5. Explain how an occupation can be considered from the standpoint of the *values* it provides. How are these important to the individual?

6. What methods are suggested for studying the values of an occupation?

7. Take a look at the classified advertising section of the telephone book, and make a list of a dozen types of occupations represented in it—occupations you had not thought much about as providing job opportunities.

8. What is meant by the "pattern of the job"? Write a brief description of the pattern of a job in which you are interested.

9. Explain what is meant by an occupational survey.

10. Explain the nature and use of the *Dictionary of Occupational Titles*.

11. Take an occupation such as teacher, machinist, electrician, or farmer, and show how many varied kinds of work may be found in it.

12. What might be said about the difference in education or training required for professional and nonskilled jobs?

13. How does an individual's occupation affect the pattern of life of his family? Give an example.

14. What might be some of the difficulties of adjustment that could arise if a person were unable to secure and hold a good job?

15. Why should a young person study the world of work and the occupational opportunities provided before making a final decision as to his own choice?

## Study the World of Work

1 STUDY what broad areas of work would be best for you. See the United States Government check list. Survey the world of work around you.

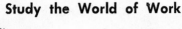

2 SELECT certain jobs or occupations in the area of your choice for further study. See entry on occupational classifications. Talk with counselors.

3 GET all the information you can about the occupations that interest you. See books and monographs. Talk with people in these occupations. Seek tryout experiences. A vast literature on occupations is available. Use it!

4 AFTER narrowing down your choice, test it carefully against what you know of yourself. Do you know enough about the world of work to know what the occupational opportunities are? Keep reading and investigating until you are satisfied on this point.

**Chart A**

## Study Yourself

**1** YOUR job will be a major factor in determining what life will mean to you. What kind of a pattern of life are you looking for? What are the values, goals, and purposes you hope to realize through your work?

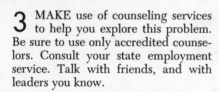

**2** BY-PASS tests unless you take them under the direction of competent persons. What do tests show about you? What do they show about your (1) intelligence, (2) interests, (3) aptitudes, and (4) personality?

**3** MAKE use of counseling services to help you explore this problem. Be sure to use only accredited counselors. Consult your state employment service. Talk with friends, and with leaders you know.

**4** EXPLORE your interests and abilities through (1) part-time jobs, (2) activities in and out of school, and (3) hobbies and tryouts of your own. Courses and training programs can help you. Ask yourself: Have you evaluated your own abilities, interests, and aptitudes *realistically*? Are there some things you could still do along this line?

**Chart B**

## Evaluate Any Specific Job Proposal

1 HOW does the proposed job "check" in terms of what it can do for you? How does it suit your goals, your purposes, your ambitions? Is it in line with your interests?

2 HOW do the specific things to be done in the occupation check with your talents and abilities? Is the occupation in line with what you *can* do? Be realistic.

3 HOW does the proposed job check with regard to conditions of work? Will they be satisfactory to you? Don't tackle an occupation unless you're willing to meet the conditions.

4 DOES the job or occupation have a future? Are there definite lines of advancement and opportunities for training? Look ahead a little. You are planning for a long time. If the proposed occupation meets all tests—for you—up to this point, you are probably justified in selecting it for the big test of training and experience.

**Chart C**

CHAPTER SEVENTEEN

# LEARNING TO LIVE AT HOME

This chapter is given over to the study of what our homes mean to us, and what conditions are necessary for establishing and maintaining a home which can do the things for us that a home should do.

It takes up the psychological values of the home. These are just as important, if not more important, than physical values having to do with food and shelter.

The chapter is very specific about some of the things which can cause unfavorable situations at home. It is also specific in suggesting how we can go about improving home relations.

It emphasizes the fact that, as in other problems of psychology, much depends on the extent to which we understand what the "other fellow" needs and wants, that is, what his values are.

Perhaps the most important part of this chapter is the section having to do with specific guidelines—both for preparation for family life, and for better adjustment in the home itself. These practical suggestions are the result of what psychologists have learned about human nature, of actual experience, of work with case studies, etc.

## QUESTIONS THIS CHAPTER WILL ANSWER

1. How do psychologists consider the home? Do they regard it as having special influences on the life of the individual? What are some of these influences?

2. What are some of the common causes of difficulty in the home?

3. Can we do anything to improve home relationships? What beneficial suggestions can psychology give us on this subject?

4. What particular problems of the home must parents understand?

5. What is the responsibility of children in the home?

6. Are there any suggestions that can be made to help young people who are planning to establish a home?

## The Social Importance of a Home

Perhaps we could all have better homes if we realized how important they are. Having lived in a home most of our lives, we tend to take it for granted. It is a place of refuge and a center from which to take off for all the various activities we call life.

Actually, the home is the vital core of society. Without the home, it is impossible to see how society could amount to anything other than a primitive, uncivilized roving band. Basically, the home is the place in which parents bring up their children; the one place where stability and security are provided for each individual. Privacy, freedom from outside annoyance, and security are necessary for family life and for bringing up children. The home is intended to provide these, and our customs and laws for generations have been intended to make sure they can be provided.

We realize that these conditions are necessary for all people as well as for children. Consequently, the home is important as a center for adult living, too. Society now recognizes that a good community is fundamentally a community that is made up of good homes and that poor homes invariably make a poor community.

## Learn How To Live in a Home

Since the home is so important for everyone, it would seem that everyone ought to know how to live in a home.

Yet, if we may judge by what is going on in our society today, people are not always successful in this. Homes are being broken up on all sides, and the divorce rate is high. In some of our recent years, our country has had one divorce for every four marriages. In 1956, there were 1,585,000 marriages in the United States and 382,000 divorces.[1]

Other signs that people are not always successful in living in homes appear in the complaints that we hear about homes. We find some homes which are not broken up by divorce, but in which, nevertheless, there is a great deal of argument and conflict. Some of the nervous and mental diseases of our generation may be caused by difficulties in the home; situations where people are living together but at the same time have more conflict and insecurity than they should.

Young people have indicated that they have frequent conflicts with their parents, another sign of "trouble" at home. These conflicts

---

[1] National Office of Vital Statistics, 1959.

may not be as serious as some people might think—probably, in most cases, both parents and children soon "get over" the emotional upset involved. Yet they may be serious in some cases. They add to the "wear and tear" of modern living.

In a study of adolescent attitudes, Remmers and Radler[2] found that the following actions or attitudes of parents were most annoying to teen-agers:

> Parents play favorites
> Parents interfere with spending money I earn
> Too strict about family car
> Too strict about dating
> Too strict about my going out at night
> Wish parents would treat me like a grownup
> Afraid to tell parents when I've done wrong
> Too strict about dates on school nights
> Family always worried about money
> Parents nag about studying
> Parents interfere in my choice of friends
> Parents hate to admit I'm sometimes right

The study also showed that parents and children often disagree over how situations should be handled. For example, 26 percent of the young people said that their parents usually treated them as if they were much younger than they really were, but only 8 percent of the mothers and 7 percent of the fathers said that this was the case. Thirty-five percent of the young people said that their parents understand the kind of problems modern youth have, but 60 percent of the mothers said that they usually understood them. The fathers weren't quite so sure—46 percent of them said that they usually understood young people's problems.

Yet, in some matters, young people and their parents seemed in rather close agreement. Both parents and young people, in general, agreed that the parents should know where their children were when they went out for an evening. Both agreed that parents should try to protect young people from making mistakes they themselves made in their youth. Both young people and parents agreed that members of the family should get together and talk over each other's problems.

In another study, 528 high-school students said that the causes of difficulty with their parents include such things as:

[2]H. H. Remmers and D. H. Radler, *The American Teenager* (Indianapolis-New York: The Bobbs-Merrill Company, Inc., 1957), pp. 117, 118, ff.

Insists upon nagging me regarding what I wear and how I dress
Complains about my hands, neck, or fingernails being dirty
Won't let me attend the church I want to attend
Holds my sister or brother up as a model to me
Won't give me a regular allowance
Won't let me entertain at home

One authoritative study of adolescent behavior reports that most of the difficulties between young people of high-school age and their parents spring from the desire of the adolescents to gain independence in connection with their social lives and activities.

Specifically, the most common conflicts relate to the hour of returning home at night, the number of times the adolescent goes out on school nights, the person the adolescent dates, the boys or girls the adolescent selects as friends, home duties, spending money, the use of the family car, grades in school, parental behavior, Sunday School or church attendance, and the clothes worn for different occasions. There are relatively few quarrels about political views or the adolescent's choice of a vocation.[3]

This writer also points out that most of the girls' conflicts with parents have to do with their social activities.

They also have more conflicts about the clothes they wear, home duties, and the clubs they belong to, while boys have more conflicts relating to spending money, the use of the automobile, and grades at school.[4]

There is also a tendency, it is noted, for girls to have more quarrels with their mothers, than with their fathers—perhaps due to the fact that girls have more contacts with their mother than with their father.

Girls, it has been reported, have more conflicts with their fathers about dating and mate selection, and more with their mothers about standards of values in the world outside the family other than dating, and about parental behavior.[5]

It was interesting to note that from one to five quarrels a month were reported as being not uncommon.

---

[3]Elizabeth Hurlock, *Adolescent Development* (New York: McGraw-Hill Book Company, Inc., 1955), p. 460.

[4]*Ibid.*, p. 420.

[5]*Ibid.*, p. 460.

**"THE PARENT PROBLEM" AS TEENAGERS SEE IT**

| | Parents Play Favorites % | Parents Interfere With Spending Money I Earn % | Parents Trying to Decide My Vocation % | Parents Too Strict About Family Car % | Parents Too Strict About Dating % | Parents Won't Let Me Make Decisions % | Parents Don't Respect My Opinions % | Parents Don't Trust Me % | Parents Expect Too Much of Me % | Parents Too Strict About My Going Out at Night % | Get No Encouragement at Home % | Wish Parents Would Treat Me Like a Grownup % | Want to Gain Confidence of My Parents % | Feel Like Leaving Home % |
|---|---|---|---|---|---|---|---|---|---|---|---|---|---|---|
| Total | 10 | 11 | 7 | 16 | 13 | 8 | 8 | 8 | 9 | 18 | 9 | 12 | 7 | 7 |
| Boys | 8 | 15 | 9 | 24 | 8 | 7 | 8 | 8 | 9 | 16 | 9 | 10 | 6 | 7 |
| Girls | 12 | 7 | 6 | 9 | 17 | 8 | 8 | 5 | 8 | 19 | 8 | 14 | 9 | 8 |
| Grade 9 | 11 | 13 | 7 | 15 | 16 | 8 | 9 | 7 | 10 | 22 | 9 | 14 | 8 | 6 |
| Grade 10 | 10 | 11 | 8 | 18 | 15 | 9 | 9 | 8 | 11 | 19 | 10 | 12 | 6 | 7 |
| Grade 11 | 12 | 10 | 8 | 17 | 11 | 7 | 9 | 9 | 8 | 18 | 11 | 13 | 8 | 10 |
| Grade 12 | 8 | 6 | 6 | 15 | 6 | 5 | 6 | 5 | 6 | 9 | 8 | 9 | 6 | 7 |
| East | 10 | 8 | 7 | 9 | 15 | 6 | 6 | 8 | 8 | 16 | 9 | 11 | 6 | 10 |
| Midwest | 10 | 12 | 8 | 19 | 12 | 7 | 9 | 7 | 10 | 19 | 9 | 13 | 7 | 6 |
| South | 14 | 6 | 8 | 18 | 11 | 11 | 9 | 8 | 8 | 18 | 11 | 13 | 9 | 11 |
| Mountain-Pacific | 6 | 8 | 3 | 15 | 11 | 8 | 6 | 8 | 3 | 14 | 9 | 11 | 8 | 7 |
| Rural | 12 | 10 | 9 | 15 | 16 | 8 | 8 | 8 | 8 | 19 | 9 | 12 | 7 | 9 |
| Urban | 8 | 11 | 6 | 17 | 10 | 7 | 9 | 7 | 9 | 17 | 9 | 12 | 7 | 6 |
| Protestant | 10 | 11 | 7 | 17 | 12 | 8 | 9 | 8 | 9 | 18 | 9 | 12 | 7 | 7 |
| Catholic | 10 | 9 | 8 | 13 | 15 | 6 | 8 | 7 | 9 | 20 | 8 | 11 | 7 | 8 |
| Jewish | 9 | 11 | 7 | 20 | 8 | 7 | 7 | 7 | 10 | 11 | 11 | 11 | 5 | 10 |
| None | 10 | 11 | 5 | 14 | 15 | 8 | 7 | 5 | 8 | 16 | 9 | 15 | 11 | 10 |
| Low Income | 11 | 11 | 7 | 16 | 14 | 8 | 8 | 8 | 8 | 18 | 10 | 12 | 7 | 8 |
| High Income | 7 | 9 | 8 | 18 | 10 | 8 | 10 | 6 | 11 | 16 | 8 | 12 | 7 | 5 |

From *The American Teenager* by H. H. Remmers and D. H. Radler (Indianapolis-New York: The Bobbs-Merrill Company, Inc., 1957), p. 117.

## Adjustment at Home

An individual will not be able to enjoy his work outside of the home unless the home situation is good. Teachers have found that many problems of students are due to difficulties at home.

One boy who was failing in his schoolwork was found to be almost entirely neglected at home because his mother had died and there was no one to take her place. The father was away all of the time. The boy had little or no home life and had to work every morning from four until eight o'clock delivering milk. Another child in the same school could not get his work done satisfactorily and seemed to be in poor health. It was learned that his parents kept a small grocery store, which took all of their time, and that they rarely had any cooked meals. Usually the "kids" were told to go get some candy from the counter if they were hungry. This boy was suffering from malnutrition due to improper care by his family, who worked in a grocery store surrounded by large quantities of food.

In one case of a high-school girl, it was found that her mother had become embittered against men because of the behavior of the father. She would not allow her daughter to have "dates" with any of the boys. Her mother was actually teaching the girl to hate men and to mistrust them. As a result the girl was unhappy, maladjusted, and out of step with her group.

In another case, a girl could never make up her mind about anything and had to "ask mother" to settle every question and problem. This even continued after the daughter was sent away to college. She was so dependent on her mother that she could not decide even the simplest matters without having to write home first. Being away from home and with people who expected answers, she began to have serious difficulties. Nothing could be done until the mother could be induced to give up her hold on the daughter, allow her to begin to live her own life, and stand on her own feet.

In still another case, a boy of very good ability was depressed and unhappy because his parents were constantly telling him that he ought to quit school and go to work, that he was wasting his time, and that no one with any sense would go to school.

It would not be true to say that all problem cases are due to improper adjustments at home, but such conditions have certainly been found to be important in most cases. A study of accidents in a large city transportation system showed that in a majority of cases the motormen of streetcars involved in accidents were having troubles at home.

Home can give us a good start or a bad start each day. It is a fact that modern home life is not always what it should be. Home reflects the qualities, hopes, and needs of the people who live in it. Homemaking is a very co-operative enterprise. It is by no means an easy job. Yet it is undoubtedly the most satisfaction-giving and the most important job anyone can have.

It is possible that in a majority of cases where there are troubles at home, the individuals involved either have not been prepared to establish homes or have failed to make adjustments in meeting the normal stresses and strains of life. This is merely saying that they have not *learned* how to live in a home.

## Study the Causes of Home Difficulties

Sometimes the causes of home difficulty are *economic*. For example, a young boy who was sullen, "mean," and always getting into fights was found to be living in a small three-room apartment in a slum section. He shared his home with seven other members of the family. A widow and a small child occupied one of the three rooms. The family depended on the daily earnings of the mother, since the father was sick, and frequently the children did not have enough to eat.

Under such conditions it would be hard to expect that the children coming from this home would be carefree, happy, and well-adjusted.

This is an extreme case. There are many problems in home life, however, which do grow out of economic causes. Sometimes the family is unable to buy the necessities of life. Sometimes it is unable to afford the little luxuries of life which lighten the burden of daily living and add to enjoyment for parents and children.

Long-continued inability to purchase needed things can become a cause of friction and annoyance. When the difficulties are of this sort, it is necessary for all of the members to help out, either by contributing to the family income (that is by getting jobs and actually helping to pay the bills) or by being careful to do their share to hold the family expenses within reason.

Sometimes the troubles are caused by lack of harmonious adjustment between the parents. Specific causes of marriage disharmony are numerous, but, when they are not economic, they are often related to physical or sexual adjustment difficulties, or to difficulties growing out of personality likes and dislikes.

Sexual adjustment difficulties are rarely due to physical causes, although they may be. But when husband and wife are found to be physically sound, sexual adjustment difficulties are due, if they exist, to one or both of the partners having unsatisfactory habits and attitudes.

Sometimes husband and wife fail to learn the techniques of sex relationships and do not establish harmony in them. There are numerous books which describe these techniques, and competent doctors can explain them to young married people or people who are about to get married.

Young people should realize that sexual disharmony can be a cause of home friction and should be concerned with this side of preparation for marriage. The attitude toward sex is the important thing.

Closely related to the physical side of marriage is the necessity for having children. Many married men and women fail to achieve happiness in the home because, for one reason or another, they try to avoid having children. Having children is the normal relationship of marriage. If young married people will accept this responsibility, working out the related economic problems as they go along, they will usually find that it has a lot to do with achieving happiness in the home. The most important reason for this is the fact that it is *biologically desirable* for a woman to become a mother. If she has children, she is carrying out the function for which she was intended, and this is wholesome and necessary from the psychological point of view.

**Lack of Common Interests.** Another factor is the contribution which having children makes toward establishing common interests for husband and wife. Married people who have children have a strong bond in their mutual love and devotion to their children. Without this, one of the greatest potential elements for binding them together is missing.

Another important cause of marriage failures is the lack of common interests and a possible clashing of personalities. Sometimes two persons who marry for love find that they have so little in common that they are unable to enjoy life together because their energies and desires are always running in different directions. While this might be an excuse to cover up other causes of difficulty, it is often a real situation. Young people are advised, therefore, to consider their mutual interests and enjoyments before marriage. If they are in harmony, to a certain extent, it will be very helpful. However, it is unlikely that they should be exactly parallel.

The personal relationships of marriage are just like the personal relationships of all people to one another. How to get along with people is the important fact in this as in any other personal relationship. The same requirements of tact, consideration, thoughtfulness, and mutual give-and-take are present. Sometimes married people act as though they did not need to pay any attention to these requirements, and then causes of friction are sure to develop.

In addition to lack of harmonious adjustment between the parents, difficulties at home are sometimes caused by the influence of "outsiders" in the home. All too often, persons are found living in the home who have ideas, wishes, and ways of doing things which are in conflict with those of the parents and the children.

The classic example of this is the presence in the home of one of the parents of the married couple. For example, a young wife's mother, or a husband's mother, living in their home, may take an undue amount of the time and attention of one of the married partners, and this may lead to exasperation and bitterness. Sometimes the older parent may wish to dictate what goes on. Often the grandparent will want to interfere in the way the children are being handled. The resulting division of authority causes difficult prob-

The environment of the home has a great influence on our behavior.

lems for the young mother or the young husband.

This is such a serious matter that it cannot be overemphasized. If possible, the presence of some visiting mother or grandparent, for an *extended* period of time, should be carefully avoided by younger married couples, unless a definite agreement can be reached as to the relative *role* of the people involved.

Each individual can play a part in promoting harmony in the home by doing what he can to reduce or eliminate occasions of friction. All of the suggestions made with regard to getting along with people apply in the home.

The young person can judge his home, and he can make an effort to understand it. He can analyze and try to understand the interests of those who share it with him.

## Home: A Good Place to Practice Psychology

Home is a good place in which to develop and practice those rules of tolerance of the other fellow. It is an excellent place to practice being "grown up" in one's own emotional adjustment.

Try to understand the people who share your home with you. Respect their needs and their wishes. Don't try to reorganize your home or to change your mother's or father's pattern of life. Usually that only makes for more trouble. Try, instead, to adjust yourself to the situation at home as you find it. Above all, don't assume a superior attitude toward your home. If you do, you haven't learned much about the psychology of getting along with people.

If a young person can learn how to adjust successfully to his parental home, he has a good chance of adjusting successfully to his own home.

Another suggestion which can be made is that when you can't find all of the satisfactions and conditions you would like to enjoy at home, you might remember that there are many other opportunities for you in other groups and in other places in society. Seek to find and to enjoy what the community offers you at school, in the church, and on the job.

One of the most difficult adjustment problems which came to the writer's attention was that of a young college student whose home life was unsatisfactory. For a while the student resented this and was always fighting or quarreling with one or the other of his parents. Finally, he began to realize that he was not going to be able to change his parents' attitudes or ways of doing things, so he decided to seek satisfaction in the life of the school. He spent more time at school, took part in activities, and devoted himself to achieving school success. It was not long until he not only began to have a great deal of satisfaction in his school life, but he found a better life at home as well. His parents began to develop a pride in their son's accomplishments, and the situation generally, though never ideal for him, became satisfactory enough for him to go on with his schooling and to share his parental home through the rest of his college years.

The family picnic is a popular way of finding happy hours for all. Doing things together not only cements close ties but also adds much to the worthwhile experiences of life.

One thought which comes to mind is this: Children, as well as the parents, are responsible for the success of a home. As they grow older, children should be able to share in solving the problems of the home, in lessening the strains, and in promoting the general well-being of the home. If they do not do this, they must accept some of the responsibility, themselves, for the failure of the home.

## Problems Which Parents and Children Must Meet

The following group of problems are given to show the leading areas in which parents and children must learn to work together for successful home living.

**Educational Problems.** As the children grow, their school interests will extend and increase. School will make demands on their time. School activities will require money, and parents will be asked to help in paying the costs. Children should learn, as they grow older, the desirability of keeping these demands on their parents at a minimum. They should be willing to help in meeting them and should share in the work of the home as a means of justifying these added expenses.

The parents, on the other hand, should become familiar with the work and activities of the school and with the requirements made upon their children. The children can help by sharing these experiences with the parents. All too often there is very little sharing of experience; all the parents know about it is that they are always being asked for this or that.

Educational goals are also tied in with vocational goals, so it is important for the parents to know something about the vocational purposes which their children are working out.

**Recreational Problems.** Recognizing the importance of recreation in the lives of their children, parents should make provision for the children to enjoy these experiences. We know that through recreation, games, and activities such as school activities, children learn how to live with other people. They explore occupational opportunities, and they develop life-long interests of great value from a mental hygiene viewpoint.

At the same time, children, as they grow older and develop, should see the relationship between these activities and family expenses as well as home responsibilities. If they do recognize these relationships, and do not use recreation as an escape from home duties and responsibilities, a happier atmosphere in the home will result.

Children, as they grow, must learn to respect the recreational needs of their parents as well. Once in a while, they ought to put some extra time and effort into helping with the work of the home so that their parents can have a day off or an evening out. Co-operation of this sort eases the pressure on the parents and makes them feel that they are getting the help of the children in making a home.

Both parents must respect the recreational needs of each other. In line with other things which have to be considered, husband and wife should respect each other's need for opportunity to follow his or her recreational interests within reason. These interests must not be discontinued or supplanted by the work of the home to such an extent that the well-being of the individual will suffer and be endangered. If they are, the balance of the home will be impaired. For example, it is unfair and unwise for the husband to expect freedom from his wife to go hunting or fishing and at the same time feel that she is going out of bounds to spend an afternoon or two a week with her friends.

Perhaps, from the standpoint of the young man or woman who is learning to live at home, this could be summed up by saying that parents are also human. They need the help of their children to live a normal life.

**Vocational Problems.** It is especially important for families to respect the occupational opportunities and interests of the various members of the group. Parents, and those learning to be parents, must remember that the individual will only derive advantages from his occupation if it is his to choose, to prepare for, and to succeed in.

All too often parents wish to dictate the occupational choices of their children. One of the main beliefs of modern vocational guidance workers is that the individual must make this choice for himself.

Parents are not only dictating an occupation, they are dictating a way of life, and this must not be done if there is to be good feeling and harmony in the modern home.

Respect for the occupation of the other fellow must be present in the home as well as outside of it. Similarly, children need to respect the occupations of their parents. If they can learn the importance of this, it will support and give encouragement to the parents as they go on with their tasks. Few parents can be found who like to feel that their children are ashamed of them and their occupations. A young man or woman who makes fun of his parent's occupation has not learned much about getting along with other people.

**Religious Problems.** Modern psychologists take the position that religious conviction is an individual matter and that it is unlikely that any individual will derive much benefit from a religious view that is forced upon him.

Parents will be able to help their children by giving them opportunities and encouragement to obtain religious experience. They may show interest in their problems and desires along this line. However, because of its close relationship to self-realization and basic personal security, there must be freedom for the individual to choose a religious point of view or belief. This is part of the task of growing up. Arguments over religious beliefs are likely to be very fruitless in a home. Respect for each other's beliefs and rights can serve as a foundation stone for good home relationships.

**Problem of Friendships.** The only point to be made in this connection is that, like religious conviction, it might be said that each individual has to learn how to choose his own friends. Here again the choice of friends will depend on the individual's own tastes and needs. These in turn are determined by our experiences in life. If children are given opportunities to develop good habits, good attitudes, wholesome interests, and if their basic needs are being met, it is reasonable to suppose that they will be wise in choosing friends, because they will want to choose friends of similar interests and values.

It is very unlikely that parents can dictate their children's choice of friends or that it would do any good for them to try to do so. One girl was told that she couldn't bring some of her high-school friends into the home because they "weren't the right sort." She began to disappear from the home in the evening on various kinds of excuses so that she could meet these same friends on the street corner. This continued for a long time until eventually the girl began to get into trouble because of the unnatural conditions under which she was being forced to find the friends she wanted.

While parents cannot dictate their children's choice of friends very successfully, they can, by their own choice of friends, have an indirect effect. They can bring into the home friends who are worth while and stimulating. This will have an indirect effect on the kind of people the children like and will want to associate with.

**Problems Concerning Property and Clothes.** As a last group of considerations to discuss, we might mention the problems which come up in connection with property, clothes, and allowances. These problems should be handled in accordance with what we know about human needs and values.

For example, what clothes parents will allow a young high-school girl to buy or wear might not depend so much on what the parents "think" would be "best" for her but on what would actually be best for her in terms of the social and personal needs which she has in connection with her life in her own group. Older people will remember a comic strip called "Buster Brown." Buster had to wear "sissy" clothes to please his mother, and the boy was always getting into all sorts of trouble with his rough-and-ready friends because he was forced to wear what she thought was right.

Parents should provide, or help the child to provide, for his basic needs of clothing, spending money, and other goods, being careful not to overshoot or undershoot the mark. Some children have been harmed by having too much; others by having too little. The worst thing a parent can do is to hand out, or refuse to give, spending money or any of these necessities indifferently. The child *must* know that the parent understands and appreciates his problem and is doing what he can to help him with it. We frequently find young people who are ashamed and unhappy in their social groups because their parents are not helping them to have the clothes they feel they need—just the essentials, not extravagant clothes. On the other hand, a boy might be put into many difficult situations by receiving, as did one boy of the writer's acquaintance, a weekly spending allowance about ten times as great as that given to any of the other boys in his group.

The basic rule might be to share, within the limits of the family possibilities, and to develop the feeling on the part of the children that the parents want them to share.

From the point of view of the young person in the home, it should be said again: In your requests for help, or in what you expect from your parents, be considerate of their needs and their problems in relation to yours. If they feel that you are considerate, they will in turn do everything they can do for you, within reason. Unless they are very unusual people, they will be anxious to help you all they can.

When there is friction about money, clothes, use of the car, or other problems involving material things, it is usually because on one side or the other there has been disregard for the real needs and problems of the other person. This is just the same point that is involved in all relationships between human beings, and it is not peculiar in any way to family life.

## Preparing To Have a Home

The discussion brought out in this chapter is in itself a guide to preparation for having a home. Life in childhood and in young adulthood is a kind of preparation for homemaking. As we learn how to live and get along with people, we are also learning the attitudes and skills needed to establish a successful home.

In summary:

1. We must learn how to adjust to other people.

Homemaking involves adjustment every day to another person—often without the softening and restraining influence of social custom. A man who would be restrained in raising his voice in public might not feel this same restraint in his home where it is really more necessary for him to be restrained.

However, the point here is simply that one of the best things anyone can do in preparing to have a home is to learn how to meet with, work with, talk with, and associate with other people in a great many different ways. Each successful adjustment we make to another individual is the best training imaginable for having a successful home.

2. We must consider our future partner's interests, purposes, and values.

In establishing a home it will be more successful, other things being equal, if there are some common interests to be shared. It is not necessary for each person to share every interest that the other one has, but there must be *some* interests in common. They will furnish a basis for planning and working together.

3. We must accept the principle that an important purpose of the home is raising children.

This is important because it is the means of establishing a common center of affection, loyalty, and a basis of mutual concern. Equally important, it is the natural physiological expression of the man and woman involved, particularly of the woman.

4. We must make some study of the problem of sexual or biological mating, and we must understand what is involved.

The need here is for a knowledge of sexual adjustment that will permit us to enter into these relationships without the damaging interference of superstition, inhibition, or fear. Particularly, we must accept the biological necessity and fact of sexual activity in marriage. We must see it as a fundamental and necessary part of human experience. We must regard it as desirable and be prepared to accept it in that way.

5. We must develop our own interests and abilities in a wide variety of ways. We must recognize that a man or woman of broad interests and education will have the background that is best for establishing a good home and raising children.

If we lead active and interesting lives ourselves, it will be reflected in the atmosphere of our homes. Putting it another way, if we are worth while, our homes will be worth while.

The test of a good home is in whether or not it contributes to the basic needs of the people who live in it. No other grouping in society has so important a task. In the home we expect to find security, comfort, assurance, and stimulation. We also expect to find satisfaction for our physical needs.

Since so much is expected of a home, much must be put into it. This is the supreme measure of what the human being can do because it requires the greatest contribution he can make. In return, it offers the greatest possible satisfaction, and the greatest reward.

## Practical Suggestions for Family Adjustment

There is no magic formula for a secure and happy home life because it is so tied in with each person's all-round personality. It is a matter of interaction between people in a group. Each member's difficulties, as well as his successes and failures, are reflected in the life of the group.

Nevertheless, there are some specific things we can do to "keep the right side up," and each of them contributes to the all-round goodness of living in the home, which is our goal.

*First*, remember that every human being is looking for physical, emotional, and social satisfactions. This applies to your mother, father, brothers, sisters, or your husband or wife.

In the things you do and say at home, are you taking this into account?

Remember that what your mother does, or what your wife does, is very likely to be influenced by how well she is succeeding in her own personal adjustment to life. Therefore, you will be wise to extend to her the same tolerance and understanding that you would want her to show toward you when you have problems.

Parents are very likely to be annoyed by things their children do or don't do, but they seldom carry a grudge. What we are looking for here is *understanding* of why the other fellow does the things he does. Bitterness does not develop when there is understanding, no matter how great the provocation of any particular incident may be.

*Second*, are your habits and ways of doing things at home reasonably agreeable from the point of view of the other members of the family? There are some "little things" that most of us can correct that help smooth over human relations. Give this some thought and attention.

*Third,* do you let people at home know what your plans are and what you are going to do, especially when it affects them? One of the commonest causes of friction is "not letting the other fellow know" about things that are going to happen which will affect him. For example, when the folks are expecting you at a certain time for dinner, do you let them know if you can't make it, or do you just fail to show up?

*Fourth,* do you share in the work and responsibilities of the home? Eventually, everyone gets tired of doing the other fellow's work for him. Children should share in the responsibility and work of the home as they grow older and become capable of it. In too many homes, they evade this responsibility. This is hardly the way to build a happy home life for all. The same principle that applies in life outside of the home, the principle of *sharing,* must be brought into the home.

*Fifth,* one of the biggest causes of difficulty mentioned by young people in relation to their parents is "nagging." Probably, there are a good many husbands whose wives "nag" them, and vice versa.

This is something that can be controlled. You are being "nagged" when the other fellow (your husband, wife, mother, or whoever it may be) repeatedly "gets after" you about something you feel you should have a right to decide or about some matter in which you feel you ought to have freedom of action.

It is entirely possible that you should *not* have the freedom of action you think you should have. A co-operative group requires that we give up a point here and a point there in order to develop a feeling in the group that all are sharing in the work, responsibility, or problems.

But we need to be definite about our relations and responsibilities. Nagging often occurs because the lines of responsibility aren't clear-cut. Let's try to straighten them out so that we and the other members of the family have better and clearer ideas of the actions and areas in which we are free to make our own decisions. For instance, one mother was making life miserable for her son because she would not allow him to use water colors or paints. She said he was always "messing things up." Finally, it was agreed that he could use one room for a workroom and that he would confine his work along these lines to that particular room. After that, her "nagging" on this subject stopped.

For our part, let's try to avoid the temptation to nag someone else. This is just common sense because nagging never does any good and usually does a lot of harm.

*Sixth,* if the problems of your home are economic, make sure you are doing your share in two ways: (1) by economizing in your expenditures and requirements, and (2) by doing something to add to the family income, if possible.

If this is a cause of trouble in your home, check up to see whether or not all that could be done is being done. Stop making foolish or unnecessary purchases. Help out with the housework and upkeep of the home so that these tasks will be less of a burden on any one individual. Look around for ways to add income to the family, on the theory that every little bit helps. Make the improvement of your family's economic situation a number one project and try out ideas that might help. For example, unless you live in a densely settled district, a garden in the growing months can add immensely to the well-being of any family.

*Seventh,* re-examine the recreational side of your family life and your responsibilities. Knowing how important this is, are you helping with activities that will promote this? Are you sharing in the work so that other members of the family can have some recreation, too? Are you planning, or helping to plan, for occasional outings, trips, or vacations that will stimulate or tone up the whole family outlook on life?

Do you do things to brighten up the routine existence of members of the family; for example, bringing home some flowers or other things that will be appreciated and make the family feel that you are interested?

*Eighth,* have a good balance of outside interests that will keep you active. After all, the individual who has some good out-of-home activities will be enriched by them and stimulated, and this will be reflected in the attitude *he brings home.* This is true for every member of the family, young or old.

*Ninth,* reread the discussion of the major purposes of a home. Is your home achieving these purposes? Is it neglecting important things? You might analyze it from this point of view and see where the weak points are.

*Tenth,* don't start a one-man drive to reform or reorganize your home! Make your contribution gradually. Familiarize yourself with the basic ideas that make for a good family life. Do what you can when you can do it. Make useful suggestions at the right time, but be sure that it *is* the right time.

In the home situation, remember that each person wants to enjoy the feeling that he is wanted, that he is respected, and that his interests are being considered. You can't do it alone, so use the same tact in carrying out these suggestions that you would apply in any other group or social situation in life.

## Ten Rules for Better Home Living

1. Develop an understanding of why folks do the things they do.

2. Check yourself for annoying little habits and get rid of them.

3. Let people in the family know about your plans when your plans will affect them.

4. Do your share of the work.

5. Eliminate nagging by getting a clearer understanding of responsibilities.

6. Cut out unnecessary spending; see if you can't add to your own or the family income.

7. Lend a hand to help in providing good recreation for the family.

8. Develop good outside interests that will keep your own general attitude cheerful and constructive.

9. Evaluate your home from time to time to see whether or not you are keeping in sight the big goals and purposes for which a home exists.

10. Be tactful and considerate in your contributions to better home living; keep clear of the reformer attitude.

## QUESTIONS AND PROBLEMS FOR STUDY AND DISCUSSION

1. What would you say as to the importance of the home to the individual?

2. What would you say as to the importance of the home to society?

3. Discuss the importance of a home in terms of the *psychological* needs of a man or woman.

4. What indications are there that American homes are not always successful?

5. What are some of the topics on which parents and children are not always in agreement?

6. Give an example of how a home situation can interfere with the success of an individual at school or on the job.

7. Show how economic conditions can create an unsatisfactory home life.

8. What attitudes toward sex are considered necessary for satisfactory home adjustment?

9. Why is it said that having children may increase the likelihood of success in marriage and in the home?

10. What is the importance of common or mutual interests in home adjustment?

11. Why do we say that getting along in marriage is much the same as getting along with people generally?

12. Explain the suggestion that children, as well as adults, have a responsibility for the success of a home.

13. What suggestions are made as to the attitude of parents toward their children's choice of friends?

14. What should be the parental attitude toward a child's choice of a vocation?

15. Look at a daily newspaper and note the official announcements of wedding licenses and divorces granted. How many are there of each?

16. For your own information, go to the library and make a list of three or four books giving information relating to marriage and family life which you could use to advantage.

17. Make a list of ten questions with which you feel that you need help in connection with marriage and family adjustment. Keep these as a check list in connection with further reading you will do on this subject.

18. Describe a happily married couple with whom you are acquainted and write down some of the probable reasons for their apparent success in this respect.

# CHAPTER EIGHTEEN

# LIVING IN SCHOOL, BUSINESS, AND INDUSTRY

The problem of getting along with other people has many ramifications, or, as people sometimes say, there are a good many "angles" to it. The study of psychology does help us to understand the kinds of attitudes and behavior which make for better human relations. In this chapter some of these are outlined in connection with the problem of adjusting to groups, at school, in business, or in industry.

We discover that there are similarities in all of these situations. Whenever we are newcomers in a group, we face the problem of securing acceptance. We find that the people who were there before we came look upon us with some degree of suspicion. They are, at the very least, likely to be a little guarded about accepting us. Possibly they feel that the newcomer may offer a threat to their own security. There is always the matter of competition to think about.

There are many ways in which groups influence us. Often, they support us or add to our sense of achievement, belonging, or importance, through the mechanism of identification. The psychological aspects of this are pointed out.

The chapter also takes up a number of the common causes of annoyance and friction, showing how, by a little care, some of these can be eliminated to our advantage.

## QUESTIONS THIS CHAPTER WILL ANSWER

1. What are the basic principles we need to know in order to get along well with people, especially as we deal with them in groups?

2. How do groups affect us, and we them? How can we become accepted as members of a group?

3. What is the extent of group influence on our behavior, for example, in comparison to other influences?

4. How should a new person, in a school or in a shop, conduct himself in order to gain acceptance by the group?

5. What are some of the things which annoy people—things which we, as individuals, need to know about and guard against?

6. What practical suggestions can be made for getting along with people who happen to be in positions of authority with reference to us?

## Groups and Our Relationship to Them

When a person learns to adjust himself to each social situation as it comes along, he is learning the habits which will serve him to advantage all through life.

Here are two guiding principles for working out wholesome adjustments with other people:

In whatever groups you are, contribute what you can—whether it is a game, a discussion, a recitation, or conversation with a friend.

Keep in mind that other people, like yourself, are striving to meet their needs and to establish their *personalities*.

It will help to remember that every human being is trying to seek and maintain those conditions which will help him and promote the goals he has set for himself. He is also trying to avoid those things which will interfere.

We should also remember that social adjustment is not something which comes automatically. We have to work for it. And to keep good relations with people, after we have established them, we have to work just as hard.

It seems difficult to realize that friendship is something one has *to work for,* but it is a fact.

The psychologist is interested in the way in which people form themselves into groups. Groups have certain ways of behaving, and they undoubtedly influence very greatly the people who belong to them.

**How Do Groups Influence Us?** In the office, in the school, and in the shop, we are much influenced by the groups we belong to or work with.

The family is the first group to which the individual belongs. As he grows older, he associates with other people on the playground or in the school. Later still, these associations widen to include people from the same neighborhood or community.

Groups are usually formed on the basis of the common interests or needs of the members. The family exists primarily because it is necessary as a means of raising children. It is what the sociologists call a *primary* group. The groups we form with our friends and associates are not so vital, but they are important in many ways.

Some writers have shown that the individual usually joins groups because they contribute something to him. They help him to have the feeling of being worth while and the feeling of "belonging" considered so important by the psychologists. To satisfy these needs, the individual will often join groups whose purposes and ideals are very different from those of his family. Then there may be conflict between loyalty to the group and loyalty to the family.

The individual hopes to gain something from the group, and the group expects to gain from the individual. Usually the group makes an effort to see to it that the new member is as much like the others in the group as possible. To provide for this the group may use initiation ceremonies; it may provide rules for admission. This is to ensure, at least as much as possible, that the newcomer will act in a manner in harmony with the group's interests and values. The member must submerge his own interests and tastes to those of the group or forego membership.

The average person is so anxious to obtain the friendship of the group and the prestige that comes from belonging to it, that he will put up with many indignities and jokes in connection with being initiated. The practices of high-school clubs, college fraternities, and community gangs illustrate this. Sometimes these initiation practices are carried in the wrong direction. In fact, it is not uncommon for some gangs to have unsocial or immoral initiation practices. For example, one gang in a large eastern city had as a part of its initiation a requirement that anyone who wanted to qualify for membership would have to show that he could "run" twelve red traffic signals without being caught.

The individual likes to keep the respect of his group. As a result, he will not often depart from their ways of doing things, even if it means violating the teaching of his own parents or the customs of his own home or family. This is understandable, for the good will and respect of one's associates count for a great deal in life. Perhaps the individual assumes that the family, in which his position is already secure, will forgive him more readily than the members of the group.

**What Are the Characteristics of Groups?** Groups have their own characteristics. One of them is the tendency to think that their group is superior to all other groups. "We've got the best outfit in the school," illustrates this. No college student ever belongs to a fraternity without agreeing that it is by far the best fraternity in the country.

We recognize this as a form of *identification*. To the extent that the group prospers or enjoys prestige, we prosper and enjoy prestige. It is to our interest that any group we belong to shall have the highest possible reputation. We *identify* our well-being with that of the group. Hence we and others belonging to the group take every possible opportunity to proclaim its good points. This is the basis of group loyalty, school spirit, patriotism, and civic pride.

Of course, this tendency can be harmful. If, instead of working for good purposes, a group chooses to seek goals or advantages of a harmful nature, much damage can be done. In a whole country, it can be disastrous. The world had an example of this in Germany when the Nazi group sought to establish itself as the master race, and the German nation as the ruler of the world. This is an abuse of the psychological principle of identification. It is well to understand how this principle works.

Another psychological mechanism involved in group loyalties is what the psychologist calls *facilitation*. Various elements in our surroundings become *conditioned stimuli* which *facilitate* various attitudes, feelings, and ways cf doing things in us. For example, we feel more comfortable in our own homes surrounded by familiar books, chairs, pictures, and people. We work best with our own tools; write most easily with our own fountain pens. We are more able to relax in our own beds.

In the same way, the familiar scenes of our community, state, or nation become capable of influencing us greatly. We are happy and content with them. Separated from them, we may be homesick and disappointed. This is another ingredient in patriotism. "I love thy rocks and rills, thy woods and templed hills."

How deeply these feelings affect us is suggested by Rupert Brooke's poem, *The Soldier*.[1]

> If I should die, think only this of me
>    That there's some corner of a foreign field
> That is forever England. There shall be
>    In that rich earth a richer dust concealed:
> A dust whom England bore, shaped, made aware,
>    Gave, once, her flowers to love, her ways to roam,
> A body of England's, breathing English air,
>    Washed by the rivers, blest by suns of home.

---

[1] Rupert Brooke, *The Collected Poems of Rupert Brooke* (New York: Dodd Mead & Co., 1931).

## The School as a Miniature Society

A school is very much like a small-scale community or state. The same influences which affect the part we play in groups are important here. The school contains groups. Individuals are sought by them, and the individuals strive to join. Group loyalties are formed.

There are admission standards and entrance tests to see whether or not the student "will belong."

The students are likely to have initiation ceremonies for the new students, formal and informal, and the groups within the school do likewise.

The school and its supporters think it is the "best" school. They tend to favor its graduates. They have certain attitudes toward other schools and toward people who support other schools. These loyalties tend to make the school a good one, if directed in the right way. If wrongly directed, they can produce unfavorable effects, too.

When a new employee joins this group of telephone operators, there will be a period of adjustment before she will feel at home in the group.

*Southern Bell Telephone and Telegraph Co.*

**School Problems Are Similar to Those of Industry.** In a business or industry, there are similar influences at work. There are entrance requirements to see whether or not the prospective worker "belongs"; whether or not he can do the work assigned or learn to do it.

Consideration is given to whether or not the newcomer can get along with other workers; whether or not he is the type of person they will want to associate with.

There are formal or informal initiation ceremonies. The group within the business or industry usually sees to this. A worker may be accepted in the group or "get the cold shoulder."

There are group loyalties and company loyalties. Within larger industries there are shops, branches, and divisions, all with their customs and loyalties. There are labor organizations which are conducted along similar lines.

In other words, a business or industry, like a school, has at work within it many of the same influences and conditions which affect your behavior and mine in other groups in society. Consequently, learning how to get along with any group will help us to learn how to get along with these groups. What we learn in one group situation will help us in another group situation. Learning how to get along in school helps a young person to get along in industry.

Industries are interested in the activity record of college or high-school students. The student with a record of taking part in activities is a good risk for taking part in the personal and social relationships of a business or organization.

**Adjustment in the Home Room.** The home room is a student's headquarters at school. Here he reports for daily duty, and here, probably, he keeps some of his possessions. Here his first associations of each day occur.

A friendly "good morning" can alter the whole day's course for someone. In many schools, a new student must speak to everyone he meets. Members of the armed forces are required to salute superiors, and officers are expected to salute in return.

There is a reason for this. It is the fact that people get along better if they act with respect and consideration for others. One should not be so preoccupied with his own affairs that he "passes up" the little custom of greeting his associates and neighbors.

The psychology back of this is that you and I like to be recognized. We ought to think of this as it affects the other fellow, and we hope that he will think of it as it affects us.

Addressing the other fellow by *name* helps. Learn the names of your fellow students, your teachers, and your associates. Address them by name as soon as you can. Everyone is quite pleased to find that the other fellow thinks enough of him and values his friendship enough to take the trouble to learn his name.

Incidentally when meeting a person with whom you have had no contact in a long time it is wise and helpful to mention your name to him. Don't assume that he will remember it. Help him out by reminding him: say, "I'm Mary Nichols," or "I'm Bill Edwards, who used to be in your class."

So often students embarrass their teachers by saying, "Don't you remember me?" After all, your teachers have to deal with hundreds of people. It is even more stupid to call someone on the telephone and start out by saying, "Guess who this is!"

If we mention our name to the person encountered after a long absence, it pleases him to think that we were thoughtful enough to help him recall the name. Inwardly he says to himself, "Now there's someone who has some *sense*."

In the home room it is necessary to be prompt and neat in the care of our personal belongings. If the place is well ordered and pleasantly managed, every individual concerned will profit. We are *identified* with that room; what helps the room and the group adds just that much to our own well-being and to the respect others have for us.

**Adjustment in a Class.** Each class to which we belong is a social group. It is a society in miniature, and with some of the members we will be on close and familiar terms. To others, we will be just acquaintances in passing.

However, each class or group is an opportunity to form friendships and associations. Each class is a *social* learning situation as well as a *subject* learning situation. It is desirable that we accommodate ourselves to the practices and customs of the class; just as it would be wise, in the world at large, to accommodate ourselves to the customs and ways of any group with which we might find ourselves.

# Respect the Customs of Your Group

Annoyance is sometimes created when an individual fails to act in a manner in which he is expected to act. When the left fielder just stands indifferently and lets a fly go by, the fans are irritated. When someone pushes his way in front of us in a line in the cafeteria, we don't like it. We are annoyed if someone jostles us as we get on a bus. We expect a man to brush a fly off his nose, if one alights there, and we are irritated if he doesn't. Perhaps one of the basic causes of annoyance is the failure of the other fellow to do what he is expected to do. Let's turn it around. One of the reasons we annoy other people is that we frequently fail to do the things they *expect* us to do.

Everyone needs plenty of sleep but left-field is
not the place to get it.

In class, we expect the other student to conform to the ways of the class. He expects us to conform, too.

Hence it is good, in each new class, to become acquainted with the customs of the teacher and the group and to conform to them as much as possible. Disturbing the class, or disturbing the work of other persons, is definitely not an expected form of behavior.

This is the underlying meaning of the old adage, "When in

Rome do as the Romans do." It simply means that we should respect the customs and ways of doing things of the group with which we associate ourselves.

## Learn What Your Responsibility Is

What *is* the behavior that is expected of a student in the work of a class? The student is expected to make a reasonable contribution to what is going on. He is not fulfilling his responsibilities if he always keeps quiet and fails to carry his share of the discussion. Just as a member of a crew in a boat is expected to "pull his weight" on the oars, so is the student expected to enter into class activities.

This doesn't mean that the student should carry more than his share. When he talks too much, offers his opinions too freely, or asks too many questions, he becomes distinctly disagreeable to everyone. This is something students should guard against, especially able students. The same caution applies to any group or meeting.

Students resent the person who talks too much or who "hogs" the recitation because he is inconsiderate of their interests and of the purposes they have in being there. Each student must develop tact and judgment about when he should participate and when he ought to keep quiet.

## Can You Make These Adjustments?

**Adjustment in the Shop.** It is evident that a great many of the same principles which apply to adjustment in a school or class will also apply in a shop.

The friendly "good morning," care in the use of equipment and respect for the other fellow and his tools, addressing the other man or your fellow worker by name, loyalty to the group—all of these apply just as strongly to the shop.

In entering a job situation or shop, the new worker is "on trial." His best policy would be to keep his eyes open to learn what is expected of workers in the shop and to adjust himself to that situation. It is not desirable for the new worker to be "stand-offish"

These operators in the railroad switchyard control tower have been at their jobs a number of years, indicating that they were successful in making the necessary adjustments to their jobs.

*Chicago and Northwestern Railway*

or a "cold fish." He should seek friendly association with the others, at the same time avoiding the appearance of being over-eager or of pushing himself forward.

"Be yourself," but be careful not to make yourself a nuisance. Be careful about the other fellow's interests and values.

New workers should remember that the older workers have developed certain loyalties and certain ideas as to their rights and privileges. It is very unwise for the new worker to disregard these. He should take the view, "I know I have a lot to learn but I'm willing to try." No matter how much education and training the new worker has had, it is unlikely that he can possibly know as much about many of the tasks to be done, and the ways of handling them, as those who have been "on the job."

A willing learner, who shows a desire to like and respect the men and women who have been there first, will usually be welcomed.

You may, as a new worker, think that many of the older workers are arrogant and conceited. Try to keep this feeling under control; remember that it is human nature to develop a kind of "vested interest" in a job or in a place after you have been there a while. This is an *adjustment mechanism* of the older worker to protect his interest and his status on the job.

The older workers may try to test the new worker out. They may try some informal initiation stunts. These must be faced and expected, and the success of the newcomer will usually be judged by how he reacts to these stunts. If he "gets sore," there is trouble ahead. If he takes the "kidding" good-naturedly, he is almost assured of success in winning the group.

A "know it all" attitude, or an attitude of resentment toward antics of this sort, will be hard to overcome. A worker may be sent for some nonexistent tool or may be "baited" to say something known to irritate someone in the shop. This is where a good-natured willingness to "laugh it off" comes in handy. The other workers expect the newcomer to be annoyed or irritated to a certain degree, but they also expect him to react quickly with a smile and to see the funny side of it, too.

If a new worker knows that these experiences are likely to happen, he will not become hurt or depressed but will take them in his stride.

**Adjustment in the Office.** What has been said about the shop is just as true of the office. In addition, there are one or two other types of behavior to be avoided.

One of these is *talking too much*. The people already working in the office are familiar with the routine and know something about their work and its problems.

Sometimes the newcomer has an impulse to suggest better ways of doing things. He wants to make use of knowledge he has gained while in training, or elsewhere, before taking the job. It makes for good human relations to hold back on these suggestions until the newcomer has made a place for himself and has earned the right to talk.

A little later on his opportunity will come when someone asks for his opinion. In due time, he will have a chance to express it.

It is bad taste to start in by criticizing what is going on. The psychology of this is that it is something of a slap at the people who have already been working there. It is a reflection on *their* judgment, and they can't help resenting it. It is much better to accept even undesirable practices until the period of apprenticeship is over, and it is known that the suggestions will be welcome.

The following suggestion has to do with *making friends*. It helps to get to know the personnel of the office as individuals. The newcomer should not make the mistake of immediately becoming so absorbed in his work that he does not take the time or exert the energy necessary to get acquainted; he should let the other people feel that he is glad to have an opportunity to work with them and to know them.

It is very easy for a newcomer, unwittingly, to give the impression that he is self-seeking and indifferent to the other people around him. It takes time to make new acquaintances, but it pays great dividends in the extent to which the newcomer will be accepted into the group.

Sometimes it takes time to develop new friendships because the workers already there are resistant. It takes energy, and the newcomer has to "put himself out" to do it. He has to be a little patient and must not resent it if the older employees are, at first, a bit aloof and not too friendly. That is just another aspect of the "tendency to protect one's own status" that has been mentioned as characteristic of the "ones already there."

In line with what has been said about carrying one's own share of the load, it is important to avoid any behavior which might result in putting responsibility or work which should be yours on the other fellow. By coming in late, by taking excessive time out for personal errands, by spending too much time away from the desk, or otherwise neglecting duty, the result often may be that someone else in the office has to do the work for which you are responsible. This is always irritating to the worker who is faithful and responsible. It makes for unpleasant human relations.

A person's fellow workers will not appreciate being left to "hold the bag" or do work which is not their responsibility. There is a sharing here that is important. Moreover, when situations do come up in which the co-operation of the workers is needed, they will be far more willing to give it and to help out if they feel that you have been fair with them.

Whether it be business, industry or education, most workers have the responsibility of performing their work to the satisfaction of a supervisor—someone who holds responsibility at a higher level. Whoever this person may be, he will always be better impressed if the worker has done a good job and has been faithful to his work.

**Some Minor Things Which Often Annoy People.** There are some other minor annoyances to guard against. They might include (when in a group) such things as whistling softly or humming, shuffling the feet, "cracking" one's chewing gum, drumming with the fingers, tapping with a pencil, opening packages or handling "crunchy" paper, moving around more than is necessary (for example, in a classroom, too many trips to the pencil sharpener), unnecessary talking or whispering (especially where other people are really trying to be quiet, as in a library), and excessive coughing or nose-blowing (when a person has to blow his nose or cough or sniffle beyond a certain point he ought to leave the room, *even if he has to miss something*).

**Adjustments in Conversation with Others.** Much social life centers in conversation. In social conversation it is just as true as it is in a classroom, that the individual must learn to carry a fair share, but no more, of these exchanges of ideas and opinions.

Perhaps the most important thing is that of showing respect for the other fellow's opinion. It hurts the other person's self-respect if you imply that you have no interest in what he says. That is like suggesting that you don't think his ideas or comments are of much value.

If you do disagree with what he says, try to bring it out in such a way as to show that you are considerate of him. You might say, for example, "I wonder if you have been properly informed on that," or "I wonder if you knew that . . . ," or "I wonder if what you have said takes into consideration that . . . ."

One of the most important things we need to learn is the habit of *paying attention* to what the other person says. We like to have the other fellow listen to our opinion. If he stands with a faraway look in his eyes while we are talking, or keeps looking around, obviously not following or listening to us, we are annoyed or disappointed. If it is worth while to converse with someone *at all*, it is worth while to make the effort to pay attention to him.

Here it is well to add that the same thing applies to following a lecture or a speech. Nothing is so disconcerting to a teacher or a speaker as to see evident wandering of attention on the part of the audience or class. It is good taste to give the speaker the courtesy of attention, even though it takes an effort to do it.

**Adjustment to Your Superiors.** Respect for persons in authority makes for better social adjustment. In a school, the administrative officials and the faculty members are charged with the responsibility of managing the school. Students must assume that they have an honest interest in the welfare of the students. If the students indicate that they desire to co-operate with the staff members, and that they recognize this authority and responsibility, they will be more likely to enjoy the confidence and good will of the staff.

The student who approaches the principal or dean with "a chip on his shoulder" may run into difficulties. This is just as true of any worker in any situation where he and his superior officer is involved.

The point is that the principal, superior officer, boss, supervisor, or whatever he may be called, may be broad-minded and sympathetic, but he is, after all, a human being. As a human being he may feel that he has to defend himself and establish his authority first. He goes "on guard" when the "trouble maker" appears. No one who has been given authority or responsibility will like ridicule or criticism which will make it seem that he is incompetent or not faithful in carrying out his duties.

## Suggestions for Intelligent Behavior

**Taking Too Much of Someone's Time.** Respect for the time and interests of the other person is important. For example, if a student wants to see the principal or a faculty member, he should observe whether the time is appropriate or not for approaching him for a consultation.

It isn't good policy to "barge in" when the person you want to see is very busy on some other matter. One of the best ways is to ask for an appointment that can be made at the other person's convenience as well as yours. This shows that you are considerate of his time, and will usually respond in a friendly manner when so approached.

In a school situation, the student who takes up too much of the teacher's time by asking numerous questions and making comments after class or after school should consider whether or not he is overdoing it. If he remembers that the teacher has other people to talk to and other duties to perform, he will be conservative in demanding the teacher's time.

**The Undesirable Effect of Flattery and Overfamiliarity.** The sensible student will avoid what is known as "apple-polishing," that is, flattery of the teacher beyond what is reasonable and proper. He will be friendly and courteous when he meets faculty members on the school grounds or elsewhere, but he will try to act toward them in about the same way he would act when meeting other friends he respects and whose good wishes he hopes to enjoy. He will certainly not be exaggerated in his attention to them or do or say anything likely to place them in an embarrassing situation.

Contacts with the office staff members, in a school or in any office or business establishment, should be friendly but not overfamiliar. If you are a student, don't get confidential with the principal's secretary. Be honest in explaining absences or tardiness. "Putting one over" on members of the office staff can only subject the student to the risk of being considered unreliable.

It is good to remember that the little comments which office secretaries and other workers make about individuals may carry more weight than one might suppose. Our impressions of people are formed on the basis of all we see, hear, and experience in connection with them.

People are resentful of those who take unfair advantages. Seeking unfair advantages from superior officers may be resented by one's associates. Those who are honest and fair in accepting credit or blame will resent the individual who "gets away with something," or who gets credit or praise when he does not deserve it.

This would apply strongly in the matter of cheating on tests or examinations. No one likes the person who gets promotions by fraud. Honest students usually tend to dislike the classmate who receives a high mark or other distinction without the necessary effort.

**Straightening Out Misunderstandings Which Lead to Friction.** When misunderstandings arise, the individual should analyze the situation. He should try to find out what is back of the difficulty. For example, a student in school will sometimes find himself misunderstood. Circumstances might make something he has done seem wrong when in reality he was not to blame.

In such cases, he should go to the teacher who has misunderstood things and explain them. Most teachers will listen to a straightforward and honest explanation.

If the teacher does not seem to accept the explanation, it is sometimes necessary to enlist the support of a third person as a kind of mediator. In most schools, a dean or the principal could handle this without much difficulty. If a person has actually made a mistake, it is better to explain it than to let it go. *Remember that most people in life are not looking for trouble but are trying to avoid it.*

This is true of employers and employees alike. In a shop or office, employers or supervisors are not usually trying to have trouble with their employees.

**Learning To Get Along with Those in Authority.** It is important to analyze one's relationship with those in authority because that is a problem that will confront the individual throughout life. In any job or vocation, there will always be someone in a position of authority who must be dealt with. To learn how to deal pleasantly and intelligently with one's superiors is a very practical matter indeed.

In business and in industry, it has been found over and over again that one reason why people fail is not lack of ability to handle the job but lack of ability to get along with fellow workers or with people "higher up."

A few suggestions for guidance in this respect might include:

1. Remember that the person in authority has a job to do and is responsible for it.

2. Remember that the person in authority naturally feels that he has to maintain his "status" or position of leadership.

3. Remember that he is a human being and may feel criticism or disrespect as much as anyone else.

4. Be straightforward about explaining errors for which you have been responsible—don't beat around the bush.

5. Don't hesitate to help others out when you see a way of doing it—they will appreciate your co-operation.

6. Don't embarrass others by overfriendliness, solicitation, or "apple-polishing."

7. Remember that they are not looking for trouble any more than you are.

## SOMETHING TO DO

Interview someone in a position of responsibility or authority. In the interview, try to find out what some of the things are that his employees (if a school official, the reference might be to students) do which he likes and which make him feel that things are going well. Also try to find out some of the things that his employees do which he dislikes.

Then write a brief report on "What Employers Like and Dislike About Their Employees" or "What a Principal Likes or Dislikes About His Students." Go over this with your friends and discuss it. Find out what conclusions you can reach that might be helpful to you in your future relationships.

## QUESTIONS AND PROBLEMS FOR STUDY AND DISCUSSION

1. Why is it advisable to take some part in any group or class to which you may belong instead of sitting quietly without participating?

2. What must be kept in mind in considering how many questions to ask, or how many comments to make, in a class situation?

3. Why should you identify yourself when meeting a former employer, or former professor, whom you have not seen or talked with for some time?

4. Explain the "group psychology" back of rules for admission and initiation ceremonies.

5. What are some of the problems a new worker must expect to face in starting a new job in a shop or in an office?

6. Can you give an example of where a group has demanded certain behavior from its members which was in conflict with the customs and practices some of them had been accustomed to in their homes?

7. Explain the meaning of *identification* and show how this operates in connection with groups and their influence on their members.

8. Bring out some of the psychological principles involved in school spirit.

9. Is there such a thing as *company loyalty* in a business or industry? What are some of its good and bad points?

10. What are some of the minor habits which people have which annoy other people? Can you add any to those described in the text?

11. Make a list of some of your own habits which might annoy other people.

12. Give an illustration of how people sometimes annoy others by not behaving in a manner which is expected.

13. The next time you have a chance, listen in on an argument in the conversation of your friends, neighbors, or associates. Note what is said which seems to make for good human relations; note what is said that

makes for friction. What are some suggestions for conversation which would make for better relations?

14. What would be some good guiding principles to follow in connection with your first days in a new school?

15. What are some of the psychological considerations which help to explain the attitude of older workers toward new workers or of older students toward new students?

CHAPTER NINETEEN

# ACTIVITIES AND ORGANIZATIONS

This chapter takes up the importance of activities from the standpoint of their effect on the individual. It presents the point of view that every individual human being needs social activity. He needs to associate with groups, not only because this satisfies a human need, but because it is through such activities that one learns much, can enrich his or her life, and contribute to and enrich the lives of others.

In this chapter you will find some suggestions for finding and making contact with worth-while groups. Some of these suggestions, especially those concerning procedure and behavior, are very practical.

Many individuals do not realize how many different kinds of activities and groups there are in their own neighborhoods. Often these groups are looking for people with similar interests.

Possibly the main point in this chapter is the fact that it takes an effort to secure social participation. It is something which requires us to take the initiative. Having friends takes time, effort, and energy. This chapter reviews the practical aspects of this problem.

## QUESTIONS THIS CHAPTER WILL ANSWER

1. Should every person take part in activities and organizations?
2. What are some of the values in this type of activity, as the psychologist sees them?
3. What kinds of activities should be considered?
4. How can an individual find out about these activities, and how can he manage to share in them?
5. What are some guiding principles for joining and taking part in organizations?

## The Value of Group Activity

This discussion is directed to students who are in school and students who are out of school. The same purposes apply to both. It is intended to emphasize the great psychological value of taking part in activities and organizations.

At the present time, and mainly as a result of the great growth of cities, it is possible for an individual to be more or less "lost." He can pass by almost unnoticed and be alone even though he lives in a great city inhabited by hundreds of thousands of people.

If this is the case, his well-being is disturbed and his chances of developing into a happy, worth-while person are interfered with. Human beings need the association of other human beings for full development and real satisfaction in life. Every human being needs, and should seek, opportunities of this kind. The opportunities are there, but sometimes the individual fails to realize it or fails to take the necessary steps to secure these benefits.

Most schools are provided with clubs and activities which are open to any individual in the school. In all communities, there are many organizations which are interested in securing good members. Churches and religious organizations support numerous clubs and young people's groups. During the 1950s and 1960s the growth of community churches with their accompanying Sunday Schools and social activities has been phenomenal. Many towns, cities, and suburban areas have organizations like the Y.M.C.A. and the Y.W.C.A. which welcome any individual who wants to enjoy the benefits they provide.

The point which should be emphasized is this: club, school, and community activities offer one of the finest means of securing friendly association, with other people and for doing things with and for them. The opportunity to contribute to the needs of *others* is a rich and rewarding condition of human satisfaction, probably because doing something for others contributes to one's own need for a feeling of personal worth. Such activities give a wonderful opportunity for social experience. They give us a chance to develop skill in getting along with people. They give us opportunities to try out our abilities along various lines. They provide for two of our most important psychological needs: the need for a feeling of belonging and the need for a feeling of personal worth. Unless we satisfy these basic psychological needs, we will experience unhappiness and frustration.

## Suggestions for In-School Students

*Each student should make it a point to belong to one or more activities.*

The student who "doesn't particularly feel like it" should make it a special point. In a large school, the interests of each individual will not be known to his fellow students automatically. Since most activity leaders are interested in finding students who may make a contribution to their activities, they will usually welcome the new member.

Usually the activity will not come to you. *You will have to go out for the activity.* This means that you will have to find out what the activities are, find out who the leaders are, when meetings are held, and then make it a point to attend one or more of the meetings and let your interest in it be known. Don't be backward about doing this. Keep in mind the fact that unless it is a most unusual activity, the people who are taking part in it will be looking for interested new members to join their group.

Of course, the new student may find that there are some leaders who will want to challenge the newcomer because all groups like to test out or try out any prospective members. One of them may say, "It's going to be tough," or "Maybe you can make it." That's to be expected. In reality, the leaders are anxious to get good students to tie-in with their activities.

## Suggestions for Out-of-School Students

Young people (or older people, for that matter) should also make it a point to identify themselves with one or more activities or organizations. The same values mentioned in connection with school clubs apply here. The young person who "doesn't particularly feel like it" is the one who should make a special effort.

"What organizations can I join?" comes the question.

In all communities, in addition to such groups as the "Y," there are first of all many church and church-related groups. Some of the larger churches have many groups ranging from church-supported boy scout organizations to men's clubs, athletic groups, and bowling leagues.

Many unions have social and recreational groups connected with them.

Many fraternal organizations exist which might be considered, and it is usually expected that the young person who is interested should take the initiative in making inquiries concerning possible membership in them.

Some communities have political organizations with active programs, social and recreational as well as political in nature.

Many business and industrial organizations have athletic and recreational groups, and some of them are very active. Some bowl-

Common interests bring people together. Thousands of modern Americans are especially enjoying outdoor activities, such as boating.

*Evinrude Motors*

ing leagues, soft-ball leagues, and similar activities have quite elaborate schedules and programs which provide much interest and fellowship to their members. Some industrial activities become very highly developed. An example: The Westinghouse Electric and Manufacturing Company of East Pittsburgh has a male chorus which presents exceptionally fine concerts and travels to various parts of the country for this purpose.

The point is that the individual will be able to find suitable activities to take part in. They are there. But it is necessary to look around and take some initiative.

Larger communities often have hiking groups and nature study

364       PSYCHOLOGY FOR LIFE TODAY

groups or hobby groups. Keep a lookout in the newspapers for
their announcements, and when it says, "everyone is invited,"
that means you! Remember that *most groups are really anxious to
get interested members, and you will be more than welcome.*

It ought not to be necessary to remind people that they ought
not to join organizations just for the sake of belonging to more
organizations. Americans call such people "joiners"—and the term
has come to indicate a rather undesirable tendency which some
people seem to have. In our discussion we are thinking of joining
organizations for the real contribution that they can make to
the well-being of the individual, and from the point of view that
the individual, if he belongs to groups which represent *his* values
and purposes, can make a real contribution to the groups and thus
participate in things worth while.

Accordingly, it is to be hoped that no one will, after reading
this section, rush out and join organizations without considering
their appropriateness for him. The thought to be emphasized is that
it is to one's advantage to participate with other people in worth-
while activities, and there are few, indeed, who can thrive and be
happy as "lone wolves" in a social world. Yet, satisfactory adjustment
to groups of people does not come with equal ease to all of us. Sometimes it takes some effort, and that is the point of this chapter. By
a little thinking and planning, most of us *can* find the ways and
the means of joining with others in worth-while social activities,
and we should certainly try to do so if we want to lead wholesome
and satisfying lives.

## How to Join an Organization

When an individual attends a meeting of an activity or approaches an activity leader with the idea in mind of becoming a
member of the organization or taking part in it, he must conduct
himself with tact and good judgment. Here is a social situation
which will be repeated many times in life. It is the situation of
seeking to be accepted in a group.

All that has been said about tact in dealing with the "other
fellow" comes in here. The newcomer will want to show the
leader of the group that he is genuinely interested in the organization or activity and that he is ready and willing to help with
whatever skill he has to make the group or activity a success.

Usually the members of any group or activity are self-respecting individuals who are interested in their organization and proud of its work and its members. The newcomer should indicate that he is also interested in their work and that the activity appeals to him.

If his position were to be put into words, it might be something like this:

"I am very much interested in the activities of this organization. I would consider it an honor and a privilege to have a share in it. I am here to learn what I can and do what I can to help the group. I would appreciate the opportunity very much."

The psychology of the situation is that the individual is endeavoring to express his own individuality and his own interests. At the same time, he should give the others a feeling that *their* values and interests would be promoted by accepting him into the group. This is a normal social situation. Each individual needs to develop skill and judgment in social behavior *on both sides* of the situation. Thus the attitude of the members of the group toward the newcomer is a matter for some consideration, too.

**Take the Initiative in Finding Worth-while Activities.** Any person who realizes that he is not enjoying the benefits of taking part in a school or community activity should look around for a group in which he is likely to have an interest. Then he should take some step toward becoming affiliated with it. The in-school student may seek the advice of any student counselor or dean in this connection. *Choosing school activities intelligently is certainly next in importance to choosing school courses wisely.*

Modern educators regard school activities as an essential part of education. They will certainly be only too glad to help the individual student who wishes to take advantage of these opportunities.

It is equally important for the person no longer in school to take the initiative in looking for activities. Just as he would expect to take the initiative in looking for a job, so he must expect to take the initiative in looking for worth-while clubs and recreational or social groups as has been noted.

Most people probably expect the organizations to come to them. This is not what happens in modern life in our complex cities and neighborhoods. *We have to take steps to find the organizations* we need for successful living.

Often we become interested in activities *by trying them.*

Just as we say to the six-year-old who doesn't want to eat some-

Hobby groups, such as this model railroad club, are always interested in acquiring new members.

*Modern Railroader*

thing, "You'll never know whether you like this food or not if you aren't willing to try it," so the student must make the effort if he is to find the satisfaction that comes from these things.

**Some Characteristics of Organized Groups.** As we realize, groups have characteristics of their own. They tend to have members who are alike in at least some respects. They are not likely to have many persons in them who differ very much from the average member.

This should be kept in mind in sizing up a group as to possible membership. If the members are of the kind you like, go ahead. If they are in general not similar to you in tastes and interests, try to find a group more likely to suit you. However, this suggestion must be applied with care. We can hardly expect to find groups of people who will suit us exactly, even if we wanted to.

Furthermore, it is wise to realize that even though groups do tend to be made up of people with similar habits and interests, there are always some individuals who differ.

Sometimes we forget the fact that there are individual differences. We run across an individual who is unlike the members of a group, and, unless we have given some thought to it, we are likely to think that all of the members are like the one we have encountered. People have been known to criticize churches, for instance, because a few of the people in the churches do not behave as faithful church members are supposed to behave. Certainly this should not condemn the whole church!

Psychology demonstrates that we must expect individuals to differ, and we must expect to find some individuals who differ at times *even from their own customary behavior.*

This is why we must develop an attitude of tolerance toward groups and realize that if we are to enjoy the undoubted benefits of associating with them, we must not be unrealistic in what we expect to find in their members.

Above all, we must remember that it is absurd to generalize about all the members of a group as a result of what we observe about one of them or a few of them.

**Find Associations with the Opposite Sex.** Since one of the most desirable purposes of social life should be to learn how to enjoy and derive satisfaction from associating with members of the opposite sex, it is worth while for the student to belong to at least one organization in which persons of both sexes are active. The girl who limits her school activities to the activities in which only girls take part is depriving herself of an opportunity to learn how to get along with boys.

Half the people in the world are members of the opposite sex! Take whatever opportunities you can to learn how to meet them, to associate with them, and to enjoy them.

Many of the associations and groups mentioned previously are made up of members from both sexes—the groups connected with churches, such as young people's groups, the hiking and nature study groups, and some of the political groups. Most of the school activity groups include both boys and girls. Many fraternal groups have joint activities with related women's organizations.

## Too Much Conformity

Sometimes, in order to be a "good fellow" or in order to win the praise of one's fellows, an individual will go too far in the direction of conforming to the customs of the group. This could happen when the individual himself does not want to be "different." In *The Organization Man*,[1] the writer suggests that one of the phenomena of modern American life is the individual who in a very real sense loses his individuality by submerging himself in his community, or in the business or professional group with which he is identified. Although his relationship to society is complex, and the problem should not be over-simplified, he is often in danger of losing his individuality in the highly organized society that we have today. In a way he considers it more important to belong to the group and to get along well with the group, than to express or find ways of expressing, his own individual creative powers.

## Adjustment to Groups and the Community in General

Adjustment to a school, to a business, or to a fraternal group is probably only a way of talking, since adjustments are usually to people or to things, specifically. That is, as we learn to get along with the individuals in a group, we develop a group consciousness along with it.

If adjustment to each individual and to each group is good, a general satisfaction of feeling a part of the community develops.

The point here is that we never really feel as though we belong to a community unless we have friends in it and unless we are sharing in some of its group activities. Unless we share in the life of the community, we may feel that it isn't much of a place.

Psychologically, we have to share in the activities of an organization before we feel that we are a part of it. In the same way, we have to share in the life of a community, or we may feel apart from it.

If you find yourself thinking, "This sure is a dumb town," you might ask yourself the question, "Am I really sharing in any of the activities around here?"

When you are a part of the activity of the community, you may come to the conclusion, "This isn't such a bad place after all."

Sometimes when people move to a new community, they find it dull and uninteresting in comparison to the place in which they

---

[1]William H. White, Jr., *The Organization Man* (New York: Simon and Schuster, 1956).

formerly lived. Often this is due to the fact that they have not yet become *active* in the new community. They haven't begun to share in what is going on.

Perhaps it is a good rule to take part in the life of any new community in which you find yourself as soon as possible.

## Prestige of Institutions You Belong To

A school or an industry is an institution. It has an identity, traditions, customs, and a reputation. The institution means much to the individuals connected with it because each individal is identified with its successes or failures. Whatever the reputation of the school may be, it reflects on each student enrolled.

For example, when a group of high-school boys get a can of paint and a brush and write on the side of the courthouse "Down with Smith High," or "Blanktown 6—Dashville 0," people are likely to think the students of the entire school are rowdies who have no regard for the appearance of costly public buildings. The behavior of each student is, to the outside world, a demonstration of what the school stands for.

One large American industrial organization has definitely ordered the dismissal of any employee found to be drinking excessively. In explaining this order, the general manager said, "We don't want people to think that our company employs a lot of drunken bums."

If a student or an employee is well-mannered, intelligent, and responsible, on the other hand, the entire school or the entire organization gets the credit, and everyone connected with the organization benefits from his behavior.

The importance of *identification* as a psychological force can hardly be overemphasized.

**Effect of the Appearance of Buildings and Grounds.** Care of the building and grounds is important in respect to *identification*. Many a stranger gets his impression of a school or a factory by observing whether or not things are orderly and clean. Writing on the walls and in lavatories; trash in the corridors, on the sidewalks, or on the grounds; these make an impression.

It is not merely "talking theory" to say that each time a careless person throws away a banana peeling, or leaves some waste paper on the floor, it is an act of *aggression* against each and every other person in the organization.

Cleanliness of grounds and buildings enters into the question of loyalty to the organization. Educated men and women take pride in such things. Most men and women react favorably to attractive places.

Just as the appearance of a school is important, not only to the students in the school but also to the whole community, so is the appearance of a store, a factory, or any other place of business or daily living.

How many communities realize this? An untidy, dirty business street has an adverse effect on the whole town. People will drive on through without stopping to patronize the business establishments found there. The whole area will get a reputation for uncleanliness. This obviously means that all of the people in the area will suffer indirectly because of the loss of trade. This is certainly one of the reasons why many large and important American cities are making strenuous and costly efforts to rebuild old and unsightly downtown areas, and to rid themselves of "blighted" sections.

If we notice the practices of the really successful businesses and industries in this country, we will find that orderliness, cleanliness, and appearance are evidently *valued very highly*.

The industries and businesses which are at the highest level of economic success are *clean*. The implications are very clear. It pays each person to give considerable attention to this in his own life and in his own activities.

To the extent that we are identified with the better classes of institutions, businesses, or groups, we will be successful in our own social and business lives.

The poorest states, the poorest towns, the sections with the lowest standards of living and the lowest income, are usually run-down, untidy, and more or less disreputable. We venture to suggest that in many cases the poverty is a *result* of the failure of the individual people concerned to realize how important, to them, good standards for the group or the community can be.

## SOMETHING TO DO

In order to discover the extent of activity opportunities in your school or community, make a table showing what they are. Think of activities or groups carrying on activities in which you might, if you wanted to, take part.

Make the classification under the following main headings:

1. Athletic
2. Arts and crafts
3. Economic (such as chamber of commerce)
4. Educational
5. Gardening
6. Hiking
7. Hobbies (cameras, electric trains, etc.)
8. Musical
9. Nature study
10. Outdoor sports
11. Political
12. Professional or occupational
13. Religious
14. Other organizations (including fraternal or groups which would cut across several interests)

## QUESTIONS AND PROBLEMS FOR STUDY AND DISCUSSION

1. In a group to which you belong, check each name according to how well you feel you know the person. Check those you know very well with a "2"; those you know fairly well, with a "4"; those you know least of all with a "6." How many persons fall within each group? What is your average score; that is, for the entire group, do you secure an average score which is near 2, 4, or 6? What does the result mean?

2. Note an instance in which someone in a group has acted in a way out of line with the behavior usually expected in the group. What happened? How did the group act about it?

3. How many organizations do you belong to? List them from top to bottom in accordance with the extent to which you are interested in them.

4. What psychological needs are met by organizations—needs important to every person?

5. What are some of the organizations usually found in every community in which almost any individual, if he wanted to, could secure membership?

6. What are some of the characteristics about an individual which might be considered by a group in determining his eligibility to membership?

7. How do most groups, in school or out, feel about acquiring new members?

8. Give an example of an industrial group or a business group which exists for the purpose of providing fellowship or recreation for the members.

9. Why is it pointed out that people have to take the initiative in becoming identified with groups or activities?

10. Discuss the extent to which members of a group or activity will be like each other. Will there be any in the group who differ?

11. Watch the newspapers for an announcement of a proposed trip or meeting of a hiking club, hobby club, nature study group, or other similar organizations.

12. Why is it stated that adjustment to the community comes through participation or sharing in the activities of the community?

13. Give an example of a business concern or industrial establishment which pays considerable attention to orderliness and cleanliness. Does this, in your opinion, affect the people who are employed in the concern?

14. Can you think of any town or community which has a reputation for cleanliness and good appearance? The opposite?

15. In what respects could your own neighborhood be improved from the standpoint of appearance? Do you think this would have any importance to you personally? Why?

CHAPTER TWENTY

# CONDITIONS OF JOB SATISFACTION

Psychologists have indicated a number of factors which make for job success. Some of these are presented in this chapter together with some additional observations on what goes into the matter of job satisfaction.

It is necessary to remember that the job gives the worker certain practical benefits, such as wages, but it also provides him with some very important psychological values such as the feeling of security and the feeling of achievement. The psychological factors are outlined in this chapter.

In this discussion you will note how to size up a job in regard to all of the benefits it is possible or desirable to consider. This is a problem of job evaluation. We all need to know how to do it.

The things the average person is looking for in his occupation are defined, explained, and illustrated. You will find some practical hints on how to get along with employers, and some suggestions on what they will be looking for in you.

## QUESTIONS THIS CHAPTER WILL ANSWER

1. What are the things we should look for in a job?
2. In connection with deciding on an occupation, what things are important besides questions of hours of work, pay, etc.?
3. Why is so much stress laid on the kind of environment and the kind of people with whom one will work?
4. What personal or psychological considerations come up in deciding on the suitability of a job?
5. Are there any factors concerning a job which the worker, rather than the employer, should consider as his responsibility?
6. How do employers usually decide the worth or value of an employee?

## What To Expect from a Job

People should consider a job from two points of view. They should consider what the job has to offer in a practical way regard-

373

ing such matters as salary, working conditions, and in relation to their own particular ability and training. In the second place, they should consider the job from the point of view of its contribution to their personal needs and to their way of life and ultimate goals in life.

From the viewpoint of job satisfactions, what are the advantages and disadvantages of working in a highly automatized industrial installation, like the above for reducing the thickness of ingots?

*Terre Haute Division AA Co.*

Possibly the first question you should ask about a job is: Is it suited to my ability and my training? A young woman just starting out as a secretarial worker had two jobs to choose from, both immediately available. One job required what might be called overall supervision of an office, meeting many kinds of people, making decisions concerning their needs, and much responsibility in addition to taking dictation and typing. The other job called for answering the telephone, writing letters, and attending to the business correspondence of one person. She took the latter job, feeling that her lack of previous training and experience made her better suited to it than to the complex job. For someone else, it might have been that the complex job would have been the best opportunity.

It would be foolish, generally speaking, for an individual to apply for a job for which he has had no training and which would be entirely out-of-line with his abilities.

However, we realize that many jobs are similar to each other in the training and abilities they require (belonging to what we call a job family, a group of related jobs in the sense that they call for similar training and some common types of work). It would be inadvisable to jump to the conclusion that a certain job would not suit you, if the job could be thought of as belonging to a job family related to the kinds of work you could do. Some people give up too easily. If there are numerous points of similarity between the job you are offered and the particular one you wanted to get, it would be a good idea to consider carefully whether or not you might be able, with some experience and possibly further training, to handle the job available.

A simple example might be the case of a young man who went to a department store expecting to get a job as a shoe salesman but was offered a job as an assistant in the rug department instead. This would be a related job, although not the job he was looking for. He took it and in a short time discovered that he could hardly have made a better choice.

A young person expecting to become a teacher of history should not refuse to consider a teaching position in English, or speech, or some other subject at least related to his training. Employers sometimes find that people narrow their own possibilities too much by getting a preconceived notion of the exact thing they want when other similar or related jobs may be the ones which are actually available.

In attempting to find out what kind of work he can do, the proposed worker should think of the skills required, the amount of knowledge needed, the experience necessary, the chances of succeeding, the amount of responsibility involved in the job, and the specific duties of the job in relation to his readiness to take them on.

He should also consider, when the job involves duties in which he has not had previous experience, whether or not there will be opportunity to secure training in these duties on the job; they might be duties he could learn readily after getting started.

In the following paragraphs we will summarize some of the *practical* suggestions which ought to be thought of in connection with "What To Expect from a Job."

**Is the Pay Satisfactory?** This should be determined in accordance with what people generally get for the type of work involved and in accordance with your own ability and experience. The amount of pay should be enough to meet your own minimum daily requirements. After a few years, your pay ought to do more than that for you. It should enable you to live in more comfort, provide for your family, give you something for savings, and provide some of the good things of life.

The beginning worker has to accept a satisfactory minimum wage and recognize that he, like everybody else, will have to consider that the first few months, or even years, on the job will usually be thought of as part of his training for greater rewards to come later.

Sometimes it is more important to know whether there is a chance for the rate of pay to increase as time passes than it is to secure a high return right at the start. In connection with pay, on any job, give some thought to the likelihood of later promotion and advancement.

**Is There Opportunity for Promotion?** Other things being equal, enter a job with promotion possibilities. (Unless, of course, you are working for yourself, in which case you should consider whether, by application and effort, you are going to be able to secure an increasing return as you put time and experience into your work.)

Promotion is necessary to most people, and it would be important to know whether or not the proposed job has this advantage. Some industries lack clear lines of promotion. They should be avoided in favor of business or industrial opportunities where the lines of promotion are established or at least possible.

**Is There Opportunity for Training and Further Learning?** Other things being equal, choose a job which has further learning possibilities. Choose a job which is in an organization which believes in training. An organization which has a training program is also likely to have good promotion and other personnel policies.

Some fields, particularly aviation, have developed an aura of glamour which makes job evaluation a difficult process. This stewardess is providing hospitality for passengers aboard a modern jet plane.

*Eastern Air Lines*

**Are the Hours of Work and Related Conditions Good?** Since the job will have considerable effect on your general pattern of life, consider the hours of employment, the length of your work week, and your opportunity for days off and vacations. This will be somewhat related to your own personal tastes and interests. But you should check on whether or not the policies of your prospective employer in this connection are reasonable.

It is better to work under conditions that are satisfactory to you than to work under conditions which are to your disadvantage to such an extent that they will interfere with your enthusiasm and loyalty.

**What Will Be the Conditions under Which You Will Work?** Consider whether or not the work will be under conditions which will be healthful, clean, comfortable, and relatively free from danger. A worker ought to recognize that his health is important to him, and he ought to size up a job with this in mind. With regard to cleanliness and comfort, of course, work is work. But the overall conditions should be right for the particular job. This varies so much from job to job that it is hard to make generalizations. It would be well to suggest considering these aspects of the job, though, before a decision is made.

Of course, each individual's personal physical qualifications have to be considered, especially with reference to any special conditions. For example, a person with limited eyesight ought not to take a job involving a great deal of close work with the eyes. A person with hearing limitations should avoid a job requiring sensitiveness to sound.

**What Kind of Environment Will You Work In?** If you don't like indoor work, it would be foolish to look for a desk job in an office. If you don't like outdoor work, it would be foolish to consider being a truck driver or a telephone lineman.

An engineer who works for one of the telephone companies likes his particular job because about half the time he is required to make surveys out-of-doors.

A teacher enjoys his job because part of the time he is in a shop where he has an opportunity to work with machines and tools, which he enjoys.

A government worker enjoys his work because he has to travel around from one building to another and enjoys "getting around town."

A secretary likes her work because she has a desk in an attractive office, beautifully furnished, and very comfortable.

A store worker likes his job because he works in very comfortable surroundings in an air-conditioned building, his hours are such that he doesn't have to get up early, he has ample "off-duty" time during the day for personal relaxation, and he has some unusually good recreational opportunities.

In other words, the environment, or the place where the work is done, is important to many individuals and should be given consideration by them.

**What Kind of People Will You Work With?** The practical matter of daily association with people, and people of a certain kind, should be considered. If work is play for some people, it is often because they enjoy working with their associates. The human relations advantages of a job are important.

A young woman resigned from what seemed like a very good secretarial job because, as she said, "I never see anybody. The boss is away three-fourths of the time, and no one ever comes near the place."

Although it is hard to generalize, people usually enjoy working with other people who have had somewhat similar backgrounds.

There is a difference between people in terms of their interests, tastes, and what they like to talk about which shows up here.

On the other hand, practically all people have good human qualities which will be found to be very satisfying, if the new worker looks for them and starts in with a friendly attitude.

**What Kind of People Will You Work For?** Although in many ways this is like the preceding question having to do with the kind of people you work with, it is well to point out the importance of having good supervisors. In individual jobs it is well to have a feeling of confidence in the particular supervisor or supervisors involved.

This is where the human side enters greatly. In business, industry, or the professions, we still have many people in supervisory positions who have little regard for good human relations. To the extent that we have the privilege of choosing our jobs, we should endeavor to find employers who will respect us as individuals and who, in turn, can justify our respecting them.

As a matter of fact, if you can say, "I think I would like to work with that man," it is a good indication that the job would be worth considering favorably.

**What Kind of People Will Work for You?** In many jobs, even from the begininng, the worker is responsible for other people. No one should accept a supervisory position unless he is ready and willing to associate with, and have around him, the men and women for whose work he will be responsible. Anything else leads to an aloofness and distance which makes it unlikely that there will be satisfactory working relationships in the organization.

Consequently, before "rushing into" a job, it would be well to think of this from the standpoint of whether or not the people for whom you will have to be responsible are the kind of people you want to be responsible for.

**Will the Job Satisfy Your Basic Needs?** Turning to the second large group of factors which a person ought to consider in connection with what to expect from a job, we need to recall the basic needs which people have and for which they are seeking satisfaction in life.

The average person:

1. Wants to have a chance to satisfy his own personal needs. He wants rest, exercise, food, and bodily comforts.

2. He wants to feel secure.

3. He wants to "get somewhere and be somebody."
4. He wants to have the feeling of "belonging."
5. He wants to respect himself.

There are other basic needs, and there are other ways of expressing the basic needs mentioned. However, these basic needs listed have come to be accepted widely by psychologists and educators, and they are rather generally agreed upon as being important.

When a person is able to meet these needs reasonably well, he is likely to be well-adjusted and to get along all right. To the extent that he can't meet these needs, he becomes (to use an expression widely prevalent in psychology) *frustrated*. Then, as we know, he tries to make up for this feeling in one way or another, and the results are not always happy either for himself or for other people.

The question of "What to expect from a job?" becomes very important at this point. We realize that a person's job has much to do with the extent to which he can satisfy these needs. In a practical way it has, for most people, everything to do with it. Most people depend on their jobs for a living. A poor man can't meet these needs entirely and lives in constant fear of not being able to meet them. He is basically "off on the wrong foot," and often his job has much to do with it.

But the other needs, the "psychological" ones, are just as important: the need for security, for a feeling of belonging, etc. We know that a job has much to do with how well an individual can achieve these satisfactions, and we recognize that a job to a very great extent sets one's pattern of life.

The following paragraphs present suggestions which apply to this aspect of the problem.

*Will the Job Enable You To Satisfy Your Basic Personal Requirements as a Human Being?* The answer depends on whether you will get enough pay to be able to afford adequate food, shelter, clothing, and the other necessities; whether the job will enable you to have adequate rest and recreation; whether the job will help or hinder you in associating with people who can prove beneficial to you in your daily living.

*Will the Job Enable You To Have a Feeling of Security?* Within reason, will the job be a secure one? Some occupations are seasonal (such as certain kinds of agriculture, some of the building trades in certain sections, and some of the amusement occupations.) Some occupations are not likely to be long-lived (especially where mechanical or industrial improvements are occurring which will affect them). Some organizations are not as securely organized as others.

The general question is: How good are the chances of my keeping this job? Avoid jobs where there are dangers of being fired according to the whims of the employer; avoid "low security" jobs. When conditions of employment are good, many people give little thought to this. Then when business conditions become unfavorable, they would like to do something about it, but it is too late.

This is where intelligent planning comes in. Think about the security aspects of the job while conditions are good, rather than when it is too late.

*Will the Job Give You an Opportunity To Feel That You Are Getting Somewhere?* The essential difference here, between jobs, is that some of them are "blind alley" jobs; whereas others lead to improvements, promotions, or some worth-while goals. Whether a job is a blind alley job or not depends on the alertness of your employers, your own ability and initiative, and the general situation. You can't predict what will happen with certainty because there are too many unpredictable factors. But you can estimate how the prospects look with all of these in mind.

Basically, everyone likes to feel that he is getting somewhere. The farmer has the satisfaction of seeing his crops grow; the carpenter has the satisfaction of seeing a building take shape or a piece of furniture "begin to look like something." On your job, whatever it may be, you will need to see that progress is being made. You will like to feel that you are getting some credit for what you do, and that your efforts are being rewarded. If a job does not provide this, or the people who are in a supervisory position over you do not consider it, then to that extent it is not a good job. Make this a criterion for judging your job, among others. Please note, however, that some supervisors, who are in other respects very good men and women, do not give much thought to this point.

One man quit a good job because, as he put it, "The guy never said, in twenty years, whether he liked what I was doing or not." The boss just had a "blind spot" on this particular point; in other respects he was a good man to work with.

*Will the Job Give You the Feeling That You Belong?* This is a personal reaction. A person should feel that he belongs, that he fits in, that he is wanted in the organization. It ties in with the preceding poin'; but it also has something to do with the nature of the work done, the attitude of one's fellow-workers toward him, and the general atmosphere of the office or shop.

Unfortunately, many people never find out that they were really wanted until they are about ready to quit. Again, it is a human trait not to let the other fellow know that we value him until something threatens to disrupt things. If he gets sick, or is going to retire, we think of it.

Actually, the feeling of being appreciated is based on more than mere words or open expressions made by one's associates. It is a *feeling* more than anything else. We can usually sense whether we are liked or not; whether we are fitting in.

Elsewhere, we discussed what we need to do in our relations with others to gain their friendship and to promote a favorable attitude on their part toward what we are doing. If, after a period of time, we still find that this feeling is missing on a job, it suggests that we are not yet in quite the right place, or that our way of doing things has not been quite appropriate to the situation. It could be either of these, or both.

A new school was being completed recently, and one of the instructors who might have been moved to the new building (very modern and comfortable in all respects) was asked if he intended to move. "No, thanks," he replied, "I like it very well here, and I feel at home here. I think I'll just stay here where I know the principal and he knows me, and where I have my friends."

This man had a feeling of belonging that was important enough to him to make him feel justified in turning down the opportunity to work in what some people would have thought was a much better environment.

*Will the Job Give You a Feeling of Self-Respect?* This has to do with the self-satisfaction that the worker gets from his job. If the work is adapted to your abilities and needs, if it challenges you, you will probably feel this inner satisfaction.

But when a man's job does not call for his best, or when it is out of line with what he feels he can do or should do, he may miss this very important element in job satisfaction. Entirely too many people miss the point in this connection. They have thought about the money reward for the job, or the promotions that might be possible, but have never felt that it was really the job best suited to their own inner drives and values.

When you can do better, or make more of a contribution to

your fellow men, and you know that you can, you ought not to be satisfied with a job at a lower or less satisfying level. Possibly this is what the poet had in mind when he wrote, "Hitch your wagon to a star." The star need not be an inaccessible one, one you can never hope to reach, but for you and your own abilities it should at least be a star. The man who does less than he can never feels the inner satisfaction that is one of the finest rewards of work.

## What the Job Expects from the Worker

This discussion on what the job expects from the worker must take into account the fact that the problem varies from one job to another. The first answer we might make is that the person who is employed is expected to get the job done.

If a boy is hired to deliver papers, then he must deliver the papers. If a professor is employed to teach classes, he ought to be there at the times when the class meets, ready to teach. The first thing any worker has to do is to find out what is expected of him and prepare to do it.

However, assuming that this is done and that this condition is being met, there are some other things the employer expects of the worker that ought to be given consideration. They are among the values the employer holds, and his attitude toward the worker will depend on how well the worker is living up to or meeting these values.

The employer expects a reasonable service for the investment he has made. He expects the papers (if we are talking about the newsboy) to be delivered regularly and on time, and he expects all of them to reach their destination. A newsboy who would fail to deliver a few, or who would be late too often, would not be rendering a reasonable service. Other jobs could be evaluated in the same way.

The employer expects friendliness and co-operation. He does not expect to have the employee "talk back" to him or make his life miserable by complaining, fretting, and worrying. Human nature is like this. If the employer has made a reasonable effort to provide suitable conditions for you, as his worker, and you still insist on complaining, his reaction is most likely to be, "Well, if you don't like it here, you can go somewhere else."

An employer expects loyalty. He does not appreciate the worker who goes around "running down" his business or engaging in constant criticism outside of the shop or plant. In most groups, some criticism "inside" is to be expected. But few organizations like it if the workers carry on the attack "outside."

This is quite understandable, since the criticism outside has a tendency to make difficulties for the employer and to decrease the effectiveness of the business. This in turn hurts the employees as well.

**Responsibility and Improvement.** The employer expects the workers to be responsible, to be dependable. No employer likes an employee who is usually late to work or who is missing when he wants to call on him for help. The worker who must, for some good reason, be late or absent, owes it to the employer to let him know beforehand (within reason, of course). If a job is to be completed by a certain time, the supervisor will expect to find it completed then. In modern business and industrial life, this is almost unavoidable, because the effectiveness of every individual's work is, so largely, dependent on the other fellow doing *his* job on *time*. It is difficult to see how satisfactory supervisor-worker relations could be kept up unless the workers accept this need for being *responsible*.

He (the employer) expects some improvement as the worker goes along. Supervisors and employers continually have the problem of breaking in new workers. They do not expect perfect performance at the start, but they do like to see improvement. Wouldn't you? It seems obvious that we should get better with practice. As we go along, we should, even to satisfy ourselves, make some progress in improving our work.

**How Employers Evaluate a Worker.** The discussion at this point is intended to refer to the common practice rather than to go into the question of "rating scales" or other technical devices. Actually, rating scales are not too common, since there has been difficulty in developing useful ones.

The usual methods of employers in evaluating workers are rather obvious and usually quite subjective. By that we mean that they are to a large extent dependent on opinion, either the employer's or the opinions of others. Opinions are good, if they are checked by others equally competent to judge. For example, if two people say that Bill Jones is dependable, it is probably so. If a third person, independently, also says that he is a responsible, dependable man, it is likely that he is. In other words, opinion is good when it is *verified*.

Employers will gather opinions concerning their workers from persons who observe their work. The immediate supervisor of the worker is the one whose opinion counts most. But usually the supervisor's opinion is checked by informal noting of what other workers say and what other supervisors, who might happen to know the worker, say.

The points on which the worker is checked conform closely to the items mentioned under the discussion of "What the Job Expects from the Worker."

Employers are influenced by the extent to which they are getting: good service, co-operation, loyalty, dependability, and improvement.

How important any one of these is depends somewhat on the nature of the job. Some jobs call for more dependability than anything else. For example, it is necesary that the night watchman, the gateman, and the time-keeper *be there* more than anything else. A telegraph company employed a man of very low intelligence and found him to be a very satisfactory employee. When given a telegram to deliver he would always deliver it, no matter how long it took or what the difficulties might be.

There certainly is no doubt about the fact that employers are impressed by dependability, regularity of performance, and attention to business. There have been cases where men of unusual skill and ability have been careless or indifferent to requirements of this sort; but usually this indifference does not last long. Eventually the employer tires of the lack of dependability and acts accordingly.

**How Job Success Is Judged.** Job success is judged pretty much in accordance with who is doing the judging. There are cases where the worker thinks one way and the employer another. Jim Edwards thinks he is a pretty valuable employee of Bell Telephone; he judges himself quite a success. Bell Telephone's opinion could be somewhat different.

One of the least successful teachers in a certain high school is certain that she is one of the best. On the other hand, there are many successful people in every walk of life who consider themselves to be anything but successful.

It is probably more important for the individual to consider himself a success than it is for anyone else to do so (though this must be said guardedly). Psychologically, the effect on a man is much worse when he considers himself a failure than it is for someone else to consider him a failure. But it is seldom necessary to go to such extremes.

We may conclude that the employer of any person will consider him a success if he delivers the desired results in terms of the items mentioned under "What the Job Expects from the Worker."

The individual worker will consider job success to be a matter of how many of the things expected from the job are realized. He will think in terms of income, security, power or authority, prestige, and the return from the job in terms of the satisfaction he feels or needs.

Lucy Ogden Norton, Assistant Supervisor of Personnel of the General Electric Company, Erie, Pennsylvania, told an audience of personnel workers that job satisfaction depended on such things as pay and extra benefits, good working conditions, good supervision, job security, respect for human dignity, promotion, information about the company and what was going on, establishing the sense of belonging, and finding the work interesting. Possibly these would be measures of job success.

Actually, job success is probably measured by the extent to which the worker himself and the supervisor or employer *agree* on his adaptation to the work and on his effectiveness in carrying out assignments. In simpler terms, if I like my job, and my employer likes me, I have a considerable amount of job success. If one or the other of these is off balance, we are falling short of the ideal situation.

**Long Range Evaluation of Job Opportunities.** From time to time a worker should *evaluate* his situation. He should look ahead to see where he is going. This is not to suggest that he ought to stir up dissatisfaction within himself; but he ought to check his goals and direction to make sure that he is realizing the best that is within him and to make such changes as may be necessary to secure the best results.

We think of goals as highly important. Unless we are careful we may find that we have lost sight of our goals. A periodic check-up would make for good occupational health, just as a check-up from time to time is desirable to provide good physical health.

The look ahead helps us to size up the value of the things we are doing, the way we are spending our time. It helps us to correct errors. It helps us to secure additional training and guidance when needed. It has a good effect, especially, on our *motives*. By restating the goals, every once in a while, we sharpen our enthusiasm for the job. This helps to keep us from falling into the proverbial "rut."

**Employee's Responsibility for Good Working Conditions.** Modern business and industry puts more and more emphasis on the idea of sharing. That is, it is becoming more and more customary to think of workers, as well as management (the supervisors and employers), as having a mutual stake in what is going on; workers and management should help each other, as they are all working toward the same end.

This is ideal, but it is what we are trying to shoot at in modern industrial relations.

In line with this, workers ought not to put all the responsibility for good working conditions on management. Sometimes workers are very careless in this respect: they are careless about equipment, they are slovenly, they are extravagant, and they are thoughtless about the other fellow. If we would practice what we know about good human relations this would not be so.

If we would remember the importance of identification, that is, how things that affect our school, business, or industry also affect us, we would be more interested in this idea of sharing.

Of course, workers will take the responsibility of sharing more enthusiastically if they feel that others are doing it too. The willingness of the group can help very much; but it is also a personal responsibility of each individual, if the advantages are to be realized.

Many businesses have suggestion boxes which are useful in improving conditions.

You and I can do a great deal about job satisfaction. We can, and should, carry to the job the attitudes that will help us to enjoy the job and our relations with the people around us, including our supervisors. If we feel that the job is pretty much lacking in the elements that we, as persons, need for bringing us up to our best level of work, then we should cast about for more favorable opportunities. With more than 17,000 different kinds of jobs in our country, and with employment at an unprecedented high peak in our industrial age, this ought to be possible. But before we make a move, we ought to evaluate intelligently the job we now have. We should make our plans and our moves in the light of full understanding as to what is *our* responsibility and what is the other fellow's responsibility.

Unfortunately, too many individuals move at random through the labor market. They go with remarkable lack of planning from city to city, from job to job, and then wonder why they have not been able to make more of a success of it. Most of this is due to a lack of knowing what goes into job satisfaction and to an almost total disregard of the simplest elements of planning.

## SOMETHING TO DO

### A Check-up on Job Satisfaction

Using the elements of job satisfaction as a basis, it is a profitable exercise to compare one's present job with another possible job.

This is done quite simply by writing pertinent comments on either side of a line down the middle of the page, paragraph by paragraph, for each of the important elements affecting both jobs. The over-all picture should give an interesting comparison.

| Job A | Job B |
|---|---|
| Description | Description |
| Compensation or pay | Compensation or pay |
|   Present: |   Present: |
|   Future: |   Future: |
| Opportunity for promotion | Opportunity for promotion |
| Opportunity for training | Opportunity for training |
| Hours of work | Hours of work |
| Vacations | Vacations |
| Working conditions | Working conditions |
| Environment I work in | Environment I would work in |
| Kind of people I work with | Kind of people I would work with |
| Kind of people I work for | Kind of people I would work for |
| Security of the job | Security of the job |
| Opportunity to feel sense of achievement | Opportunity to feel sense of achievement |
| Extent to which I feel that I *belong* | Extent to which I would feel that I *belong* |
| Opportunity for basic satisfaction | Opportunity for basic satisfaction |
| Extent to which job suits my training and abilities | Extent to which job would suit my training and abilities |

## QUESTIONS AND PROBLEMS FOR STUDY AND DISCUSSION

1. What are you looking for in a job? How do your own personal ambitions check with the elements usually considered in job satisfaction?

2. Have you had any experience in which you have had an unusually high degree of satisfaction on a job? To what do you attribute this?

3. Have you held a job which did not produce much in the way of job satisfaction? What were the reasons for this?

4. What, in your own words, are the main elements involved in job satisfaction?

5. Describe a job which you think would be a good job *for you.*

6. Look at the "help wanted" column of a newspaper. Note one or two jobs which you think might be of interest to you and one or two which you feel would not be of interest. Then try to write down or note the reasons for your accepting or rejecting them.

7. Give an illustration of a job situation involving a high degree of cooperation between employee and employer.

8. Give an illustration of a job situation involving a high degree of cooperation between fellow employees or fellow workers.

9. Think of an industry or business in your community which has a reputation for good employee-employer relations. What are some of the reasons why this good reputation exists?

10. Why is it suggested that job success should be judged in terms of *both* the employer and the employee?

11. Discuss the question of pay or compensation. What considerations should guide a person in deciding whether or not a job opportunity is a good one in this respect?

12. Why is it suggested that the worker himself has a lot to do with conditions of job satisfaction?

13. What do you consider to be the most important single consideration involved in job satisfaction, aside from the matter of compensation (pay)?

14. Why is planning important in connection with job satisfaction?

• 15. Ask several people what they like or dislike about their jobs. Make a little summary of the reasons given, and see whether or not they fall under the headings given in this chapter.

# CHAPTER TWENTY-ONE

# THE PSYCHOLOGY OF
# LABOR RELATIONS

In this chapter the point is made that, at times, all of us are employers. We usually think, though, that the employer is someone else. How would we "rate" as employers? It is very easy for the workers to be critical of their employers, but it is not often that we think of this problem from the point of view of the one who is the employer.

The chapter introduces some basic principles of good job relations. During World War II, some excellent suggestions were made by government agencies on how to handle workers and how to get better working relations. They have stood the test of time in the intervening years and have widely influenced industry-labor relations. Some of the suggestions were made under the J.R.T. or Job Relations Training program, described in this chapter.

Everyone can benefit by putting into practice the rather simple rules of J.R.T.

In this chapter there is some discussion of the importance of good job relations for a democracy. We live in a time of huge industrial organizations. The close personal touch between employer and employee is not always possible. At the same time, all workers work with supervisors, and some of the requirements of good supervision are outlined in this chapter.

## QUESTIONS THIS CHAPTER WILL ANSWER

1. Why should everyone be concerned about employers and their responsibilities? Why is it said that, at times, everyone is an employer?

2. What are the practices that distinguish good employers from poor employers?

3. There are often times when people are working for *us*. What are some of the methods of handling them which we should consider?

4. How can we tell whether or not we are good *employers?*

5. What specific suggestions can be made to assure good working relations between employers and employees?

## Employer's Responsibility for Good Working Conditions

Everyone is an employer. This may seem like a bold statement to make, but it is true. The father is an employer of his children in many situations around the home. The husband is an employer of his wife; the wife of her husband.

Although we don't ordinarily think of these relationships in this way, the point is that in any situation in which one person is performing services for another under direction, it is essentially an employer-employee relationship.

Ordinarily, we think of this in a different light, however. We usually think of an employer in the business, industrial, or economic sense. In this sense, the employed person is working on a job—performing some definite service or series of services—for pay. Even in this sense, everyone is at some time or other in his life, an employer. A man who is himself an ordinary employee, perhaps working for a company for pay, is also an employer when he hires someone to build a house for him, to paint for him, or to do any of a great many ordinary jobs we run across in everyday life.

Even in business or industry, due to the way in which modern life is organized, a great many people are at one time employees and at another time employers. Many people who do not think of themselves as employers are in reality employers. They have to supervise other people who work for them.

*This makes it important for all of us to understand the basic principles involved in good employer-employee relationships.*

Employers at any level—whether the big employers in big business or the lesser employers in supervisory jobs—must know something about good conditions of work. They must know how to provide good conditions, since that is their responsibility. Anyone who is responsible in any degree for directing the labor of others has an obligation to know what he is doing and what his responsibilities are.

## Essentials of Good Relations with Workers

Possibly the simplest and the most satisfactory analysis of what is necessary for good employer-employee relationships was the analysis developed and widely used during the Second World

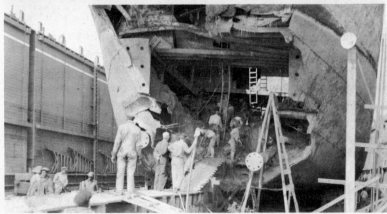

Where heavy equipment and materials are used, as in this dry dock, it is the employer's responsibility to provide safe working conditions.

*Merrill-Stevens Dry Dock and Repair Company*

War by the Federal Security Agency (War Manpower Commission).
This was known as the J.R.T.—Job Relations Training.

The J.R.T. was a program, or way of handling workers, which
was explained and taught to thousands of persons who found
themselves in supervisory positions.

J.R.T. called for several basic principles which are herewith
presented for consideration and discussion because they actually
give, without a great deal of formality, the framework for good
human relations on the job. They are:

1. Let people know how they are getting along.
2. Give credit where credit is due.
3. Tell people about changes that are going to affect them.
4. Make the best use of each person's ability.
5. Never stand in a person's way.

These simple rules are the foundations of good job relations.

**Let People Know How They Are Getting Along.** This is based
on the principle that people like to feel that they are getting
somewhere; that they are succeeding. It is considered to be the
responsibility of the employer or supervisor to let his workers
know whether or not they are doing a good job. Silence is damaging
to morale. A judicious mixture of praise and constructive criticism
is helpful to any worker. Criticism, properly phrased and timed,
can be of great instructional value.

Since we can assume that most workers are interested in succeeding, we can be sure that they will welcome constructive criticism.
Workers will work better if they get constructive criticism than they
will without it, even if the criticism is of a simple sort such as: "Maybe it would be easier if you did it this way," or "How would it be if
you handled it just a little differently, say for instance, like this?"

As to letting a worker know how he is getting along, a suggestion
may often be equally simple when expressed in such comments as:
"It looks to me as though you've about got the hang of it, now," or
"Well, I see you've covered that first assignment; going to start on
the next one now?"

The important point is that the supervisor recognizes that the
worker is accomplishing something, and the worker is happy to
know that it is recognized.

**Give Credit Where Credit Is Due.** Again, the worker likes to
know that he is getting somewhere and that his efforts are appre-

ciated. This is in line with the psychology of motivation which recognizes that praise, giving credit or reward, stimulates good workmanship.

Since most jobs are conducted in a social situation, most workers like to have their work recognized so that other workers will appreciate what they are doing.

We all recognize that no one likes to be blamed for something he didn't do. Likewise, no one enjoys seeing someone else get the credit for something he himself did. This grows out of the fact that we are all individuals, and we are all working according to our different abilities and skills. If we all had exactly the same skill, the same energy, and the same drive, probably this would not concern us. But since the existence of individual differences is a fact, it is important that we get some credit for the use we make of our ability and skill.

To disregard this side of human nature is to disregard the facts. It is hard to conceive of anyone, no matter how high up the scale of human affairs, who would not be influenced by this kind of motivation.

As an example of how this works, we might consider first the attitude of a baseball player. He looks at the newspaper account to see his name. He would like to see a write-up of his part in the game.

The wife hopes for a word of praise from her husband when she has prepared a particularly good meal or a dish. He hopes that she will comment on his new tie, his haircut, a "raise," or word of recognition he gets at the office.

Good job relations require that the supervisor give credit where credit is due. In addition to the simpler kinds of reward and recognition, good employee relationships require that men or women who do good work be rewarded by increases in pay, promotions, or other concrete benefits.

The rewards must go to the people who deserve them. This is a fundamental principle in good job relations. It is something an employer must not disregard.

**Tell People about Changes That Are Going To Affect Them.** Again and again personnel workers have pointed out the importance of this rule in job relations; but it is one of the most neglected of all. The rule simply means that if you are going to take some action that will affect what one of your workers does (as for example changing the nature of his duties, changing or moving his equipment, or in any way planning to take some step which will *affect him*), you should let him know about it ahead of time.

We can understand why this is necessary. Studies have shown that workers in factories become very much annoyed when their duties are changed without their approval or consent. They don't like being moved to another department without being asked. A man doesn't appreciate having his office changed around while he's on vacation. He doesn't like to discover that his ways of working, his tools, or his helpers have been suddenly "shifted on him" over the week-end or while he has been out of town.

The interesting thing about this is that when changes are explained ahead of time to workers, they will usually accept them quite readily. Studies have shown that the fact of letting them know what is to be done is the important thing.

**Workers appreciate being told of changes that affect them.**

One man was disgruntled for a whole month because he was assigned to a desk in an office, and overnight the desk was assigned to a fellow worker and another desk moved in for him. Another man was unhappy because his office was shifted to a new location (actually a better one) without his having been asked about it.

A secretary was hurt because a file for which she had been responsible was made the responsibility of someone else. People don't like to have duties taken away from them without warning, even though the action actually lightens their work and improves conditions for them.

One office was thrown into a bad state of affairs for months because the men who had been used to writing their reports in longhand found suddenly that new typewriters had been installed and they were expected, from then on, to write their reports on these machines.

Changing the rules about when the workers can go to lunch, the length of the lunch hour, the time of starting work in the morning, the location of the washroom available for their use, or any one of a hundred different things *affecting them or their work without taking them into account first and letting them know about it* can make for bad relations, or even result in their deciding to quit the job and go somewhere else.

**Make the Best Use of Each Person's Ability.** This is somewhat more obvious than the other rules. If a worker feels that he has some skill or ability and is not given the opportunity to use it, a very important essential of job satisfaction is neglected. We all like to have our abilities recognized.

Men have literally pined away wishing that they really could be given certain job assignments which would enable them to use their skill. They have experienced continued frustration because the supervisor or employer, for some reason, refused to let them have the chance.

Of course, this means that the supervisor or employer needs to know his workers; he needs to be aware of what they can do. If he does not have this information, he may unconsciously neglect to give them the opportunities they deserve.

How deep-seated this is in all of us can be seen almost any day in a home. The child when given an opportunity by the parent to do something shows his delight. The teen-ager when given a chance to learn to drive the family car has a great feeling of satisfaction. The principle is the same in job relations.

**Never Stand in a Person's Way.** Good employers or supervisors are always ready to give the worker a boost along the way. This means that when a worker has shown skill and has an opportunity to improve himself possibly by promotion "up the line" or to another department offering better pay or better opportunities, one should help him along, not stop him.

Yet, for selfish reasons, an employer might do that very thing. Supervisors have been known to "soft pedal" reports on a good employee so that they could keep him.

Little more need be said on this particular point. An employer or supervisor who gets the reputation for holding his men back has little chance of establishing a reputation for fair dealing. His gain from so doing can, at best, be just temporary.

A good job-relations situation can't develop in such an atmosphere. All we have to do is think of how we would like it if we were in the position of the one being blocked.

Another comment should be made at this point. It is advisable for any employer to see to it that all of the supervisory officers are trained to follow the basic lines of J.R.T. Often a "top" man has the principles in mind, but they are short-circuited by supervisors further down the line.

One can easily see the application of these principles in any job situation in industry, in the management of people working in a store, in the management of the staff of a college newspaper, in the direction of a group of people working voluntarily in a Sunday School, or even in the management of a home.

## Evaluating Job Relations

If you are employing someone, or several people, you can get an evaluation of how well your supervision is going by considering a few questions.

**1. Do Workers Like to Work for You?** You can tell whether people like to work for you or not. They will be friendly and agreeable if they like you; somewhat aloof and noncommunicative if they don't like you. It will show in their tone of voice in answering questions or replying to instructions. As often as not they will tell you that they like to work for you, if that is the case. (They are unlikely to tell you if they *don't*.)

**2. Do They Stay on the Job?** When workers stay away from the job, are late, or "home sick" frequently, it is referred to, in industry, as *absenteeism*. Of course, there are good reasons for absenteeism, as in the case where someone is forced to remain away by illness or injury; but many times absenteeism is a sign that the employee or worker does not like his work very much. He wouldn't stay away if he liked it, or if he was taking it seriously.

**3. Do They Comment Favorably on Their Work to Others?**

Methods of establishing good relations with their workers are discussed by employers at their annual business conventions.

*Fred Hess and Sons*

Workers are quite likely to show their attitudes toward you as an employer or supervisor in their talk with other workers. You won't hear these comments; but they will get back to you indirectly. For example, one of your associates will say, "What's the matter with Joe? I hear he's griping about his job."

Indirectly, you can obtain evidence either favorable or unfavorable to your employer-employee relations.

**4. Are There Many Complaints?** There is probably a close connection between the number and frequency of complaints and the harmony of employer-employee relationships. Of course, it seems to be an old American custom to "gripe," but there are legitimate complaints and too many of them are certain evidence that something is wrong somewhere.

It has long been considered a fact that when men like their employer or leader, they will accept, uncomplainingly, quite a few hardships and unpleasant circumstances. Hence any considerable number of complaints is in all probability a danger signal.

**5. Do They Accept Extra Assignments or Overtime Duties Cheerfully?** Occasionally it is necessary to ask a worker to do something out-of-hours or at some personal sacrifice of convenience. The cheerfulness or willingness of his acceptance of such assignments is an indication (other things being equal) of his loyalty to you as a supervisor or employer.

Of course, no employer or supervisor should be thoughtless in making such assignments. However, it is quite common. The employer often thinks of his own convenience instead of the convenience of his workers. This is a sign of careless thinking and lack of realization of the responsibility which goes along with good management.

When an overtime or extra job has to be done, it is desirable to call the people involved in, ahead of time if at all possible, and explain to them and discuss with them "the situation." If they can share in accepting the responsibility for working out a problem of this sort—instead of just being expected to do it or ordered to do it—the situation will be enormously better for all concerned.

## Specific Suggestions for Good Working Relations

The idea of treating other people as you would like to be treated yourself is the best guiding principle for good employer-employee relations.

There are still some employing officers who take the "well, what do you want" attitude toward a person applying for a job. In line with the known need of each individual to have some feeling of self-respect or personal worth, the employer should be courteous to the job-applicant—whether he has an opening for him or not.

One personnel manager puts this first at the top of a list of specific suggestions for employers who would like to have good working relations,[1] suggesting that a business or industry should have:

A considerate and orderly hiring procedure which insists upon the same kind of courteous and sympathetic treatment for each applicant that management would like to have if it were the applicant.

[1] Arthur Guy, Jr., American Thread Co., in an address before the Southern Conference on Human Relations in Industry.

This personnel executive describes a "real boss," and in doing so goes into some of the specific things which any employer or supervisor should keep in mind:

The next thing you and I would like to have if we were starting in a new organization is a real boss. We would want to talk to him before we accepted the job. We would want a man we would enjoy working for and with. A man who could answer questions regarding company policies, our pay checks, and our status. A man who could and would help us to get ahead. A man who would listen to our grievances and really do something about them. A man who would explain things to us so we would understand what he wanted us to do and how he wanted it done. A man who would make us understand when we were wrong and who would admit it when he or the company erred. A man who would not "pass the buck" and whose hands were not tied by top management. A man who would give us a fair deal and treat us as he would like to be treated. We would have confidence in such a person and really respect him.

The thing to note is that throughout this discussion there is the idea that an employer, or "boss," if he is to get along well with his employees, must be a person who understands them and wants to help them.

This is quite contrary to the idea that a worker is just a paid hireling who does what he is told to do "or else." Modern life, with its emphasis on democracy and on education, has developed a different idea as to what is worth while in life. By setting the goal of sharing in the good things of life, democracy has brought an end to the period of time when a man's labor was something he sold to the highest bidder on the market place, and, after selling it, accepted a place little higher than that of the slave of ancient times.

A modern employer has to understand this. If he does not, he will be beset with difficulties, one after another, because his practices will be out of step with what democracy in our modern industrial world requires.

## What Workers Look for in Good Management

In addition to the specific things which have been mentioned, workers look for several qualities which they have come to expect management (employers) to have.

They expect human qualities more than anything else. Probably the most frequently heard expression of approval, when workers are talking about an employer or boss or superior officer, is "He's a good guy." This is simple American for "a man who is really human and who is like the rest of us."

This is without a doubt a result of our American tradition which puts much emphasis on *democracy*. We have come, over a period of many years, to want men and women in superior positions to show that they have not lost "the common touch." We resent "high-brows" and dislike social distinctions. We actually have social distinctions; but, when it comes to labor-management situations, we don't like to admit it, and any employer who displays very much of the "I am better than you" attitude will be disliked.

Workers like management to be interested in them as people. This includes the idea of sharing plans with them and sharing the credit with them for successes and accomplishments.

As industry has become larger and larger, in the modern age of machinery, it has been harder for management to maintain this personal interest. It is difficult for the manager of a plant employing 15,000 people to know them all personally and share their joys and sorrows.

However, at the level of the office or the shop, the supervisor or immediate employer can know his people and share with them, and this is what the worker expects. Most people have sense enough to know that there is a limit to how far personal relationships can can go in a big organization.

At the same time, when personal relationships are involved, they look for courteous and humane treatment.

Workers expect management or employers to be considerate of them in emergency situations. It is true that sometimes there will be pressure to get a big job done. Then, when the workers are taken into the picture and given an understanding of what the problem is, they will usually be glad to help. But they do like to be taken into consideration. The situation here is the same as it is in the individual relationship of the supervisor to the individual worker, which has been discussed.

Workers also expect management to place as much value on the human side of the work as they do on the technical side. This is one reason why they object to efficiency experts who seem, sometimes, to think only of the work that is to be turned out and never about the human beings involved. It sometimes happens that a machine is introduced which changes the work of individuals. They may not like this if it makes their work less interesting, less responsible, or less important. They may need to be consulted about the operation and to be given a chance to offer opinions as to how the improvement can best be used to the advantage of all.

In such cases it is best if the workers can be used in some other equally important capacity, and their services should be terminated only as a last resort. In such cases they should be given help in readjusting or in finding other suitable employment. These are problems of industrial relations which are hard to handle, but it is necessary for the employer to know about them and to approach them with the welfare of the workers in mind.

## SOMETHING TO DO

### Check List for Evaluating Job Conditions

A simple check list can be used by any employer to evaluate his own methods of handling employees.

| *J.R.T. Items* | Good | Fair | Inadequate | No Provision |
|---|---|---|---|---|
| 1. Letting people know how they are doing | | | | |
| 2. Giving credit where due | | | | |
| 3. Telling people about changes affecting them | | | | |
| 4. Using their ability to best advantage | | | | |
| 5. Helping them to progress | | | | |

| *Other Items*[2] | Good | Fair | Inadequate | No Provision |
|---|---|---|---|---|
| 1. Courteous hiring | | | | |
| 2. Good policies on hours of work, vacations, etc. | | | | |
| 3. Sound pay scale | | | | |
| 4. Provisions for promotion (upgrading) | | | | |
| 5. Provisions for training | | | | |
| 6. Provision for providing good working conditions | | | | |
| 7. Provision for considering grievances | | | | |
| 8. Provision for fair dealing when services of worker are no longer needed | | | | |
| 9. Fairness in discipline | | | | |
| 10. Provision for keeping employee or worker informed on plans and policies | | | | |

---

[2]Adapted from suggestions by Arthur Guy, Jr.

## QUESTIONS AND PROBLEMS FOR STUDY AND DISCUSSION

1. Why is it suggested that everyone is, at one time or another, an employer?

2. State, in your own words, the principal points in the J.R.T. program.

3. Give an example of "letting the worker know how he is getting along" from your own experience.

4. Give an example of "giving credit where credit is due" from your own experience.

5. Have you ever been in a position where you felt that you did not get credit when due? Describe.

6. Explain some of the points that are involved in carrying out the policy of making the best use of each person's ability.

7. What do you consider to be the best way of finding out whether or not people like to work for you?

8. Have you ever applied for a job? What were your experiences? Were you favorably or unfavorably impressed?

9. What is meant by the suggestion that Americans like employers to be *democratic* in their manner?

10. Do you know any employer or supervisor who is undemocratic? Describe him, and discuss the effect of this attitude on his workers.

11. Explain what is meant, in labor relations, by the term *management*.

12. Consider your own experience on a job. How many of the points presented in this chapter as contributing to good labor-employer relations were put into effect? Which ones were neglected?

13. Would you yourself consider the principles emphasized in the J.R.T. program as important? Why?

14. Can you give an example of where workers or students have been disregarded by having policies put into effect without their having been consulted?

15. What do you understand by "upgrading" and "promotion"? What should be taken into consideration by both employer and worker in this connection?

# CHAPTER TWENTY-TWO

# UNDERSTANDING YOUR SOCIETY

Scarcely a day goes by without some reference in the newspapers to minority groups. We hear of class conflicts, labor-management troubles, segregation, and other similar issues. It seems that we all belong to a variety of groups and that these groups are often in conflict for various reasons.

This is all part of the life around us, and we need to know what some of these forces are and how they work. The more important ones are presented in this chapter.

This is not just a mental exercise, because some of these issues come close to home. Many of us belong, ourselves, to one or more minority groups. The more we can understand about group attitudes, the easier it will be not only to understand these pressures, but also to adjust to problems as they arise.

Some of the influences which cause people to move in different groups and circles are discussed, and their importance is shown.

In the latter part of the chapter some suggestions are made to help us in evaluating political programs—something we greatly need to understand in our democracy.

Throughout this chapter there are suggestions that should help us to correct some very faulty ideas we sometimes get about certain groups and the people who belong to them.

## QUESTIONS THIS CHAPTER WILL ANSWER

1. Since we are all concerned with the groups around us, what are some of the things we should know about groups?
2. What are some of the larger groups commonly found in our country? What about classes and class distinctions—do they enter into the picture of life in America?
3. Why is it that we have difficulties with minority groups in this country, and in other countries?
4. What is the psychology involved in problems of dealing with minority groups? What particular problems do members of minority groups have to face? How did these problems come to exist?
5. What are *stereotypes?*

6. What can we learn about groups and group attitudes that can help us to understand the social problems of our own communities?

7. What practical suggestions can help us in analyzing political activity?

## How American Communities Are Organized

Groups are of two types, as we know. The chief *primary* group is the family. The family is organized to provide for the raising of children and to give each individual a living-center from which to go forth to the activities of the work-a-day world. *Secondary* groups of many kinds exist, such as school classes, political clubs, fraternities, and others. When a group is very intimate and dominates the lives of the individual members closely, it may be, along with the family, thought of as a *primary* group. Most groups we belong to, however, are *secondary* groups. We belong to many of these.

American communities are formed from large numbers of people living together in many families and groups. One of the interesting things about communities is the way in which people in them have contact with one another through various groups and situations. Some writers speak of these as *associations*.

The associations of people differ somewhat according to the sections in which they live, the wealth or standing of their families, the amount of education they have had, their occupations, their religious affiliations, and other things.

In primary groups, individuals are more or less protected and sheltered. The people they live with understand them and tolerate their weaknesses, more or less. In the secondary groups, individuals face problems of getting along with others who have similar problems, and there is a certain amount of competition involved.

We all move in different groups and circles. The particular ones we move in reflect, to a considerable extent, the social standing of our families.

The geographical location of our homes in communities is important. Some homes are in quiet residential sections, some are in less pretentious sections, some are in hotel and apartment house districts, and still others are in "in-between" areas located between industrial sections and the better residential streets.

We have all heard the expression, "He comes from the other

Lives of many people are affected by major redevelopment projects either under way or planned in large cities. In the top picture above the first of five 19-story apartment buildings in Chicago, Prairie Shores, replaces many blocks of housing and business property. The lower picture shows some of the old which has yielded to the new.

*Chicago Land Clearance Photo*

side of the tracks," meaning that the individual lives in a less favored area of town.

It is certainly true that the boy or girl who lives in a less favored area has obstacles to contend with not known to the more fortunate ones whose homes are in the better residential districts. The magnitude of the slum problem is indicated by a report published in the *Denver Post* during the summer of 1960 which showed that although one of the city's blighted areas covered but five percent of the city's area, and housed just ten percent of the population, it consumed 35 percent of the total city budget, 50 percent of the total welfare budget, 50 percent of the health and hospitals budget, produced 50 percent of the city's crime, 70 percent of the city's fire calls and 80 percent of the city's juvenile delinquency.

In the usual American city, around the edges of the central business district are areas in which both business and residences are found (often interspersed with rooming houses and apartments). Then further out from the center there are quieter, more attractive streets of residences; and quite a distance out are the very attractive suburban sections of homes and neat shopping districts. Here and there, usually along railroads, highways, or rivers, there are areas given over to industrial plants and buildings.

The character of the stores, restaurants, taverns, and other buildings is very different in these various areas. The whole picture is necessary if we are to understand the make-up of a typical American community.

## City Life and Country Life

There are many differences between the surroundings of city and country children, and there are many differences in the experiences they have.

The city children have a tendency to be "more sophisticated" or more "in the know" about modern life. They are quite ignorant of many things about nature and animals which are commonplace to country children. On the other hand, the country boys and girls are lacking in information about the ways of the city, and they have little or no idea of the kind of people found in many sections of the city.

One effect of the place where children live is that it influences their chances of getting an education. Although the widespread development of junior colleges has brought the opportunity for college attendance to many living in smaller towns and rural areas, there remain many sections in which the opportunity to go to college is limited. Another factor brought to our attention is the influence of the family. It tends to be stronger and to be more of an influence on country children than on city children. Many country children have a more restricted social life, and, when they do go to city high schools or move to town areas, they have problems of adjustment because of this limited background. There are many other influences, but these few illustrate the point.

## Neighborhoods

The neighborhood is a section of a city or of the country in which any group of people live. Strictly speaking, it is a section in which the people are brought together by geographical boundaries or by transportation facilities (along a certain bus line or car line, for example, or in the area served by a particular school).

Neighborhoods have some of the influences on people that we used to associate with small towns. The people who live in a neighborhood tend to be somewhat alike and to have common interests. These, in turn, are affected by the nature of the neighborhood, as we noted in the discussion of groups and family backgrounds.

One point to note is that a person is likely to be thought of according to the neighborhood he lives in. It *places* him in the minds of people. It is probable that, lacking other information, people will think of him as being more or less like those who they *associate* in their minds with that particular neighborhood.

## What About Suburbia?

A new or at least expanded form of neighborhood has developed in America, labeled *suburbia*. This is the region, or perhaps we should say regions, which surround American cities in great numbers, occupying tremendous areas of the countryside.

The effects of suburban living were treated in considerable detail in reports made to the 1960 White House Conference on Children and Youth. Suburbia has become the increasing subject of attention in books, magazine articles, and in the theater. Sociologists, also, have become concerned about the influence of suburbia on American attitudes and values.

The principal characteristic of suburbia seems to be that all of the people are more or less alike—there isn't the diversity of population that has customarily been found in the large city or the small town. Alike in their homes, their customs, and their values, the people of suburbia seem to have been developing a new kind of provincialism and self-centeredness which may or may not be good for society. In 1960, one estimate indicated that 47,000,000 Americans were living in the suburbs.[1] This constituted a larger population than lives in the cities or in isolated towns or on the farms.

While some writers see in suburbia an opportunity for many people to enjoy the good things of life, and for families to spend more time together, others see some dangers that these people will have a different way of living that will tend to alienate them from others.

Typical of one criticism is the following:

The one-class community does not provide the child with a realistic picture of the world around him. There has been observed a lack of spontaneity in play of young children. The child's school time is overorganized. The pressures on children to be popular, to be like all the others and yet maintain their individuality, create conflicts. There is general lack of accepted community standards for teen-age behavior. The inexorable pressure to make good grades in order to get into the "right" colleges has frequently created hostilities toward academic curiosity.[2]

Our purpose is to indicate that there are problems emerging in connection with life in the sprawling suburbs, but the exact nature of these problems and their impact on society remains to be seen.

## Are There Classes in America?

Because we recognize the importance of social attitudes and the influence they have on people, it is fair to consider this question. The answer will surprise many Americans: it is *yes*.

---

[1] Dan W. Dodson, "The Effects of Suburban Living," in *Children and Youth in the 1960s Survey Papers*, for the 1960 White House Conference on Children and Youth, p. 14.

[2] *Ibid.*, p. 16.

The classes are not exactly like those in older European or Asiatic countries, but there are classes. A class in America is made up of people who do not (unless they have thought about it) even realize that they belong to a class. They might deny it if they were accused of it because the class idea is so out of harmony with our American ideas of democracy and opportunity.

The fact that classes exist in America is made obvious by a visit to one of the nation's resort centers, such as the Boardwalk at Atlantic City, New Jersey.

*Fred Hess and Sons*

At the same time, there are classes. They are organized according to prestige, family background, money, education, religious affiliation, and some other considerations.

People who belong to the highest of these class levels are sometimes thought of as "the best families" or "the old families." There are various levels, according to the social groupings and customs of the people; and the people in these so-called classes have their own ways of doing things, their customary ways of thinking, and many attitudes of importance to our democracy.

## How Social Distinctions Affect Attitudes

A few comments will show how the social distinctions which we recognize in America affect people's attitudes.

In the higher level or "upper" classes, "the old families," it is not considered good taste to associate with people from the "lower" classes. Seldom, if ever, will members of these families invite members of the less favored families into their homes; rarely will they associate with them in a social way. In the same way, members of the less favored groups will not be likely to associate, or want to associate, with members of the "old families."

The opinions of people at these different levels will vary on matters of politics. Their attitude toward political parties and toward political candidates will be very pronounced. In the South, the old families will tend to be conservative Democrats; in the North they tend to be conservative Republicans.

Members of the higher level groups will frown on dance halls and public amusement places. Some of the very old families may even frown on public schools, preferring to send their children to the older private schools for boys or girls.

People's customs in dress will also vary according to the group they commonly associate with. The churches they attend will be different. The fraternal organizations and clubs they support may be different.

The point is simply that people are *conditioned* in many of of their viewpoints, habits, and attitudes by the kind of homes they come from and the kind of groups or classes with which they are identified. If we will keep this in mind it will help us to understand the various points of view various people seem to have and which they sometimes express quite vigorously.


## Psychological Considerations in a Democracy

In a democratic society such as ours, it is important to recognize that these distinctions and differences in attitude occur, because then we can make allowance for them in our political economic, and social life. We must not allow these considerations to damage our society.

We know enough about human nature to realize that people are going to associate with the people they like—with the people whose customs and habits are somewhat like their own. Accordingly, we cannot, nor could we if we wanted to, force people to associate with people they don't want to associate with. But we can see to it that our political and economic ways of doing things do not create harsh barriers which work hardships on people.

In our educational system, we must be constantly alert to provide equal opportunity for all men and women to make the wisest and best use of their abilities. We must guard against permitting individuals with selfish or strictly personal interests to misuse schools or institutions for their own ends.

Sometimes people misjudge other people and adopt unwise ways of living. In a Pennsylvania town a man and his wife, who had many friends, were very successful in their business. The man built a big house on top of a hill. But the old friends, although they accepted invitations to visit the "house on the hill," never could feel at home there. There was something missing, and the old freedom of association was gone. It was a serious price to pay for the privilege of living in a mansion.

Keeping in mind what we know about the psychology of human nature, it is better to apply the usual rules of treating other people "as we would like to be treated" and to associate with them on a friendly basis, respecting their rights and their values and interests. If we have a wholesome respect for the other fellow's values and his customs, we may avoid a good many difficulties which grow out of the great differences in background and opportunity.

Psychologically, democracy is an ideal form of society because it protects the right of the individual to be an individual and it insists on each member of the group recognizing this right. At the same time democracy provides for teamwork and co-operation so that our best interests can be protected.

## Juvenile Delinquency—Challenge to Young Americans

Juvenile delinquency has increased in mid-century America and throughout the world. There are several types of juvenile delinquency, but perhaps the most notorious kind is that which has to do with gang warfare and acts of violence. Another kind involves the individual in developing bad personal habits of a destructive kind like alcoholism and drug addiction.

The young parent is concerned about this problem, because it affects not only some of the young people with whom he comes in contact from day to day, but also the future of his own children. We should note that juvenile delinqency is a form of self-expression, a bad, anti-social form. Long continued frustration, as we have learned, can provide a "build-up" for later violence, and when the spark is ignited it can spread through a group of people with unfortunate results. Among the sources of frustration for young people in our society are the absence of suitable and challenging job opportunities for those who leave school at an early age, and the failure of schools to provide educational programs equally appealing and worthwhile to all of the many kinds of young people enrolled in them. These are contributing factors which make for juvenile delinquency, in addition to all of the individual, psychological adjustment factors operating in our individual lives, which have been discussed and dealt with in this book.

When there are socially approved outlets for our behavior there is less likelihood of it taking a delinquent form. Therefore young people should support efforts of the community to provide suitable jobs and work programs for youth; they should support the schools in providing more suitable courses of work and study; and they should help our communities in developing more and better recreational outlets and programs.

But perhaps even more important than these factors is the need for young people to have goals and purposes which challenge their loyalty and inspire the best that is in them. We can all work toward the development of such worth-while goals, through our schools, through all of our group and personal contacts, and through our social institutions such as churches, fraternal orders, political parties and other agencies which bring us together.

Democracy, which gives us our sense of freedom and our feeling of personal worth and dignity, is a much looser form of social organization than is totalitarianism, and consequently we must work harder to maintain and extend it. The problem of juvenile delinquency is not simply explained or easily solved, but a part of the problem is due to the fact that too many people, young or old, do not have challenging and worth-while goals in life. It is our responsibility—especially if we are young parents—to recognize this and to do what we can to correct it.

## Minority Groups

A minority group has been described as one which is smaller or less able to influence affairs than the majority group. This concept lays emphasis on the ability-to-influence idea and associates size with power or dominance. A minority group usually has a racial, religious, cultural, linguistic, or other common characteristic of some sort with which it is identified.

This indicates that the bases for classification are many—that there are minorities of many kinds according to the base selected as a criterion.

It is quite conceivable that a person could be recognized as one of a minority as far as his race was concerned, as a member of the majority on the basis of his religion, as a member of a minority on the basis of his politics, as one of the majority as far as his occupation was concerned, and so on according to the bases selected for purposes of comparison and contrast.

That groups do exist in society is a reality which involves a wide variety of psychological factors.

History recounts the sorry fact that minority groups have often been subjected to mistreatment by those in the majority in various societies from ancient times to the present day. The fact that the minority differed from the majority in some more or less pronounced characteristic offered a pretext for discrimination. Not infrequently, the many assumed that the differing characteristic of the few was an inferior trait—one which marked the few as being people of less value according to a scale of prideful pretension. The more that a difference was stressed, the wider became the cleavage between the two groups. Claims of superiority on both sides usually went in favor of the many because of their very numbers.

In self-defense, minorities frequently developed habits and attitudes to counteract the attitudes of the majority. For protection, they often bound themselves together with close ties which tended to make them seem even more distinct from the many.

Hostility between groups—hostility born of prejudice—often opened opportunities for unscrupulous members of a majority to exploit people of minority groups for material gain. The chances for persons thus exploited to acquire an education, to live healthfully, and to become practiced in cultural refinements were accordingly diminished, with the result that the oppressed people did appear to be inferior as a group.

That certain strains of mankind are inherently inferior is a theory disproved by the research and observation of science. That such a theory is false is evidenced by the attainments in the arts and sciences of persons of every race, creed, and nationality who have had opportunities to perfect their talents.

The case record of a very young girl found lost in a jungle, a child born of primitive parents, provides a very excellent example of the universal sameness of human nature. The child was not immediately recognized as being human when found; she was momentarily thought to be some creature less than human. The waif was brought out of the jungle and reared in civilized society. Today, she is a grown woman living in Paris, a very intelligent and well-educated person who can speak French, Spanish, and Portuguese, and who occupies a responsible position in a scientific laboratory in the capital city of France.

Concerning what man is biologically, anthropologists—almost without exception—emphasize that no race is a "pure" one and that all people are of the same genus and species.

Physical differences among various peoples such as the predominant color of eyes, the contour of eyelids, the shape of nostrils, and the texture of hair, readily occur to us as examples of dissimilarities in mankind. These dissimilarities and others are, in most cases, only external traits.

The essential differences that do exist between groups of people are mainly the result of environmental influences and training, of tradition, of conditioning, and the formation of attitudes through experience.

Psychologists have noted that we derive many of our attitudes toward groups from persons with whom we are closely associated —persons having established attitudes. Parents exert a very strong influence on their children in this respect. The attitudes that we find prevailing in our churches and places of work affect our own attitudes in greater or less degree.

Social problems involving minorities have received a great deal of attention throughout the world in recent years. Interracial and intercultural relationships have been sensitive. Often increasing this sensitivity, minority groups have elected to meet prejudice in so militant a way that new prejudices have been born.

In the United States, tradition and customs, including some brought over from the Old World, play a part in the relationships between majorities and minorities. Of greater importance are the convictions and spirit prevailing in American society that derive from the doctrine of human rights and principles of democracy upon which the nation was founded. Government by consent of the governed and the recognition in our basic laws of the inherent worth of each individual give strength to popular belief in freedom, justice, and tolerance for all men.

This belief in human values, supported by widespread education, has found ever greater expression in our national life, despite the fact that there have been interludes of slow progress, even setbacks, in our history.

## Social Attitudes and Politics

Most of what has been said about groups applies to political parties. We tend to think of Democrats and Republicans as groups made up of people who think alike and who act alike. Actually, we find that there are many differences among Democrats and many differences among Republicans.

One of the tendencies of human beings is the tendency to generalize; another is the one which causes us to seek for ways of classifying people into hard and fast groups. We try, in our thinking, to fit people into these groups.

We have a great tendency to "size up" people and put them in a certain category. Once we have done this, it is hard for us to change our minds about them, even if we find out new facts or new information which *should* cause us to change our minds.

This process of placing people in a given class by "fixing" them with certain characteristics is called *stereotyping*.

A stereotype is a device used in printing. Instead of printing directly from movable type, a metal cast is made of a whole page of type, and the printing is done from this cast. Since the stereotype is hard, fixed, and unchangeable, the word is used in psychology or sociology to refer to hard and fixed characteristics which fall into a pattern or group.

We might classify one particular person as a "tough guy" because he has an appearance we have come to associate with "tough guys." A bespectacled college student is a "drip," or maybe a "square." A person whose social habits or mode of dress is somewhat conventional might be described as an "old maid."

When we "spot" a person as belonging to one or the other of these or other stereotypes, we have a tendency to think that the person has *all* of the traits or qualities usually found in such people, whether he does or not. We might even put a person in the wrong stereotype altogether. Yet the custom of putting people in stereotypes continues all the time.

Classifying individuals according to supposed characteristics is called stereotyping.

This labeling of people is exceedingly powerful and creates attitudes toward them. Accordingly, if a man is labeled a "politician," we all have a certain stereotype for politicians which "places" the man who is given that label, and it may not be necessarily good. To label a man as a communist is—at the present time—extremely damaging to him in our American society. A "fair dealer" or a "new dealer" is a particular kind of Democrat. A "hillbilly" or a "cracker" is a particular kind of country or small-town person.

In politics, in newspapers, on the radio, and on the stage, stereotypes are used deliberately to fix in people's minds the qualities of any person or group of persons. Yet the actual individual who is supposed to fit into the stereotype may not be of that type at all.

So influential are these stereotypes in our thinking that when we actually meet a capitalist, socialist, banker, politician, or teacher we are frequently surprised to find that he is not at all similar to what had been expected.

For a simple exercise in understanding stereotyping, try this: What sort of a person do you think of when you think of Italians? Of Frenchmen? Of Yankees? Of members of the House of Lords? Of gamblers? The fixing of certain ideas or pictures in our minds of people, of organizations, and of national groups, plays a dominant role in our attitudes. It is a matter of strenuous effort sometimes, to think objectively and clearly instead of, in terms of "stereotypes."

Ideas are also given labels or forced into a stereotype. For example, in many places if an idea is called "socialistic," it is immediately condemned. If a plan is promoted which some people don't like, and they can tie an "un-American" label to it, it will seriously affect the chances of the plan's succeeding.

The point is that people don't *think* when they are unduly influenced by stereotypes.

One more example of how stereotypes influence our ideas may be given. The teacher, in the conventional and prevailing stereotype, is still apt to be thought of as an "old maid" type who wears high shoes, long dresses, perhaps a shirtwaist and skirt, hair piled up on her head, and glasses with a ribbon on them. The professor is pictured as an absent-minded man with a long coat, a beard, and an umbrella.

The political life of the country can be greatly influenced by attitudes and conditioning which, unless we are careful, cause us to act unintelligently. We need to be alert to the fact that unless we see through the propaganda and the deliberate efforts of people to throw us off the track by giving people and plans labels and by playing on our weakness for stereotypes, we may unwillingly allow the wrong side or the wrong man to win. A thinking person votes for ideas on their merits, not because someone calls names or gives them labels.

**How the Individual Should Evaluate Political Activity.** As a citizen, each person has to make up his own mind as to what is right and what is wrong, what candidate to support, and what party to favor.

We have already emphasized the great importance of deciding about issues and about people on the basis of *facts*. Name-calling should be disregarded. Stereotypes used to mislead us should be recognized.

Since we are called upon to decide what people to support, the suggestion comes to mind that we ought to do it in terms of their ability for leadership and in terms of the values and goals which we think are important.

We usually find that we are called upon to support *a man* and *a program*. The right man with the wrong program can do a lot of harm. The wrong man with the right program may not be able to accomplish much, and may even bring the right program into disrepute.

Consequently, our problem is to find the right combination of man and program. Of course, we may end up by having to compromise, since it is unlikely that any candidate or any program will suit us exactly. It is unnecessary to repeat here the qualities that are important for leadership. It should be said, however, that the leader must be one who shares the same values and purposes that we have, at least to a reasonable degree, and he must have the qualities of behaving and thinking that will cause people to want to support him.

We can only decide about the issues of the campaign according to what we think will promote the type of government and the kind of government policy which we believe is good for us and for the country or community. Here we will find that people have honest differences. If it is a fair election, the views of the majority will decide.

The hardest task for the average person in connection with political activity is to decide what the candidates really stand for and what the issues really are. As we have noted, there will be smoke screens deliberately intended to keep us from getting at the answer to such questions. But we must make the effort. We must then support the group or the individual whose purposes are in accord with what we believe.

Political parties are quite necessary in a democracy. It is only through organized effort that a large number of individuals can make their wants known or their influences felt. People living in a democracy who believe that politics is an undesirable thing have not thought very carefully about the facts. Of course, politics is necessary. But the methods of politics may or may not be good, and it is the purpose of this discussion to indicate that whether they are good or not depends on how well they harmonize with the actual facts, the actual goals or purposes of the group, and the abilities of the leaders.

The "fanfare" and "propaganda," as we know, are merely methods of stirring up interest and promoting loyalties. They are liable to be good, or they are liable to be dangerous. We must watch them.

## SOMETHING TO DO
### Analyzing a Political Campaign

It is very instructive to take a political campaign and subject it to careful analysis. The psychological forces which affect people appear when this is done. The following method may be used.

Let us suppose that Jim Henderson is running for the position of United States Senator. Make an analysis of his campaign under the following three headings:

1. The man and his qualifications for office
    a) Education and experience
    b) Personal qualifications
    c) Beliefs and viewpoints in general
2. Issues of the campaign
    a) Issues as stated by the party
    b) Issues as shown in the speeches or publications of the candidate
    c) Issues as stated in the speeches or comments of those who are supporting the candidate
3. An evaluation of the man and the issues
    a) Comparison of his purposes with his previous record
    b) Comparison of his purposes with his training and experience
    c) Comparison of his purposes with his probable ability to carry them out in terms of initiative and personality.

Watch for truths, half-truths, and alleged facts which are not true at all. Watch for use of stereotypes, for labeling ideas, and for propaganda devices. Watch for appeals based on prejudice and for appeals for or against minority groups.

## QUESTIONS AND PROBLEMS FOR STUDY AND DISCUSSION

1. What do we mean by *associations* in the community? What are some of your associations in your community?
2. Do you agree or disagree with the conclusion of investigators that there are *classes* in our society?
3. What are some of the important differences between classes, according to investigators?
4. Some psychologists have indicated that there are four or five *classes*: upper, lower upper, middle, upper lower, and lower. Which class would you put yourself in according to this breakdown? Could you think of anyone who might fit into each of these so-called classes?
5. In your own community are there distinct areas like the ones described in the text?

6. Would there be any area in your community in which you would expect to find a higher percentage of arrests or cases of delinquency?

7. Describe the stores, shops, restaurants, etc., found in the least desirable section of your own community. Are they patronized by all of the people in the community?

8. What is a neighborhood? Can you identify one or more neighborhoods in your community? Do they have names which are commonly used by the people of the community in referring to them?

9. What minority group or groups exist in your community?

10. Do you agree that the attitudes of people toward minority groups are largely the outcome of *experiences*? Can you give any example of how the psychological principle of *conditioning* has entered into this situation?

11. Some psychologists have noted that our attitudes toward groups are often caused by the fact that we are in close association, in our families, with older people who have already established certain attitudes toward them. Do you agree with this? Can you give an example?

12. What is a stereotype? Give an illustration.

13. What stereotypes have you noted in your own experience, especially in relation to political parties or political ideas?

14. An example of a stereotype might be the athlete. Describe an athlete according to this.

15. Write a short statement of your own views in relation to politics and your own participation in them.

# INDEX

effect of changes on, 192-193
how emotions are the result of, 192
learning by, 92-94
Conformity, 367-368
Conscience, 48-49
Control of emotions, 210-223
Conversation, 354-355
Counseling, 241, 312-314
Country life, 407-408
Crusoe, Robinson, 152
Curie, Madame, 258
Curiosity, 50-51
Customs, 348-350

## D

Dashiel, John Frederick, 61, 63
Davey, Mildred A., 306
Davis, Robert A., 162
Daydreaming, 234-236
Delinquency, juvenile, 412-413
Democracy, 411-412
Desire
for social status, 39-40
to escape monotony, 40-42
to feel important, 42-43
Detjen, Mary Ford and Erwin W., 306
Development and growth, 75-76
Dewey, Governor, 177
Dewey, John, 153
*Dictionary of Occupational Titles*, 286-288
Difficulty
a felt, 153
locating and overcoming, 153-155
suggestions of possible solutions, 155
Displacement and projection, 233-234
Divorce, 323
Dodson, Dan W., 409
Dreams, 234-236, 238
Drives and emotions, 213-216
Drug addiction, 413

## E

Edison, Thomas A., 258
Emotions
and experience, 218
and group activity, 219-220
and habits, 211-212
and heredity, 21
and knowledge, 221
and the adrenal gland, 196-197
anxiety, 197-198
as drives, 213-216
balance of, 201-207
conditioning, 192-196
control of, 210-223
importance of, 188-189
pleasurable, 199-201
reconditioning of, 216-218
sharing of, 220
tests of, 199
undesirable, 223
Employee-employer relations, 373-388, 390-402
Energy, outlet for, 197
Environment
and adjustment, 327-340, 342-358, 373-388, 390-402, 404-420
and heredity, 18-33
importance of, 29-31
Escape mechanisms, 232
Exercise
law of, 90
physical, 35-37
Experiences
and attitudes, 131-135
and concepts, 144-147
and emotions, 218-219
and interests, 71-73
and learning, 86-106
of parents, 20-21
sharing, 220
vicarious, 132
Extravert, 252

## F

Facilitation, 345
Families